The Centralist Tradition of Latin America

The Centralist Tradition
of Latin America

Claudio Véliz

Princeton University Press
Princeton, New Jersey

Copyright © 1980 by Princeton University Press
Published by Princeton University Press, Princeton, New Jersey
In the United Kingdom: Princeton University Press,
Guildford, Surrey

All Rights Reserved
Library of Congress Cataloging in Publication Data will be
found on the last printed page of this book

Designed by Bruce Campbell

This book has been composed in VIP Bembo

Clothbound editions of Princeton University Press books
are printed on acid-free paper, and binding materials are
chosen for strength and durability.

Printed in the United States of America by Princeton
University Press, Princeton, New Jersey

This book is for María Isabel

Contents

Abbreviations

AJS	*American Journal of Sociology* Chicago
AESC	*Annales, Economie, Societés, Civilisations* Paris
AUCH	*Anales de la Universidad de Chile* Santiago
BID	Banco Interamericano de Desarrollo Washington, D.C.
BACH	*Boletín de la Academia Chilena de la Historia* Santiago
CHR	*Catholic Historical Review* Washington, D.C.
DE	*Desarrollo Económico* Buenos Aires
EHR	*Economic History Review* Economic History Society
EI	*Estudios Internacionales* Santiago and Buenos Aires
FA	*Foreign Affairs* New York
FI	*Foro International* Mexico
FO	*Foreign Office Papers (Chile)* Public Records Office, London
HAHR	*Hispanic American Historical Review*
HTR	*Harvard Theological Review*
IADB	Inter American Development Bank Washington, D.C.

JEH	*Journal of Economic History* New York
JLAS	*Journal of Latin American Studies* London
LARR	*Latin American Research Review* Austin
LE	*Land Economics* Chicago
RCHG	*Revista Chilena de Historia y Geografía* Santiago
REP	*Revista de Estudios Políticos* Madrid
RLACS	*Revista Latinoamericana de Ciencias Sociales* Santiago
TA	*The Americas* Washington, D.C.
TAJS	*The American Journal of Sociology* Chicago
TC	*Trabajos y Comunicaciones* La Plata
TSAHQ	*Texas State Historical Association Quarterly*
TV	*Teología y Vida* Santiago

Preface

Work on this book started in 1971 at the Institute of International Studies of the University of Chile. It had to be interrupted soon afterwards as a result of the increasing severity of a political crisis that, although external to the normal activities of the institute and the university, eventually brought both to a virtual standstill. It was resumed more than a year later in the Department of Sociology of La Trobe University in Melbourne. However, I was only able to complete it under the auspices of a generous fellowship from the John Simon Guggenheim Memorial Foundation, which, taken together with sabbatical leave from La Trobe University, enabled me to devote the whole of 1976 to research and writing.

An important part of this work was done in the Reading Room of the British Museum, now disconcertingly renamed The British Library, and was greatly facilitated by the courteous cooperation of the staff of that unique institution. The problem of accommodation that so frequently hinders the work of visiting scholars in the British capital was efficiently and pleasantly solved by the Nuffield Foundation, to which my family and I are most grateful. I also wish to thank Mr. Dietrich Borchardt, Chief Librarian of La Trobe University, and his staff for many years of truly selfless and expert assistance. The La Trobe University Library houses an excellent and growing collection of Latin American materials that has proved indispensable for my research.

Throughout the enjoyable process of preparing this book I have been honored with valuable advice and assistance from colleagues in Australia, Britain, and the United States, as well as Latin America. It is not possible to name them all, but it would be unjust not to express my gratitude to those who, though not necessarily agreeing with what I have written, devoted time and reflection to help me correct errors and misconceptions. I am grateful to Professor J. H. Parry of

Harvard University; Professor R. N. Burr and Dr. Temma Kaplan of the University of California, Los Angeles; Professors E. L. Jones and P. A. Tomory of La Trobe University; Professors R. M. Morse and R. N. Adams of the University of Texas; Dr. A. W. Martin of the Australian National University; Father Gabriel Guarda, O.S.B. and Father Mauro Matthei, O.S.B. of the Benedictine Monastery in Las Condes, Santiago; and especially to Professors Osvaldo Sunkel and Darcy Ribeiro, and to Mr. Richard Gott, who in countless seminars and conversations at the Institute of International Studies of the University of Chile enriched my understanding of the complexities of Latin American history and society.

My good friends Miss Hermia Oliver and Miss Katharine Duff and my daughter Zahira assisted me with tact and firmness in the revision of the first draft of the book. Mr. Sanford Thatcher of Princeton University Press was more encouraging and more truly helpful than anyone I have yet met in publishing. The demanding work of editing the text for the printer was done with meticulous care by Miss Rita Gentry. I am deeply grateful to all of them for their invaluable help, and I hasten to add that the infelicities of language remaining in the text are solely a reflection of my stubbornness. Mr. Nicholas Baring has most generously made the Rugendas painting available. I appreciate his kindness very much.

Even in the most favorable circumstances, to type and retype untidy drafts revised often over several years is a hard and unattractive task. In this case the difficulty was exacerbated by unexpected and complicated moves from Chile to Australia, then to Britain and Italy, and back to Australia, as well as by unavoidable and prolonged interruptions. I would like to express my gratitude to Mrs. Norma Cann and Miss Susan Summerhayes in Melbourne and Mrs. Vera Williams in London for performing this exacting work with patience and efficiency.

The final version of the book was carefully prepared by Mrs. Ann Brown, who also devoted much time to the last revision of the text, discovering and correcting many errors that had escaped previous scrutiny. It gives me pleasure to acknowledge her generous and most valuable cooperation.

This book would not have been started, let alone completed, without the loyal and imaginative support of my wife, to whom it is gratefully dedicated.

The Centralist Tradition of Latin America

Introduction

Disillusionment and perplexity appear to be the most obvious consequences of recent attempts to reform, modernize, revolutionize, or otherwise transform the countries of Latin America. I am convinced that this is a result of the mistaken belief that the experience of the industrialized countries of northwestern Europe and the interpretative models derived from it are precisely applicable to the peoples of the southern regions of the New World. I am also convinced that the proliferation of authoritarian regimes during the past few years is not an aberration of moral and political taste, but a manifestation of a style of political behavior, a secular disposition of Latin American society that under different forms—of which the military may well prove most transient—will be with us for some time yet. The main hypothesis presented in this work affords a basis for these assertions. This hypothesis is founded on the description and analysis of the principal factors that distinguish the social, economic, and political character of Latin American society from that of the countries that share in the northwestern European tradition. These factors had a decisive influence on the genesis and formation of Latin American society; they are also of contemporary importance and will, I believe, continue to be of major significance in the future. Although I shall list them separately here, they are not discrete but interpenetrate and interact with each other, and in the body of this work they will be found interwoven with the historical treatment of the theme. Four of these factors are inversely related to what I choose to call the "centralist" character of Latin American social and political arrangements: the first is the absence of the feudal experience from the Latin

American tradition; the second is the absence of religious nonconformity and the resulting latitudinarian centralism of the dominant religion; the third is the absence of any occurrence or circumstance over time that could conceivably be taken as the counterpart of the European Industrial Revolution; the fourth is the absence of those ideological, social, and political developments associated with the French Revolution that so dramatically transformed the character of western European society during the past century and a half.

These are negative factors that, although strongly supporting the argument presented in this book, may be insufficient to explain the special characteristics of modern Latin America. I shall, therefore, further propose that Latin American society exhibits features that elsewhere, notably in the countries of the northwestern European cultural stream, are associated with the consequences of the Industrial Revolution, but here have a distinct preindustrial origin and temper. These are a tradition of preindustrial bureaucratization and rationalization on which is founded the centralism that has shaped the processes of change and continuity, and a *sui generis* preindustrial urban culture within which a vast tertiary sector has developed intimately bound up with bureaucratic institutions and habits.[1]

---

[1] The Spanish historian José Antonio Maravall has impugned those who, as he sees it, interpret Spanish history in a negative manner, singling out what is presumably not found in it: feudalism, the bourgeoisie, the Enlightenment, etc. He believes that for historical work to be acceptable it can "never be the negative profile of a void. What must be said is what is positively there." (author's translation.) He also suggests that it can be misleading to pay attention to these overdramatized absences, for they may simply reflect the fact that the Spanish instances of some general phenomena are very unusual; there existed a Spanish bourgeoisie, but it was strikingly different from the more familiar Orleanist or Tuscan varieties.

Though full of admiration for the work of this historian, I am not prepared to follow him here. I find it useful as well as reasonable, for instance, to ascertain whether medieval Spain experienced what we normally refer to as "feudalism." I am not convinced by Maravall's assertion that positive statements are necessarily more worthwhile than negative ones. Surely to say that the king survived can be as helpful as to indicate that he is not dead. Also, it is admittedly difficult to know precisely when minor differences are plentiful

The argument presented in this book could also be summed up by stating that Latin America has been bypassed by the Industrial and French Revolutions and by their most significant consequences. The rationalizing and centralizing tendencies inherent in its bureaucratic establishment were there two centuries before the fall of the Bastille and have retained their preindustrial character. If the Industrial Revolution resulted in massive social change mainly because of the demands posed by a labor-intensive technology, in Latin America industrialization introduced a capital-intensive technology that necessitated different adjustments. If the Industrial Revolution can be justly linked with the exertions of an industrial bourgeoisie that in turn generated an industrial proletariat, in Latin America industrialization was neither the result of the activities of an industrial bourgeoisie nor has it resulted in the formation of an industrial proletariat.

From Marx to Weber and Talcott Parsons most students of social change have concurred that "the modern type of society has emerged in a single evolutionary arena, the West, which is essentially the area of Europe that fell heir to the western half of the Roman Empire north of the Mediterranean."[2] They have also agreed that the fundamentals of modern Western society can best be understood as "responses to the problem of order created at the beginning of the nineteenth century by the collapse of the old regime under the blows of industrialism and revolutionary democracy . . . two forces, monumental in their significance."[3] Monumental, indeed, for they marked "the transition from the early phase of

---

enough to warrant major changes. But, is the Spanish bourgeoisie Maravall has in mind so different as to cease being a bourgeoisie? Maravall, of course, is referring to Spanish history only, but, as the history of Latin America inevitably emerges from that of Spain, I consider it appropriate to point out that in this work I shall attempt to make legitimate use of both positive and negative statements, and that these uses are absolutely without reference to the disquiet expressed by the distinguished Spanish historian. See José Antonio Maravall, *Estado moderno y mentalidad social*, Madrid, 1972, I, 7-8.

[2] Talcott Parsons, *The System of Modern Societies*, Englewood Cliffs, N.J., 1971, p. 1.

[3] R. A. Nisbet, *The Sociological Tradition*, London, 1972, pp. 21-22.

western modernity to the one that has crystallized in the mid-twentieth century."[4] More emphatic still is the affirmation by Hobsbawm that the dual revolution "which broke out between 1798 and 1848 . . . forms the greatest transformation in human history since the remote times when men invented agriculture and metallurgy, writing, the city and the state."[5] Exaggerated or not, I find it unnecessary to quarrel with the spirit of these assertions, and it is on this agreement that I base my understanding of the crucial significance that the absence of the Industrial and French Revolutions have had for the historical development of Latin American society. I also find that this conveniently emphasizes the crucial importance of a centralist tradition preceding the coming of industry by several centuries and constituting the common denominator of the transformations and continuities discernible throughout the economic, social, and political history of the nations of Latin America.

Here it would be legitimate to expect a careful definition of the term "centralism" that would otherwise remain diffuse and open to a variety of interpretations. However, I would rather allow the considerations put forward in this study to intimate the significance and limitations of the concept. In this respect, I am happy to rely on Professor Gellner's wise dictum that "it would be an absurd requirement to restrict sociological interpretation to clear and distinct concepts. These are historically a rarity, and there is nothing to make one suppose that vague and broad notions, whose logical implications for conduct are ill-determined, do not in fact, have a powerful and specific impact on actual behaviour."[6] I certainly think that, during the past five centuries centralism has had a most "powerful and specific" impact on the behavior of Latin Americans, and I am content to let the matter rest there

---

[4] Parsons, *The System*, p. 74.

[5] Eric J. Hobsbawm, *The Age of Revolution: Europe from 1789 to 1848*, London, 1962, p. xv.

[6] Ernest Gellner, "Concepts and Society," in *Sociological Theory and Philosophical Analysis*, ed. Dorothy Emmet and Alastair MacIntyre, London, 1970, p. 116.

subject to only one qualification: "centralism" as used here should not be confused with "patrimonialism," an essentially different concept, in some ways antithetic to the bureaucratic temper of Latin American centralism.[7] In patrimonialism, ancestry, heredity, and personality play a definitive role; in centralism their role is exceptional or accidental. The concept of patrimonialism falls within the Weberian category of "traditional authority" while centralism should certainly be classed under Weber's "rational" type of domination. Whatever its shortcomings and excesses—and these are not rare in five eventful centuries—the centralist bureaucratic tradition has found expression through the office rather than the man, thus satisfying the key Weberian condition for a modern bureaucratic establishment.[8] The victory of La Gasca over Pizarro—the loyal civil servant over the dissident military hero—has been echoed through the centuries down to our time, affording abundant evidence to support the affirmation of de Tocqueville that "the incessant increase of the prerogative of the supreme government, becoming more centralized" leads eventually to situations when "the very men who from time to time upset a throne and trample on a race of kings bend more and more obsequiously to the slightest dictate of a clerk."[9]

That centralism and patrimonialism differ substantially, I would submit, is clear. It must now be added that the phenomenon of centralism that both Weber and de Tocqueville

[7] There have been a number of good studies on Latin American patrimonialism among which should be mentioned: Magali Sarfatti, *Spanish Bureaucratic Patrimonialism in America*, Politics of Modernization Series No. 1, Berkeley, Calif., 1966; Howard Wiarda, ed., *Politics and Social Change in Latin America; The Distinct Tradition*, Amherst, Mass., 1974; and Riordan Roett, *Brazil: Politics in a Patrimonial Society*, Boston, 1972.

[8] "It is decisive for the specific nature of modern loyalty to an office, that, in the pure type, it does not establish a relationship to a person, like the vassal's or disciple's faith in feudal or patrimonial relations of authority." H. H. Gerth and C. Wright Mills, trans. and eds., *From Max Weber: Essays in Sociology*, New York, 1958, p. 199.

[9] Alexis de Tocqueville, *Democracy in America*, trans. Henry Reeve, ed. Henry Steele Commager, London, 1959, pt. 2, p. 574.

were describing was a result, and both saw it in this light, of the Industrial and French Revolutions and was therefore closely linked to egalitarianism and industrialism, while Latin American centralism precedes these great transformations and retains to this day its preindustrial and nonegalitarian character.

This concept of centralism, not defined but carefully circumscribed, is essential for the understanding of an Ibero-American historical development that has undergone several alternating stages of relaxation of central control and recentralization. Although this study is not arranged in chronological accordance with these steps, I think it useful to set them down here, even if succinctly, to highlight the fact that centralism has not had a steady, uneventful progress, but has undergone notable fluctuations.

The first period extends from the second half of the fifteenth century, when the Catholic monarchs successfully initiated the arduous process of Castilian centralization at the Cortes de Madrigal in 1476, to the latter years of the sixteenth century, when the Catalan revolt of 1591, the great financial collapse of 1596, and the death of Philip II marked the end of an era and the commencement of the prolonged decadence associated with the Hapsburg relaxation of central control. The second period would cover approximately one century, from the accession of Philip III to the death of the last Hapsburg monarch in 1700 and the coming of the Bourbons to the Spanish throne. No matter what the causes of the decline experienced by Spain during the seventeenth century, one of its major consequences was a *de facto* weakening of the ties that bound the imperial and bureaucratic periphery to the central authority. The return to the centralist mainstream of Castilian and imperial policy was heralded by the enthronement of the duke of Anjou, with the title of Philip V. Although the main thrust of the recentralizing Bourbon reforms was not felt until the latter part of the century, the new administrative and political mood was apparent from the beginning of Philip's reign, albeit under the guise of French influence. This third period, of Bourbon recentralization, ran parallel to the recentralizing reforms of the Pombaline dictatorship in Portugal, and both extended their influence beyond the years of the revolutionary movements for independence and the first decades of republican government to the middle of the nineteenth century, when the centralism of the Iberian Enlightenment was overwhelmed by the rising tide of European commercial and political liberalism.

The "liberal pause" began in the mid-nineteenth century, started to crumble with the Great Depression of 1929, revived for a while during the Second World War and its aftermath, and came fitfully to its end during the economic malaise of the late sixties and early seventies. For the past half century—with the expected variations from country to country—Latin America has been finding its way back to its centralist mainstream. Regardless of the intentions of revolutionaries and reformers, every major reconstruction has resulted in increased central control, and the greater the revolutionary upheaval the more emphatic the centralism of the resulting institutional structure. Hence, the three revolutionary movements that are generally considered to be the most important to have taken place this century in the region—those of Mexico, Bolivia, and Cuba—all resulted in single-party systems of government with virtually all power vested in the center. Lesser attempts to reconstruct the institutional structure of society share this centralist style of politics, and the extension of central power has become a long-term characteristic of every country, no matter what the political coloring of its government.

That a comparable process has occurred elsewhere in the world is beyond doubt, but while the centralizing tendencies induced by improvements in communications, administrative techniques, and the like in nations such as Britain, Sweden, Australia, New Zealand, Holland, the United States, Denmark, Canada, or the German Federal Republic encounter a stubborn resistance on the part of the body politic and the traditional institutional arrangements, in Latin America the centralist mood is supported and strengthened precisely by a political tradition that has always been centralist and has only exceptionally departed from that course.

Britain's North American colonies proved a rewarding ambit for the realization of one of the most significant private utopias of modern times; they provided a *tabula rasa* "on which Puritanism was able to develop relatively freely without the interposition of extraneous factors."[10] The Indies afforded as much freedom for the unimpeded construction of one of history's great public utopias; there the fledgling Renaissance state of the crown of Castile was able to bring into being a centralized political structure without the hindrance of feudal traditions or the opposition of a baronial periphery. As Maravall has felicitously put it, the prowess of the Indies was an incomparable Renaissance feat of inventiveness; America was invented by sixteenth-century Spain.[11] The Indies were created from the metropolis as a centralized structure by political minds who contemplated the Renaissance from Madrid, the imperial capital of a nation full of confidence after great military victories, and ruled by a bureaucratic establishment carefully designed to prevent any encroachments on the central power. Aged and hardened by centuries of struggle, at the time of the great discoveries Castile had evolved an efficient form of centralized government, a reasonably well-organized bureaucratic establishment, a settled relationship between Church and state, and a system of laws sufficiently developed and complex to be imposed wholesale over a conquered people. It was on these civilian and bureaucratic foundations that the Castilian crown erected its imperial edifice; this is why very early after the military invasion of the Indies, "the

[10] Robert Ashton, "Puritanism and Progress," *EHR*, n.s. XVII (April, 1965), 582. One ought not to forget that there was purpose in that venture. As Johnson has explained, "The birth of Protestant America was a deliberate and self-conscious act of Church-State perfectionism." Paul Johnson, *A History of Christianity*, London, 1976, p. 421.

[11] Maravall, *Estado moderno*, I, 38-39. Or, as Raymundo Faoro has expressed it, referring principally to Portuguese America, it became possible at that time for princes and their advisors "to organize a State as if it were a work of art, a conscious and calculated act of creation." (author's translation.) Raymundo Faoro, *Os donos do poder, formação do patronato político brasileiro*, 3rd ed. rev., Porto Alegre, 1976, I, 16.

conquistadores, adventurers, crusaders quickly gave way to administrators, lawyers and judges."[12]

The consolidation and institutionalization of the imperial hold was accompanied by the emergence of a centralist, civilian, bureaucratic, and legalistic style of politics from which neither the imperial Indies nor the independent republics of Latin America have ever departed with much conviction or success. When these departures did occur, they did not modify substantially the institutional edifice but allowed only for a *de facto* relaxation of the centralist authority. W. B. Yeats delineated utter anarchy and dissolution in his celebrated "Things fall apart; the centre cannot hold." To this, one could reply that in the Latin American historical tradition the center very seldom fails to hold, and even when it apparently succumbs, it soon revives, perhaps invigorated.

During the three centuries of Iberian dominance over Latin America, the major departures from centralism occurred by default; the decline of Spain in the seventeenth century was reflected in indifference toward the Indies or, worse, incapacity to discharge the imperial responsibilities of government. Since independence, the "liberal pause" marks the most important departure from the centralist tradition, and this was largely the result of an outward-looking nationalist surge that attempted to discard everything Spanish and to replace it with the more attractive culture then flourishing in France and Britain. The concept of a strong centralist and authoritarian government was correctly identified with the colonial tradition and rejected in favor of the dispersal of effective political and economic power embodied in the contemporary liberal and radical creeds. The intelligentsia and the dominant commercial, agricultural, and mining interests coincided in their feverish and sincere espousal of the ideologies that stood at the vanguard of civilization; their enthusiastic advocacy was made possible by the exportation of primary commodities re-

---

[12] J. H. Parry, *The Spanish Theory of Empire in the Sixteenth Century*, Cambridge, 1940, p. 1.

sulting in a generalized prosperity enjoyed principally by those in the upper groups of society.

The Great Depression of 1929 marked the beginning of the end of the easy affluence based on primary exports, but the dependent mood did not vanish overnight. The perplexity, the confusion, and disillusionment of the last decades have at their root the essential paradox of a vast centralist social conglomerate, many of whose intellectual and political leaders have not resigned themselves to being what they are, but persist in pretending stubbornly that they can still lead their peoples into becoming acceptable imitations of Europeans, be it British liberals, French radicals, Russian communists, Italian Christian Democrats, or any other fashionable variety.

A few years ago, in his magnificent essay entitled *The Hedgehog and the Fox,* Sir Isaiah Berlin made use of an obscure fragment from Archilochus that reads, "The fox knows many things, but the hedgehog knows one big thing." Noting that possibly all that the Greek poet wanted was to point out that for all its cunning the fox is defeated by the hedgehog's single defense, Sir Isaiah, nevertheless, suggests that the words, taken figuratively, could be made to yield another, richer meaning, marking one of the most profound differences that divide writers and thinkers or human beings in general. "For there exists a great chasm between those, on one side, who relate everything to a single central vision, one system less or more coherent or articulate, in terms of which they understand, think and feel—a single, universal, organizing principle in terms of which alone all that they are and say has significance, and, on the other side those who pursue many ends, often unrelated and even contradictory." The first kind, according to Berlin, would lead centripetal lives, the second, centrifugal—"The first kind of personality belongs to the hedgehogs, the second to the foxes"—and he goes on to suggest that Dante, Plato, Pascal, Lucretius, Hegel, and Proust are hedgehogs, while Herodotus, Aristole, Erasmus, Goethe, Pushkin, and Joyce are foxes. No doubt, as he himself points out, this is an oversimplification, a dichotomy that, if examined, becomes "artificial, scholastic, and ultimately absurd. But if it is not an aid to serious criticism, neither should it be rejected as being merely superficial or frivolous; like all distinctions which embody any degree of truth, it offers a point of view from which to look and compare, a starting point of genuine investigation."[13]

It is in this guise that I am content to accept Sir Isaiah's dichotomy. If writers can be classified as foxes or hedgehogs, why not nations, perhaps with the interesting difference that while human beings are either one or the other throughout their brief productive lives, nations may change over time, and the Roman hedgehog evolve into an Italian fox, or the German fox into a hedgehog. Again, without pressing the point too far, I would suggest Latin America is a hedgehog that since the middle of the nineteenth century has been desperately trying to become a fox, with indifferent results. The avid imitation of foxlike western Europe was not sufficient to achieve the transformation during the affluent years of the late nineteenth and early twentieth centuries; since the Great Depression of 1929 and the relative decline of the liberal democracies, the hedgehog quality of Latin American centralism has reasserted itself assisted, no doubt, by a universal trend in the same direction. At times, this centralism is paradoxically established in the name of liberalism, as has happened often enough with military regimes wishing to impress foreign investors, but this should not obscure the fact that in such cases policies of economic liberalization and even what is described as political decentralization are instituted by executive degree and administered under severe central control.

At the risk of appearing needlessly dilatory, I feel it is necessary to explain that, although few, if any, generalizations about Latin America are capable of withstanding rigorous scrutiny, I shall in the course of this study make fairly free use of this conceptual instrument. The differences between Honduras and Argentina, or Haiti and Chile, are as great as those between, say, Norway and Hungary, or Liberia and

[13] Isaiah Berlin, *The Hedgehog and the Fox, an Essay on Tolstoy's View of History*, London, 1953, pp. 1-2.

Tanzania; moreover, it is by now fairly clear to serious students of Latin American contemporary history that each nation demands careful detailed and separate study. For all its nineteenth-century eminence, Latin American historiography is particularly unimpressive when dealing critically and imaginatively with the more recent past, and it is almost mandatory for anybody wishing to understand contemporary political or economic phenomena to go fairly deeply into the antecedents.

This has been convincingly demonstrated by Hugh Thomas's masterly study of the Cuban revolution. After originally planning to start with Fulgencio Batista's coup d'etat in 1952, he decided that such a proximate date would leave out too much. Therefore, he took 1899, the year when Spain abandoned the island to the United States, but, to use his own words, "that also omitted the absorbing question of slavery and how that decisively affected the character of Cuba, not to speak of the golden age of Cuban sugar in the nineteenth century; and so, after wondering whether there could be such a thing at all as a starting point to the book I had in mind (other than Columbus's journey to Cuba in 1492), I finally selected 1762, the year of the first Anglo-Saxon capture of Havana. . . . Afterwards, it seemed to me in Cuba that this decision was wise since so much that seems obscure in the present Cuban scene becomes more comprehensible if set against the experiences of the previous four or five generations."[14]

The need for detailed and scholarly national histories does not, of course, exclude the validity of wider studies, and these must include generalizations that could be made more acceptable were they preceded by numerous qualifications, but this would be cumbersome and not necessarily helpful. At any rate, despite the limitations of generalizations used in this context, they are perhaps less vulnerable than one would suppose, as they refer to a group of nations that stems from a common Iberian stock, share largely the same historical and

[14] Hugh Thomas, *Cuba, or the Pursuit of Freedom*, London, 1971, pp. xxi-xxii.

cultural traditions, the same religion and—considering the intimate link between the Spanish and Portuguese languages—use the same linguistic vehicle to communicate with each other. Much can be said about the differences between these nations, but this should not obscure the fact that they have much in common that is of definitive importance in the construction of their present and their future. As Marx indicated, although men make their own history, they do not make it out of the whole cloth: "They make it out of conditions not of their own choosing, but such as lies ready to hand. The traditions of all past generations weigh (like a nightmare) on the brain of the living."[15] In Latin America, in addition to a common language and religion, the significant traditions weighing on the decisions of the living also include a centralist disposition that has given a distinct shape and texture to the cloth out of which history is presumably made.

[15] Karl Marx, "Der achtzehnte Brumaire des Louis Napoleon," in *Karl Marx Friedrich Engels Werke*, Berlin, 1960, viii, 115. (author's translation.)

1

Postfeudal Conquest

The Iberian countries of the Western Hemisphere entered
the modern age as administrative, legal, and political creations of a postfeudal Castilian monarchy committed to the
principle of central control.[1] The political and administrative
structure of Hispanic America owes its centralism to an emphatically centralist Castile and not to a more or less pluralis-
tic Spain. The new realm was given order, system, and
hierarchy by ministers and monarchs who contemplated the

[1] If this appears unfairly to minimize the importance of the pre-Columbian
cultures, it is merely the appearance of unfairness disguising an essential
truth; for although the rich pre-Columbian heritage has survived to this day,
especially in the arts, the language of many Indian communities, and some
aspects of rural organization, it fails to impress as an essential component of
the juridical, political, or administrative arrangements of the region as a
whole. This is not to say that it should not be a component, simply that it is
not. There is but a tenuous continuity between the great empires of the time
before Columbus and the colonial and republican institutional structure of
the last five centuries. There are, of course, exceptions, and in this case the
author can offer one from his own efforts. In an earlier article the author
suggests that there appears to be an intriguing continuity from pre-
Columbian to republican forms in the propensity toward centripetal political
arrangements in the Andean region. See "Cambio y continuidad: el Pacto
Andino en la historia contemporánea," *El* IV, no. 16 (February-March, 1971),
62-92. The continuity that may well exist between the centralist tradition of
the Iberians and the special forms of centralized control characteristic of the
Quechua *Tahuantinsuyo* has been noted by Jacques Lafaye who states that
"the *Tahuantinsuyo* was a highly centralized state which can be compared—in
spite of other differences—with that of the Spanish Empire under Philip II."
(author's translation.) This may or may not be so, but at any rate it is reasonably clear that the centralism of Castile did not represent a drastic departure
from the general modes of political control associated with the *Tahuantinsuyo*. Jacques Lafaye, *Los conquistadores*, México, 1970, p. 45.

world of the Renaissance not from a cultivated cosmopolitan city in a divided Italy, but from the cold, windswept, and introspective capital of a united Spain. This Castilian character persisted throughout the period of imperial ascendancy and beyond, as vigorous and stern under Philip as it had been under the Catholic monarchs.[2] The style was Castilian indeed, hence perhaps the lack of humor, the concern with administrative punctilio, the bureaucratic diligence and rigorous adherence to the requirements of the royal prerogative. Although distant from the Castilian center, Brazil was not an exception to the centralist impulse. It could be argued that it was in Brazil where the transfer of centralist institutions from the peninsula to the Indies achieved its most telling embodiment: the wholesale transportation of the court and the imperial capital from Lisbon to Rio de Janeiro. More will be said later about the far-reaching consequences of the centralizing momentum imposed on Portugal and Brazil by the Pombaline dictatorship; in this chapter attention will be concentrated on the postfeudal Castilian conquest of Hispanic America.

Shaped by Renaissance circumstances and Renaissance minds at a time when feudalism had all but vanished from the western European scene, Latin America was spared an experience that elsewhere played such a decisive role in the formation of institutions: feudalism was never part of the Latin American cultural and political tradition. It could not have been transplanted from Spain or Portugal because, by the time of the great discoveries and the conquest, even the very special variety of Iberian feudalism had ceased to be a significant feature of the political organization of these metropolitan nations.[3]

[2] According to Braudel, "The fundamental characteristic of Philip II's empire was its Spanishness—or rather Castilianism—a fact which did not escape the contemporaries of the Prudent king, whether friend or foe." Fernand Braudel, *The Mediterranean and the Mediterranean World in the Age of Philip II*, London, 1975, ii, 676.

[3] This variety is indeed so special as to prompt Maravall to state that the Spanish medieval tradition is "the least medieval of all those found in Europe." Maravall, *Estado Moderno*, i, 23. (author's translation.) The feudal

This relatively simple fact has become unnecessarily complicated by the erratic way in which the word "feudal" has often been employed to describe the relations between landlord and peasant or to comment on the patterns of land distribution in parts of Latin America. The Bolivian sociologist Arturo Urquídi, for instance, maintains that "Spanish feudalism is reproduced in Latin America with absolute fidelity, and this reproduction which offers an almost biological similitude because of its hereditary character, affects the psychological and spiritual fields, as well as that of institutional organizations."[4] Addressing himself to those he calls "North Americans," the Mexican writer Carlos Fuentes also indulges in a lax use of the term "feudal" when he describes the historical tradition of Latin America: "You (the United States) started from zero," he states, "a virgin society, totally equal to modern times, without any feudal ballast. On the contrary, we were founded as an appendix of the falling feudal order of the Middle Ages. . . . the Latin American drama stems from the persistence of those feudal structures over four centuries of misery and stagnation." Fuentes later affirms that "the formulas of free enterprise capitalism have already had their historical opportunity in Latin America and have proved unable to abolish feudalism."[5] Another contemporary observer of the Latin American scene Moisés Poblete Troncoso, writing about Costa Rica, states that "the nineteenth century marks the beginning of the feudal oligarchy, which originated from the widespread cultivation of coffee."[6] Hernán Ramírez Necochea goes further and firmly declares that the Chilean latifundia of

---

institutions of Castile, Asturias, and León developed in ways substantially different from those of the rest of Europe, and it is arguable whether they are strictly comparable. See Claudio Sánchez-Albornoz, *Estudios sobre las instituciones medioevales españolas*, México, 1965, pp. 791-822.

[4] Arturo Urquídi, *El feudalismo en América Latina y la reforma agraria boliviana*, Cochabamba, 1966, p. 46. (author's translation.)

[5] Carlos Fuentes, "The Argument of Latin America: Words for the North Americans," in *Whither Latin America?*, ed. Paul M. Sweezy and Leo Huberman, New York, 1963, pp. 10-11.

[6] Moisés Poblete Troncoso, *La reforma agraria en América Latina*, Santiago, 1961, p. 28. (author's translation.)

the nineteenth century were the basis of a "purely feudal" economic and social structure.[7] Holding views wholly different from those of Ramírez Necochea on most issues Régis Debray is not above making as enthusiastic and unrigorous a use of the term as the Chilean historian. When referring to the controversy over the appropriate revolutionary program for Latin America, he states: "To the sectarian thesis . . . of the immediate socialist revolution without preliminary stages is counterposed the traditional thesis of certain Communist Parties, of the antifeudal agrarian revolution." A few lines further on he stresses, "Even a cursory analysis of Latin American capitalism reveals that it is organically bound to feudal relations in the countryside." And then he goes on to explain that "Cuba is admired . . . as the only country which has succeeded in liquidating feudalism."[8] Finally, he suggests that the Alliance for Progress failed "because the liquidation of agrarian feudalism required the transformation of the relations of production as a whole, since agrarian feudalism is an integral moment of the development of the commercial and agrarian-export bourgeoisie."[9]

[7] Hernán Ramírez Necochea, *Historia del movimiento obrero en Chile*, Santiago, 1956, p. 49.

[8] Robin Blackburn, ed., *Régis Debray, Strategy for Revolution*, London, 1970, pp. 71-72, 78.

[9] Blackburn, *Debray*, p. 120. The French historian Jacques Lafaye concludes from the same assumption of the existence of feudalism at the time of the conquest, "This feudal organization of the conquest of the New World had as a natural corollary, in the spirit of the conquerors, a great freedom of action at first, and freedom of administration later." *Conquistadores*, p. 55. In the course of this work it will be shown that both these propositions are unwarranted. In fact, Lafaye contradicts himself a few pages on when he writes, accurately this time, that "if one wanted to sum up the relationship between the conquerors and the Spanish state one would have to say that the former had to face all the risks and the latter came in to share in all the profits," p. 61, and then further on, "the *Casa de Contratación* in Seville was the only permanent and omnipotent institution for the administration of the New World," p. 68. (author's translation.) It would be fair to ask whether omnipotent central institutions are in fact compatible with feudal administrative freedom, even as narrowly defined as M. Lafaye suggests. Possibly it is in the more recent work of Johan Galtung that the word "feudal" has undergone its most demanding metamorphosis, for here, apart from being adorned with a re-

Such unrigorous use of this important word should not be allowed to obscure its precise political meaning. Without attempting to propose a satisfactory definition of the term it can be said that serfdom, ill-treatment, and the division of land into large estates are not distinguishing characteristics of Western feudalism. Human beings were cruel and nasty to each other for centuries before feudalism appeared on the political horizon and have continued to behave in objectionable ways after it vanished. As for serfdom, even if, stretching definitions to their limits, one were to consider that the relationship between the conquerors and the native inhabitants of the Indies was similar to that found in European medieval serfdom—a highly questionable assumption—and were further to accept that serfdom "is the characteristic existence-form of labour power in the feudal mode of production,"[10] the argument would still have to overcome the objection that much more than serfdom is needed to produce feudalism. Sweezy indicates that "some serfdom can exist in systems which are clearly not feudal; and even as the dominant relation of production, serfdom has at different times and in different regions been associated with different forms of economic organization."[11] As for the large estates, it does not

---

markable amount of what is commonly known as "sociologese," it is freely used as if it were synonymous with the term "authoritarian." Of course, it would be far more appropriate for the concept of feudalism to be associated with the absence, or the relaxation of central authority, but surely there are better words to describe either situation, and it only confuses the issue to persist in the loose utilization of words such as "feudal" to describe contemporary power arrangements. See Johan Galtung, *Feudal Systems, Structural Violence, and Structural Theory of Revolutions*, Oslo, 1969.

[10] This is the position adopted by H. K. Takahashi in support of Maurice Dobb's explanation of the decline of feudalism. See *The Transition from Feudalism to Capitalism: A Symposium* by Paul M. Sweezy, Maurice Dobb, H. K. Takahashi, Rodney Hilton, and Christopher Hill, New York, 1963, p. 32. In his well-known book on the development of capitalism, Maurice Dobb defines feudalism primarily as a mode of production and, as such, "virtually identical with what we generally mean by serfdom: an obligation laid on the producer by force and independently of his own volition to fulfil certain economic demands of an overlord." *Studies in the Development of Capitalism*, London, 1946, p. 35.

[11] Sweezy et al., *The Transition*, p. 1. To support this view Sweezy cites

demand much erudition to discover instances—Britain afforded a classical one to Marx when he was trying to prove the same point—of countries where the formation of large estates has been one of the consequences of the demise of the feudal system.

The concept of feudalism used here refers specifically to that particular system of distribution of political power that became widespread in much of western Europe roughly between the seventh and the thirteenth centuries. A principal shared characteristic of this system was the transformation, often by gradual and functional delegation of power, of public duty into private obligation formalized through the holding of a fief. This process lessened the power of the monarchical center and augmented that of the baronial periphery. The assumption of judicial, legislative, and military duties turned the barons into an effective and politically important intermediary between the vassals and their sovereign. In addition to many other significant consequences, this rearrangement led to the development of diverse practices and habits of compromise and understanding permitting the coexistence of the different holders of effective political power. Pragmatic notions of equilibrium and balance of power issued from such arrangements, and schemes were devised to ensure the continued functioning of the body politic even though perfect agreement or the absolute subservience of the lesser holders of limited power to the central monarchy did not occur.

This does not pretend to be a definition of feudalism, but merely a brief enumeration of those features that are important for this study. Obviously there are others perhaps equally important; Dobb lists six that appear eminently acceptable: a low level of technology; a system of production for immediate use (which would rule out the whole of the Spanish

---

Engels who in a letter to Marx indicates that "it is certain that serfdom and bondage are not a peculiarly [Spezifisch] medieval-feudal form, we find them everywhere or nearly everywhere where conquerors have the land cultivated for them by the old inhabitants." As for the presence of serfdom outside western Europe, it is usually associated with political and economic arrangements so dissimilar that it is virtually impossible to establish generalizations applicable to them as well as to the European phenomenon.

and Portuguese overseas empires); demesne farming, often on a considerable scale, by compulsory labor services; conditional holding of land by lords on some kind of service tenure (which again would exclude much of the Hispanic and Portuguese American empires); possession by a lord of judicial or quasi-judicial functions in relation to the dependent population (again not applicable to the Indies); and finally—and possibly most important—political decentralization.[12]

The end of feudalism was not a simple result of a lineal sequence of events; many factors contributed to it and their interaction is certainly not a subject that can be described superficially; those who have examined it closely do not agree.[13] For the purpose of this study it is enough to point out that there is a discernible parallel between the decline of feudalism as a workable form of social and political organization and other changes such as the increase in the circulation of money, the regularization of taxation by central governments, the purchase by monarchs of the military services that permitted them to challenge the power of the peripheral barons, the development of a learned professional judiciary that gradually took over the legislative functions of the nobility, the overexploitation of serfs apparently resulting in mass migration into the towns, and, generally, the development of commerce on a vast and unprecedented scale. Feudalism declined when the need for balance was no longer mandatory; it ended when the central monarchies secured sufficient power to enforce acceptance of their writ.

This feudal experience has been a cardinal factor in the development of the Western political tradition and is certainly found at the very root of European parliamentarism, liberalism, and all the social democratic variants that evolved from them. Trevelyan makes this point when he writes: "un-

[12] Dobb, *Studies*, pp. 33-37, also Sweezy et al., *The Transition*, pp. 1-2.

[13] The Symposium to which reference has been made earlier is precisely the outcome of yet another controversy between distinguished Marxist scholars over the factors responsible for the decline of feudalism. In the Foreword Maurice Dobb frankly notes that "no one of us could claim that finality has been reached on these issues."

less we become a Totalitarian State and forget all about our Englishry, there will always be something medieval in our ways of thinking, especially in our idea that people and corporations have rights and liberties which the State ought in some degree to respect, in spite of the legal omnipotence of Parliament. Liberalism, in the broadest sense, is medieval in origin, and so are trade unions. The men who established our civic liberties in the Seventeenth Century, appealed to medieval precedents against the 'modernizing' monarchy of the Stuarts."[14]

And of course he is right; representative institutions and parliaments are distinctly a product of the Middle Ages and directly a result of the development of feudalism; the parliamentary limitations that proved so tiresome to the absolutist rulers of the "New Monarchies" after the end of the medieval period were certainly an echo of medieval practices in matters of political representation. It is difficult to disagree with R. H. Lord when he suggests that the hallmark of the period from the thirteenth to the seventeenth century was the limitation of the power of the crown by assemblies, "in part elective, whose members, though directly and immediately representing only the politically active classes, were also regarded as representing in a general way the whole population of the land."[15] This was probably true of most of western Europe, but the country where it least applied was certainly Castile. Modern absolutism developed strongly in France and Britain, but it came earlier and more successfully to Castile where the assertion of the royal authority was virtually unrestricted by institutional obstacles. This historical circumstance has afforded a basis for intriguing suggestions regarding the origins of the modern state. Sánchez Agesta, for example, believes that it is in sixteenth-century Spanish thought, firmly founded, of course, on political experience, that "the architecture of a theory of State; perhaps the first theory of the State" can be discerned. According to Maravall, sixteenth-century

[14] G. M. Trevelyan, *English Social History*, London, 1964, p. 96.
[15] Robert Howard Lord, "The Parliaments of the Middle Ages and Early Modern Period," *CHR*, XVI (1930), 125-144.

Spanish politics are intelligible only if considered as a consequence of the early rise of the modern state in the peninsula.[16]
And as it was from the heart of Spain, from Castile, that the
Indies were conquered, colonized, and organized, the dying
political feudalism in the kingdom of Isabella was never given
the opportunity to prosper overseas, and consequently the institutional habit of compromise between alternative holders
of effective political power did not have an early opportunity
to become established in Latin America. When it appeared at
all, it was as a result of the eager imitation of nineteenth-
century western European institutions on the part of the independent republics that emerged after the collapse of the
Spanish Empire.

Reference has been made to the directness with which the
central monarchical authority was exercised over the empire,
and it is useful at this stage to comment on two common mis-
understandings that plague much of the historical writing
about the overseas Spanish Empire. The first one arises from
an erroneous interpretation of the well-known dictum, "*Se
obedece, pero no se cumple*," whose approximate meaning is
"One obeys, but does not enforce," suggesting that the formal act of acceptance of a royal order was not necessarily followed by its enforcement, usually on the excuse of seeking
clarification or further information. This legalistic delay,
which was certainly not rare, has been interpreted as a dilatory tactic designed to avoid compliance without openly challenging the metropolitan authority. Basing themselves on this
interpretation, some students of these problems have been led
to believe that the power exerted by the crown was more apparent than real. Julio Alemparte, for instance, roundly states
that "the kings were not in Spain, but in the Indies; the real
sovereigns, in a way, were the colonial masters." While the
crown was in Castile, as were the official sources of power
and juridical order, the real sovereignty was "that which
emerges from the effective control of the land and the mass of

---

[16] Luis Sánchez Agesta, *El concepto del Estado en el pensamiento español del
siglo XVI*, Madrid, 1959, also, Maravall, *Estado Moderno*, ɪ, Introduction,
chaps. 1 and 2.

the people" and that was in the colonies. It might be said, according to Alemparte, that in the New World there was a curious mixture of feudal nobility and bourgeoisie, both at one and the same time: "Is more power possible? Fiefs indeed could be called those enormous extensions of land given to the *encomenderos* and the Indians and *mestizos*, their serfs. . . . The inhabitants of the Indies, both creoles and Europeans, and particularly those of Peru . . . as long as they remained loyal to the kings of Spain and unshaken in their faith, could hardly wish for a more advantageous government, with greater freedom than they enjoyed and more security for their properties."[17] Of course, the operative phrase is "as long as they remained loyal to the kings of Spain." Comfort and well-being must not be confused with power, even when distances and slowness of communications permitted the colonial authorities to attenuate the full rigor of the crown directives. Power ultimately must mean power to disagree; latitude of enforcement, perhaps more the result of geographical distance than of political intent, cannot be accepted as evidence that there were in the Indies groups of men with effective power to stand up successfully against the metropolis.[18]

The second misunderstanding, also mentioned by Alemparte, is based on the belief that the privileges of the *encomenderos* were such as to make them veritable feudal barons and the lands they controlled through royal grants the equivalent of fiefs. Some of the characteristics of the *encomienda* and the

[17] Julio Alemparte, *El cabildo en Chile colonial*, Santiago, 1966, pp. 84-85. (author's translation.)

[18] Braudel has reminded us of the true dimensions of Philip II's Mediterranean, "certainly not within the measure of sixteenth century man," but an immense area, mastered only at the cost of great efforts with delays in communications so frequent and prolonged that as the Cardinal de Rambouillet complained to Charles IX when the royal dispatches did arrive "the time when I could have availed myself of them and had occasion to execute the orders contained in them is often, to my great sorrow, past." There was no procrastination or political intent here, simply great distance and poor communications. Such difficulties must have multiplied when orders had to sail across the Atlantic and then travel overland to the capitals of the distant Indies. Fernand Braudel, *The Mediterranean*, I, 355-358.

land grants given by the Spanish crown to the settlers superficially resemble the institutions associated with military feudalism in parts of western Europe and Prussia. It would be a mistake, however, to assume that in the case of Latin America these constituted the basis for a feudal system. As Mario Góngora has pointed out, "the *encomienda* lacked all the political characteristics of the western seigneurial domain, the jurisdiction, the immunity, the *Ban*. The Spanish State in the Indies jealously retained the judicial supremacy for itself." He adds that it is not possible to speak of a politically effective feudal enclave in the Indies, for "the authorities that represented the king retained a key position in the distribution of power . . . the holders of *encomiendas*, even in those places where they constituted an important force through their weight in the local council [*cabildo*] necessarily had to have recourse to the authority of the Crown and its administrative entities without which there was no legal sanction. . . . The institution [of the *encomienda*] was part and parcel of a modern bureaucratic state." Góngora further points out that the *encomienda* was "an administrative concession . . . which evidently resulted in the creation of economic privileges and military duties," but these practices were merely an expedient utilized by the Spanish bureaucratic empire. In his opinion the bonds holding the state together certainly lacked the profound feelings that arose in personal relationships based on feudal oaths of loyalty. The monarch remained as important and central a political juridical figure for the *encomendero* as he was for other common subjects. According to Góngora, "The *encomenderos* are not, in fact, vassals; they are simply a privileged group of subjects. The feudal ethic does not exist in America."[19]

Feudalism has never existed in Spanish America; there have been no grand dukes or warlords or even local chieftains strong enough to raise taxes and organize armies in defiance of the central power.[20] There has been no functional need for

[19] Mario Góngora, *Encomenderos y estancieros, 1580-1660*, Santiago, 1970, pp. 118-119. (author's translation.)
[20] Neither has it existed in Portuguese America. This has been shown con-

the political center to divest itself of effective power or to compromise at the highest level the exercise of political responsibility. The problem of coexistence of various centers of more or less equivalent importance has not been an issue; the political center has not been endangered partly because there have been no effective challengers.

It is also important to point out that the hypothesis presented in this study is in no way related to the deceptively similar argument advanced by those who feel that the absence of a feudal experience extinguishes the possibilities for "bourgeois democratic reform" in Latin America and that because of this, the only way to further progress is through violent mass action. Possibly the most candid spokesman for this position is A. G. Frank who maintains that feudalism never took root in this part of the world, but that from as early as the sixteenth century a capitalist "satellite colonization" established an iron framework within which the stunted and dependent economies of Latin America developed. The fault, therefore, would not lie with outdated, oppressive feudal institutions, however residual, but with peripheral capitalism. If this is true, then Frank infers that "the historical mission and role of the bourgeoisie . . . is finished . . . in Latin America as is [sic] elsewhere, the role of promoting historical progress has now fallen to the masses of the people alone. . . . To applaud and in the name of the people even to support the bourgeoisie in its already played out role on the stage of history is treacherous or treachery."[21]

---

vincingly by Faoro in his seminal work, first published in 1957, *Os donos do poder*. See especially vol. I, 127-133, "O chamado feudalismo brasileiro."

[21] A. G. Frank, *Capitalism and Underdevelopment in Latin America*, New York, 1967, pp. xii-xiii. It should not be very hard to think of good reasons for refraining from accepting Dr. Frank's thesis. In my opinion, one of them would be the extreme vulnerability of one of its premises—namely, that the only possible alternative to "feudalism" was "capitalism," and further that these forms of social and political organization necessarily follow each other on a rather fixed schedule, so that once feudalism is out, capitalism must come in. If capitalism and its leading exponents the "bourgeoisie" are, as Dr. Frank puts it, "finished," then they must be immediately discarded, and whoever fails to do this leaves himself open to the charge of treason. Perhaps

This may or may not be so, but apart from the fact that this argument is based on views of the nature of history, politics, and retribution that are at least arguable, I should naturally feel unhappy if anybody were to relate the present study to such an unusual thesis.

---

one may be allowed to hope that human beings and human society are a little more complex than Dr. Frank would lead us to believe. Another author who impugns the thesis of the feudal character of the colonization of the Indies for what can be fairly described as political reasons is Luis Vitale. In his *Interpretación marxista de la historia de Chile*, Santiago, 1967-1971, II, 15-25, he argues that this thesis was first advanced by nineteenth-century liberal historians and has now "been brought up-to-date in a biased way by contemporary reformist writers." (author's translation.)

2

Castilian Origins

Castile under Ferdinand and Isabella was the strongest centralized monarchy of its time able to exercise effective control over Spain and vast overseas territories in a manner that justifies the description of the Spanish Empire as the "first world power."[1] This was not the result of good fortune or dynastic accident, but of policies pursued tenaciously over a long period of time. The feat was achieved when the power of monarchs was on the increase, but whereas elsewhere feudal establishments were able to obstruct the authority of crowned heads, in Castile the political and military might of the nobility was effectively neutralized. When the temporal power of western European kings was still limited by feudal survivals, Ferdinand and Isabella had undisputed political control over the largest empire the world had ever seen and virtually absolute ecclesiastical authority as well.

That the "New Monarchies" of the sixteenth century were the precursors of the modern state is sufficiently clear, but the fact that it was in Castile, under Ferdinand and Isabella, that the earliest successful moves in this direction were undertaken has possibly received less attention from Latin Americans than it deserves.[2] For these seminal developments occurred in Castile a good quarter of a century before the legendary hero of Russian centralism Ivan the Terrible had even been born and at a time when France was still torn by domestic struggles

[1] John Fraser Ramsay, *Spain: The Rise of the First World Power*, University, Ala., 1973.

[2] In Spanish historiography there has been no such inattention. Two most pertinent modern authors in this respect are Luis Sánchez Agesta and José Antonio Maravall.

between the crown and nobility. Moreover, during the early years after the accession of Henry VIII to the English throne, it was the counsel of a mature and experienced Ferdinand of Aragon that apparently influenced the young king. This occurred from 1509 onwards, five years after the death of Isabella, when the construction of Castilian centralism had been completed and the task had commenced of extending it overseas. The Catholic monarchs had an early opportunity to influence vast territories as yet untouched by European institutions, and their imperial policy carried the imprint of the vigorous Castilian centralism justly identified with their reign.

The successful consolidation of a centralist political and administrative structure under the rule of Ferdinand and Isabella was not shared throughout Spain. A number of the ancient corporations and lesser kingdoms in the peninsula retained some of their medieval privileges, albeit in a residual form, not only throughout the reign of the Catholic monarchs and their successors, but well into the twentieth century. This is an important theme of Stanley and Barbara Stein who state that, "perhaps the greatest myth assimilated into the European thinking of this period was the myth of 'Spain' itself." According to the Steins, in the late fifteenth century the political geography of Spain had not yet become consolidated nor had its internal structure as a nation-state been developed. "The marriage of Ferdinand and Isabella, often considered the birth of the modern Spanish state, resulted not in the unification of the kingdoms of Aragon and Castile but in condominium in which the two parts of the 'Spanish Crown' coexisted as separate entities with separate laws, taxation systems, coinage, and trading patterns."[3] Regardless of the merits of this statement with respect to Spain generally, it certainly does not apply to Castilian domestic political arrangements and it was not intended to—and, more importantly, it does not apply to the relationship between the

---

[3] Stanley J. and Barbara Stein, *The Colonial Heritage of Latin America*, New York, 1970, p. 14.

crown of Castile and the Indies. Perhaps its greatest short-coming is that it does not adequately consider the dominant position of Castile within Spain during the life of Isabella or the fact that after her death Ferdinand established an almost unchallenged authority over both kingdoms and passed it on to rulers as strong as himself. At the time of the marriage of Ferdinand and Isabella, Castile had 73.2 percent of the population of the Iberian peninsula, including Portugal, and covered 65.2 percent of the territory. Together with the crown of Aragon, Castile accounted for 82.4 percent of the total Iberian territory and for 85.2 percent of the population. The population density in Castile was 22 inhabitants per square kilometer while in Portugal it was only 16.7, in Aragon, 13.6 and in Navarre 15.4. It is therefore legitimate to assume that the political weight of Castile, let alone that of Castile and Aragon combined, was of overriding importance. No other kingdom or region outside these two attained even the shadow of the central power exercised from Madrid.[4]

The policy of centralization of particular relevance to Spanish America was that of the kingdom of Isabella. The rest of Spain may or may not have been completely and uniformly integrated at all levels of political and administrative control, but this did not affect the centrally devised arrangements for the Indies originating from Castile. Its government was unencumbered by impediments to temper the views of rulers who never faltered in their conviction that power was absolute, that it should be absolutely centralized and exercised absolutely.[5] The fact that the empire in the Indies was incorporated as a fief of the Castilian crown to the exclusion of the other Spanish kingdoms from a formal participation in its af-

[4] J. H. Elliott, *Imperial Spain, 1469-1716*, New York, 1966, pp. 24-25.

[5] This ought not to be taken to mean that at the national and imperial levels Spain lacked all unity. As Maravall has indicated, writing from a decidedly sceptical vantage point and granting very little indeed to the idea of unification, "the mere circumstance of being united under the same Crown (imposed) common tasks, and a destiny . . . that generated long lasting ties of a supranational character . . . under which the unifying process . . . was facilitated." (author's translation.) See Maravall, *Estado Moderno*, I, 101.

fairs facilitated the centralization of administrative and political decisions. The Indies were indeed formally "the Indies of the Crown of Castile, and all major decisions were made, in theory, by the monarch, advised by the Council of Castile." Moreover, in practice, questions of administration and policy affecting the overseas territories rarely came before the full body of the council. The king referred these affairs to individual councillors, notably Juan Rodríguez de Fonseca and Lope de Conchillos, so that in fact, "the government of the Indies . . . was a narrow and tightly centralized bureaucracy controlled by Fonseca in the name of the King."[6] This concentration of executive power under the Castilian crown ensured that even if there had been variations within a heterogeneous Spain, these did not affect the government of the Indies. As it was, Ferdinand and Isabella reigned with the greatest harmony, and serious disagreement as to the manner in which power should have been shared between them is almost completely unknown. There was some initial difficulty in defining their respective powers over the kingdom of Castile, but this was settled amicably after close consideration of the legal points involved. Isabella was recognized as monarch and given the responsibility of dispensing patronage, "looking after the fortresses and administering the finances of the kingdom."[7] It was clear after this, that in matters pertaining to Castile and the Indies, the crown was Isabella's, and she was not the sort of ruler to part lightly with power and responsibility.

This single-handed control of the affairs of Castile and the Indies during the formative decades of the late fifteenth and early sixteenth centuries becomes even more important when considering the fact that in the vast panorama of western European feudalism the phenomenon as it evolved in Castile

---

[6] This firm centralization of control was symbolized in the creation in 1514 of a special royal seal for the authentication of all enactments and decrees pertaining to the Indies left in the keeping of Fonseca, J. H. Parry, *The Spanish Seaborne Empire*, London, 1966, pp. 57-58.

[7] Fernando del Pulgar, *Crónica de los Reyes Católicos*, Madrid, 1943, I, 70-74. (author's translation.)

was noticeably exceptional. Toward the end of the sixth and the beginning of the seventh century, most of western Europe, and the kingdom of Aragon as well, though at a later date, witnessed the growth of feudal immunities that meant precisely what the word implies; that is, they were a legal emancipation of the baronial periphery from the direct sovereignty of the monarch. This was accepted by the crown and greatly valued by a baronial class increasingly conscious of its rising power. But as Sánchez-Albornoz has shown in his careful studies, in Castile the development of feudal immunities assumed a radically different character; the royal prerogative emerged juridically undiminished, although an intermediate, aristocratic status was allowed to evolve *de facto* between the person of the monarch and the common subjects.[8] Moreover, these differences, as well as those between regions within the Iberian peninsula were further emphasized and modified by the formidable impact of the Moorish invasions.

The Arabs conquered the peninsula in a few years, but it took the Christian kingdoms seven centuries to dislodge them. That intermittent, at times savage, war left its mark everywhere on the Spanish world, including, of course, on the development of institutions. In addition to other factors of importance, the order in which different regions of Spain were reconquered determined the eventual political, social, and economic climate. The kingdom of Aragon, comprising roughly what is now known as Valencia, Aragon, and Catalonia, was recovered early, during the second half of the thirteenth century, and the population was able to direct its energies to the development of Mediterranean trade. Barcelona became the center of a commercial empire of consequence, and Catalans were the masters of Sardinia, Sicily, and part of Greece, as well as comptrollers of important trading outposts in North Africa, Venice, Genoa, Bruges, and Antwerp. Such diligence and the resulting prosperity nurtured a powerful urban business patriciate, almost a bourgeoi-

---

[8] Sánchez-Albornoz, *Estudios*, p. 796.

sie, that made its opinions count in the affairs of the kingdom, eventually introducing into the political arrangements of Aragon a distinct constitutional system founded on the idea of a contractual obligation between the ruler and the ruled with a mutual recognition of rights and responsibilities. It was on this that the Catalan Cortes based their traditional power and prestige. Halfway through the long reconquest of Spain, these Cortes had already secured the power to legislate and even to limit the king's power to issue legislation under certain conditions.[9]

While the kingdom of Aragon went its constitutional way, Castile was engaged in war, either against the Moors or against herself, and torn by internecine feuds that caused as much anarchy and destruction as the intermittent campaign against the foreign invaders. A poor land with a pastoral economy, little opportunity, and possibly less inclination to engage in commercial or industrial pursuits, Castile evolved differently from Catalonia. In the Castilian hinterland it was the warlords, not the merchants, who were influential, and the crown saw its power circumscribed *de facto*, not *de jure*. This was not the consequence of a successful royal resistance to such encroachments, but rather of the reluctance of the warrior-barons to institutionalize their gains partly because of their ignorance or dislike of juridical procedures and also in part because to do so would have established a contractual, legal relationship with responsibilities they were unlikely to accept.

In Castile, as in Aragon, the medieval parliamentary in-

[9] As Elliott points out the Cortes were only one of a number of uniquely Catalan medieval institutions originally devised to protect the rights and liberties of the subjects and directly based on the existence of a prosperous and prestigious commercial bourgeoisie, others were the *Justicia* and the *Diputació*, of which Elliott writes, "The Catalan *Diputació* was . . . an immensely powerful institution, backed by large financial resources; and its obvious attractions as a bulwark of national liberty had stimulated Aragonese and Valencians to establish similar institutions in their own countries by the end of the fifteenth century. As a result, all three states were exceptionally well protected at the end of the Middle Ages from encroachments by the Crown." Elliott, *Imperial Spain*, p. 30.

stitution of the Cortes existed, but were seldom summoned as the monarch was not under an obligation to do so. Their influence was minimal, and as nobility and clergy were exempted from financial exactions that could conceivably join them with the representatives of the towns in resisting additional levies by the crown, they did not pose a credible challenge to the power of either the king or the barons. To revoke laws, it was necessary to obtain the consent of the Cortes, but to make new laws, the crown could act alone. The Cortes were allowed to address petitions to the monarch, but, as Elliott has indicated convincingly, they never succeeded in transforming this into the right to legislate, "partly because of their own lack of unity, and partly because of their failure to establish the principle that redress of grievances must precede supply."[10] Furthermore, the military foundations of Castilian society made it unlikely that the military commanders, nobles, and warlords who wielded direct power under the crown should be particularly inclined to seek juridical ratification of that power from institutions, such as the Cortes, that represented the views of burghers with limited economic and political influence. Hence, when the barons were able to make inroads into the royal power during the fourteenth and fifteenth centuries as a result of the incapacity of the monarch, these were not institutionalized and remained *de facto* usurpations, easily redressed under a strong king, as in fact happened when Ferdinand and Isabella assumed leadership.

At the time of the accession of the Catholic monarchs, there was near anarchy in Castile; the authority and prestige of the crown had been seriously eroded during the undistinguished tenure of Henry IV, and the nobility had made good use of the opportunity by usurping in form and essence many of the royal prerogatives.[11] In the country at large there was little

---

[10] Elliott, *Imperial Spain*, p. 34.

[11] Eighteenth and nineteenth-century historians of Spain appreciated this critical situation and conveyed its significance to their readers perhaps more forcibly and convincingly than their more restrained twentieth-century successors. For example, according to the inimitable Prescott, Isabella is reputed to have observed, while in the middle of one of her confrontations with the

respect for the crown's judiciary, and the state of lawlessness was forcing citizens to look to their own devices for protection. As one historian describes it, Isabella corrected this situation through the relentless use of "centralization, repression and assertion of the supremacy of the Crown."[12] A number of reforms, some far-reaching, were efficiently implemented, and results were already in evidence by 1482, before the outbreak of war in Granada and a decade before Columbus's first voyage.[13] A high priority was assigned to ensuring a workable system of law enforcement, and this was mainly achieved through the reorganization of the ancient paramilitary institution of the *Santa Hermandad* that in the past had been used by the municipal corporations and sometimes by the nobles themselves as a defense against banditry and against attempts to limit their privileges.[14] Isabella transformed this organization into a militia loyal to the sovereign and active throughout the kingdom. Not surprisingly, the nobility was strongly opposed to the creation of what was, in certain ways, a precursor of a centrally controlled police as well as a royal armed force, but their resistance was unavailing. And more was to follow. Reforms were introduced into the procedures for filling public posts, basing them on merit instead of rank or connections. All pensions granted to the nobility in previous ad-

---

nobles, "so long as Heaven permits us to retain the rank with which we have been entrusted, we shall take care not to imitate the example of Henry the fourth, in becoming a tool in the hands of our nobility." William H. Prescott, *History of the Reign of Ferdinand and Isabella the Catholic*, London, 1885, pp. 135-136; see also William Robertson, *History of the Reign of Charles V*, London, 1774, I, 177-190.

[12] H. Butler Clarke, "The Catholic Kings," in *The Cambridge Modern History*, edited by A. W. Ward, G. W. Prothero, and Stanley Leathes, Cambridge, 1904, I, 352.

[13] Prescott classified the reforms under six headings: the efficient administration of justice; the codification of the law; the depression of the nobles; the vindication of ecclesiastical rights belonging to the crown from papal encroachment; the regulation of trade; and the pre-eminence of the royal authority. Prescott, *Ferdinand and Isabella*, pp. 135-136; see also Tarsicio de Azcona, *Isabel la Católica*, Madrid, 1964, ch. 5.

[14] Antonio Alvarez de Morales, *Las Hermandades, expresión del movimiento comunitario en España*, Valladolid, 1974.

ministrations were forfeited entirely unless it could be proved that they had been awarded because of outstanding service to the state. The nobility were forbidden from imitating in any way the regal style of address in writing, from quartering the royal arms on their shields, from being attended by macebearers or bodyguards, from erecting fortresses without specific authorization from the crown, and, perhaps as grating as any of these measures, duelling was strictly prohibited.[15]

The interests of the baronial periphery were best represented by the wealthy and powerful military orders of Castile. Unless these were neutralized or destroyed, the crown could not succeed in achieving complete mastery over the country's affairs. Isabella dealt with this problem by seizing control of the grandmasterships of the orders as they fell vacant. The first such opportunity occurred in 1477, and, in a brilliant and totally unexpected last-minute move the nobles were unable to counter, she proposed the name of her consort as candidate. Ferdinand was thus elected grandmaster of the Order of Santiago, establishing a precedent that later gave him control of the Orders of Calatrava and Alcántara as well.[16]

The successful policy of bringing the nobles under central control was paralleled by the recovery for the crown of Castile of the powers that had been relinquished to the Holy See. This required unusual determination on the part of rulers as devout as these. Prescott has summarized the situation admi-

---

[15] The passage of so many new laws highlighted the need to bring the vast, unwieldy mass of existing and often contradictory or obsolete codes, statutes, precedents, and assorted existing legislation into order. This task was entrusted to the learned Alfonso Díaz de Montalvo who produced the *Ordenanzas reales* of 1485. With alterations, these ordinances remained in use until the time of Philip II and then provided the basis for the *Nueva recopilación* that became the core of Spanish law until the nineteenth century.

[16] Ferdinand valued these grandmasterships so much that after the death of Isabella when he had to resign the regency of Castile in 1506 for what turned out to be a very brief period he insisted in retaining them together with the portion of the Castilian revenues bequeathed specifically by the queen in her will. Robertson, *Charles V*, I, 192-193.

rably by pointing out how courageous it was for the Catholic monarchs to assume an attitude of such defiant independence, and he added, "whoever has studied their reign will regard this measure as perfectly conformable to their habitual policy, which never suffered a zeal for religion, or a blind deference to the Church, to compromise in any degree the independence of the Crown."[17] This policy, however, was not maintained without friction. An early clash took place with Sixtus IV over the appointment of the bishop of Cuenca. Contrary to the wishes of the queen, who wanted the post for her chaplain, the Castilian Alfonso de Burgos, the pope had named his nephew, Cardinal San Giorgio. The intricate confrontation that followed reached a critical point when Isabella ordered all Spanish citizens, lay and ecclesiastical, to quit the papal dominions without delay. Faced with such resolute opposition, the pope acceded to negotiations that eventually led to the issuing of a bull in which His Holiness "engaged to provide such natives to the higher dignities of the Church in Castile as should be nominated by the monarchs of that Kingdom."[18]

This bull, issued in 1482, was followed by other concessions, some secured after acrimonious confrontations with the Holy See, others the result of skillful diplomacy on the part of Ferdinand during the complex international difficulties that beset the Italian states at the turn of the century, and yet others the expression of papal support for the Castilian crown in the prosecution of the war of Granada.[19] In 1486, for in-

---

[17] Prescott, *Ferdinand and Isabella*, pp. 491-492.

[18] Prescott, *Ferdinand and Isabella*, p. 157.

[19] For a differing view, see for instance Darcy Ribeiro's *The Civilizational Process*, Washington, D.C., 1968, p. 85, in which he argues that "the association of the Iberian monarchs and the Papacy was so close as almost to constitute a fusion of the economic resources and salvationism of Madrid with the anti-reform zeal of Rome. Under this state of affairs, Iberia obtained from the Pope the title to exclusive domination over all lands discovered west of an imaginary line, and the Spanish monarchy was granted the privileges of creating and directing the Sacred Inquisition, of conferring the title of 'apostolic vicar' with the status of 'universal patronage' and even of collecting tithes and other Church income. In this way, an aristocratic-ecclesiastical power struc-

stance, when this conflict was claiming the better part of the energy and resources of the kingdom, the bull of Granada was issued, *Orthodoxe fidei propagationem*, conferring on the Castilian crown the right of nomination to all monasteries, churches, and episcopal sees in the conquered Moorish kingdom. This gave Ferdinand and Isabella a degree of *de jure* ecclesiastical governance over reconquered Granada that exceeded not only their authority elsewhere within Spain, but also that of any other monarch in Europe.[20] No doubt taking advantage of the fact that the pope was a Spaniard, the Castilian monarchs acted as if the general dispositions of this bull allowed for an extension to other parts of their dominions. Alexander VI proved amenable, but his successor, Julius II, was less easy to deal with.[21] However, in 1508 with Italy once again threatened with a French invasion, the pope was virtually forced to negotiate for Spanish support. This coincided with Ferdinand's full assumption of power as regent of Castile after the death of Isabella and the complex problems of

ture was established that henceforth controlled the destinies of the Iberian people." In fact, the concessions described were not related to Rome's antireformist zeal, but were the outcome of very worldly political negotiations that reflected the Vatican's practical interest in Italian and European diplomacy. After all, the bull *Universalis ecclesiae regimini* was granted in 1508, while Luther's ninety-five theses were nailed up at Wittenberg in 1517.

[20] These concessions were gradually extended, mostly under the pressure of war. Partly as a result of an ambiguous commitment on the part of Ferdinand not to intervene, the French armies of Charles VIII invaded Italy in 1494. This emergency prompted the pope to propitiate Spain with additional important concessions. The Castilian crown received in perpetuity the *tercias* or two-ninths of all the tithes collected in their dominions; also, bulls of crusade were promulgated granting a tenth of all ecclesiastical revenues in Spain to the crown on the lightly honored understanding, that this money would be used for the defense of the Holy See. It was at this time that the pope conferred the title of "Catholic" on the Spanish monarchs to mark the successful conclusion of the war of Granada. Parry, *Seaborne Empire*, pp. 153-155.

[21] In 1504, replying to a carefully worded Spanish request for papal legislation, not approval, to establish new episcopal sees in the Indies, Julius issued an equally carefully worded bull, *Illius fulciti presidio*, erecting three new bishoprics, but ignoring the scarcely disguised claim for royal patronage independently exercised. Parry, *Seaborne Empire*, ch. 8.

succession had been favorably resolved. It was in these negotiations that Ferdinand proved his mettle as arch diplomatist
securing at one stroke what he and Isabella had sought for so
many years. By the bull *Universalis ecclesiae regimini* the pope
conceded to the crown of Castile in perpetuity "the privilege
of founding and organizing all churches, and presenting to all
sees and livings, in all overseas territories which they possessed then or might acquire in future."[22]

The victory of Ferdinand's regalism was complete. As the
Mexican historian Joaquín García Icazbalceta commented,
"by virtue of the bull of Julius II . . . the Spanish monarchs
came to exercise a power in the ecclesiastical government of
the Indies which, except in purely spiritual matters, was almost pontifical. Without the authorization of the King no
church, monastery or hospital could be founded, nor could
bishoprics or parishes be established. No priest could cross to
America without a specific royal permit. The King named the
bishops and sent them to their duties without awaiting papal
confirmation."[23] The bull of 1508 was followed in 1510 and
1511 by additional enactments dealing with matters such as
the tithes that the crown was entitled to collect, the recognition of Seville as the metropolitan Church of the Indies, and
the exemption of the production of precious metals from
payment of tithe. Ferdinand responded in 1512 with the Concordat of Burgos in which the principles were established for
the exercise of his ecclesiastical prerogatives. A most important item in this concordat referred to the redonation of tithes

[22] This bull, without doubt the single most important concession wrested
from the pope, was the basis for the royal *patronato*, a source of much disputa-
tion after 1810 between the new republican regimes and the Vatican, as those
naturally tried to retain it as heirs of the ousted colonial administration while
the pontiff saw in the crisis of independence an opportunity to recover the
ground lost to regalism three centuries earlier. For a useful description of the
patronato see N. M. Farriss, *Crown and Clergy in Colonial Mexico, 1759-1821:
The Crisis of Ecclesiastical Privilege*, London, 1968, pp. 15-38 and W. Eugene
Shiels, S.J. *King and Church: The Rise and Fall of the Patronato Real*, Chicago,
1961.

[23] Joaquín García Icazbalceta, *Don Fray Juan de Zumárraga*, México, pp.
128-129. (author's translation.)

in perpetuity to the bishops of the Indies. This was less generous than it would appear at first sight because what the monarch did was simply to establish formally that the collection and distribution of tithes in his dominions was the responsibility of men appointed by him and was to be carried out in a manner he determined. And, of course, subject to the exemptions, notably on the production of gold and silver, ordered by him.

An apt symbol of the relationship between Church and state secured by the skill of Ferdinand could be construed from the fact that the Spain of the time produced no Thomas à Becket, but instead a less renowned yet significant Bishop Gaspar de Quiroga who braved the pope by refusing to publish a bull in a manner contrary to instructions from the king. He was excommunicated for his defiance, but Philip II rewarded his loyalty by promoting him in quick succession to the post of royal councillor, grand inquisitor, archbishop of Toledo, and primate of Spain. Openly and at grave spiritual risk, Bishop Quiroga chose obedience to the king; in doing this, he reflected the regalism prevalent in the Spanish Church.[24] The contrasting parallel can be carried further; ac-

---

[24] The regalist policies of Ferdinand were continued by his successors. Charles V, though considerably more cosmopolitan in outlook, pursued similar nationalistic aims in matters relating to Church and state. As the Spanish scholar Luciano Ildefonso, who examined in detail the relations between pope and emperor, writes, "the spirit which dominated the politics of Charles V, above all in his relations with the papacy, was that of a nationalistic minded Spaniard and whoever ignores this fact, fails to understand the secret of sixteenth century politics." "Primeras negociaciones de Carlos V, rey de España, con la Santa Sede," *Cuadernos de Trabajo de la Escuela Española de Arqueología e Historia en Roma*, II (1914), 68, quoted by Lewis Hanke, "Pope Paul III and the American Indians," *HTR*, III, no. 2 (April, 1937), 77. On Bishop Quiroga, see Leopold von Ranke, *La monarquía española de los siglos XVI y XVII*, México, 1946, p. 106; also W. H. Prescott, *History of the Reign of Philip II, King of Spain*, London, 1855-1859, III, bk. 6, pp. 365-366. The social implications of the right of *patronato* as it was exercised by the centralist monarchs are rightly stressed by Ranke who sees in this concession a powerful instrument that allowed the king to choose ecclesiastical dignitaries from all ranks of society effectively weakening the quasi monopoly traditionally enjoyed by the aristocracy. Ranke, *Monarquía*, pp. 105-106.

cording to Sir Hugh de Morville's justification for the murder of Becket, as presented by T. S. Eliot in *Murder in the Cathedral*, the king's wishes, had they been carried out, would have led to "an almost ideal State: a union of spiritual and temporal administration, under the central government." Such an aspiration, thwarted in England by Becket's resolution, was achieved in Spain under Ferdinand. Though it is arguable whether an "ideal State" was the result, unparalleled ecclesiastical as well as political power was secured by the Castilian monarch abundantly justifying the admiration of one of his more formidable contemporaries. In the eyes of Machiavelli, Ferdinand was "for fame and glory, the first king in Christendom," worthy of being presented as a model for other princes to imitate: "if you regard his actions, you will find them all very great and some . . . extraordinary." There were other reasons, in addition to Ferdinand's successful quest for central monarchical power, that excited the admiration of the great Florentine. Almost a generation before the publication of *The Prince*, Ferdinand created a militia force loyal to the king in the place of the traditional feudal or mercenary levies so despised by Machiavelli. As early as 1496, one in every twelve inhabitants of Castile aged between twenty and forty-five was ordered to enlist in the military service of the central state. The remaining eleven were also liable to be called in case of need. The recruits were paid during their period of service and were exempt from taxation. Thus were laid the foundations for a modern, popular armed force directly under the control of the crown and available for regular and disciplined training. From these beginnings emerged the famous and dreaded Spanish *tercios* that dominated the European theater of war during the greater part of the century.[25] It was from such positions of self-conscious central control, political as well as ecclesiastical and military, that Ferdinand and his ministers proceeded to create the earliest administrative and political structure for the New World.[26]

[25] For Machiavelli's views on Ferdinand, see *The Prince*, ch. 21; also Herbert Butterfield, *The Statecraft of Machiavelli*, London, 1955, p. 92.

[26] Pierre Vilar went further, stating that "Ferdinand, prince of Machiavelli,

Dissimilarities are immediately apparent when comparing the origins and early development of the English settlements in North America and those of the Spanish Indies. Amongst these one of the most striking is that between the attitudes of the Castilian and the English metropolitan authorities toward their respective overseas establishments.

Left largely to their own devices, the North American colonists developed practices of regional self-reliance suited to their new surroundings and strongly influenced by that dissent from established central authority that had moved them to emigrate in the first place. The English government showed little interest, and it could even be said that the settlers survived and prospered in spite of the attitude of their mother country. Not only did they not carry with them to America an explicit legal nexus that could have facilitated the exercise of central authority, but they rejected it. Far from representing the policies of the metropolis in the New World, they were in fact outspoken members of a dissenting periphery.

In the Spanish Indies the situation was radically different. These were lands discovered as the result of what can well be described as a private venture on the part of the crown. The expectations of gain that were immediately aroused made it all the more necessary, from the monarch's point of view, to institutionalize a direct and exclusive control over their development. Given the legalistic bent of the Spanish political tradition, this was inevitably reflected in a flow of legislation that from vigorous beginnings soon attained the proportions of a flood. By 1635 over 400,000 decrees had been issued—2,500 annually since Columbus first sailed to the Indies.[27] The legal

established the modern mercantilist state." (author's translation.) Citing Vilar, Maravall objected to the implied suggestion that it is in Ferdinand's "Machiavellism" where we must search for the explanation of the rise of the modern Spanish state, or any other modern state. Such an influence, of course, would be anachronistic, for, by the time the great Florentine began work on *Il Principe* in 1512, the political work of Ferdinand was completed. See Pierre Vilar, *Crecimiento y desarrollo*, Barcelona, 1964, p. 439; also, Maravall, *Estado moderno*, I, 28-29n.

[27] Thomas, *Cuba*, p. 46.

minds of Castile regarded the incorporation of the Indies as a great expansion requiring conceptual and legal unification. A durable link was needed between the crown and these new subjects, peoples of alien nature and unknown legal traditions. At the same time, it was clearly understood that the link must be sufficiently strong "to resist the centrifugal tendencies of an avaricious and disorderly colonial society." The task of forging such a link was, as Parry has observed, "naturally entrusted to benches of professional judges."[28]

Even though private expeditions were encouraged, these were strictly regulated and at no time left to proceed independently of supervision from the metropolis. It is a mistake to make much of the private sources of finance used by many expeditions setting out from Spain to conquer and colonize the Indies. Some authors have seen in this method of financing either an indication of political laxity on the part of the crown, or a portent of what was to come in the way of effective freedom of action for the settlers. These suppositions are incorrect. Even when the larger portion of the funds for these expeditions came from private sources, the political, administrative, legal, and religious control was never out of the hands of the central authorities. Possibly the opposite point could be made with some confidence; that is, that the position of the crown was so strong it could secure private finance for these early and most risky ventures without relinquishing the exacting control of the process of empire building.[29] Hugh Thomas is absolutely right when he points out that "the main mark of the Spanish Empire (was) its centralization. In contrast with Anglo-Saxon America, the Crown had been the decisive factor in colonization, government and town planning."[30]

When the process of Castilian centralization reached its successful culmination in the peninsula, Columbus discovered a New World for the Catholic monarchs. The centralizing

[28] Parry, *Seaborne Empire*, p. 194.
[29] For dissenting views see Jacques Lafaye, *Conquistadores*, pp. 54-55 and Alvaro Jara, *Guerra y sociedad en Chile*, Santiago, 1971, p. 17.
[30] Thomas, *Cuba*, p. 46.

momentum was far from spent and reached the Indies in full force, finding there a vast scenario, uncluttered with feudal residues and easily directed by the ambitious conception of dutiful Christian power exercised from Madrid. It was soon filled, mostly with Castilian *dramatis personae*.[31] The origins of Latin American centralism are not to be found in Spain generally, but in the Castile of Ferdinand and Isabella.

[31] During the first century of colonization emigrants to the Indies came from every region of Spain, but by far the greatest number was from Castile and León. See V. Aubrey Neasham, "Spain's Emigrants to the New World, 1492-1592," *HAHR*, xix (1939), 157.

3

The Regalist Indies

By the time of Columbus's discovery Castilian feudalism had ceased to exist as a viable political arrangement; it was not resurrected to be carried across the Atlantic by the conquerors. But this did not wholly exclude the possibility of anachronistic feudal practices, habits, and, eventually, institutions emerging from the unspoiled and conveniently distant political soil of the Indies, either as independent growths or as responses to circumstances similar to those that gave rise to Old World feudalism.[1] What is known about the character of those who participated in the conquest would of itself suggest this possibility; ruthless and cunning survivors, soldiers of fortune with a keen understanding of the price and the rewards of power—of all the subjects of the Castilian crown, the conquerors of the Indies were probably the least inhibited by conventions, proprieties, or fear, and it was the most successful among these who received grants of land and Indians during the formative years of the empire. They constituted, if not a class apart, at least a group of men bound by a common experience of warring and conquest and an interest in retaining and extending the privileges secured by their efforts.[2] No

[1] A thesis that includes these possibilities was advanced by Lesley Byrd Simpson in 1929. The pertinent paragraph reads as follows; "The circumstances which gave rise to feudalism in the Old World were repeated in the New, and it was inevitable that the Spaniards should apply the only system with which they were familiar to a situation that it fitted. The result was the establishment of little principalities isolated from one another . . . self-supporting and self-sufficient." *The encomienda in New Spain*, Los Angeles and Berkeley, Calif., 1929, pp. 188-189.

[2] On the sociological characteristics of this group and its evolution see Alfonso García Gallo, "El encomendero indiano," *REP*, xxxv, (1951), 141-161.

other group could have been, or was, as committed as this one to the institutionalization of feudal or quasi-feudal arrangements.[3] Moreover, with its control of much of the wealth and military power in the Indies, it was in a most advantageous position to resist and, if necessary, to defy the distant crown of Castile. That it proved unable to do this and to generate feudal institutions even in such exceptionally favorable conditions is one of the crucial factors in the formation of Latin American political society.

The themes of greed and cruelty, gold and slavery, silver and serfdom, dominate the better-known historical accounts of the Castilian conquest of the Indies. Settlers hungry for riches and saintly men fired with a selfless concern for the fate of the Indians are seldom absent from the scene; their difficulties with each other and with the crown are a persistent feature throughout the sixteenth century. It is beyond dispute that the principal economic and religious aspects of the problem posed by the conquest were reflected in the attitudes of settlers and priests. Less well-known and appreciated is the fact that these economic and religious considerations were subordinated to the political necessity of preventing distance from the mother country, private wealth, *de facto* military strength or even tactical necessity to create quasi-feudal foci of effective power that could inhibit the authority of the crown in the Indies. What Ferdinand and Isabella so strenuously and successfully endeavored to eliminate from their Iberian realm they were most unlikely to tolerate in their overseas empire.

The forcible incorporation of large numbers of Amerindians into the body politic of Catholic Spain resulted in a

[3] It is arguable whether this espousal of feudalism was necessarily the consequence of retarded political evolution, as suggested by Silvio Zavala when he states that "if the Spanish priests and soldiers had not evolved towards the modern world of strong, centralist monarchical states, this had certainly been achieved . . . by the House of Austria, which, encouraged moreover by the defenders of the Indians, would not permit the reproduction of the European medieval world in the new territories." *La encomienda indiana*, Madrid, 1935, p. 105. (author's translation.) It ought to be noted that restraints on the demands of the settlers were first imposed by Ferdinand and Isabella before the advent of the Hapsburgs.

situation of considerable legal, social, and theological complexity. Nevertheless, I think that one can make use of a legitimate oversimplification and say that, notwithstanding a keen awareness of economic and religious factors, the crown was primarily concerned with its political aspects, the settlers, though important matters of social prestige and political power were involved, with economic aspects, while in the case of the Church the principal concern was religious and humanitarian. For purposes of analysis, a qualified acceptance of this oversimplification is more useful than exaggerated assumptions about the greed of churchmen, the cruelty of settlers, or the venality of officials. Each of these groups of churchmen, settlers, or crown officials, or individuals within the groups, understood there were compelling reasons for defending policies and interests that were at variance with those of the others; no group was lukewarm in the defense of what it thought would advance its own or what it understood to be the kingdom's best interests. But, after an incredibly involved sequence of philosophical, legal, political, and military confrontations that continued for over a century, it was the crown that emerged victorious having maintained its political pre-eminence without conceding any of the basic principles it had espoused during the early years of the sixteenth century.

Seen through the eyes of the conquerors and early settlers, the Indian problem had a straightforward definition and an even simpler solution. Land was plentiful in the Indies and so was mineral wealth, but good soil and rich mines were useless without an abundant and docile labor force. The conquerors were few and did not count among their numbers many manual laborers; though some crossed the Atlantic as foot soldiers, they saw no reason why they should work in farms and mines as a reward for their courage and enterprise. There were early attempts to colonize the Indies with Spanish farmers; the best known is possibly that led by Father Bartolomé de las Casas who planned to settle one such colony in Cumaná in 1521, on the northern coasts of what is now Venezuela. The plan was put into effect after some politicking in the Spanish court, but it was a tragic failure, with many of the settlers killed by the Indians. Las Casas retired to a Dominican monastery for almost a decade and a half; his major work on behalf of the Indians still very much in the future.[4] Although slavery was introduced during the first years of colonization, it was only of marginal importance as the slaves did not constitute more than a relatively small group of unfortunate Africans and perhaps a slightly greater number of Amerindians enslaved as legal punishment for offenses or because they had been captured in battle.[5]

There was an iron logic in the argument, as presented by the settlers, that the most satisfactory solution to the problem was to allow, indeed, encourage, the full integration of the Indians into the colonial economy by compelling them to work in farms and mines. This objective was achieved early; Columbus had first tried to impose tribute on the Indians, but this proved impractical and unenforceable; then, responding to the demands of the settlers, he allocated to them the labor services of three hundred Indians.[6] Only at this stage, appar-

[4] See Ramón Menéndez Pidal, *El Padre Las Casas. Su doble personalidad*, Madrid, 1963, pp. 37-46, and Lewis Hanke, *The Spanish Struggle for Justice in the Conquest of America*, Philadelphia, 1949, pp. 54-71.

[5] In all probability the first African slaves arrived in the Indies in 1502, with Nicolás de Ovando. Isabella, who was much concerned about the conversions of the Indians, was advised of the corrupting influence of Africans in the Indies, and she cancelled the import permits in 1503. The suspension did not last long for she died the next year and the traffic, trifling at that stage, was renewed. José Antonio Saco, *Historia de la esclavitud de la raza africana en el Nuevo Mundo*, Barcelona, 1879; p. 62. As is well-known, Father las Casas recommended the importation of African slaves to alleviate the lot of the Indians. His advice was partly responsible for the influx of African slaves to work the sugar plantations and alluvial gold fields. The first import licenses granted for these purposes permitted the introduction of 4,000 slaves into Hispaniola, San Juan, Cuba, and Jamaica. See Fray Bartolomé de las Casas, *Historia de las Indias*, in Colección de documentos inéditos para la historia de España, Ed., Marqués de la Fuensanta del Valle and José Sancho Rayón, Madrid, 1876, LXV, bk. 3, ch. 129, p. 29. According to Juan López de Velasco, writing in 1575, the number of African slaves in the whole of Spanish America was only 40,000. Ricardo Beltrán y Rozpide, *América en tiempo de Felipe II segun el cosmógrafocronista Juan López de Velasco*, Madrid, 1927, p. 7.

[6] According to Antonio de León Pinelo, writing in 1630, Columbus also sent some Indians to Castile, presumably as slaves or vassals, and these were

ently, did he write to the queen "begging that the colonists be
allowed to use the labour of the Indians for a year or two,
until the colony should be on its feet."[7] On receiving this
news, an angry Isabella is said to have asked, "By what power
does the Admiral give away my vassals?" A departure from
the Queen's original policy, a general enslavement was out of
the question for the Indians were regarded legally as subjects
of the crown of Castile and although enslavement, even in
Spain, was sometimes used as punishment for serious crimes,
notably for armed rebellion, "no self-respecting prince could
permit the enslavement of his subjects for economic gain by
private persons."[8] The admiral's ad hoc measure was rejected
by Isabella, and friar Nicolás de Ovando, the first governor of
Hispaniola, who was about to sail for the Indies, was instructed to rescind it on arrival, placing the Indians once more
under the direct protection of the crown and requiring them
to pay tribute out of the wages they were expected to earn
with their labor, like any other Spanish subject.[9] Ovando arrived in Hispaniola in 1502, promptly informed the Indians
that they were free men and on hearing the good news, they
disappeared into the jungle leaving the settlers to their own
devices. Faced with this unsatisfactory result the crown had to
make allowances, and the governor was ordered to compel
"the said Indians to trade and converse with the Christians in
the said Island, and work in their buildings, and extract gold
and other metals, and produce [supplies and provisions] for

---

returned to the Indies by the indignant queen. See *Tratado de confirmaciones
reales*, 1630; facsimile rpt. Buenos Aires, 1922. Pt. 1, ch. 2, para. 5.

[7] Simpson, *The encomienda*, p. 27. In this study it is suggested that Columbus "was in all probability seeking the regal recognition of a *fait accompli*, because the Spaniards could not have lived six months without the forced services of the Indians."

[8] Antonio de León Pinelo, *Confirmaciones*, Pt. 1, ch. 1, para. 5, and J. H.
Parry, "A Secular Sense of Responsibility," in *First Images of America, The
Impact of the New World on the Old*, ed. F. Chiappelli, Berkeley and Los
Angeles, Calif., 1976, p. 290.

[9] The royal instructions given to Ovando in 1501 read in part "because it is
our will that the Indians should pay us the taxes and tributes . . . in the same
way that our other subjects do who reside in our kingdoms." Zavala, *La encomienda*, pp. 2-3. (author's translation.)

those Christians . . . and you must pay each of them for each day they work a wage and subsistence; that according to the quality of the soil, of the person, and of the task you consider appropriate . . . each chieftain [*cacique*] must come with the number of Indians that you determine . . . to work . . . on payment of the wage that you have assessed. . . . all this (the Indians) will fulfil as free persons, as they in fact are, and not as serfs: and you must ensure that the said Indians are well treated."[10]

These instructions, contained in the Cédula de Medina del Campo of 20 December 1503 and signed by Isabella, institutionalized at one stroke the principles of the freedom of the Indians but also the compulsion to work that was to confound the legal relationship between settlers and Indians for the next century.[11] At the same time they set down in unmistakable fashion both the problems and the practical solutions as defined by regalist Castile. Thus, to solve the problem of labor scarcity, the Indians were compelled to work for a fair wage; to solve the pressing problem of the true nature of the Indians, they were declared to be free men, subject to the same duties and responsibilities as any other subject of the crown.[12] The crown responded to the problem of jurisdiction

[10] Zavala, *La encomienda*, p. 4. (author's translation.)

[11] The apparent incompatibility between the principles of freedom and compulsion did not present insurmountable obstacles to the legalistic talent of Spaniards. As the eminent and scholarly jurist Juan de Solórzano y Pereyra explained, "to compel and retain the Indians by force in such labour services does not contradict . . . their freedom; because when there is a just cause or the universal welfare is at stake, any well governed republic has the authority to compel its citizens to work, and this does not mean that they cease to be free. . . . one thing it is to be a serf and another thing altogether to serve. . . . Because according to Archilochus, the only true freedom, and the most important consists in all of us being servants or slaves of the law." *Política indiana; antología*, ed. Luis García Arias, Madrid, 1947, I, bk. 2, ch. 6, p. 178. (author's translation.) It should be noted that this massive study was first published in 1648 and that Solórzano was a senior civil servant who for many years occupied a principal post in the viceroyalty of Peru before being appointed to the council of the Indies, the supreme governing body for Spanish America.

[12] Silvio Zavala observes, differing from Solórzano, that the establishment of the juridical principle of the freedom of the Indians as well as of their capac-

and seigneurial authority by refusing to delegate these at all, symbolizing the retention of central control by imposing on the Indians a tribute due to the monarch. The solution to the problem of how to reward the conquerors and settlers for their exertions was to grant them those tributes. To the problem of just compensation for the Indians; that is, to the problem of the definition of the duties of the crown or its representatives with respect to its subjects in the Indies, the answer was to offer protection, both physical and spiritual. Hence, the crown by its armed presence assured the Indians of defense against their earthly enemies and by Christian education and conversion presumably opened to them the door of spiritual salvation.

These responsibilities and privileges were implemented not by delegating jurisdictional authority, but only the functions of that authority. Those selected to carry out these tasks or receive tributes did not constitute intermediate juridical entities between the monarch and her subjects in the Indies, but rather they became, after a fashion, informal civil servants representing the monarch, acting on behalf of the central government with limited tenure, and liable to have their duties terminated at the royal will. They could also be considered an extended clientele dependent on the good will of the monarch for the continued enjoyment of their privileged position. The Indians therefore were not given away as feudal vassals in perpetuity, but "commended" for limited periods in *encomiendas* granted to those among the conquerors and settlers who had distinguished themselves in the service of the monarch and were thought worthy of discharging the attendant responsibilities.[13] These *encomenderos* undertook by oath

ity to reason "created the greatest theoretical obstacle to the conquest of America, for it left only two ways open to proceed; to convince the Indians using peaceful means, or to fight them, but as the first did not happen and the second was forbidden, the conquest of the New World should have been abandoned." (author's translation.) The explanation of why this did not happen is a theme in one of the Mexican historian's most impressive works. *Las instituciónes jurídicas en la conquista de América*, Madrid, 1935, pp. 55-56, and also chs. 6 and 7.

[13] The best brief definition of *encomienda* is probably that found in Solór-

to teach their "commended" Indians the rudiments of Christianity and to offer them protection. In exchange, the tributes due to the crown were paid directly to them in kind, or in labor services, or occasionally in money or gold. The precise manner in which tributes were paid varied considerably from time to time, but from the middle of the sixteenth century there was a clear and rapid trend toward the abolition of labor services and their substitution for money payments.

The sixteenth was a harsh century everywhere and Spanish America was no exception. The conquerors had endured much suffering during their epic discoveries and were not inclined to behave kindly, or even justly, toward those they regarded as "naturally lazy and vicious, melancholic, cowardly, and in general a lying, shifty people."[14] Laws to make people behave well toward each other have seldom been very successful; the legislation promulgated in Castile to ensure the good treatment of the Indians would certainly fall under this vast category. In spite of the evident good intentions of the monarch and her advisors, there was sufficient distance between Spain and the Indies and enough scope for interpretation of the letter of the law to permit the most unbelievable brutality and exploitation.

Ill-treatment of the Indians under the *encomienda* was, obvi-

---

zano's monumental work; "a right conceded by royal grace to the meritorious of the Indies to receive and collect for themselves the tributes of the Indians commended for their lifetime and that of one heir in accordance with the law of succession with the charge of looking after the spiritual and temporal welfare of the Indians and of dwelling in and defending the Provinces where they are commended and of fulfilling all this and homage by a personal oath." Solórzano y Pereyra, *Política*, II, bk. 3, ch. 3, pp. 21-22. (author's translation.)

[14] The text continues, "their marriages are not a sacrament but a sacrilege. They are idolatrous, libidinous and commit sodomy. Their chief desire is to eat, drink, worship heathen idols, and commit bestial obscenities." These are the views of the historian Gonzalo Fernández de Oviedo, a well-known enemy of the Dominicans who played so prominent a role in the defense of the Indians. He was perhaps an illiberal man, but certainly not an uncultured one, and if he found it possible to espouse these views, one wonders what the average soldier thought about his indigenous enemies in the Indies. See Hanke, *Spanish Struggle*, p. 11.

ously, only one of the factors leading to the rapid increase in
mortality among the Indians of the Caribbean Islands first
colonized by the Spaniards; the introduction of European diseases was undoubtedly more important. At any rate, it is
quite clear, as Hanke has indicated, that though there was undeniable brutality on the part of some settlers, this was not
necessarily true of all, and there were enough Spaniards concerned with the plight of the Indians to wage a vigorous and
eventually successful campaign on their behalf. According to
Hanke, the conquest was characterized for its "spirited defence of the rights of the Indians, which rested on two of the
most fundamental assumptions a Christian can make:
namely, that all men are equal before God, and that a Christian has a responsibility for the welfare of his brothers no matter how alien or lowly they may be."[15] As for the crown's
participation, elsewhere Hanke writes, "the Spanish colonial
system has usually been considered a rigid, uncompromising
autocracy, impervious to the demands of time and place.
However justified may be this description . . . it certainly
does not apply to the Spain of Charles V. . . . the Emperor,
far from exhibiting an impassive inflexibility in his early Indian policy, was imbued with a spirit not unlike that of a
modern sociologist."[16]

The first public attack on the system of the *encomiendas* was
launched by the Dominican friar Antonio de Montesinos in
1511 from the pulpit of the church on the island of Hispaniola. In an impassioned sermon, Montesinos accused the
encomenderos of being in mortal sin because of the cruelty with
which they treated their "commended" Indians and assured
them that if they persisted they would have as much chance of
being saved as the heretical Turks or Moors.[17] First astonished and fearful, then indignant, the settlers reacted

[15] Hanke, *Spanish Struggle*, p. 1.

[16] Lewis Hanke, *The First Social Experiments in America*, Cambridge, 1935,
p. xi.

[17] The sermon of Montesinos is known from the supposedly paraphrased
version included by las Casas in his *Historia*, bk. 3, ch. 4; see also Menéndez
Pidal, *Las Casas*, pp. 2-5.

swiftly; verbal and written protests were followed by the decision to send the Franciscan friar Alonso de Espinal to represent their views before Ferdinand in Castile.[18] Montesinos, loyally supported by his Dominican superiors in the island, also travelled to Spain to put his case and, as las Casas reports, was able to convince Ferdinand that awful excesses and misuses of the king's authority were being perpetrated without his knowledge.

Faced with what looked like an involved problem, Ferdinand reacted in a manner characteristic of that bureaucratic empire by appointing a commission, a junta, of civil servants, jurists, and academic theologians under the chairmanship of the bishop of Palencia, a senior member of the council of Castile, to look into the matter. After meeting with remarkable assiduity, the junta agreed on seven propositions that were submitted to the king. The first stated that, "as the Indians are free and Your Majesty and the Queen (in Holy Glory) ordered that they should be treated as free men, that this be obeyed." Then the regal undertaking to Christianize the Indians was ratified with a passing mention of the papal bull to that effect, but the third proposition, which according to las Casas "smelled and tasted of things in support of tyranny," also ratified the principle of compulsory labor: "that Your Majesty can order [the Indians] to work, but the work should

[18] In addition to an obvious concern for the future of their farms and mines if compulsory labor were to cease, the *encomenderos* centered their attacks on Montesinos's apparent denial of the royal authority over the Indies. According to las Casas, the Dominican friar had said "by what right or justice do you keep these Indians in such a cruel and horrible servitude? On what authority have you waged a detestable war against these people, who dwelt quietly and peacefully on their own land?" Ferdinand, naturally, reacted angrily, and in a letter to the governor of Hispaniola, Diego Columbus, after explaining the juridical basis on which the authority of the crown rested, stated that it would be reasonable "to use some severity" (*algún rigor*) with the man who had preached the offending sermon as well as with those priests that following his lead had refused absolution to the settlers, "because their error has been very great." See Hanke, *Spanish Struggle*, p. 17, and Zavala, *La encomienda*, p. 12. Montesinos, however, turned the settlers' arguments against them by explaining that he did not question the authority of the monarch, but that of the *encomenderos* to misuse it.

be such that it should not impede their religious instruction and it should be rewarding for them and for the Republic and Your Majesty should receive tribute (*aprovechado y servido*) on behalf of the seigneurial rights and services due to him for teaching [the Indians] matters of faith and ensuring the dispensation of justice."[19] The report drawn up by the junta was the basis of the Laws of Burgos promulgated in 1512, and these largely ratified what had first been decided upon in 1503: forced labor was legalized, but there was also a determined effort to mitigate abuses by the introduction of detailed regulations with respect to the feeding, clothing, hours of work, wages, and education of the Indians. These reflect a touching naiveté and at the same time the undoubtedly sincere concern for the welfare of the Indians that moved Ferdinand and his ministers. For instance, when ordering the *encomendero* to instruct his charges in religious matters, the legislators add, "but all this shall be done with great love and gentleness, and the person who fails to obey this shall incur a penalty of six gold pesos." Also, in a notable decision that anticipates much twentieth-century social legislation, the Laws of Burgos ordered that "no pregnant woman after the fourth month shall be sent to the mines or made to plant hillocks but shall be kept on the estates and utilized in household tasks . . . and after she bears her child she shall nurse it until it is three years old and in all this time she shall not be sent to the mines or made to plant hillocks or used in anything else that may harm the infant." Perhaps reflecting more accurately the existing day-to-day relationship between settlers and Indians, the laws add, "no person or persons shall dare beat any Indian with sticks, or whip him, or call him dog, or address him by any name other than his proper name alone."[20]

The Laws of Burgos did not satisfy the demands of those who, like Montesinos, were absolutely opposed to the *encomiendas*, but they did meet more practical requirements.

---

[19] Zavala, *La encomienda*, p. 14. (author's translation.)

[20] Charles Gibson, ed. *The Spanish Tradition in America*, New York, 1968, pp. 65-74.

The granting of *encomiendas* remained firmly in the hands of the monarch; there were no perpetual concessions, and seigneurial or quasi-seigneurial jurisdictional powers were not allowed to crystallize during that delicate formative period in the Indies. From the vantage point of the settlers, not all of whom were *encomenderos*, the laws usefully ensured a continuing supply of Indian labor although under what for many of them must have been annoying limitations.

Passive acceptance of this legislation did not last long, and agitation was renewed with greater fervor both by those who wanted the *encomienda* abolished and those who wished to have its privileges extended. Once their more immediate need for Indian labor was satisfied, the *encomenderos* moved on to greater demands. Their principal aspiration became the attainment of that social status associated in Europe with the holding of land and perpetual seigneurial rights over vassals. Such aspirations fit the penuries and ambitions of lowly men who had crossed the Atlantic armed solely with their courage and who now saw a way open in the Indies to ascend to exalted positions entirely beyond their reach in the Old World.[21] This was particularly apparent after the Spanish conquest advanced from the islands of the Caribbean to the mainland of America and majestic civilizations were discovered that absolutely overshadowed those simple tribal communities first encountered by Columbus. It is worth pointing out that Cortés conquered Mexico sixteen years after Isabella signed the Cédula de Medina del Campo establishing the basis for the *encomienda* system, while the conquest of Peru was undertaken by Francisco Pizarro twenty-nine years after 1503. The richness and sophistication of that truly New World had a formidable impact on the social expectations of the conquerors and colonists.

[21] The conquerors were a mixed crowd, of course, but as Hernán Cortés reported to the king in 1524, "it is notorious that the greater number of the Spaniards who come over here are of lowly condition and riddled with diverse vices and sins." Letter from Hernán Cortés to Charles V, dated October 1524 in *Colección de documentos para la historia de México*, ed. Joaquín García Icazbalceta, México, 1858-1866, II, 471. (author's translation.)

To the shrill requests for land and Indians from those
settlers who had none were added the more muted, perhaps
more worldly and ominous, demands for seigneurial rights
from those *encomenderos* who already had land and Indians but
who realized that more was needed if they were to acquire
prestige sufficient to pass on to their descendants.[22] They
wished their children to become *hidalgos* (the derivation is
from *fijos de al* or *fijos dalgo* meaning well-born or, literally,
sons of something or somebody).[23] But for this to come
about they themselves had to become something more than a
sword on horseback: wealth did not suffice—they knew, if
anybody ever did, how quickly it could be gained and lost—
so they wanted a name tied forever to the land they had conquered. They felt, perhaps correctly, on the very threshold of
achieving this, and their exertions were directed precisely to
this end: the earliest grants of *encomiendas* had been for two
years renewable, then for one lifetime, then two lifetimes, but
soon afterwards the *encomendadores* were insistently demanding grants in perpetuity.[24]

---

[22] In a letter to the king dated October 1524, Hernán Cortés advocates the
granting of *encomiendas* in perpetuity arguing that "in this way each (*encomendero*) would look on the Indians as their own and would care for them as an
inheritance to bequeath to his successors." García Icazbalceta, *Colección*, I,
474-475. (author's translation.)

[23] The derivation from *fijo de al* comes from Solórzano who takes it from
the *Partidas*. See Solórzano, *Política*, II, bk. 3, ch. 25, p. 285.

[24] A. de León Pinelo, *Confirmaciones*, Pt. 1, çh. 1, para. 12, Provisión de
Valladolid, 14 August 1509. This document mentions the practice of awarding *encomiendas* for 2 years. The earliest document allowing, but not necessarily granting, *encomiendas* for one lifetime is the *Declaración de Valladolid of 28
July 1513*, quoted by Zavala, *La encomienda*, pp. 16-17. The awarding of *encomiendas* for two lifetimes is first documented as early as 1514, in the Albuquerque grant quoted in full by las Casas in his *Historia*, bk. 3, ch. 37, and
reproduced by Zavala, *La encomienda*, pp. 8-9. The fullest and most useful
explanation of the controversy that raged for so long about the granting of
encomiendas in perpetuity is probably that found in Solórzano, *Política*, II, bk.
3, ch. 32. At any rate, as Parry indicates, "perpetual inheritance, though often
asked, was steadily refused. Only in rare and special cases were exceptions
made. Two of Montezuma's daughters received Indian towns in perpetual
hereditary *encomienda*, but the Cortés *marquesado* was the only perpetual hereditary *encomienda* ever granted to a Spaniard in the Indies." Parry, *Seaborne
Empire*, pp. 185-186.

The exertions of the *encomenderos* were matched by the zeal of the ecclesiastical enemies of the system. Many clerics were ready to follow in the footsteps of Montesinos, and their struggles on behalf of the Indians make an impressive story that has been told often and well. It is important to notice, however, that the efforts of these churchmen were almost without exception directed to ensuring that the laws of the realm were obeyed; they were largely in accord with the crown and only in a few instances were they prepared to go beyond and advocate the abolition of the *encomienda* system. Nevertheless, this relationship between a regalist monarchy and an enthusiastically humanitarian band of clerics was less simple than it would appear at first glance, and one incident should be cited to illustrate how punctilious the crown was in retaining absolute central control over these matters in the Indies.

A Dominican friar Bernardino de Minaya, who had travelled to the Indies during the decade of 1520, returned to Spain shocked by the inhuman treatment that the Indians were receiving at the hands of the Spaniards. Feeling that his protestations in the Spanish court were unavailing, he decided—with the knowledge of the empress who gave him a letter of introduction to the Spanish Ambassador—to go to Rome to place the problem before Pope Paul III.[25] He succeeded in this, and the result of his conversations with the pontiff was the promulgation of the bull *Sublimis Deus* of 9 June 1537. In this document the pope stated that "notwithstanding what may have been or may be said to the contrary, the said Indians and all other people who may later be discovered by Christians, are by no means to be deprived of their liberty or the possession of their property, even though they be outside the faith of Jesus Christ; and that they may and should freely and legitimately, enjoy their liberty and the possession of their property: nor should they be in any way enslaved."[26]

---

[25] A full account of this incident is found in Hanke's article "Pope Paul III and the American Indians."

[26] Hanke, "Pope Paul III," p. 72.

Having succeeded so signally in bringing the moral weight of the Vatican's voice against the *encomenderos* and, as he saw it, in support of the policies of the crown, the active friar made a number of copies of this bull and sent them to his friends in the Indies without first consulting with the Council of the Indies.

When news of what Minaya had done reached Madrid, the emperor's reaction was swift and unequivocal: the earnest Dominican was gaoled for two years, and after his release he was kept in Valladolid, preaching to the prisoners; for good measure, the emperor issued an order forbidding him to return to the Indies. At the same time, wishing to leave no doubt whatsoever about his views on the matter, Charles obtained from the pope a brief revoking "all other briefs or bulls issued before in prejudice of the power of the Emperor Charles V as King of Spain and which might disturb the good government of the Indies."[27] With this in hand, the emperor wrote to Antonio de Mendoza, then viceroy of New Spain, explaining that "having been informed that a friar Bernardino de Minaya, of the Order of Santo Domingo, moved by good intentions had beseeched our Holy Father and obtained certain bulls or briefs concerning the natives of that land, their instruction, their freedom and manner of life, prejudicing thereby our Royal pre-eminence the maintenance of which we have arranged with such great care, we ordered that all the

[27] Hanke, "Pope Paul III," p. 72. The brief revoking whatever documents Minaya had obtained from Paul III was issued on 19 June 1538, almost to the day a year after the promulgation of the bull *Sublimis Deus*. During the month of June 1538, the pope, Francis I, and the emperor Charles were together in Nice trying to reach agreement on the future of Europe. The outcome of these negotiations was a ten year truce that represented one of the pope's signal diplomatic achievements. No doubt Charles had little difficulty, given the circumstances, in extracting the needed assurances from the pontiff in the case affecting Minaya. Also, at the time, Paul III was interested in marrying his grandson Ottavio Farnese to the emperor's recently widowed natural daughter Margaret of Austria and was consequently most unlikely to quarrel with the emperor for the sake of an obscure Dominican and the well-being, material or spiritual, of some very distant Indians. Robertson, *Charles V*, III, 162-165.

original copies of those bulls and briefs be recovered and informed His Holiness so that he would have them revoked." Further on, Charles explains he has received information that Minaya had sent copies of these documents to the Indies and instructs his viceroy "to find out if there are any copies in New Spain and if so, to recover them and send them to the Council of the Indies." He concludes by extending the instruction to include any bulls or briefs "concerning the good government of that province and the preservation of our patrimony and our royal jurisdiction" and ordering that, if these had not been sanctioned by the Council of the Indies in Spain, they be taken and returned to the Council so that "if it be judged that they should be executed, then they should be, but if not, to pray before our Holy Father so that His Holiness being thus better informed, will have them revoked."[28]

This severe response was dictated by the crown's meticulous regalism in the Indies. Nothing in *Sublimis Deus* contradicted the emperor's views on these matters, but its political implications did not go unnoticed. As Hanke has explained in his detailed study of this incident, it is conceivable that the pope may have acted prompted solely by humanitarian considerations, "but it is possible that this shrewd and tenacious ruler also intended the bull to be the opening wedge for a more aggressive papal programme in the affairs of the Indies. . . . Paul manifested a greater interest in the Indies than had any earlier Pope—an interest which a king jealous of his prerogatives might look upon with suspicion."[29] This Charles most certainly did, for he greatly valued the ecclesiastical power that Julius II had conferred on the Castilian crown with the bull *Universalis ecclesiae* and was not prepared to let it be watered down, even if by default.[30]

[28] Mariano Cuevas, S.J. *Historia de la Iglesia en México*, México, 1921, 1, 228. (author's translation.)

[29] Hanke, "Pope Paul III," p. 76.

[30] Almost ten years before the incident with Minaya, the emperor had obtained an explicit ratification of the crown's ecclesiastical rights in the Indies from Clement VII in the bull *Intra arcana* of 1529 thus continuing the regalist policies initiated under Ferdinand. Hanke, "Pope Paul III," pp. 73, 76-78.

As if to prove that the crown's objections to Minaya's efforts were not moral but political, scarcely four years after the revocation of the documents obtained by the Dominican, the emperor appended his signature to the drastic New Laws of 1542 abolishing the *encomienda* outright. The promulgation of these New Laws and their subsequent modification led to the most serious confrontation between the crown and the settlers in the whole history of the Indies and afford a most telling illustration of the nature of the centralist hold over Spanish America.

Though questioned by the crown from time to time during the first four decades of the sixteenth century, the legal existence of the *encomienda* had not really been at issue.[31] Twice ratified *de jure* and many times *de facto*, it appeared safe from the reformist zeal of its ecclesiastical enemies; the *encomenderos* were devoting their energies to secure extensions of privileges and duration rather than to defend the institution itself. The question appeared to be not whether the *encomienda* ought to be abolished, but whether the settlers would succeed in using it to wrest effective seigneurial and jurisdictional power from the distant crown.

It was against this background of rising ambition and amid frequent reports of the abuses of the *encomenderos* and their persistent disregard for the spirit as well as the letter of the laws regulating their *encomiendas* that the bishop of Chiapa, the famous Bartolomé de las Casas, brought his formidable moral authority and eloquence to bear on the emperor and convinced him and his counsellors of the need to abolish the *en-*

---

[31] In the instructions sent to Hernán Cortés by the emperor on 26 June 1523, the monarch explained that having seen the bad effects the system of *encomiendas* had had on the inhabitants of Hispaniola and other islands and having consulted with his council, he commanded Cortés not to make any further grants of Indians in *encomienda* in New Spain, but "to let them live in freedom, like our vassals do, here in our kingdom of Castile." As is well-known, Cortés felt unable to comply with these instructions and wrote back explaining his reasons. He was supported by the Franciscans and Dominicans of New Spain who adduced that *encomiendas* granted in perpetuity would result in better treatment for the Indians. Zavala, *La encomienda*, pp. 45-51. (author's translation.)

comienda system altogether. According to Hanke, the passage of the New Laws was a great social experiment undertaken by the Spaniards in their "struggle for justice in America."[32] However, it would be more appropriate to describe the New Laws as a departure from orthodoxy, largely the consequence of the skill and persistence of las Casas in fanning the monarch's known concern about the threat of potential feudal enclaves in the Indies.[33] For almost half a century the crown had successfully resisted all demands for an extension of privileges to the *encomenderos* while retaining the arrangements that most efficiently appeared to answer the economic needs of the colonies. By abolishing the *encomienda*, the crown was not ratifying an established policy, but making inroads into the position of the settlers that would allow it later, though this can only be conjectured, to negotiate from a position of strength.

The arguments of las Casas were presented in the form of written propositions before a junta convened by the emperor to reexamine the problem. Two of these embodied the essence of his theological and political theses. The first established that the papal concession of the Indies to the crown of Castile had been made expressly because of the "dignity and the industry of the royal persons," and therefore responsibilities as great as those relating to the Christianization of the Indians could not be delegated by the monarchs to lesser private persons, whether with or without jurisdiction. Proposition fourteen presented the political argument that may possibly have had the greatest effect on the emperor: "the Spaniards, haughty and arrogant as they are, seeing themselves as [feudal] lords (*señores*) over the Indians, their loy-

[32] Hanke, *Spanish Struggle*, p. 83.

[33] Precisely at the time that the New Laws were being discussed, it was discovered that some of the more senior members of the council of the Indies, including the most eloquent supporters of the *encomiendas*, had been receiving bribes from settler leaders such as Pizarro, Almagro, and Cortés. The councillors were tried and punished. There is no doubt that this brutal evidence of the power of the emerging lords of the Indies must have strengthened the king's resolve to stamp out the quasi-feudal challenge before it became too powerful. Hanke, *Spanish Struggle*, p. 94.

alty to the King will diminish. The King should never grant earldoms, marquisates or dukedoms."[34]

Charles was convinced and the New Laws were promulgated. The *encomienda* was abolished; grants were either to terminate immediately or would revert to the crown at the death of the imcumbent; deserving settlers could still receive from the crown the right to collect tribute from the Indians, but the laws established that the Spaniards would have no power over the native inhabitants other than that of receiving those rents.[35]

The reaction to the New Laws in the Indies was predictably hostile, and, as it was known that he had a major responsibility in their promulgation, las Casas was the object of violent attacks; "a friar unread in law, unholy, envious, vainglorious, unquiet, tainted by cupidity, and, above all else, a troublemaker." As for the New Laws, the *encomenderos* declared themselves "as shocked as if an order had been sent telling us to cut off our heads."[36] Distance from Spain and the sincere feeling on the part of many of the old conquerors that the crown was ill-using them because of the distorted advice of a handful of troublesome friars contributed the moral conviction needed to justify defiance. Nowhere were these factors as significant as in Peru where protracted feuds between the conquistadores had kept the settlers armed and open to the charge of "criminal participation" in the quarrels between Pizarro and Almagro, thus liable to lose all their privileges and properties under the terms of the new legislation. Most importantly, Peru had a leader. Gonzalo Pizarro was at the

[34] This proposition echoed the advice given by Sebastian Ramírez de Fuenleal a few years earlier when he presided over the *Audiencia* of New Spain; "the King must never grant vassals or jurisdiction to the settlers . . . because in addition to the maltreatment of the Indians, such concessions would weaken the authority of the Crown; the only concessions the King should make are those of tributes, rents and personal services." Zavala, *La Encomienda*, p. 94. (author's translation.)

[35] Zavala, *La Encomienda*, pp. 95-99.

[36] Murdo J. Macleod, "Las Casas, Guatemala, and the Sad but Inevitable Case of Antonio de Remesal," *Topic*, Washington and Jefferson College, no. 20 (Fall, 1970), 54.

time engaged in mining silver at Potosí, but the arrival of a new viceroy especially sent by the emperor to enforce the New Laws brought him back at the head of an enthusiastic army. His military skill and popularity were too much for the uncompromising and rigidly legalistic viceroy who, having antagonized the moderate settlers, was defeated in battle and beheaded by the rebels.

The news of this first important uprising by the New World settlers caused consternation in the Spanish court where it was immediately understood that unless the challenge was met there was an imminent risk of other parts of the Indies following the Peruvian example. Unable to send an army strong enough to face Pizarro on his own ground, Charles entrusted the task of putting down the rebellion to the statesmanship and experience of Pedro de la Gasca, an austere ecclesiastic and senior civil servant who arrived in the Indies alone and unarmed but with full powers from the crown to deal with the situation as he thought best. Cajoling, threatening, compromising, and distributing rewards, in a brief period he raised an army, routed Pizarro in the Battle of Xaquixaguana, and ended the revolt by publicly executing the leader and his principal officers and, according to custom, having their severed heads prominently displayed in the capital of the viceroyalty.[37]

In the achievement of this momentous triumph, the regalist legitimacy of la Gasca's patronage and the social ambitions of the settlers were at least as important as his diplomatic resourcefulness. It must be borne in mind that not all the settlers held *encomiendas*; in fact, merely as a result of demographic factors, including immigration from Spain, the *encomenderos* were a dwindling minority throughout the century.[38] Those settlers who had not received *encomiendas* in the first instance were, of course, passionately opposed to the abolition of the

[37] Modern scholarship has not dimmed Prescott's magnificent account of the crushing of Pizarro's rebellion by la Gasca. In my opinion, it will remain unsurpassed for a very long time. William H. Prescott, *History of the Conquest of Peru*, London, 1847, bk. 5.

[38] García Gallo, *El encomendero*, p. 141.

institution, for they hoped in time to obtain grants; they were equally opposed to making existing grants perpetual, for that would effectively prevent them from ever holding the better *encomiendas* themselves. Their social aspirations, moreover, took them beyond simple greed for land and wealth: those who held *encomiendas* wanted perpetual seigneurial rights, with jurisdiction over vassals. These rights a chieftain like Pizarro was quite incapable of granting; the only legitimacy the conquerors and settlers knew or could conceive—there were no republican stirrings at that time—issued from the central monarchy. Land and laborers without legitimacy were a poor prize indeed for revolutionary loyalty.

Pedro de la Gasca was able to exploit the conflicting sentiments by ignoring the articles in the New Laws that abolished the *encomienda* and granting to those settlers who took arms against Pizarro the *encomiendas* of the rebels "so that with the hope of these rewards the loyalists would be encouraged and the rebels depressed, as in fact they were."[39] As Antonio de León Pinelo described it later, Pedro de la Gasca took this opportunity to give away one hundred and fifty *encomiendas* valued at considerably more than one million pesos in rents, "an amount that no Prince in the world, without granting away States and Kingdoms, has ever distributed as reward for services, in one day, and through the hands of a vassal."[40] These grants were made without sacrificing major principles; in spite of the rhetoric surrounding their revision, the New Laws were not revoked, but only altered to suit the requirements of the unprecedented crisis. Earlier it was stated that the abolition of the institution of the *encomienda* was a departure from orthodox monarchical policy, largely, if not solely, the result of the personal intervention of Bartolomé de las Casas. Perhaps for this reason, la Gasca wisely chose to regard this part of the New Laws as expendable, and the con-

[39] A. de León Pinelo, *Confirmaciones*, Pt. 1, ch. 3, paras. 28, 29. See also Enrique Torres Saldamando, *Libro primero de Cabildos de Lima*, Paris, 1900, Pt. 2, p. 105. (author's translation.)

[40] A. de León Pinelo, *Confirmaciones*, Pt. 1, ch. 3, paras. 28, 29. (author's translation.)

cessions made in Peru were tacitly based on the assumption that the clause abolishing the *encomienda* would be revoked. On the other hand, he strengthened those provisions that restated what had been crown policies in these matters since the beginning of the century; there were no extensions of the privileges of *encomenderos* and no jurisdiction given to them over the Indians. On the contrary, labor services were to be commuted for payment of a fixed tribute thus returning to the original policy of Isabella, from which the crown had departed reluctantly in pragmatic response to what then appeared as an otherwise insoluble problem. All told, the laws on the abolition of Indian slavery were not only retained, but substantially enforced. On the other hand, *encomiendas* were permitted once again, but with a fundamental difference: *encomenderos* were entitled only to the tribute of the Indians.[41]

The commutation of labor services proceeded gradually until they were eventually phased out completely. This was not readily acknowledged by nineteenth-century liberal historians of Latin America, notably Diego Barros Arana, who were reluctant to find much to praise in the colonial administration of the Indies. Even in Chile, where the Araucanian wars imposed exceptionally severe conditions, the commutation of personal services proceeded steadily until they virtually disappeared before the middle of the seventeenth century. Fifty years earlier, as Alvaro Jara's researches have indicated, the funds accumulated by the Indian communities from their share of gold production were already substantial enough to be used regularly as a source of credit by the Spanish settlers. Barros Arana unwittingly demolished earlier assertions to the effect that the crown directives about the commutation of labor services had not been obeyed when he explained that the decline in Chile's gold production was a direct consequence of the royal decrees regulating labor in the mines and establishing a salary for the Indians.[42]

[41] Parry, *Seaborne Empire*, p. 186.

[42] See Alvaro Jara, *El salario de los indios y los sesmos del oro en la Tasa de Santillán*, Santiago, 1960, and Diego Barros Arana, *Historia de Chile*, Santiago, 1884–1903 IV, p. 262.

At the minimal price of withdrawing the clause of the New Laws that abolished the *encomienda* the crown gained a major victory, and the regalist hold over the Indies was consolidated. An appropriate commentary on the mood that prevailed among the majority of the settlers, who did not hold *encomienda* grants, after the Peruvian crisis came from an anonymous memorialist who wrote to Charles V in 1554 saying that great care should be exercised when distributing the Indians among the settlers, because, if they are granted to lords (*señores*), each lord would regard himself as a king, "as they do not love the King and care nothing for the increase of the Crown of Spain, but think only of themselves and their families, and as they are so far away . . . they are within a hair's breadth of rebellion. As the experience of a few years ago showed, neither lords nor *encomenderos* guarantee the land (to the King); rather they make it ready for rebellion." Therefore, the memorialist concludes, "His Majesty could maintain peace and tranquility throughout the New World . . . by giving it well-paid governors, who should be required to resume their residence in Spain after a certain brief term of office."[43] This was preaching to the converted, but while before the Peruvian uprising there was an element of doubt about the future development of the *encomienda* with at least the possibility of it acquiring a seigneurial or even a quasi-feudal character, after the defeat of Pizarro this was ruled out, and the crown followed the direction suggested by the anonymous memorialist from New Spain. At any rate, as Zavala has explained, "the possibility of creating a general system of nobility in the Indies became even more remote," and "the political system of the colonies moved nearer to the centralized and bureaucratic type of the modern European states."[44] As for

[43] The same anonymous author put forward the example of the Turkish system of imperial administration as something worth following by the Spanish Crown in the Indies: "the Turks keep all their territories in safe subjection . . . by refusing to grant city, village, or fief to anyone." Silvio Zavala, *New Viewpoints on the Spanish Colonization of America*, New York, 1943, pp. 72-73.

[44] This trend was accentuated by the growing fiscal needs of the crown

the *encomienda* itself, the failure of Pizarro's challenge was its undoing; "by the end of the sixteenth century the *encomienda* had ceased to be a major factor in the economy of the Indies. By the end of the seventeenth it had almost disappeared. . . . In its insistence on the personal liberty of the Indians the Crown had won a notable victory."[45] It had indeed, and re-galist central power was successfully reaffirmed, both with respect to the sympathetic interference of humanitarian clerics and the open rebellion of settlers with seigneurial aspirations.

---

that persistently endeavored to acquire a larger proportion of the tribute paid by the Indians, and, as Zavala has indicated, "by the end of the eighteenth century these efforts had resulted in the almost total absorption of this income by the royal treasury, and the old *encomiendas* or the pensions paid for the royal treasury to their former owners, continued to exist in only a few prov-inces." Zavala, *New Viewpoints*, p. 79.

[45] Parry, *Seaborne Empire*, p. 186.

4

Bourbon Recentralization

Among modern empires, the Spanish American has been the largest and the longest lived; it encompassed a considerable portion of the world, and it lasted for just over three hundred years before its dissolution early in the nineteenth century.[1] During this period, Spain was an active and at times a principal participant in European politics. In addition to the political and economic stresses imposed by its external stance, Spain had to endure dynastic and domestic difficulties that were naturally reflected in the imperial arrangements. Such vicissitudes reacting on each other produced a varied and extremely complex historical process that is not amenable to simplistic classification. Nevertheless, for the purpose of this study, two periods of singular importance in the development of the empire can be safely identified: the first one covers the latter part of the seventeenth century when Spain was under the administration of the Hapsburgs and is justly associated with recurrent crisis and the relaxation of the imperial hold; the second period is marked by reform and recovery and, with equal justice, is commonly associated with the administration of the Bourbon monarchs especially with that of Charles III and his regalist ministers.[2]

[1] "At the Congress of Vienna the pretensions of Spain were dismissed as those of a *cour secondaire*; at the accession of Charles III in 1759, such an attitude would have been inconceivable and unrealistic. The Spanish Empire, which stretched over the American continent from California to the Straits of Magellan, was the most imposing political structure of the Western World; to Napoleon it was still the greatest supplier of silver and to British merchants, the greatest unexplored market." Raymond Carr, *Spain, 1808-1939*, Oxford, 1966, p. 38.

[2] The nature of the recovery following the Caroline reforms has been vari-

During the decades of decline under the later Hapsburgs, laxity, inefficiency, and at times plain corruption weakened the central control of the empire. This has led some authors to think such a development marked the beginning of an irreversible dispersal of power that proceeded unchecked until it became a factor in the eventual secession of the Indies more than a century later. This type of interpretation should be examined more closely, for, if true, it would largely invalidate the working hypothesis presented in this study—namely, that the centralism of the formative decades of the empire survived as a significant factor throughout the colonial period and the nineteenth century and is with us today.

The Steins in their book on the Spanish colonial heritage, suggest it was probably in the seventeenth century that the large landowners in America emerged as the dominant figures of both the colonial society and economy. Against a darkening background of economic depression, declining trade, infrequent ship sailings, and a visible relaxation of central control, landowners and miners in the Indies appeared almost as quasi seigneurs. According to the Steins social and political power shifted "from the metropolis to the periphery—to the colonial *hacendado*, mineowner, merchant. At the same time the compartmentalization of colonial regions was enhanced . . . sectionalism, regionalism, provincialism . . . undoubtedly helped produce among Spaniards born in America an incipient nationalism, an ill-defined sense of greater rule in

---

ously interpreted by students of the period; O. Carlos Stoetzer, for instance, has attributed the eventual dissolution of the empire precisely to those reforms, "the revolution in Spanish America was certainly prepared, even though unconsciously, by King Charles III and his enlightened reforms." *El pensamiento político en la América española durante el período de la emancipación 1789-1825*, II, Madrid, 1966, 256, et seq. (author's translation.) John Lynch goes further in his study of an important aspect of the reforms and concludes that, "by giving Americans a vision of better government and denying them a significant share in its operation, the reforms of Charles III, both in their administrative and in their commercial aspects, helped to precipitate the collapse of the imperial regime they were intended to prolong." *Spanish Colonial Administration, 1782-1810: The Intendant System in the Viceroyalty of the Rio de la Plata*, London, 1958, p. 289.

America than that enjoyed by European-born administrators and merchants."[3]

Although there is no doubt that during the second half of the seventeenth century the affairs of Spain and her empire were in a critical condition,[4] it is less clear whether this necessarily devolved responsibility to the periphery, and if this happened in reality, whether it went to the *"hacendado, mineowner, merchant,"* as suggested by the Steins. In the absence of a detailed study of this question, one would suppose that as it became gradually evident that the metropolis was not prepared, mostly through lack of interest, to discharge the responsibilities of imperial leadership, the importance of these tasks must have declined until they were reduced to matters of administration planned and executed for the most part according to precedent. There is no reason to suppose that the responsibility for maintaining the administration of affairs at this level was left in hands other than those of the civil servants in the Indies. These men were by necessity the most zealous followers of established practice in the well-founded expectation that whatever it was that they were compelled by circumstances to do in the absence of clear metropolitan direction, would eventually be either approved or overlooked by the central authorities.

It must be noted that the imperial decline was not accompanied by juridical changes in the formal structure of administration. At least on paper, the empire of the Hapsburgs was as

[3] Stein and Stein, *Colonial Heritage*, p. 66. There is a temptation to generalize from the situation inside Spain during the second half of the seventeenth century to the rest of the imperial territories. However, such a temptation ought to be resisted for the consequences of the Hapsburg decline inside Spain and in the Indies were quite different.

[4] Max Beloff, in his well-known *The Age of Absolutism, 1660-1815*, London, 1954, ch. 4, p. 79, describes the domestic state of Spain: "Spain had been in the grip of an economic decline; a falling population; chronic unemployment and land falling out of use. The power of the Crown had decreased; the great estates, the *latifundia* had grown in size and number." See also Lynch, *Colonial Administration*, p. 1, and the useful collection of essays by Antonio Domínguez Ortíz, *Crisis y decadencia de la España de los Austrias*, Barcelona, 1969, especially "La crisis de Castilla en 1677-1687."

centralist and legalistic as ever, and the severe system of inspection and control functioned with sufficient regularity to ensure that even the most exalted officers of the crown in the Indies, including viceroys and captain-generals, were not forgetful of the dreaded judicial review: the *residencia*. As has been pointed out by Lillian Estelle Fisher, in Spanish America the *residencia* was "the principal means employed by the king to keep viceroys and other functionaries under control." On the expiration of their term of service, all officials had to undergo this official investigation of their conduct. The fear of the *residencia* was frequently an incentive to serve the monarch well; it also limited any autonomous inclinations of ambitious civil servants in the periphery of empire. This was not the only means of control; other limitations were imposed on senior colonial officials that brought them effectively under the direct control of the metropolis. As Fisher has indicated, they were commanded "to report to the king with the greatest detail on all matters, so that nothing might escape his eye. The *audiencia*, which communicated directly with the sovereign, was one of the principal checks upon the viceroy's authority, and the Viceregal council also had a slight restraining influence upon him. . . . There was danger of the king deposing the Viceroy if he was not careful of his conduct, and reprimands were received frequently."[5]

The sobering effect of such constraints was reinforced by the legal training of many of the higher civil servants in the Indies. Although these lawyer-bureaucrats from unavoidable necessity often made decisions without specifically consulting with Spain, or without receiving satisfactory instructions, they almost invariably took care to spread responsibility by seeking advice locally, not necessarily from *hacendados* and merchants but from the *oidores*, the judges of appeal who, also had administrative and advisory duties. At any rate, irrespective of the extent of the dispersal of administrative responsibilities to the periphery as a result of metropolitan indiffer-

---

[5] Lillian Estelle Fisher, *Viceregal Administration in the Spanish-American Colonies*, New York, 1926, p. 44.

ence, these responsibilities continued to be exercised solely in
the name of the crown, and at no time did the imperial civil
service take advantage of the situation to adopt a posture that
could be considered rebellious.

This, of course, does not mean that there were no rebellions in the Indies. In the seventeenth and eighteenth centuries
there were rebellions indeed, but "their causes were usually
local, often merely personal or factious. They never—or very
rarely—implied conscious rebellion against the Crown or
against the tie with Spain. There were no Massachusetts sepa-
ratists, no premature mutterings of colonial self-government,
of independent kingdoms or commonwealths."[6] Going
deeper into the nature of the sporadic uprisings that occurred
before independence, Richard Morse suggests that if one ex-
cepts seditious revolts that were the result of personal ambition for power, the rest share "the characteristics one could

---

[6] Parry, *Seaborne Empire*, p. 274. The reverence with which the crown was
regarded even by those who presumably rebelled against it, is worthy of a
special study as a subject in social and political psychology. The case of the
famous revolt led by Tupac Amaru in the eighteenth century merits consideration. At the peak of his military success, Tupac Amaru managed to capture the *Corregidor* of Tinta, an unfortunate civil servant called Arriaga, who
was subsequently executed in the central square of Tungasuca after an elaborate trial. Both trial and execution, however, were performed in the name of
the Spanish crown and the revolutionary leader indulged in the revealing
farce of pretending that he had received direct instructions from Charles III to
proceed with the execution; thus, this most important revolt against authority in the Indies, was conducted in the name of the distant king. One wonders
whether this aspect of the history of the Tupac Amaru rebellion escaped the
notice of the young Uruguayans who more recently have been conducting
terrorist activities under the name of *Tupamaros*, obviously inspired by the
eighteenth-century Peruvian uprising. See Oscar Cornblit, "Society and
Mass Rebellion," *Latin American Affairs*, ed. Raymond Carr, St. Anthony's
Papers no. 22, Oxford, 1970, pp. 40-43. As for the significance of the Tupac
Amaru rebellion as an antecedent for the movement for independence, a recent study of the period indicates that "had creole support been forthcoming,
it might have developed into a separatist movement. However, seen in the
light of conditions in 1780, it makes more sense as a story of fruitless attempts
to secure the legal redress of grievances, followed by a sudden, unplanned,
violent outburst." J. R. Fisher, *Government and Society in Colonial Peru. The
Intendant System 1784-1814*, London, 1970, p. 23.

define as 'legitimate' for revolt within the framework of the Thomist patrimonial state" for such actions according to L. Machado Ribas tended "always toward the immediate resolution of a severe and urgent crisis" and not to the establishment of a separatist entity or the overthrow of the imperial arrangement.[7] Possibly the most convincing evidence of continuing centralization is that the revolts that did occur were very few and invariably unsuccessful, even at the time when the central regime was at its weakest.[8]

More important, it would appear, were the consequences of the new policies of recruitment into the civil service. These were practically forced on the imperial administration as a result of public indifference to the affairs of the Indies during much of the Hapsburg period. Because very few peninsular civil servants of sufficient merit and ability were willing to serve overseas, a large proportion of civil service posts in the Indies were staffed with American-born creoles. As will be seen later, this was the cause of considerable difficulties once the Bourbon reforms got under way in the eighteenth century.

The crisis of the Hapsburg period resulted in a widespread feeling that Spain had entered a period of decline and that only forceful and far-reaching reforms could lead to an effective recovery. This was the attitude of those who were entrusted with the responsibility of planning and executing the changes associated with the Enlightenment under the Bourbon monarchs. From the point of view of this study, the important aspect of the vast complex of eighteenth-century re-

---

[7] Richard M. Morse, "The Heritage of Latin America," in *The Founding of New Societies*, ed. Louis Hartz, New York, 1964, p. 158. The second quotation comes from L. Machado Ribas, *Movimientos revolucionarios en las colonias españolas de América*, Montevideo, 1940, p. 23. (author's translation.)

[8] A Bolivian historian has observed that although some have tried to describe these disturbances as a prelude for independence, "the truth is that they had no concerted plan of any kind and were only sporadic explosions of discontent against the local authorities, mostly in protest against some new exaction, or simply acts of pillage and banditry headed by irresponsible brigands." Enrique Finot, *Nueva Historia de Bolivia*, La Paz, 1954, pp. 119-120. (author's translation.)

forms is its regalism and, closely bound with it, the intention
to recentralize the political, economic, and ecclesiastical life of
the empire in pursuit of a nationalistic program of recovery
and growth. Whether the changes resulted in the prosperity
and increased power its initiators hoped for is a question that
demands separate consideration; what is of importance here is
to ascertain whether the traditional centralist arrangements
described in earlier chapters survived into the nineteenth century.

The recentralizing reforms were imposed on the aging empire by ministers who passionately believed in the virtues of
rational, modernizing, central control and who, under
Charles III, were strongly supported by a monarch who took
a personal interest in their realization. Resistance against reforms was weak and became serious only when the changes
ordered were distinctly unpopular, as in the case of the Esquilache riots.[9] Although it is possible that, in comparison
with the most advanced European nations of the time, the
Caroline reforms did not create an outstandingly efficient regime, it can be fairly stated that the imperial administration
under the later Bourbons "was more efficient, more tightly
centralized, than any government which the Indies had
known before."[10] From a different point of view, the Mexican author Octavio Paz indicates that "the reforms undertaken by the Bourbon dynasty, particularly Charles III, improved the economy and made business operations more
efficient, but they accentuated the centralization of admin-

---

[9] Leopoldo de Gregorio, Marqués de Squillace (Esquilache) the Neapolitan
Minister of Finance for Charles III was "grasping, coarse and tactless, but
well-meaning and progressive. He cleansed and improved the city, turned on
hard the screw of taxation. . . . he improved street lighting in Madrid, where
he installed 5,000 lamps, in order to check crime and vice at night, and with
the same end in view prohibited wide-brimmed hats and flowing cloaks. The
cloak is indispensable to the Spaniard. . . . The Spaniard's cloak is the Englishman's castle. Madrid rose in revolt on Easter Sunday 1776, in a fury
against the Neapolitan Minister. . . . The King was forced to dismiss Esquilache and rescind the unpopular decrees." Salvador de Madariaga, *The
Fall of the Spanish American Empire*, London, 1947, pp. 276-277.

[10] Parry, *Seaborne Empire*, p. 326.

istrative functions and changed New Spain into a territory strictly controlled by the centre of power.''[11] Regarding the process from yet another and broader perspective, Max Beloff sees the policy of centralization as a principal and relatively successful feature of Bourbon rule. But he also thinks that Spain presented only the appearance of absolutism and firm central control since "the condition of its existence in theory was to refrain from exercising it in practice.''[12] In view of what actually happened to Spain and her empire during the half century following the reforms, such a statement could appear almost self-evident; yet it would be a mistake to think that the formal recentralization had a less than formidable impact throughout the vast empire. It was quite the contrary.

The effect of the Caroline reforms in the Indies was momentous. Old institutions inherited from the Hapsburg period were either overhauled or had their jurisdiction and powers severely reduced by the establishment of modern administrative departments and the appointment of new officials. Those who held office under the old order were frequently native Americans who came to resent bitterly "the sudden influx of young men from the peninsula, chosen . . . to manage the new monopolies and other offices of State. At the same time, the organization of a fairly rapid, efficient royal postal service throughout the empire put an end to that former freedom of action conferred by distance and bad communications.''[13] Here indeed, among many other sig-

[11] Octavio Paz, *The Labyrinth of Solitude*, New York, 1961, p. 117.

[12] Beloff, *Absolutism*, p. 78.

[13] D. A. Brading, *Miners and Merchants in Bourbon Mexico 1763-1810*, Cambridge, 1971, pp. 33-34. According to one modern student of these problems, the degree of efficiency of the Caroline reforms was responsible at least in part for the generalization of conflict in late eighteenth-century Latin America; "The reform measures which the administration introduced signified a growing threat to almost every portion of the established network of interests. . . . Faced with [the] sustained pressures from the central government, the local dominant classes had no other recourse but to try to mobilize the lower sectors of the population: this was done in many of the disturbances which broke out in 1780. As it was progressively clear that the activities of the new bureaucrats were not going to be stopped easily, more and more

nificant consequences of the reforms, may be found a major
factor in the rivalry between creoles and peninsular Spaniards
that was to play such a decisive role after 1810. It was the
creole civil servants, not merchants and landowners with a
feeling of "incipient nationalism" as suggested by the Steins,
who nursed a grudge against the Spanish-born. Having
laboriously reached the senior levels of the bureaucracy during the latter Hapsburg and early Bourbon administrations,
the creoles found themselves superseded and replaced by the
new professionals sent from Madrid. As Brading explains,
whereas the first Bourbon kings had promoted creoles on a
liberal scale to all offices in colonial government, except those
of viceroy and bishop, Charles III's enlightened ministers intent on a thorough reform relied mainly on soldiers and
bureaucrats brought in from Europe. Consequently the government reforms entailed not just the creation of new institutions, but also the importation of new men."[14] The main architect of this administrative policy was José de Gálvez, one
of the king's most trusted advisors. In a memorandum prepared some years before his well-known visit to Mexico in
1765-1771, he explained that "lately, in all the American *au-
diencias* many natives of the province or city in which these
courts are situated, have been appointed . . . many presiden-
cies, governorships and captaincy-generals . . . have been occupied by creoles." This he considered unsatisfactory on the
grounds that the creoles were much too closely bound by ties
of "family and faction in the New World to provide a disin-
terested, impartial government." The misgivings of the eminent civil servant were partially confirmed during his visit to
Mexico where he discovered that, contrary to existing legislation, the majority of the members of the *audiencia* were na-

---

elements of the higher and middle classes were ready to support the demands
of the Indians." Cornblit, "Mass Rebellion," pp. 40-41. This is perhaps an
excessive claim, but it is significant that the whole argument rests on the
premise that the Caroline reforms were effective, or at least effective enough
to pose a threat to the established order.

[14] Brading, *Miners*, p. 35.

tives of the country. This was true not only of New Spain; in the *audiencia* of Lima, five of the eight *oidores* were creoles.[15]

The Bourbon economic reforms were largely based on the ideas of a distinguished group of Spanish political economists, many of whom were also called to accept senior posts in the imperial bureaucracy or to serve directly as advisors to the king on economic matters. Their writings are not distinguished for theoretical originality, for they were strongly imbued with the prevailing mercantilist ideas, but their undisguised pragmatism merits attention.

They seldom ventured into the realm of abstraction, but rather proposed measures intended to bring a rapid resurgence of the ailing imperial economy. Such was the case with the writings of men like Campillo, who served in a number of ministerial posts in the decade of 1740 and was the author of the celebrated treatise *Nuevo sistema de gobierno económico para las Indias*, presumably written in 1743 and widely circulated in manuscript form among government officials until it was eventually printed in 1789. Campillo's proposals included the general freeing of trade between the colonies and the metropolis, the lowering of tariff barriers on foreign merchandise, the encouragement of agriculture in the overseas territories, the abolition of the traditional trade monopolies at that time centered in Cádiz, and the establishment of rapid, regular postal services between Spain and the Indies.[16] The mercantilist framework within which Campillo's policies were devised was well-suited to the temper of a government bent on a policy of national advancement through the strengthening of central control over the vast empire. The increased intervention of the state in the economy did not in any way con-

[15] Brading, *Miners*, p. 35, et seq. Gálvez's resulting advice to the king was very much in line with Morse's description of the imperial edifice as a patrimonial state in the Weberian sense. According to Morse, among the characteristic ways in which the ruler of such a state endeavors to retain authority are: "limiting the tenure of royal officials; forbidding officials to acquire family and economic ties of administration." Morse, *Heritage*, p. 157.

[16] Lynch, *Colonial Administration*, p. 12.

tradict the demands for greater liberalization of trade; such a suggestion referred not to the institution of free trade as understood, for example, by Adam Smith, but simply to the freeing of trade within the empire. Campillo's treatise was possibly the single most influential work on which the Caroline economic reforms were based, and it must be noted that in spite of the limitations with which the policies for economic recovery had to contend, they were remarkably successful.[17]

If in the field of economic reform Spain was well-served by her own thinkers and statesmen, when it came to the task of modernizing and strengthening her administrative apparatus, she had to turn to France for advice and assistance. Philip V was the first Bourbon monarch to seek French help in this respect. At the time, early in the eighteenth century, the country was faced with bankruptcy and its administration was in disarray.[18] Moved partly by necessity and partly by admiration for the success of the French centralizing effort and especially for the efficient operation of the system of intendants, the king appealed to Louis XIV who responded by sending a mission headed by Orry, an economist and expert in administration who for many years afterwards served as advisor to the Spanish crown.[19]

This mission laid the foundations for the adoption in 1718 of the system of intendants by Spain, but it was not until the second half of the century, after the Peace of Paris, that the Bourbon administration, satisfied with the advantages of the new arrangements, decided to extend them to Spanish America. By that time France was at least as interested as Spain in the efficient reform and advancement of the overseas

[17] Angel César Rivas, "Prosperity—the Fruit of Generous Reforms," in *The Bourbon Reformers and Spanish Civilization*, ed. T. S. Floyd, Boston, 1966, p. 11.

[18] According to some students of the period, notably Domínguez Ortíz, the slow process of recovery that culminated after the Caroline reforms of the eighteenth century, had already started by 1687. *Crisis*, pp. 216-217.

[19] Lynch, *Colonial Administration*, p. 47.

empire. She had just emerged from a disastrous war in which the rising power of Great Britain became apparent, and she was particularly interested in strengthening her Spanish ally and especially the economy of the Indies in order to restore the European balance of economic and political power. Choiseul, the French minister for foreign affairs, actively encouraged Charles III to introduce the needed reforms and offered all the help which the Bourbon monarch required. France sent a number of experts to Spain to cooperate in the momentous task. On the advice of Choiseul himself, a secret ministerial commission started functioning in Madrid to elaborate the scheme for the reform; moreover, in José de Gálvez, the Spanish Minister for the Indies, France had an additional and most influential ally.[20]

The first intendant was appointed for the island of Cuba in 1764, and by the end of the decade of 1780, the system of intendants covered practically the whole of the Spanish American empire. This is not the place to undertake a detailed examination of the introduction of the system of intendants; such a task has already been ably performed, at least for the viceroyalties of Peru and the Río de la Plata, by J. R. Fisher

---

[20] The Chilean historian Jaime Eyzaguirre attributed great importance to the foreign origins of the centralizing efforts of the Bourbon kings that he saw as a disastrous pretension "to transform the monarch into the immediate depository of the divine authority, without any limitations." This he considered a drastic departure from "the old, traditional posture that recognizes the participation of the people in the generation of power, its ethical limitations and the rejection of tyranny." He further maintained that the pragmatic Bourbon absolutism swept away the traditional religious and philosophical bonds that held the empire together, substituting them with administrative techniques and a type of monarchical rule that left the crown in a singularly vulnerable position, isolated and distant from the old sources of popular support. I find this an amiable, but untenable thesis. It would be hard to demonstrate that the rule of Charles III or Philip V was less or more absolute than that of Philip II or the Catholic Kings, harder still to maintain that the latter understood that the exercise of their power was in any way conditioned by popular acceptance or that its origins owed anything to the popular will. See Jaime Eyzaguirre, *Ideario y ruta de la emancipación chilena*, 2nd ed., Santiago, 1969, p. 82.

and John Lynch in books that have been important sources for
this study.[21] It is sufficient here to indicate that the intendant
system was centralist in conception and execution and as
Fisher describes it, "the aims of the programme were to cen-
tralize and improve the structure of government, to create
more efficient economic and financial machinery, to defend
the empire from other powers, and in general, to restore integrity and respect for law at all levels of administration."[22]
Regardless of its shortcomings and the many problems it generated, the system of intendants undoubtedly carried the imperial administration to a very high degree of centralization,
and, despite the disappointment of the exaggerated expectations of improvement in economic matters, it is possible to
perceive a correlation between its introduction and a betterment of the financial situation.[23] As Fisher has indicated, the
tribute revenue of the viceroyalty of Peru shows a distinct increase during the period, and similar results are observable
elsewhere.[24] Some have seen in the introduction of the system
of intendants the beginnings of a decentralizing tendency that
acquired momentum during the nineteenth-century republican period. This interpretation has been used with reference
to the subsequent development of a federalist movement in
what is now Argentina. It would be difficult to accept this as a
valid proposition, and for an opinion worth quoting in this
respect there is that of the Argentine historian Ernesto
Palacio, who states that the intendant system "in which some
have pretended to discover the genesis of our federalism,
meant on the contrary, the establishment in our country of

---

[21] Lynch, *Colonial Administration*, and J. R. Fisher, *Government and Society*.

[22] Fisher, *Government and Society*, pp. 1 and 156.

[23] For a description of the shortcomings, see Lynch, *Colonial Administration*, pp. 279-289, and Tulio Halperin Donghi, *Historia contemporánea de
América Latina*, Madrid, 1969, pp. 52-56.

[24] The figures for tribute revenue from 1780 to 1811 in the viceroyalty of
Peru are given by J. R. Fisher, *Government and Society*, App. no. 4. From
these, the figures for the following years have been extracted to illustrate the
general trend: (1780) 631,143 pesos; (1785) 752,835 pesos; (1790) 914,502
pesos; (1795) 948,626 pesos; (1800) 1,203,388 pesos; (1805) 1,243,732 pesos.

the most implacable centralism; the local municipalities were absorbed by the provincial *juntas* and the intendant and these together, by the viceroy."[25]

That the administrative system of intendants was centralist in all respects should not occasion surprise as its adoption by Charles III for application in the Indies was one of the consequences of a marriage of convenience between two great imperial regimes, both on the threshold of their eventual historical collapse. The modern institutions of absolute centralism, shaped by men such as Richelieu and Louis XIV, were transplanted to Spanish America to revive an equally centralist imperial hold, grown weaker more as the result of indifference than because of any triumphant challenge from without or within.

Bourbon recentralization, especially under Charles III, was as important in ecclesiastical matters as it was in administration, commerce, and politics; perhaps in the former case the effect was all the more noticeable because of the international resonance caused by measures as drastic as the expulsion of the Jesuits or the decisive royal attack on the institution of ecclesiastical immunity, both moves with lasting consequences throughout the Spanish Indies.[26] Caroline ecclesiasti-

[25] Ernesto Palacio, *Historia de la Argentina*, Buenos Aires, 1954, I, 137. (author's translation.) Of course, it will hardly do to mention Argentine federalism as an example of decentralization; the regime of Rosas, who ruled in the name of federalism, was one of the most rigidly centralized that the country has known.

[26] The expulsion of the Jesuits was not exclusively a Spanish development; they were first expelled from Portugal in 1759; France did likewise in 1761 and 1768; Spain ordered the expulsion in 1767, so did Naples; Parma followed in 1768, and Prussia decreed the expulsion in 1780. The reasons put forward varied considerably from one country to another and from one colonial territory to the next, but they coincided in regarding the Society of Jesus as a serious obstacle to national policies generally identified with the Enlightenment. As Madariaga put it, "The Jesuits were traditional upholders of the universal monarchy of the Pope as against the national monarchies of mere temporal kings." Madariaga, *The Fall*, p. 278 et seq. For a sober and scholarly view of the consequences of the expulsion in one specific instance, see Walter Hanish, S.J., *Itinerario y pensamiento de los jesuítas expulsos de Chile 1767-1815*, Santiago, 1972.

cal reforms cannot be studied in isolation; they were not the result of blind impulse, excessive influence by this or that anticlerical grouping, or the direct consequence of any particular enmity of the monarch, a devout Catholic, against the Church in general or any specific religious order.[27] Furthermore, although the reforms are of the greatest interest when examined from an ecclesiastical point of view and raise a number of complex and important theological problems as well, for the purposes of the present study their main significance lies in their relationship with the dominant, well-nigh official, doctrine on the nature of the state. Founded on a profoundly regalist and all-embracing view of the state and of the relations between temporal and ecclesiastical power its acceptance led, almost unavoidably, to the conclusion that in Spain the Catholic Church generally and the Society of Jesus in particular were moving disturbingly close to an autonomy amounting to privilege, and worse, that they espoused unacceptable concepts about the respective powers of the Vatican and the Spanish monarch. This doctrine was based on the writings and advice of Charles III's ministers, mainly those of Pedro Rodríguez, count of Campomanes, one of the most intellectually and politically influential figures of the period.[28]

[27] Although Madariaga later abundantly qualifies it, his opening statement on the expulsion of the Jesuits, "a masonic impulse was one of the forces which led to the expulsion of the Jesuits from Spain and Portugal," taken together with the perhaps excessive importance he attributes to Voltaire and D'Alembert in his study, give to the expulsion a conspiratorial character that may unfairly detract from the reasons of national policy as understood by the monarchs of the Enlightenment and their ministers, especially in the case of Spain and Portugal. Madariaga, *The Fall*, p. 263.

[28] "The key to this [ecclesiastical policy] is the relationship between ecclesiastical power and privilege and the two overriding goals of Charles III and his ministers, to which all other questions were subordinated: the first political, the extension of royal absolutism; the second economic, the development of Spain's (and the colonies') material prosperity. With these primary aims in view, the Caroline policy-makers, principally the two *fiscales* of the Council of Castile, Pedro Rodríguez de Campomanes (Count of Campomanes) and José de Moñino (Count of Floridablanca), formed a corollary programme of ecclesiastical reform which sought to limit or abolish any

It is almost impossible to study any matter of consequence during those decades without finding Campomanes involved at one or another level. The issue of ecclesiastical reform, or of the recentralization of ecclesiastical control in the hands of the monarch, is no exception. Campomanes had concerned himself with the general question of the correct relationship between temporal and spiritual power and had arrived at conclusions that, though not tremendously original, did have the virtue of absolute clarity. For instance, on the issue of the legitimacy and sovereignty of temporal power, he wrote: "the temporal power is and must be completely sovereign and independent; God has entrusted the absolute exercise of such sovereignty to the monarch who is exclusively charged with public affairs; neither the national clergy nor the Pope have any right whatsoever to interfere."[29] There was no room for confusion, doubt, or discrepancy, and, of course, having accepted such a premise, the corollaries followed swiftly. Campomanes, his ministerial colleagues, and the monarch were agreed "that the best means of achieving the revival of Spain was through a powerful monarchy, removing every pocket of independence and eliminating all privileges, social, ecclesiastical and municipal, outside the Crown."[30]

In the full blossoming of the Enlightenment this was not a novelty; the world had seen the like of it before, in theory and in practice. Whether Campomanes had studied Hobbes is not known; what is beyond doubt is that views remarkably similar to those of the reformist minister are found in the pages of *Leviathan*. Campomanes and his royal master, for instance, would have agreed without difficulty that "Christian kings

---

ecclesiastical institution that would interfere with their realization." N. M. Farriss, *Crown and Clergy in Colonial Mexico, 1759-1821: The Crisis of Ecclesiastical Privilege*, London, 1968, pp. 90-91. See also Ricardo Krebs Wilckens, *El pensamiento histórico, político y económico del Conde de Campomanes*, Santiago, 1960.

[29] Krebs Wilckens, *Campomanes*, p. 129. (author's translation.)

[30] Lynch, *Colonial Administration*, pp. 1-2.

are . . . the supreme pastors of their people, and have the power to ordain what pastors they please."[31] Ferdinand of Aragon would also have approved and so would have the Emperor Charles and Philip II. Outside Spain the robust Gallicanism of France was far from exhausted, and there is no reason to suppose that it did not constitute as well an interesting ingredient of the policies of Campomanes. To deduce from this that they were merely a Spanish version of Gallicanism would be mistaken. Campomanes's policies were rooted in the Hispanic regalist tradition and made full use of the ideas of sixteenth-century and seventeenth-century authors like Salgado, Chumacero, Solórzano, and Pimentel. As Krebs Wilckens observes, they did not constitute "a revolutionary innovation, but the continuation and culmination of a long historical process."[32]

Whether these reforms were completely successful or not is a matter of marginal relevance to the working hypothesis presented in this study; yet it is important to observe that their implementation was a major cause of disaffection among the lower ranks of the clergy in Latin America. Later on during the period of independence, they helped to alienate a considerable sector of the population who identified the cause of religion with their parish priests and with the creole revolutionary movement instead of with the ruling and ostensibly anticlerical intelligentsia of Madrid. After the triumph of the revolutionary movement, this apparent contradiction was resolved with the victory of the more conservative ecclesiastical groups who had earlier opposed the Caroline reforms. This victory, even where it was most convincing, as in Mexico, was not long-lasting as the regalism of the metropolis was

[31] Thomas Hobbes, *Leviathan, or the Matter, Forme and Power of a Commonwealth Ecclesiasticall and Civil*, ed. Michael Oakeshott, Oxford, 1960, ch. 42, p. 355.

[32] Krebs Wilckens, *Campomanes*, p. 121. (author's translation.) Also Vicente Rodríguez Casado, *Iglesia y estado en el reino de Carlos III*, Seville, 1948, p. 21. For a different view, see Farriss, *Crown and Clergy*, pp. 88-89. Miss Farriss considers that the ecclesiastical reforms of the reign of Charles III "rested on a totally new concept of the relationship between Church and State formulated by Charles's regalist ministers."

soon embraced by the emerging ruling groups in each of the peripheral capital cities.[33] In ecclesiastical matters, as well as in administration, economic organization, commercial policy, and even political ideology, the Caroline reforms successfully reimposed on the Spanish Indies a centralist style in the conduct of affairs. There were variations in the efficiency with which the reforms were established, but generally they proved sufficiently effective to permit Madrid once again after the relaxation of the Hapsburg regime to gather firmly the reins of power.

Spain crossed the threshold of the nineteenth century with the empire more centralized than ever and unknowingly making ready to pass it on to the hands of the nascent republics of 1810. At the time of the Caroline reforms, the Indies had shown no disposition to secede. There had been some outbreaks of violence, some more important than others, but none with a contemporary impact comparable to that which a century later they evidently had on liberal historians, wise after the event and busily looking for portents of the independence movement. Such discontent as there was at the time was located among the middle and upper reaches of the civil bureaucracy and was frequently caused by the metropolitan policy of filling senior posts with professionals brought in

[33] Few incidents are as revealing of the continuity between the centralism of the Caroline reforms and the centralism of the republican regimes as the expulsion of the Jesuits by Juan Manuel de Rosas. In 1833 during his second administration the Argentine strongman invited the Society of Jesus to return to Argentina especially to assist the government in its efforts to improve educational standards. There followed several years of equivocation and a most complex history of intrigue when Rosas tried to bend the Jesuits to his will and make them cooperate with the central state in ways the order considered unacceptable. In 1840 when the end of this bizarre relationship was drawing near, Rosas wrote to the governor of Salta discouraging him from inviting the Jesuits into that province before "the degree of dependence of the Order with respect to the Government has been agreed upon, and the principles and the political system which they are teaching our young men are carefully examined." The situation deteriorated further, and in 1843 Rosas ordered the Jesuits out of Argentina in terms meriting the applause of Campomanes or any other regalist of the Caroline period. See Raúl H. Castagnino, *Rosas y los jesuítas*, Buenos Aires, 1970, p. 50. (author's translation.)

from Spain. There is no doubt that the creoles had a griev-
ance, but it is equally clear that their aim was not to secede
from Spain, but to obtain access to the highest responsibilities
in the imperial administration that only the crown could in-
fuse with mandate and authority.[34] This easily understood inclination became more urgent as the efficiency, honesty, and
modernizing intolerance of the new administrators began to
revolutionize stagnant colonial practices. It was precisely the
efficacy of the new arrangements and the probity of the
Spaniards sent to put the reforms into effect that earned them
and their regalist masters the enmity of the upper levels of
creole society. Exercising wide and remarkably independent
powers, the intendants tightened the administration of the Indies, improved fiscal control and the collection of revenues,
and achieved notable success in the prevention of abuses.
Municipal authorities that had been largely inactive for generations, were prodded into activity through ambitious and
well-planned programs of public works. The result of all this
improving zeal, as Parry points out, was that "They were
cordially detested throughout the Indies."[35]

[34] There are other interpretations of the successful survival of centralism.
According to Antonio Domínguez Ortíz, cited by H. R. Trevor-Roper,
"The loyalty of Spaniards was an ocean which neither incompetence nor severity could drain." The English historian implies that it was loyalty keeping
the reins under central control, for the reformers of the Enlightenment, according to this view, thought that "it was through an enlightened, dynamic,
authoritarian state, and through that alone . . . that the obscurantist, stagnant,
obedient society of Spain could be re-galvanised. In the end, on the eve, as it
must have seemed, of success, the machine broke in their hands, but it only
broke when an overmighty minister, having usurped the authority, could incur, as a scapegoat, the penalties which none would think of exacting from
the Crown." One wonders whether loyalty, even Spanish loyalty, could account for the political fact of central control, but be that as it may, the centralist style and tempo remained, and until the Napoleonic onslaught the
crown was not effectively challenged from within. See H. R. Trevor-Roper,
Historical Essays, London, 1963, pp. 265-266, "The Spanish Enlightenment,"
an article reviewing the works of Antonio Domínguez Ortíz, *La sociedad española en el siglo XVIII*, Madrid, 1955, and Jean Sarrailh, *L'Espagne Éclairée*,
Paris, 1954.

[35] Parry, *Seaborne Empire*, pp. 324-325. See also Halperin Donghi, *Historia
contemporánea*, p. 75. The systematic efforts made by the Castilian crown to

train and recruit able men into the expanding imperial bureaucracy had other interesting consequences. It has been shown, for instance, that most of the senior civil servants of the empire were the product of the only six graduate colleges (*colegios mayores*) to be found in the Spanish universities. University friendships and educational affiliations may have played a role in promotions within the bureaucracy, but it is also possible that this concentration of highly trained civil servants is simply additional evidence that the crown did try to promote the best trained and most capable into the highest positions of the civil service. See Richard L. Kagan, *Students and Society in Early Modern Spain*, Baltimore, 1974.

5

Pombaline Recentralization

It is possible to see the history of the Iberian peninsula from earliest times until the present as an intermittent struggle between center and periphery, between a regalist, bureaucratic, legalistic, nationalistic, and relatively illiberal Castilian center and a cosmopolitan, outward-looking, trading, industrious, and relatively liberal periphery. Two observations would follow from such an interpretation: first, that the center has prevailed, notwithstanding the continued reluctance of the peripheral regions to accept its dominance (Catalonia and the Basque country may resist stubbornly, but they are undoubtedly integral parts of the Spanish nation rather than discrete cultural and political entities); second, that Portugal is the only peripheral region that succeeded in escaping the Castilian embrace.

Portugal is the exception in the Iberian peninsula; Brazil appears to be the exception in Latin America. Yet their exceptional character is not absolute. There is sufficient parallelism in their cultural and political development to justify pause in considering Portugal and Brazil as essentially different and separate from the Iberian or Latin American cultural and political traditions. Perhaps the relationship between Portugal and Spain and between Brazil and Hispanic America is adequately illustrated by the differences and similarities between the Portuguese and the Spanish languages that are different, but with enough similarities to make those who speak one feel confident, wrongly confident as it usually turns out, that they can understand the other without special training. Those whose mother tongue is Spanish can, with the aid of a dictionary, understand most Portuguese business or journalistic prose and vice-versa. It is quite another matter, however, to understand the poetry, or to appreciate the finer points of a novel written in Portuguese; the broad outline is readily detected, but the nuances are almost invariably lost. In the history of Spain and Portugal and their respective empires the pattern is inverted; the broad outlines appear dissimilar, and yet, when attention is paid to the details, there are enough similarities to suggest caution before making definite statements about their differences.[1] Even more germane to the purpose of this study is the fact that although the broad streams of Portuguese and Spanish history often diverge, there are other times when they flow in the same direction. Such was the case, for example, during the second half of the eighteenth century when the Marquis of Pombal did for Portugal and her overseas territories largely what Charles III and his ministers did for the Spanish empire.

For twenty-two years between 1755 and 1777, Pombal ruled like a virtual dictator, enjoying the confidence and support of King Dom Jose of the house of Bragança. A typical Enlightenment regalist reformer, the great minister subordinated his policies to the fundamental need of bringing about the political and economic resurgence of his nation, and, in order to do this, he made his first priority the task of recovering for the crown the effective control over the affairs of the empire. The central hold had relaxed in Portugal and its empire during the preceding century and a half, presenting the

---

[1] This is written with some feeling. In 1968, in a footnote to the introduction of a book on Latin America, the author made the following statement: "It is evidently impossible to establish valid generalizations for the whole of Latin America and the Caribbean and no such attempt is made here. However, the most important exception—that offered by Brazil—is abundantly described and analysed in this book, especially in the articles by Professor Celso Furtado and Emanuel De Kadt. It is worth noting that a significant difference between Spanish and Portuguese America is that the latter never attained the degree of political and administrative centralization typical of the former during the colonial period." Now I am convinced that I was wrong when I wrote that; Brazil is not an exception. See Claudio Véliz, ed., *Latin America and the Caribbean, A Handbook*, London, 1968, p. xix,n.

reforming minister with a situation comparable to that facing Charles III and his advisors when they assumed the responsibility of governing Spain.[2] Even so, the background of this moment in mid-eighteenth-century Brazil and Portugal is sufficiently different to warrant a separate explanation. To begin with, the Portuguese administrative arrangements in Brazil during the first half of the sixteenth century lacked the emphatic centralism of the Spanish ones. At that time Portugal was emerging from a prolonged economic crisis and did not have the men and resources needed to launch a major colonizing effort directly under the auspices of the crown. Moreover, differing again from the Spanish experience with the conquest of Mexico and Peru, the early expeditions to Brazil proved disappointing as no great wealth was discovered that could conceivably justify a firm financial commitment on the part of an exhausted metropolis.[3] It was mainly the fear of losing the recently discovered lands to France that moved the Portuguese crown to make some mild exertions and try to organize a permanent settlement.

It was under these conditions that Dom João III, of the celebrated Aviz dynasty, took the practical course of offering substantial concessions to those willing to accept the responsibility of leading the colonizing enterprise. The country was divided into twelve *capitanías* between the mouth of the Amazon and the Cape of São Vicente. Each of these varied in width from two hundred to approximately six hundred kilometers and extended indefinitely toward the west. The *capitanías* were entrusted as hereditary grants to *donatários*

---

[2] "The diminished stature of the Iberian nations in the eighteenth century had forced both Spanish and Portuguese statesmen to face the formidable problem of modernization. It became increasingly evident that governmental efficiency and imperial consolidation were essential if either country was to retain its influence in a competitive and jealous world." Kenneth R. Maxwell, *Conflicts and Conspiracies: Brazil and Portugal, 1750-1808*, Cambridge, 1973, p. 3.

[3] Eulalia María Lahmeyer Lobo, *Processo administrativo Ibero-Americano*, Rio de Janeiro, 1962, pp. 134-154. Extensive use has been made of this comparative study of the development of colonial administration in Spanish and Portuguese America.

(grantees) who, in addition to the land, were allowed important privileges, such as the raising of local taxes, the right to collect tithes, to found townships and grant municipal rights to them, to inflict capital punishment on heretics, slaves, and low class Christian free men, and to pursue, with the sole exception of crown monopolies such as the one for Brazilwood, almost complete freedom of commerce, both within and outside their territories.[4] Such concessions contrast strongly with the strict central control exercised by the Spanish metropolis over the Indies through the *Casa de contratación*. Taken together with the hereditary right to the vast *capitanías*, they gave to these extraordinary grants a quasi seigneurial appearance unlike anything to be found in the Spanish Indies.

In practice, however, the *capitanías* fell short of constituting a feudal system. As Faoro has indicated, the legendary wealth and power of the holders of these grants was precisely legendary, because grossly exaggerated, while the juridical responsibilities and confirmation of the seigneurial status were never forthcoming.[5] These were obstacles enough and there were others. The system was not a success; four of the *capitanías* were not even claimed; of the rest only two, those of São Vicente in the extreme South and Pernambuco in the North, sur-

[4] Caio Prado Junior, *Historia económica del Brasil*, Buenos Aires, 1960, p. 57.

[5] Faoro, *Donos do poder*, I, pp. 131-132. Although the feudal character of the *capitanías* had been the subject of lengthy controversy, possibly the discussion should not have continued after the publication of Faoro's work in which, notwithstanding the special characteristics of the *donatário* system, he shows as baseless the assumption that there existed a Brazilian mode of feudalism. One of the more recent contributions in this debate has the advantage of being a useful summary of the main positions. See H. B. Johnson, Jr., "The Donatory Captaincy in Perspective: Portuguese Backgrounds to the Settlement of Brazil," *HAHR*, LII (1972), 203-214. Johnson traces the controversy back to the work of Carlos Malheiro Dias, first published in 1924, in which he describes the *donatário* grants as "feudal." Johnson comments that "nothing in his description remotely conformed to any viable definition of feudalism, or that medieval Portugal never experienced an identifiable 'feudal' tradition, seems not to have perturbed him at all." See Carlos Malheiro Dias, "O regímen feudal das donatárias," in *História da colonização portuguesa no Brasil*, Oporto, 1924, III, ch. 6, pp. 217-283.

vived and attained a very moderate level of prosperity. Out-side Pernambuco and Bahia, the wealth of the *donatários* and of the leading families may have been closer to the "barefoot with spats" category than otherwise. Freyre has described it caustically as an "incomplete" luxury of lordly families boast-ing silk-lined palanquins but sleeping poorly, tormented by bed-bugs, rich enough to indulge in the superfluous and partly justify the shrill exaggerations that reached European shores, but certainly far from rich enough to take even a first step in the direction of aristocratic power.[6]

Important additional factors behind the failure of the *capitanías* were the virtual impossibility of developing an eco-nomic base to sustain the ambitious establishment decreed from Lisbon and the strategic difficulties of organizing a cred-ible defense system at a time when there appeared to be a seri-ous threat of a French military invasion. By 1549, the same Dom João III reversed his former policy and superimposed a centralized administration over the *capitanías*. These lost most of their privileges; a colonial capital was established in Bahia, and a governor-general appointed with widespread powers over the political, economic, and religious life of the whole of Portuguese America.[7]

The intention of the reform of 1549 was to bureaucratize what until then had been a private initiative encouraged by a monarch prepared to delegate effective, sovereign power as an incentive to the *donatários*. The sudden transformation of this highly decentralized system into a centralized one, exclu-sively the result of the royal will, caused little resistance in Brazil mainly for the reasons accounting for its ill-success.

[6] Gilberto Freyre, *Casa-grande e senzala*, 14th ed. Rio de Janeiro, 1966, I, 52; Charles R. Boxer, *The Portuguese Seaborne Empire, 1415-1825*, London, 1969, pp. 86-87.

[7] Francis A. Dutra, "Centralization versus Donatorial Privilege: Pernam-buco, 1602-1630" in *Colonial Roots of Modern Brazil*, ed. Dauril Alden, Berke-ley and Los Angeles, Calif., 1973, p. 20. For a dissenting view, see Faoro, who states that the office of the governor-general was not born from amidst the ruins of the colony, but from the very real prospects for its future pros-perity. It was the success of Pernambuco and São Vicente that largely invited the intervention by the metropolis. Faoro, *Donos do poder*, I, 141-146.

The only significant opposition was found in the *capitanía* of Pernambuco, ably managed by the Captain-General Duarte Coelho who protested so vigorously that the crown acquiesced, for a while, granting this region a position of exception within the new system.[8] Thus, seeds were sown for a confrontation between central and regional power that became endemic in Brazilian history during the next two centuries.

The ease with which the reform of 1549 was realized was deceptive; although most of the *donatários* were unable to resist the dramatic reversal of policy, the governor-general in Bahia representing the monarch in the colony lacked power to have his orders obeyed throughout the vast territory. He had no army and his financial resources were limited; worse, his official duties made him understandably unpopular with the principal groups already established in the colony. The *donatários* and their dependents were obviously unhappy about his rule and so were the few merchants who had until his arrival enjoyed freedom to operate without royal supervision, while the settlers who had initiated agricultural activities were strongly opposed to his efforts to enforce the liberal crown laws with regard to the enslavement of the natives. Furthermore, he could not count on the traditional support accorded the monarch by the people at large. In western Europe during the latter days of feudalism, the people regarded the king and their representatives as their best defense against the excesses of the barons; in Brazil the common people were without influence, consisting mainly of negro slaves, Indians, and very poor whites. The only sectional support on which the governor-general could rely came from the religious orders, at the time on excellent terms with the monarchy, and the civil servants. Two consequences of this situation were: first, that the opposing forces, equally powerless, settled into a prolonged stalemate that could only be broken when one of them secured the wealth to give it the

[8] Lahmeyer Lobo, *Processo administrativo*, pp. 261-262. Dutra, "Centralization," p. 26.

upper hand; and second, that the centralizing reforms were not very effective while the power of the governor-general was more nominal than real. From 1580 until 1640, Portugal was under the Spanish crown, and Brazil became part of the Spanish overseas empire. This interlude was the result not so much of Spanish exertions as of the collapse of the Portuguese house of Aviz after the disastrous reign of Dom Sebastiâo. Portugal was exhausted after the exactions to finance the king's Moroccan campaign and hardly able to resist whatever demands issued from Madrid. However, the Hapsburg efforts to systematize and integrate the Iberian colonial administration, including that of Brazil, did not develop for the most part because Spain was also experiencing a period of decline and because Brazil was viewed as a particularly poor and unattractive territory.

Portugal emerged after sixty years of Hapsburg rule with her economy in ruins, her fleet destroyed, and much of her overseas empire permanently lost. The relationship with Brazil had also undergone a substantial change; it was Portugal that was dependent on her colony after 1640, rather than the reverse.[9] For although Brazil had not been immune from the vicissitudes of the unsuccessful foreign policy of the Hapsburgs with her coasts frequently raided and the Dutch actually conquering and remaining in control of the region around Pernambuco for over twenty years, she had also developed a robust economy based principally on the cultivation and export of sugar. Until the middle of the seventeenth century, Brazil was the world's principal producer and exporter of this valuable commodity. Her population had also grown considerably both from the importation of African slaves and the steady increase in the flow of immigrants from

[9] "Portugal could not carry on her twenty-eight years' war of independence against Spain (to say nothing of fighting Holland for most and Cromwellian England for part of the time) without economic resources provided by her Brazilian 'milch-cow' as King John IV aptly if crudely characterized his most profitable colony." Charles R. Boxer, "Padre Antonio Vieira, S.J. and the Institution of the Brazil Company in 1649" *HAHR*, xxix (1949), 474-497. See also Lahmeyer Lobo, *Processo administrativo*, p. 369, et seq.

Portugal, and this in spite of the repeated efforts made by the metropolitan government to stem a tendency they considered detrimental. As Caio Prado has pointed out, the very frequency of the decrees restricting emigration to Brazil is an indication of their ineffectiveness.[10]

Pressed by the urgencies of domestic and economic difficulties, the monarchy tried again to strengthen central control in Portuguese America mainly to secure increased revenues, but it was precisely the economic weakness that rendered the attempt fruitless. The duties of the *Concelho Ultramarino* (Overseas Council), founded in 1604, augmented considerably, and both the economic and ecclesiastical affairs of the colony were placed under its direct supervision. The monarchy had in its hands the legal and administrative instruments necessary to bring the colonies under direct control; it also had the will. The only thing it lacked was sufficient economic and military power to have its orders obeyed. This was also perhaps the worst time to try and force the *donatários* into submission. Having prospered as a result of the sugar boom, they were less inclined than ever to submit themselves to distant metropolitan control. It must be noted that many *donatários* were still in possession of their hereditary land grants because the metropolitan governments had been unable to find enough funds to redeem these rights by purchase as established in the 1549 reform. Other special circumstances had given some of them additional strength. For example, the governor of Pernambuco, one of the richest sugar growing regions, had been invested by the crown with exceptional military powers that he was unwilling to surrender back to the king after the conclusion of the war with the Dutch.[11] The crown's intention of introducing a more liberal policy with respect to Indian slavery was also thwarted by the opposition of the owners of sugar plantations whose taxes provided the main sustenance of the declining metropolis.

In fact, the mere retention of Brazil within the empire must

[10] Prado, *Historia económica*, p. 54.
[11] Lahmeyer, *Processo administrativo*, p. 376.

be listed as a major accomplishment for the central government. As Boxer has indicated this was achieved against the heaviest odds possible. During the fourteen years between 1640 and 1654, Portugal's chances of survival as an independent nation appeared very slim indeed and there was a distinct possibility of Brazil becoming a Dutch possession, either in whole or in part. At the time, Portugal was engaged in formal or informal war with Spain and Holland, respectively the most powerful military and naval countries on earth. Dutch harassment of the sugar trade resulted in enormous losses that in turn jeopardized its military position with respect to Spain. The shipping losses in the Atlantic crossing were very great, but, as Boxer has observed, the truly remarkable thing was that the trade between Portugal and Brazil actually increased during the period; "This vital but generally forgotten fact speaks volumes for Portugal's resilience and powers of recovery." It certainly does, for the losses were colossal; in the first fifteen years of informal hostilities, 547 Portuguese ships were taken by the Dutch; in 1633 ninety Portuguese ships were captured by Dutch corsairs while in 1647-1648 the losses reached 249 ships, a figure without parallel in contemporary naval warfare.[12]

The Brazil trade was saved by the compulsory institution of the convoy system under the control, organization, and responsibility of the *Companhia Geral do Estado do Brasil*, the brainchild of Father Antonio Vieira. The diligent Jesuit took a keen interest in the operations of the monopolistic chartered company in general and in the organization of the transatlantic convoys in particular. No vessel of any type was allowed to leave Brazilian or Portuguese ports bound across the Atlantic unless it sailed in one of the company's bi-annual convoys. These were protected by a fleet of thirty-six warships, each carrying a minimum of twenty guns. The capital for the company came principally from the Jewish community in Portugal who were granted immunity by the Inquisition from fiscal confiscation of any funds invested in this enter-

[12] Boxer, "Padre Vieira," pp. 474-477.

prise. The company was a resounding success. As Vieira himself described it many years later, in correspondence with one of his critics, the company was always able to bring from Brazil "the sinews wherewith to sustain the war against Castile, to maintain the kingdom, to recover Pernambuco, and still today [in 1689] helps with prompt and lavish means in times of greatest need."[13] Vieira's company proved very timely as a strategic device to prevent the dismemberment of the empire, but as a purely commercial venture, it failed to live up to the expectations of its supporters mostly because of the excessive number of concessions the Portuguese government had earlier been forced to make to France, Holland, and especially to Great Britain during the war of restoration and immediately afterwards.[14]

Hence the impasse resulting from the promulgation of the 1549 reform was broken a century later, partly as a consequence of the weakness of the metropolis and partly because of the growing wealth and population of Brazil. This situation, however, was soon to change once more and this time, paradoxically, due to the finding of gold and diamond deposits in the colony.

---

[13] Boxer, "Padre Vieira," pp. 486–487 and 496.

[14] Furtado has indicated how the loss of its eastern trade and the collapse of the sugar market left Portugal without resources to defend its colonies at a time of increasing imperialist activity on the part of the principal European powers. The Portuguese government decided then that to survive as a colonial power, the country should find powerful allies, even at the price of relinquishing some of its sovereignty. England was the most attractive and convincing imperial nation at the time from the Portuguese vantage point. Treaties were signed with England in 1642, 1654, and 1661 that shaped an alliance leaving "an indelible mark on the economic and political life of Portugal and Brazil for the next two centuries." Portugal managed in this way to retain its dominions, including Brazil, the most lucrative colony in the eighteenth century. However, the privileges secured by English merchants included broad extraterritorial concessions, freedom of trade with the Portuguese colonies, and control over the custom duties levied on merchandise imported from England. All these gave them an overwhelming influence over the economic and political affairs of Portugal. Celso Furtado, *The Economic Growth of Brazil*, Los Angeles and Berkeley, Calif., 1963, pp. 33, 35, et seq.

Although the exact date of the first great gold strike is not known, it is fairly certain the gold was found between the years 1693 and 1695 in several different regions of what is now Minas Gerais by different individuals and groups of prospectors.[15] This precipitated the first modern "Gold Rush." Thousands of adventurers from all over Brazil and Portugal went searching for gold into the hinterland. This large mass of people soon ranged itself into two opposing groups: on one side the original settlers, mostly from the São Paulo region, and on the other the newcomers supported by their slaves, most of whom came from West Africa. Friction between these groups degenerated into violent skirmishes lasting intermittently for over a year between 1708 and 1709. This minor civil war gave Portugal an excellent opportunity to assert its royal authority because both warring sides appealed to the king for support; in the process of restoring peace, the crown officials managed to establish a centrally controlled administration in Minas Gerais.

Antonio de Albuquerque Coelho de Carvalho, who at the time of the troubles was governor of Rio de Janeiro and who played a decisive role in restoring order to Minas Gerais, was charged with the governorship of a new administrative unit, the Captaincy of São Paulo and the Mines of Gold, with headquarters in São Paulo. Among the main problems successfully solved by this dynamic administrator were the rationalization of the collection of the "royal fifth" in the new territory, the imposition of a "reasonable tax" on all merchandise, slaves, and cattle imported into the mining region, the official creation of some companies of soldiers for internal security, and the passage of severe and enforceable laws restricting the use of arms by slaves, mulattoes, Amerindians, and mixed bloods generally. This last regulation effectively limited the likelihood of a white leader or clique being able to muster sufficient support to challenge the crown representatives.[16]

[15] Charles R. Boxer, *The Golden Age of Brazil, 1695-1750*, Los Angeles and Berkeley, Calif., 1964, p. 35.
[16] Boxer, *Golden Age*, pp. 75-82.

In 1720 troubles over the collection of the "royal fifth" payable to the central government once again led to violence, this time between the settlers of Ouro Preto, the principal mining township, and the governor.[17] The revolt was suppressed, and the authority of the crown reasserted by force. Later in the same decade of 1720, diamonds were found in the region of Minas Gerais, precipitating another rush of fortune seekers from all over the colony. Crown officials, however, after the experience of the Gold Rush, rapidly established a strict system of surveillance and control over the diamond district, which, for instance, only allowed people in and out who carried with them a permit issued by the central authority.

This series of successful interventions gave the crown undisputed control over the rich mining districts. These had not yet generated local pressure groups sufficiently powerful and organized to be able to withstand the inroads by the central authority. This almost accidental success was restricted to the mining areas, but, of course, it was sufficient for a government desperately short of funds to direct the flow of Brazilian gold, diamonds, and taxes to Portugal where, among other things, it was used to pay for the restoration of royal power over the colony. The crisis of the sugar markets caused by the irruption of several Caribbean islands and Central American territories into production during the latter part of the seventeenth and the beginning of the eighteenth centuries also helped restore the authority of the crown.[18] Those most likely to oppose the growth of royal power, the traditional *donatários*, found themselves in the midst of a financial crisis precisely when gold and diamonds started to reach Portugal and the domestic disorders accompanying the new mineral discoveries opened the door to the successful military intervention of the central authority.

Thus once again the balance shifted, this time in favor of the metropolis that, through a combination of good fortune

---

[17] Boxer, *Seaborne Empire*, pp. 156-157.
[18] Furtado, *Economic Growth*, pp. 24-33.

and sagacity, was able to put an exceptional opportunity to some use, but without perhaps taking full advantage of all that was offered. The king of Portugal was at the time Dom João V (1706–1750), an extremely devout monarch whose religiosity became almost a mania in his latter years, but also a superficial man obsessed with personal prestige and the desire to give his reign the visible features of the greatness he associated with the France of Louis XIV. The country had then enough wealth partly to satisfy these wishes; one of the early consequences of the mineral discoveries was that Portugal was able to settle her debts with Europe in gold. The king is reported to have observed, referring to this, "My grandfather feared and owed: my father owed: I neither fear nor owe."[19] He was also able to indulge his religious inclinations, granting vast sums of money for the construction of some impressive ecclesiastical buildings: the huge monastery of Mafra, for instance, Portugal's answer to Versailles and the Escorial, was built during his reign. More mundane public works also claimed his attention and large amounts were spent on the monumental Aqueduct of the Free Waters, which for the first time provided Lisbon with sufficient drinking water. Undoubtedly under his reign Lisbon became once again one of the leading capitals of Europe; he encouraged scholarship and imposed on his court a meticulous regard for ceremony that may have contributed to the feeling the declining empire was on the threshold of a new golden age.

Under such leadership, it was almost inevitable that greater attention should be paid to the outward and more ostentatious symbols of power than to its essence. The wealth of Brazil lulled the government into a mood of passive acceptance of the imperial arrangements as they then stood with Portugal playing, as Furtado accurately points out, "the role of a mere supply station." The close association with Britain already mentioned had been formalized in treaties, principally the Methuen Treaty of 1703, that meant for Portugal the "renunciation of any industrial development" and the in-

[19] Boxer, *Seaborne Empire*, p. 158.

stitutionalization of her dependent status vis-à-vis the great power. On the positive side, however, the British alliance and its European diplomatic implications "came to be the true foundations of territorial stability for Portuguese America."[20] Mainly because of British support, Portugal was able to secure French renunciation to any claims in the Amazon region and Spanish acceptance of the Sacramento frontier of Brazil in the South.

To be fair, it must be said that under Dom João V some attempts were made to support local industries, but these were of slight importance; at midcentury, Portugal was scarcely more than a British commercial dependency that happened to have an abundant supply of gold to pay for its manufactured imports and that retained control, albeit more nominal than real, over her vast Brazilian territories, at the time the wealthiest colonial possession on earth. The stage was thus set for the arrival on the scene of the archregalist, nationalistic, and reformist Sebastião de Carvâlho e Melo.

Dom João died in 1750 and was succeeded by his son Dom José who, two days after acceding to the throne, called Sebastião de Carvâlho e Melo (who became Marquis of Pombal in 1770) to serve as secretary of state for foreign affairs and war. Pombal had until that time been an undistinguished diplomat who had held posts for a few years in London and Vienna. His influence on affairs did not begin with his ministerial appointment but was rather the result of his courage and resourcefulness during and after the famous Lisbon earthquake of 1755; he then gained the trust of the king and was able to govern the country virtually as he wished.

It is unnecessary to describe and analyze completely the

---

[20] Furtado, *Economic Growth*, pp. 36-37. Portugal's participation in the War of the Spanish Succession on the side of Great Britain resulted in a considerable financial setback, but at the peace negotiations concluding with the Treaty of Utrecht in 1715, Portugal did manage to have its rights in Brazil formally recognized. However, Boxer is probably right when he suggests that "In the light of hindsight, neutrality would have been the best solution for Portugal's delicate position between France and Spain on the one hand and the maritime powers and the Austrian empire on the other." Boxer, *Seaborne Empire*, pp. 158-159.

Pombaline period of Portuguese history, but space is sufficient to touch briefly on some aspects of his administration.[21]
The main objective of Pombal's policies was to bring about
the political and economic resurgence of Portugal; he was in-
tensely conscious of the diminished stature of his country in
Europe and was convinced that the strengthening of royal
power was essential if Portugal was to respond successfully to
the challenge of modernization. The consolidation of the empire and the increase of the administrative efficiency of the
central government were two bases of his policy. In his view,
a highly centralized and efficient administrative apparatus was
necessary for Portugal to succeed in overcoming her prostra-
tion; he was equally convinced such a structure could only be
built around the absolute authority of the monarch.[22]

During the six years he served as Portuguese envoy to the
court of St. James, Pombal studied closely the economic and
political foundations of the imperial power of Great Britain.
His library on politics, economics, statistics, and related subjects was remarkably complete, and there is ample evidence
that he brought method as well as zeal to the task he had set
himself.[23] Not untypically, however, his close study of Eng-

[21] The Pombaline period has a full bibliography that would be impossible
even to summarize here, but the following works are noteworthy: Alfredo
Duarte Rodríguez, *O Marquez de Pombal e os seus biógrafos*, Lisbon, 1947; João
Luzio Azevedo, *O Marquez de Pombal e sua época*, Lisbon, 1922; Antonio de
Sousa Pedroso, Visconde de Carnaxide, *O Brasil na administração pombalina*,
Rio de Janeiro, 1940; Jorge Macedo, *Situação económica do tempo de Pombal*,
Oporto, 1951.

[22] To secure this objective he went to some remarkable lengths. For instance, basing his action on the principle that the monarch ruled with divine
authority, he ordered that the laws and decrees of the realm issued under the
signature of Dom Jose, should only be referred to as "Holy" or "Most Holy"
laws or "Sacred" or "Most Sacred" decrees. See Boxer, *Seaborne Empire*, p.
189, and Dauril Alden, *Royal Government in Colonial Brazil*, Los Angeles and
Berkeley, Calif., 1968, p. 9. See also Kenneth R. Maxwell, "Pombal and the
Nationalization of the Luso-Brasilian Economy, *HAHR*, XLVIII (1968), 609.

[23] Carvalho e Melo's library reflected his obsessive interest in discovering
the causes and techniques of British commercial superiority. Maxwell has
made a detailed examination of the catalogues of his library in London and
notes that "with the books of Thomas Mun, William Petty, Charles Dave-

lish political economy led him to conclude that the British imperial ascendancy bore a principal share of the responsibility for the painful decline of his country.[24] Such sentiments, of course, are not uncommon among twentieth-century students of Portuguese and Brazilian history. But in the case of Pombal this conviction created an almost obsessive dislike of Britain only mildly tempered by a statesmanlike prudence that prevented him from needlessly quarrelling with his country's most important ally.

In 1760 he informed the British envoy "that the King his master was bound in duty to consider the welfare and the interests of his own subjects in the first place and preferable to all others." But, Pombal added, "That upon consideration, he was always of the opinion that the King his master should prefer, in matters of commerce the subjects of Great Britain to all other foreigners whatsoever."[25]

A pragmatic statesman, he accepted many of the ideas of industrial capitalism not so much because he was convinced of their theoretical worth, but because he felt that his country could not compete successfully in the international markets solely on the basis of her colonial wealth. He believed that Portugal had to protect her industries and commerce, and this could only be done effectively as part of a centralized program of national development under royal guidance.

For the crown to extend its control over the country's economy and administration it was necessary to improve the performance of the civil service. To do this skilled technicians

---

nant, Charles King, Joshua Child, with select reports on colonies, trades, mines, woollen manufactures, with specialized tracts on sugar, tobacco, fisheries, parliamentary acts of tonnage and poundage, shipping and navigation, fraud in customs houses . . . and above all with a heavy concentration of works on the English trading companies, his collection was a veritable treasure house of mercantilist classics." Maxwell, "Pombal," p. 609.

[24] "Carvalho e Melo came to see the control Britain exercised over his country not only as the root cause of the social and economic malaise of the Portuguese nation, but also as one of the reasons for the rapid advances of the British economy." Maxwell, Pombal," pp. 609-619, et seq.

[25] Interview with Lord Kinnoull, British envoy at Lisbon, in October 1760. Quoted by Boxer, *Seaborne Empire*, pp. 184-185.

and professionals were needed that the country's feeble system of higher education was incapable of producing. Hence Pombal's interest in the founding of technical schools, improvements in the curriculum, and, above all, in the transformation of the university into a modern academic center. His reform of the University of Coimbra "created, in effect, a new university, modern in spirit." Pombal reformed faculties, began practical classes, changed syllabuses and methods of study, and established disciplinary measures and the penalties for their infringement. Even the lecturers were selected and appointed by him. This far-reaching intervention was all the more important because of the centralization of university training for Portuguese imperial civil servants. While Spanish America boasted many universities where creole civil servants could take their first degrees, Brazil had none and all the aspiring bureaucrats born on that side of the Atlantic were compelled to travel to Portugal for their tertiary studies at the University of Coimbra.[26]

Pombal's intention, of course, was not to advance academic enquiry in general, but to transform the university into an efficient and docile center "for the pursuit of that strange novelty, 'practical studies.' " To this end he also established a botanical garden, a museum of natural history, a theater of experimental philosophy (this was a physics laboratory), a chemical laboratory, an astronomical observatory, a pharmaceutical dispensary, and an anatomy theater. A telling comment on Pombal's effort to lead a centrally controlled, pragmatic, intellectual resurgence in Portugal, came from one of that country's eminent scholars Canon Antonio Ribeiro Sánchez who wrote: "The minister wanted to achieve the impossible; he tried to civilize the nation while at the same time attempting to enslave it; to spread the light of the philosophi-

---

[26] João Cruz Costa, *A History of Ideas in Brazil. The Development of Philosophy in Brazil and the Evolution of National History*, Los Angeles and Berkeley, Calif., 1964, p. 38. See also Stuart B. Schwartz, "State and Society in Colonial Spanish America: An Opportunity for Prosopography," *New Approaches to Latin American History*, ed. Richard Graham and Peter H. Smith, Austin, Tex., 1974, pp. 22-23.

cal sciences while exalting royal power to a despotism."[27] In his efforts to modernize and streamline the country's administrative apparatus he exhibited the same authoritarian, centralizing spirit with which he had approached the problems of educational reform. A principal part of this reform was the establishment of a single fiscal entity for the whole empire, the *Real Erario*, into which flowed all the monies due to the state. This new central institution was run by trained accountants using the novel double entry system of accountancy, an innovation that, having proved its value in Portugal, was introduced in Brazil. An important aspect of this change was the establishment of "boards of inspection," (*mesas de inspeçao*) in the principal ports of Brazil, São Luiz Maranhão, Recife, Bahia, and Rio de Janeiro to provide quantitative and qualitative controls for the export of sugar and tobacco and to promote either of these commodities where its sale was lagging.[28] This readiness to acknowledge mineral and commercial developments did not blind him to the continued key role of agriculture in the colonial economy. In 1755 he created the *Companhia do Grão Pará e Maranhão* as a government sponsored monopoly with a specific responsibility for regional agricultural development; four years later he founded a similar organization for the encouragement of the sugar industry in the northeastern part of the country.[29]

With the new wealth produced by the colony, his administration finally completed the recovery of the last remaining *capitanía* hereditary grants by compulsory purchase from their private owners, and the vast regions were then placed under the control of crown officials. Even before Pombal's administration, but most certainly after, these senior colonial officials "served at the Crown's pleasure, and when they sufficiently incurred its displeasure as a result of cowardly or treasonable acts, malfeasance, serious bad judgment, or mere intransigence . . . were likely to suffer consequences ranging

[27] Cruz Costa, *History of Ideas*, p. 39.

[28] Alden, *Royal Government*, p. 12.

[29] Lemos Britto, *Pontos de partida para a história económica do Brasil*, Rio de Janeiro, 1923, pp. 227-230.

from a sharp reprimand to removal from office or even heavy fines, exile from the Court or the Kingdom itself, or imprisonment." This vulnerability was useful to the crown that in turn encouraged tale-bearing correspondence from senior officials to make it as difficult as possible for any collusion to take place against its interests. The administrators did not need to be prodded to divulge details about their rival's conflicts and difficulties; they were always anxious, as Alden has observed, "to persuade the Crown of their own devotion to duty and to protect themselves against possible charges of misconduct."[30] Thus the officialdom that took over the control of the *capitanías* on behalf of the metropolis was not allowed any more power than its less important predecessors. Pombal was not prepared to grant truly viceregal responsibilities; his reluctance to do this "stemmed partly from his deep-seated distrust of the high nobility from whom the viceroys were drawn, partly from his centralization impulses that tended always to tighten the Crown's grip on all levels of the imperial bureaucracy."[31]

To counteract some of the consequences of the Methuen Treaty, which made Portugal almost defenseless against the importation of British manufactures, Pombal supported a general program of industrial development, founding a gunpowder factory and a sugar refinery in 1751, a silk factory in 1752, and wool, paper, and glass factories in 1757 and 1759. With the same protectionist intention, accentuated by his distrust of private ventures in this field, he organized a number of chartered companies into whose hands he hoped to place the control of all mercantile activity: "I find it absolutely necessary to bring all the commerce of this kingdom and its colonies into companies, and then all merchants will be obliged to enter them, or else desist from trading, for they certainly may be assured that I know their interests better than they do themselves, and the interest of the whole king-

---

[30] Alden, *Royal Government*, pp. 471-472; see also Boxer, *Golden Age*, p. 145.

[31] Alden, *Royal Government*, p. 472.

dom."[32] Some merchants did not agree, and the Lisbon Chamber of Commerce protested against the forcible channelling of the Brazil trade into these companies. Pombal promptly dissolved the chamber and had several of its leading members imprisoned; the rest were regrouped under direct government supervision into a *Junta do Comercio* that dutifully approved all of the minister's decisions.

Not all of Pombal's policies were so illiberal; he abolished slavery in Portugal, excepting domestic servants, though not in Brazil.[33] He also conducted a determined and fairly successful campaign against anti-Semitism, forbidding the Inquisition, for instance, from persecuting "New Christians," as Jewish converts were euphemistically denominated. Moreover, he had all the decisions of the Inquisition subjected to revision by the crown, although, it must be added, he had no qualms or hesitation in using the Holy Office as an instrument to persecute his opponents.

Pombal's extreme form of regalism and his systematic policy of centralization brought him into direct conflict with the Church and the Portuguese aristocracy; in both contests he proceeded with severity, not shrinking from the most extreme of measures. For example, although this was never conclusively proved, he is said to have convinced the king that an abortive plot against his life in 1758 had been the work of members of the aristocratic and influential Tavora family. Evidence against them was produced under torture and the leading members of the family were publicly executed.[34] But

---

[32] Boxer, *Seaborne Empire*, p. 184.

[33] Boxer, *Seaborne Empire*, p. 192.

[34] Although in line with the rest of his regalist policies, Pombal's ruthless attack on the aristocracy, and especially on the Tavora family, appears to have had some additional motives. According to one careful student of the period, "The prime motive for Tavora's disaffection had probably been an intimate personal matter, for the king had taken the young marquis's wife as his mistress." But later on he adds, "The attack on noble tax privileges, the qualification of commercial men for public office, the corresponding permission for public men to involve themselves in commercial matters, and the use of ennoblement as an incentive to investment in the privileged companies,

it was in his systematic campaign against the Society of Jesus that Pombal showed himself the true totalitarian; he personally prepared a three-volume work entitled *Dedução chronologica* (Chronological Deduction), in which, through the flagrant utilization of every imaginable trick, documentary evidence was distorted to demonstrate that the ills and troubles of Portugal had been caused by the machinations of the Jesuits. This treatise was distributed widely to all official bodies, civil servants being instructed to read it attentively. Even parish priests in the colonies were ordered to use it so that they could cure the "sickly sheep" among their flock, in the words of the minister himself, with the salutary doctrines it contained. As Boxer points out, Pombal's propaganda efforts were a worthy portent of the literary outpourings the world has received from the pen of some twentieth-century leaders.[35]

A principal factor in his obsessive persecution of the Jesuits was his determination to subordinate all orders of society and all institutions to the crown. Although a devout Catholic, he did not hesitate to act against any prelate, even some very highly placed, who dared to oppose or slight him. In 1760, for example, after an otherwise unimportant incident, he ordered the Papal Nuncio, none other than a cardinal, out of Portugal, breaking diplomatic relations with the Vatican for over ten years and refusing to normalize relations until Pope Clement XIV had accepted all his demands. He was equally severe in the prosecution of his campaign against the Jesuits, concluding it with the expulsion of the order from all the

were all part of a wider policy. . . . The College of Nobles, chartered in 1761 and endowed in 1765 from, among other sources, the confiscated properties of the house of Aveiro and the Jesuits, was to purge the nobility of the false persuasion that they could live independent of the virtues." Maxwell, "Pombal," p. 630. Another author suggests that there was a degree of vindictiveness in Pombal's antiaristocratic policies, as "he seems to have attempted to cut a smart figure in Lisbon society in the 1730's but was snubbed because of his inferior lineage, a mortification for which he was later to repay the grandees." Alden, *Royal Government*, pp. 7-8. On the trial and execution of the members of the Tavora family, see also Madariaga, *The Fall*, pp. 270-272.

[35] Boxer, *Seaborne Empire*, pp. 187-188.

Portuguese dominions. This decision was later followed by Charles III and eventually by the pope himself, who had the Society of Jesus formally abolished under pressure from the Iberian enlightenment despots.

Pombal's regalism had a decisive effect on the Brazilian Church. The tutelage of the central state was embodied in an abundance of regulations, laws, and decrees, some of which would appear irritating, if not vexatious to an outside observer. Nevertheless, the Brazilian Church acquiesced without reluctance and went on to embrace the regalist doctrine with a zeal that would have pleased the great minister. Lloyd Mecham has noted the remarkable lack of Brazilian opposition to the constant and detailed intervention of the Portuguese metropolis in religious matters. This acquiescence may well be one of the more interesting indications of the success attending Pombal's centralizing policies, for throughout the early days of the empire of Brazil, regalism was dominant and continued to be strong until the latter part of the nineteenth century. Since the time of Pombal, and no doubt mainly because of his influence, both the Portuguese and Brazilian churches have shown pronounced Gallican tendencies. After the independence of Brazil, "the virus of Jansenist and Gallican heresy persisted" and the emperor and his imperial officials did not lack allies among the clergy to support their policy of subordinating the Church to the central state. In the first legislative assembly of 1826-1829 there were twenty-two ecclesiastics openly committed to the support of regalism.[36] None other than the leading Brazilian prelate of his time Father Diego Antonio Feijóo, later appointed regent for Dom Pedro II, became the direct and enthusiastic heir of Pombaline regalism in matters regarding the relations between Church and state. There was a moment when Feijóo led a substantial body of opinion to agitate for the formation of a separate and independent Brazilian Catholic Church.[37] This was not successful, and neither was another proposal formally advanced

[36] J. Lloyd Mecham, *Church and State in Latin America, A History of Politico-Ecclesiastical Relations*, Chapel Hill, N. C., 1966, p. 265.

[37] Charles Wagley, *An Introduction to Brazil*, New York, 1971, p. 215.

by Feijóo, "that it would be proper to apply to the Pope to relieve the clergy from the penalty annexed to marrying." Among the reasons put forward to justify this petition to abolish ecclesiastical celibacy was the need to restore morality to the conduct of the clergy, "for a goodly number of priests kept concubines."[38]

There is little doubt that Pombal's regalism found a fertile soil in Brazil, and his influence can perhaps be seen today in the proliferation of politically significant movements for social reform that have become almost a characteristic of the Brazilian Catholic Church.[39]

All that it is relevant to say here about the effects of Pombal's policies in the field of economic and commercial development is that, although at the start of his regime mineral wealth was pouring from Brazil, soon afterwards in 1760 production started to decline, inevitably limiting his capacity to advance the protectionist and interventionist program he had in mind. Yet during the last quarter of the eighteenth century, Portugal witnessed a period of singular prosperity in certain sectors of the colonial economy; cotton, hides, and rice became valuable exports from Brazil; even the stagnant sugar industry of Maranhão experienced a revival, while the chartered companies began to show good profits. But it is not this aspect of Pombal's program that is the most important for the purposes of this study—much of it, notably the chartered companies, was quickly dismantled after his fall—rather it is the success in bringing about, ruthlessly and efficiently, a recentralization of the administrative structure of the empire around the person of the monarch. The effects of these policies could not be undone easily, and although after his fall there was a momentary clerical reaction, the administrative

---

[38] Mecham, *Church and State*, p. 267.

[39] See, for instance, Helder Camara, *The Church and Colonialism: the Betrayal of the Third World*, London, 1969; Emanuel De Kadt, *Catholic Radicals in Brazil*, London, 1970; Cándido Mendes, *Momento dos vivos: A esquerda católica no Brasil*, Rio de Janeiro, 1966; Rowan Ireland, "The Catholic Church and Social Change in Brazil: An Evaluation" in *Brazil in the Sixties*, ed. Riordan Roett, Nashville, Tenn., 1972.

apparatus he had so painstakingly erected continued to function. More important still, his plans for creating a well-trained and, within the limitations of his epoch, permanent civil service were not effectively challenged after his departure. In fact, one of his sons retained an important post in the government, and most of his senior officials also remained in the service of the crown.

For Brazil the Pombaline dictatorship had far-reaching effects; it is quite possible that had it not been for this last minute centralizing effort, the country would have split into several independent republics after the Napoleonic onslaught. It must be remembered that in 1750 there were regions of Brazil, the Maranhão for instance, that enjoyed a status amounting to quasi autonomy, while a number of *donatários* whose hereditary land grants had not yet been repurchased by the crown were acting with increasing disregard for the central government. In less than a quarter of a century, the great minister successfully suppressed these anomalies, subordinating everybody to the authority of the monarch. By doing this, he gave the abstract concept of the monarchy an increased prestige and political validity that stood it in good stead a few decades later when, forced to flee from Portugal by the French invasion, the king established his imperial capital in Rio de Janeiro. Pombal's centralizing policies also reinforced other factors already working toward the greater unification of the vast country. Among these can be mentioned the development of an exporting agricultural economy in the southern regions, the mineral discoveries, and the rapid increase in population. The reforms introduced by the minister gave these tendencies an adequate administrative and political framework bound by the unifying symbol of the monarch.

After the fall of Pombal there were a number of republican rebellions in Brazil, partly the repercussion of the American and French revolutions, partly the symptoms, no doubt, of some regional opposition to the strong central hold exerted by the metropolis. These uprisings, in 1789, 1798, and 1817, were all successfully and rapidly suppressed after some minor military action. One of these in Minas Gerais was in part motivated by what were considered the excessive taxes imposed by a central government that had failed to consider the steep fall in gold production. This and the other rebellious movements were also encouraged by local annoyance with a system of administration that left virtually all major decisions to officials residing in the distant metropolis, a considerable change from the period before the coming of Pombal when the local authorities enjoyed what amounted almost to complete, though informal, autonomy.

As it happens, although Brazil witnessed more genuine republican uprisings than did Hispanic America, when independence did come in 1825, it was proclaimed by the king and followed by the peaceful establishment of a Brazilian Empire lasting for the better part of the nineteenth century, considerably longer than the early republican arrangements of Hispanic America. Moreover, when the Portuguese court emigrated to Brazil in 1807, it carried with it the centralizing style so successfully imposed by Pombal on the metropolis. The growth of the Brazilian civil, military, and ecclesiastical bureaucracy during the early years after 1807 was impressive; it more than doubled between 1807 and 1810 and it increased two and a half times by the end of 1815.[40] This was a reflection of the increased functions of the centralist bureaucracy in Rio as well as of the massive and jealously guarded prerogative of royal patronage. All officials from the highest positions in the state to the lowliest servant drew their wages and salaries only by authorization of the crown. Official appointments, no matter how unimportant, were not valid until the royal signature had been formally placed on the corresponding document. This required that the original petitions accompanied with supporting documents had to navigate all the appropriate channels until they reached the monarch for final action. The royal decision would then return through the same lengthy route to the petitioner. This procedure was fol-

---

[40] Alan K. Manchester, "The Growth of Bureaucracy in Brazil, 1808-1821," *JLAS*, IV (May, 1972), 80.

lowed invariably, regardless of the importance of the post.[41] Most significant still, and possibly best illustrating the meaning and influence of Pombal's reform, was the definitive establishment of metropolitan bureaucratic power in the Brazilian capital. As Manchester has indicated, "The creation of the mechanism of a sovereign state in Brazil, parallel to and coequal with the prototype in Lisbon, produced a centralized, national bureaucracy which looked to Rio de Janeiro as the source of authority." At the same time, the provincial bureaucracy was expanded within the framework of "the traditional absolutist colonial administration with its focus in Rio de Janeiro."[42] Considering the exacting manner in which patronage was dispensed by the crown as a result of the Pombaline reforms, it is difficult to imagine that the provincial bureaucracy could have evolved in ways fundamentally divergent from the pattern outlined at the imperial center located in Rio de Janeiro. The style, the techniques, the momentum of centralism were efficiently transferred from Portugal to Brazil, and it is this that may constitute the most convincing and enduring monument to Pombaline recentralization.

[41] Manchester, "Growth of Bureaucracy," p. 82.
[42] Manchester, "Growth of Bureaucracy," p. 83.

6

The Central State and the Liberalization of Trade

Accceding to Arnold Toynbee, the decline of empires is usually attended by a transfer of power from the center outwards, more often than not the result of a successful challenge issuing from the periphery that the imperial center is unable to withstand.[1] In support of this general statement he mentions plausible examples drawn from the classical Mediterranean civilizations, from the Far East, and pre-Columbian America, but the cases of the Spanish and Portuguese American empires clearly constitute exceptions, for these are not examples of imperial bastions overwhelmed by a peripheral challenge. If it were permissible to make use of a hypothesis contrary to a fact to illustrate the point, it could be suggested that had the Iberian peninsula managed to stay out of the Napoleonic wars, it is almost inconceivable that a movement for independence would have occurred in the Indies at the time it did or even for many years after. No doubt it is possible now, *a posteriori*, to discover signs of disaffection as well as significant social and political factors that would have added their momentum, as they did in fact, to a movement for independence, but it is nonetheless arguable whether such a rebellion would have taken place at the time it did in the absence of a collapse of the imperial center, an event brought about not by the actions of rebellious colonies overseas, but by a French invasion. In this respect, it is easy to agree with Humphreys and Lynch when they write, "The Napoleonic invasion of Portugal, therefore, led to a peaceful dissolution of the Por-

[1] *Survey of International Affairs 1930*, Oxford, 1931, p. 133.

tuguese empire in America, the Napoleonic invasion of Spain to the violent dissolution of the Spanish empire in America. Had these invasions not occurred, Spanish America might well have remained Spanish for some years to come, and the empire of Brazil might never have come into existence at all."[2]

The movement for independence in Latin America was the result of complex causes. It is unrealistic to attempt to isolate any single factor as having had vastly greater importance than others in determining the secession; moreover, it would appear reasonable to consider it as a diversified response to what was basically an external stimulus, a response that, by definition, and regardless of the feelings and aspirations of a number of notable precursors, lacked a preconceived and unified program of action. It did not have an alternative plan for proceeding with the economic, social, and political arrangements of society and was therefore forced to rely on the existing administrative concepts and practices even though thereafter these were directed to different ends.

This view is not shared by all students of Latin American history. Some have suggested the opposite and in doing so, have often stressed the importance of the economic determinants involved in the process. The evaluation of these determinants varies significantly from the almost mythical, transcendental quality attributed to them by Mariátegui to the dry and straightforward and perhaps orthodox mechanism implicit in Ramírez's explanation. The Peruvian José Carlos Mariátegui, for example, indicates that "the natural impulse of the productive forces in the colonies was to endeavour to break the [colonial] link. The rising economy of the incipient nationalities in America demanded imperatively . . . to break away from the medieval mentality of the King of Spain." And further, "there already existed in South America an embryonic bourgeoisie which, because of its needs and economic interests, could and should partake of the revolutionary mood

[2] R. A. Humphreys and John Lynch eds., *The Origins of Latin American Revolutions 1808-1826*, New York, 1965, p. 4. For a general development of this theme, see the Introduction. See also Jaime Eyzaguirre, *Ideario y ruta de la emancipación chilena*, 2nd edition, 1969, pp. 89-90.

of the European bourgeoisie."[3] Another historian the Argentine Rodolfo Puiggros states that "the movement in favour of freedom of trade acquired revolutionary proportions and shook the colonial institutions to their very foundations at the end of the eighteenth century."[4] Miron Burgin, the Polish-American historian, actually opens his study on the economic aspects of Argentine federalism with the following statement, "Amongst the numerous forces which caused the decline and fall of the Spanish colonial empire in America, none was as important as the economic factor."[5] The Chilean Hernán Ramírez explains that "Chile needed to break away from its economic isolation, to free itself from the restrictions which impeded its international trade, and to expand its great productive capacity. . . . essentially this meant that the economic structure of the country required independent direction. . . . [these aspirations] could only be realized through the complete disruption of the Spanish Empire." As to the economic situation of the country during the years before independence, Ramírez is equally forthright: "A high proportion of the inhabitants were wretchedly poor. . . . unemployment and poverty were endemic." He then quotes Manuel de Salas's famous report on Chile: "[Large numbers of people] suffer from the precarious condition of casual employment. . . . Every day one sees sturdy labourers in the square and streets, offering their services, and underselling them in exchange for goods which are often both useless and dear." He also quotes Anselmo de la Cruz's vivid descriptions of "so much poverty amidst so much plenty" and Cos de Iriberri, secretary to the *consulado*, writing about "the persistent contrast between the wealth, security, and comfort of the few, and the poverty, insecurity and misery of the many."[6]

[3] José Carlos Mariátegui, *Siete ensayos de interpretación de la realidad peruana*, Santiago, 1955, pp. 7-8. It is worth noting that the first edition of this book was published in 1928. (author's translation.)

[4] Rodolfo Puiggros, *Historia económica del Río de la Plata*, Buenos Aires, 1948, p. 62. (author's translation.)

[5] Miron Burgin, *Aspectos económicos del federalismo argentino*, Buenos Aires, 1960, p. 25. (author's translation.)

[6] Hernán Ramírez Necochea, "The Economic Origins of Independence,"

These interpretations rest on two unconvincing assumptions. The first is that the economic situation in the Indies was very critical indeed, that unemployment and dire poverty were rife as a direct consequence of the stagnation in agriculture, mining, and industry, and that these ills were aggravated by an extremely unequal distribution of the limited wealth available.[7] This unhappy state is attributed to the policies pursued by the metropolis, and it is also implied that the population at large was well aware that this was so. Secondly, these interpretations assume that there existed in most major centers of the Spanish and Portuguese American empires a significant and influential group of merchants, almost a budding commercial bourgeoisie, fundamentally committed to the development and expansion of international commerce with access to capital and knowledge of the market and sharing aspirations that they felt were being systematically thwarted by the imperial policies of Spain and Portugal notwithstanding the reforms of the eighteenth century. Such a group was strongly in favor of the opening of the American ports to international trade and supported the revolt against the metropolis presumably because of practical considerations arising, as it were, from its relations of production within the imperial scheme.[8]

The first of these assumptions is the most vulnerable. No doubt the reports on the economic condition in the Indies did refer to the undeniable poverty of many, but they did so in relative terms; theirs was a poverty in the midst of plenty, for, as the definitive researches of Richard Herr have established,

---

in *The Origins*, ed. Humphreys and Lynch, pp. 169-183. This is a translation of the original essay entitled, *Antecedentes económicos de la independencia de Chile*, Santiago, 1959. A new and substantially enlarged edition of this work was published in 1967.

[7] Though enjoying a modern vogue, these interpretations are not strikingly original since they are in some ways yet another version of the "Black Legend" school of Latin American history that attained a notable popularity during the nineteenth century.

[8] The opening of ports to foreign trade other than that carried in Spanish vessels is not to be confused with latter-day "free trade" that was not an issue at the time.

"The last years of Carlos' reign saw the Spanish economy flourish in a way that had been unknown for centuries." The directors of the *Banco de San Carlos* in 1785 gloated over "the progress of our industry, the multiplicity of modern factories . . . the growth of agriculture, and the increase in demand for its products." This prosperity extended from the metropolis to the empire through the trade links partly revivified by the liberalization policies of the Enlightenment.

A hundred years earlier, about one eighth of the goods shipped from Spain to America had been of Spanish origin; in 1784, Spanish products made up almost half of the total value of goods shipped from Spain to the Indies. This proportion continued to increase and four years later it had reached 53 percent.[9] In 1792 the English historian William Robertson expressed the uneasiness of the exporters of northwestern Europe who had been brought up in the belief that a declining Spain maintained an empire for the profit of others when he observed that the progress of Spain was sufficient "to alarm the jealousy and call for the most vigorous efforts of the nations now in possession of the lucrative trade which the Spaniards aim at wresting from them."[10]

One does not have to search far to find evidence of the prosperous condition of the Indies during this period. In a dispatch sent to the Foreign Office, the British consul in Lima stated that "it is just here to observe, considering the late cry which has been raised against the mother country, that during the period adverted to [1781-1795], Peru was not only in a flourishing state both in respect to her mines and to her commerce, but also as referable to the capitals possessed by individuals, to the comparative extent of her manufactures, and to her navigation."[11] As for Chile, though the economy of this captaincy-general was perhaps not as buoyant as that of

---

[9] Richard Herr, *The Eighteenth Century Revolution in Spain*, Princeton, N.J., 1958, pp. 146-147.

[10] Herr, *Eighteenth Century*, p. 147.

[11] R. A. Humphreys, *British Consular Reports on the Trade and Politics of Latin America, 1824-1826*, London, 1940, p. 114.

the viceroyalty, it was certainly not sunk in absolute back-wardness and stagnation; if it is remembered that Chile was the most remote and one of the least populated colonies of Spain in America, with less than 800,000 inhabitants in an area twice as large as the British Isles, the figures for mineral and agricultural production are not unimpressive: exports of wheat for the decade of 1790 were in the neighborhood of 20,000 tons per annum, which was roughly the equivalent of 260,000 *fanegas* of 153 pounds each. As it was generally esti-mated that a third of the total production was exported, it is prudent to assume that Chile was then producing almost 800,000 *fanegas*, which was no mean figure.[12] The production of minerals, principally gold, silver, and copper, increased steadily through the second half of the eighteenth century reaching the highest levels recorded during the colonial pe-riod precisely in the decades before independence: between 1801 and 1810, Chile produced an average of 3,110 kilograms of gold per annum, and this figure has not been surpassed since; as for silver, the average yearly production between 1781 and 1800 was approximately 5,000 kilograms, the high-est recorded during the whole colonial period, while during the fifty years following 1761, copper was produced at an an-nual rate of 11,000 tons, a level not reached again until the middle of the nineteenth century.[13]

Similar trends are apparent elsewhere; in New Spain the production of silver increased noticeably. As the Steins have observed, "the volume of silver produced in America and drawn largely from Mexico's Guanajuato mining center rose encouragingly. By 1800 Mexico produced 66 per cent of the world's silver output and Spain's American colonies contrib-uted 90 per cent of total world output."[14] In his meticulous

[12] Sergio Villalobos, *El comercio y la crisis colonial*. Santiago, 1968, p. 281.

[13] Alberto Herrmann, *La producción en Chile de los metales y minerales más importantes . . . desde la conquista hasta el año 1902*, Santiago, 1903; see also Guil-lermo Subercaseaux, *Monetary and Banking Policy in Chile*, Oxford, 1922, pp. 39–41. According to Subercaseaux, the amount of gold coined in 1810 was not equalled again until 1849.

[14] Stein and Stein, *Colonial Heritage*, pp. 100–101. For a description of the

study of Bourbon Mexico, Brading comes to a similar conclusion: "silver production, as measured by annual mintage, augmented from under twelve million pesos in 1762 to a peak of over twenty-seven million pesos in 1804. The less complete figures for transatlantic commerce indicate an equally dramatic expansion."[15] In Buenos Aires the trend was also upwards; during the five year period between 1773-1777, the average yearly returns from the customs was 23,474 pesos; in the period 1779-1783, it went up to 152,187 per year, and in 1791-1795, to 389,569 pesos per year.[16] Ernesto Palacio describing the situation in his *Historia de la Argentina* declares "Buenos Aires progressed indeed under the government of Vértiz, in part as a result of the zeal with which he advanced the reforms, in part because of the enrichment of the port and its mercantile class."[17]

The overall picture was also encouraging. Haring, in his classical study, explains that trade between Spain and the Indies probably increased by over 700 percent during the latter part of the eighteenth century and adds, "At the end of the colonial era most of the American provinces enjoyed greater prosperity and well-being than ever before."[18] Parry makes the point even more forcibly by bringing another weighty opinion to reinforce his argument: "The Spanish Indies in the late eighteenth century, if so perceptive and so thorough an observer as Humboldt is to be believed, presented an impressive appearance of prosperity, stability and order. . . . Population, productivity and trade were all increasing, and if a large part of the trade was directly or indirectly with foreign coun-

---

prosperous conditions of the Venezuelan economy during the same period, see Federico Brito Figueroa, *Historia económica y social de Venezuela*, Caracas, 1966, i, 109-110.

[15] Brading, *Miners and Merchants*, p. 28.

[16] Horacio William Bliss, *Del Virreinato a Rosas. Ensayo de historia económica argentina. 1776-1829*, Tucumán, 1959, p. 26.

[17] Palacio, *Historia*, i, 137. (author's translation.)

[18] Clarence H. Haring, *The Spanish Empire in America*, New York, 1963, p. 322.

tries that did not worry the colonists; they had a reasonable supply of European goods and good markets for their own products. Administration was reasonably effective by the standards of the time, and not unduly oppressive; dilatory and pettifogging, no doubt—it had always been that—but probably not less effective nor more oppressive than in Spain; and taxation was lower."[19]

It hardly needs restating that poverty and deprivation could still be found in this dynamic economic setting; many people lived miserable lives, and this was all the more striking in the midst of great and growing wealth, but it was not the dispossessed who rose in arms against the Spanish Empire. More important perhaps, if one excludes the anecdotal, humanitarian, and most justified complaints about the unsatisfactory conditions of the poor, contemporary evidence overwhelmingly indicates that the colonies were experiencing an unprecedented period of growth and prosperity. Alas, the misery of the laboring classes and the absence of social justice are not always adequate indicators either of the state of an economy or of its overall trends; one cannot forget that Charles Dickens painted a vivid and true picture of poverty and deprivation in England at a time when this country was at the height of its power and her economy was flourishing.

The economic prosperity of Latin America in the decades before independence was not without problems, some of them serious, but very few that were not in turn balanced by some positive development. Brazil offers a good example of the unstable transition in which the export of some products was in decline while at the same time others were entering the world market under favorable conditions. From 1760 onwards, gold production experienced a sharp decline reducing the total value of Brazilian exports by a considerable margin. However, at the same time, the chartered company organized by Pombal to develop the region of Grão Pará and Maranhão, was doing very well, for the most part because of the success

[19] Parry, *Seaborne Empire*, p. 327.

in the export of cotton and rice. This was helped along, no doubt, by the revolutionary contest in North America that hindered exports from the Southern states as well as by the increasing momentum of the industrial revolution in Britain. Thus, the colony of Maranhão that "had received only one or two ships a year . . . went through a period of exceptional prosperity . . . and began to harbour as many as 150 vessels a year while exports rose to about one million pounds sterling annually."[20] Exceptional circumstances also resulted in notable benefits for the sugar industry of Brazil when the revolt in the French sugar-producing colony of Haiti destroyed its exporting capacity. This coincided with the tremendous increase in the European demand during the Napoleonic wars, and the value of Brazil's sugar exports appreciated almost tenfold during the last decade of the eighteenth century and the first of the nineteenth. It is clear that the factors responsible for this rapid growth in exports were of an accidental character and external to the economy; yet it is doubtful whether the country would have been able to profit from these fortuitous circumstances in the absence of the Pombaline statist initiatives, especially those associated with the chartered company for the development of Grão Pará and Maranhão.[21]

Roughly similar conditions prevailed elsewhere in the Indies, with some branches of the regional economy undergoing expansion in response to changes in the international

[20] Furtado, *Economic Growth*, pp. 97-98. Furtado entitles the chapter from which this data is taken, "Maranhão and the False Euphoria." It is at the very least arguable, however, whether this was a false or a real euphoria; after all, it lasted for a generation; how long does a euphoria have to last to become real?

[21] Some of Pombal's policies had unexpected results; endeavoring to discourage the economic activities of the Jesuits, who depended on Indian labor, the minister went out of his way to try and eliminate all forms of Indian slavery in Brazil, and to do this he encouraged the importation of African slaves into the colony to work on the rice and sugar plantations. The rate of interest on loans to finance these imports was first reduced and then abolished by decree; between 1757 and 1777, 25,365 slaves were imported into Maranhão and Pará and over 30,000 into Pernambuco and Paraiba giving a significant boost to the agriculture of those regions. See Boxer, *Seaborne Empire*, pp. 192-193.

markets, and others sustaining setbacks. All told, however, the abundant available evidence comes down overwhelmingly against the thesis that there existed in Spanish and Portuguese America at the time an economic crisis so severe and generalized as to move a significant section of the population to consider secession from the metropolis as the only satisfactory solution.

More important, however, is the second assumption that during the latter years of the Spanish empire in America there existed in the main centers of the region influential and articulate mercantile pressure groups, an "embryonic bourgeoisie" according to Mariátegui, committed to the liberalization of trade, conscious of their economic interests, and convinced that these could only be advanced by securing, in the words of Ramírez, "the complete disruption of the Spanish empire." If this were so, it would undoubtedly constitute formidable evidence of the existence in the periphery of empire, of pressure groups presumably with power sufficient to challenge the metropolitan center and, considering the events that accompanied the growth of the movement for independence, to disrupt the imperial structure from within. To judge from the writings of Ramírez, Mariátegui, and others who have accepted this uncomplicated thesis and its corollary, that is, that a main cause of the secession was the economic discontent of the mercantile groups, the promulgation after 1808 of decrees opening the ports of the Indies to international trade would afford substantial proof that this was indeed a major aspiration of the movement for independence.[22] A superficial chronological view of these events could lead to such a conclusion, as there is no doubt that the authorities established in the Indies after the Napoleonic takeover of the Spanish throne

[22] A surprisingly large number of Latin American historians have accepted uncritically this rather simple deterministic explanation. In addition to Mariátegui, Puiggros, and Ramírez, on whose judgment it is reasonable to assume that political considerations may have had some weight, one should mention, Luis Peñaloza, *Historia económica de Bolivia*, La Paz, 1953, I, 258-271; Bliss, *Del virreinato*, pp. 35-41; Daniel Martner, *Estudio de política comercial chilena e historia económica nacional*, Santiago, 1923, I, 121-122; Vitale, *Interpretación marxista*, II, 153-181.

devoted much attention to trade liberalization. This started, perhaps paradoxically, with the opening of the Brazilian ports by the Portuguese Prince Regent in 1808, when he was safely installed in Rio de Janeiro with his family and court. It was followed with the opening of the port of Buenos Aires decreed by Viceroy Cisneros in 1809, and then by similar decisions by the various governing juntas formed in the other imperial provinces, greatly extending the freedom of commerce allowed under the colonial administration. It remains to be considered, however, why they acted in this way, who supported these measures, who opposed them, and for what reasons.

The relative economic well-being of Spanish America during the latter years of the eighteenth century was at least in part the result of the Bourbon liberalization of colonial trade. Despite the complaints voiced by various groups of merchants, it is clear that this had an invigorating effect on the colonial economy over several decades. The earliest of these reforms dates from 1765, when the first decree was passed granting a small degree of freedom to the colonies to trade with each other and also directly with selected Spanish ports. Next came the *real cédula* of 1778 extending these privileges to Peru, Chile, and Río de la Plata, and then the royal order of 1797 that, because of the crippling shortage of sailings from Spain, authorized the colonies to admit neutral shipping in all major ports.[23] These measures were not the outcome of a

---

[23] The crown was much more responsive to local demands for change than some authors have assumed, and all too often its better intentions were thwarted precisely by local opposition. For instance, on the strength of reports issued by the secretary of the *Consulado* in Santiago, don José de Cos Iriberri, the metropolitan authorities issued a number of decrees and enactments permitting traders to send their merchandise directly from the major ports of Chile to Panama and Guayaquil, without using Callao as an entrepôt, as had been done in the past. These enactments, however, were the object of a persistent campaign of obstruction and harassment on the part of the commercial groups in the viceroyalty of Peru who strongly objected to the Chilean trade bypassing Callao, and in the end it proved impossible to make full use of the opportunities they presented to the Chilean merchants. It should be added, moreover, that the commercial groups in Chile had been

successful agitation by mercantile circles in the colonies, but on the contrary, were based on the economic ideas of Charles III's ministers, principally Campillo and Campomanes and were decreed by the metropolis against the wishes of the local traders. Their opposition, though insufficient to stem the tide of the Caroline reforms, continued unabated after the passage of these decrees; in 1786, for instance, the merchant guild of New Spain, the *Consulado*, "after a brief experience of the greater influx of merchandise and the reduction in prices brought about by *comercio libre* . . . presented a vehement memorial to the Crown demanding the restoration of the Cádiz monopoly and the convoy system. The Crown, however, withstood this pressure."[24] Something similar happened in Lima in 1788 when the *Consulado* addressed an impassioned memorial to the king complaining of the ruinous effects of the freeing of trade that had destroyed the principal commercial firms in the viceroyalty leaving most of the trading activity "in the hands of foreigners who use it to market the produce from their factories which are the only ones to have profited from their indiscriminate dumping of their surplus manufactures into the Indies."[25]

In the same year of 1788, soon after he became governor of Chile, the Irish-born Brigadier General Ambrosio O'Higgins asked three leading merchants of the country, as representing the Chilean commercial interest, to report on the state of trade and also to give him their views on the measures so far adopted by the crown for trade liberalization. All three coincided in estimating the liberal reforms as damaging to the commercial interest. Francisco Javier de Errázuriz, one of the three merchants, stated that "Unanimously mercantile opin-

---

traditionally dependent on the trade of the viceroyalty and it was no small matter to secede from such a relationship. See Carlos Ugarte, "El Cabildo de Santiago y el comercio exterior del reino de Chile durante el siglo XVIII," in *Estudios de historia de las instituciones políticas y sociales*, Universidad de Chile, no. 1, Santiago, 1966, pp. 40–41; on the general theme of the liberalization of trade, see, Villalobos, *El comercio*, pp. 92–131.

[24] Brading, *Miners and Merchants*, p. 116.

[25] Villalobos, *El Comercio*, pp. 277–279. (author's translation.)

ion complains against the new system of free trade, source of all the ills and obstacles in American trade." Another, Domingo Díaz de Salcedo y Muñoz, attributed the damage to the "abundance of European manufactures which have flooded these provinces with luxury and inclined the people to the superfluous instead of to the necessary."[26]

Time did not make the reforms more acceptable. If in 1786 the merchants of Mexico were against the policy of liberalization, they were equally opposed in 1793. As Venezuelan historian Eduardo Arcila Farías points out: "the extension of free trade to New Spain was not greeted with enthusiasm in commercial circles in the viceroyalty. Contrary to what might have been expected, it met with very strong opposition from local merchants." The viceroy, count of Revillagigedo, in a report of 1793, states that all except two of the merchants of Mexico, "were strong partisans of monopoly and restriction, both in respect of the import of goods and of the export of precious metals."[27] The conclusion is unavoidable that in a manner typical of the Enlightenment, the Spanish monarchy imposed reforms and improvements on her colonies, including the liberalization of trade, that, though generally successful, were not welcomed by those who might have been their strongest supporters. The reason is not hard to discover; the merchant class, made up both of Spanish born and creole traders, had prospered precisely by adapting successfully to the intricate pre-Caroline restrictive regulations; they were not interested in changing them, facilitating thereby the way for a competition that could prove ruinous to their interests.[28] At least from this point of view, which appears to be soundly based on contemporary evidence and documentation, there

[26] Villalobos, *El Comercio*, pp. 286-307. (author's translation.)

[27] Eduardo Arcila Farías, "Commercial Reform in New Spain," in *The Origins*, ed. Humphreys and Lynch, pp. 165-166.

[28] In the case of Peru, for instance, one of the reasons explaining the opposition of the *Consulado* to commercial liberalization was its fear of contributing to the formation of alternative centers of power, outside its monopolistic control. See Virgilio Roel, *Historia social y económica de la colonia*, Lima, 1970, p. 392.

are no grounds for assuming there existed in the colonies a rising commercial bourgeoisie committed to liberal reforms that could only have been implemented after secession from the metropolis.

However, if there were still room for doubt, the events almost everywhere in Latin America that preceded and accompanied the decision to open the ports to foreign trade after 1808 throw a decisive light on the question.

The first "free trade" decree was promulgated in Bahia in 1808 by the Prince Regent, Dom João (later King Dom João VI), on the advice of the Viscount of Cairú and, apparently, with decisive encouragement from Britain.[29] Dom João accepted Cairú's advice as an "inevitable and necessary economic precaution" in the circumstances of the closure of the Portuguese ports that served as entrepôts and distribution centers for Brazilian products because of the French invasion and occupation: "it would have been simple madness to keep the ports of Brazil equally closed and thus condemn colonial commerce to a complete paralysis."[30] This decision extended to Brazil the dependent position of Portugal with respect to British trade; there is no doubt that it benefited British commercial interests while also rescuing the colonial economy from what could have amounted to virtual blockade.[31] It is also clear that the opening of the ports was not decreed at the behest of an active and self-conscious Brazilian commercial bourgeoisie, embryonic or otherwise, ready to secede from Portugal if its demands for the liberalization of trade were not

[29] José Wanderley Pinho, *A abertura dos portos: Cairú, os ingleses, a independencia*, Salvador, 1961.

[30] Manoel de Oliveira Lima, *Dom João VI no Brasil, 1808-1821*, Rio de Janeiro, 1908, I, 191. (author's translation.)

[31] "to merchants in every commercial centre [in Britain], and to Canning in the Foreign Office, Brazil was a land that offered relief—or even a grand opportunity. Direct trade might be more profitable than traffic through Lisbon. . . . The Rio court alone would be a good market; and if the Prince Regent could be persuaded to give British traders a substantial tariff preference over rivals from other countries, the royal exodus might turn out to have been a smart stroke of business as well as of strategy." Herbert Heaton, "A Merchant Adventurer in Brazil, 1808-1818," *JEH*, VI (May 1946), 5-6.

met. As Furtado has pointed out, "there was no conspicuous merchant class in the colony," and colonial trade was virtually a monopoly enjoyed by the metropolis, with Portuguese merchants grown accustomed to their profitable dependent relationship with Britain.[32] Hence, if anybody's interest was considered in the advice given to the prince regent, it was presumably that of the Portuguese mercantile community, and not that of the insignificant Brazilian merchant group. As it was, the decision to open the ports was welcomed in Brazil, not by the merchants, but by the producers of agricultural exports, of sugar, rice, and hides, who perceived a good opportunity for placing their commodities in a growing market without the cost and encumbrance of using Portugal as an intermediary. But there is no evidence to suggest that if the prince regent had not acted as he did, the Brazilian landed interest would have led a separatist, bourgeois, republican uprising against Lisbon.

The second free trade decree was promulgated in Buenos Aires on 6 November 1809 by Viceroy Cisneros, by virtue of one of the clauses in the treaty signed between Spain and Britain on 14 January of the same year.[33] The viceroy adopted this resolution with reluctance and after careful consultation with local interests; he had arrived only a few weeks earlier from Spain to assume his post and had found the treasury almost empty because, during the chaotic days that followed the British assault on Montevideo, the contraband trade had increased greatly while customs receipts declined in the wake of the slump in Spanish shipping. It was against this background that he had to consider an application presented by two British merchants John Dillon and John Thevaite who, having sailed from Cork for Brazil with a mixed cargo, arrived when that port was glutted with merchandise and were unable to dispose of their goods. Hearing that the port of Buenos Aires was opened to friendly flags, they went there only to discover that they had been misinformed. Burdened with mounting

---

[32] Furtado, *Economic Growth*, pp. 101-102.

[33] Diego Luis Molinari, *La representación de los hacendados de Mariano Moreno*, Buenos Aires, 1939, pp. 107-124.

losses, they were riding at anchor in front of Buenos Aires unable to sell goods for which there was an obvious demand on shore; their last hope of avoiding complete ruin was an application presented to the viceroy to allow them to sell their merchandise in Buenos Aires.[34] Funds were urgently needed in the viceroyalty, and if they were not obtained from the tariffs levied on imports, it was quite clear that local sources would have to provide them, presumably through compulsory loans. When consulted, the municipal authorities (*cabildo*) gave their approval considering that the measure was "a necessary and indispensable evil." The merchants, through the sindic of the *Consulado*, registered their vigorous opposition.[35] The only group that openly supported liberalization were the landowners, producers of wheat, hides, and tallow who unable to sell their produce were, like their Brazilian counterparts, more than willing to encourage the opening of the port to any foreign vessel as long as they could export freely. On this occasion they entrusted a brilliant young lawyer Mariano Moreno to put their case. He prepared what is considered to be the classic statement of contemporary liberalism in Latin America.[36] Moreno's famous argument for free trade was not, therefore, presented on behalf of "an embryonic commercial bourgeoisie," or any group of merchants, creole or Spanish, but of landowners intent on securing cheap transportation and good markets for their produce.[37]

[34] For the text of their application see Molinari, *La representación*, pp. 221-222.

[35] Bliss, *Del virreinato*, pp. 35-36.

[36] Mariano Moreno, *Representación que el apoderado de los hacendados de las campañas del Río de la Plata dirigió al Excelentísimo Sr. Virrey Don Baltasar Hidalgo de Cisneros*, Buenos Aires, 1874.

[37] There is another interpretation of these events that should be mentioned; according to some historians, "this decision [to open the port of Buenos Aires to foreign trade] . . . belongs to the turbulent events of the region at the start of the struggle for independence. The fact itself of the opening of the port can be interpreted as an episode in the struggle between Montevideo and Buenos Aires." See Clifton B. Kroeber, "El Consulado de Buenos Aires en el proceso de la revolución de Mayo," *TC*, no. 9 (1960), 130. (author's transla-

As soon as it became known that the viceroy was considering the British merchants' application, Moreno explained,
"the discontent and anger of some of the merchants of this
city became manifest: groups of shop-keepers were everywhere rumour-mongering and complaining." But the better
interests of the royal treasury and of the farmers coincided as
they both stood to benefit from the proposed liberalization.
"This fact should carry more weight than the protestations of
those who oppose the measure for, what could be more ridic-
ulous than the sight of a merchant defending loudly the prohibitive laws at the door of his shop where only English cloth
clandestinely imported can be found?" For, according to
Moreno, the main reason why the mercantile interests were
opposed to the opening of the port was because they were
profiting so much from the contraband trade.[38]

Whether Moreno's *Representación* convinced the viceroy or
not is a point endlessly debated.[39] What is clear is that the
support for the measure came from the producers of exportable agricultural commodities and that when it was adopted it
was against the opposition of the merchants and with the
grudging acceptance of the local authorities. Moreover, the

---

tion.) It is perfectly possible to see in the decision to open the port of Buenos
Aires, simply a response to a continuing rivalry with the only other commercial center of the River Plate; however, such an interpretation does not affect
the functional hypothesis presented here with respect to the alignment of interests on the part of landowners, traders, and bureaucrats.

[38] Moreno, *Representación*, p. 14. It has also been maintained that the controversy about the opening of Buenos Aires in 1809 reflected the clash between national and foreign interests, thus, "whilst colonial protectionism
favoured industry and the families that lived on the productive land, free
trade benefited foreign wealth and manufacturing industry." This is not an
easy thesis to defend, for, as Moreno's argument clearly indicates, the
"families that lived on the land" were in fact vociferously in favor of free
trade. (author's translation.) See Pedro Santos Martínez, *Las industrias durante
el virreinato, 1776-1810*, Buenos Aires, 1969, p. 158.

[39] Molinari's work, for instance, is devoted to trying to prove that
Moreno's *Representación* was of minimal importance in reaching a decision
that was well-nigh imposed by pressure from British interests exerted not
only on the viceroyalty of the Río de la Plata, but throughout the Spanish
empire in the Indies.

main reason behind the viceroy's decision was simply financial expediency, this being the only acceptable and most rapid way of securing the funds so urgently needed.

Two years later in 1811 the Chilean governing junta was faced with a comparable situation; having practically, though not formally, severed relations with Spain and the viceroyalty of Peru, it had to find new sources of revenue to cover ordinary administrative expenses and also to finance the organization and equipment of a new army, ostensibly to defend the country against the enemies of Ferdinand VII, the king of Spain. In the first instance, the junta proceeded to reduce the salaries of the civil service and ecclesiastics, to suspend the construction of the cathedral of Santiago, and to confiscate sums of money about to be sent to Spain.[40] All this proved insufficient and, reluctantly, the junta decided to increase the tax on tobacco, traditionally an unpopular measure. Altogether the funds collected were woefully inadequate. In this critical situation, a local dignitary José Miguel Infante, supported by the municipal council, addressed a note to the junta suggesting that instead of raising taxes, the ports should be opened to international trade: "This last measure is now an urgent necessity and it can soon provide the funds needed for the defence of this kingdom."[41] Juan Egaña, one of the most distinguished *letrados* of the latter days of the empire and later a leading figure in the movement for independence, joined in arguing that "trade must be freed because if we must assume that Chileans will buy goods from foreigners, then they would better buy them here rather than in Buenos Aires [which had already opened the port to all flags], and then the money from the customs will remain in the country."[42]

An informal meeting of the merchants of Santiago was convened to examine these proposals. Although some went so far as to agree that under strict limitations the opening of the ports could prove beneficial in the circumstances, the vast majority spoke strongly against any change in the existing

[40] Villalobos, *El Comercio*, pp. 250-251.
[41] Barros Arana, *Historia*, VIII, 270. (author's translation.)
[42] Barros Arana, *Historia*, VIII, 242. (author's translation.)

system, stating that such a step would necessarily impoverish the kingdom by forcing the export of coin: "it would prevent the establishment of manufactures. . . . it would lead to the introduction of bad quality merchandise. . . . it would propagate foreign diseases which were as yet unknown in Chile and it would also be attended by the propagation of irreligious doctrines taught by heretics and Protestants that will arrive on our coasts."[43]

After a heated debate, the meeting was adjourned without reaching a decision. A week later yet another meeting was convened. On this occasion all the required formalities were strictly adhered to. The members of the governing junta were present, but not even the solemnity and the careful explanations by the government spokesmen of the critical need for additional revenues and the ease with which the opening of the ports would solve the problem were sufficient to convince the stubborn merchants. The meeting had to be adjourned after many hours of acrimonious debate without reaching a favorable decision. Finally, a third meeting of merchants was called to consider the question in the light of the reports presented by three leading members of the Chilean mercantile community, José Antonio Rosales, Pedro Nicolás de Chopitea, and Manuel Antonio Figueroa. Their reports were not opposed, in principle, to the opening of the ports, but demanded such conditions and safeguards as to make the whole scheme impracticable from the point of view of the central authorities, and the discussion again showed the merchants were not prepared to support the measure.

Nevertheless, the central government did not feel bound to accept this verdict. It had no doubt called the meetings because it wished to appear as representative as possible of popular feeling, but the financial crisis was too pressing, and there

---

[43] Barros Arana, *Historia*, VIII, 270. (author's translation.) The passage of the free trade ordinance of 1811 has been abundantly studied; for contrasting modern interpretations see Sergio Villalobos, *El comercio*, pp. 249-257; Luis Vitale, *Interpretación marxista*, III, 13-15; Jaime Eyzaguirre, "El alcance político del decreto de libertad de comercio de 1811," *BACH*, XXXIII, no. 75 (1966), 115-161.

were no overriding reasons for it to abide by the negative views of a group of merchants who, after all, were relatively unimportant compared with the three basic creole pressure groups of the latter colonial period: the landed interest that produced wheat, hides, tallow, wines, and jerked beef for export; the mine proprietors who produced gold, copper, and silver, also for export; and the central government bureaucracy that obviously favored liberalization. Also, landowners and mine proprietors well understood that if additional revenue was not obtained from a significant increase in foreign trade, it had necessarily to be raised locally, and the main burden, if not all of it, would fall on them. They were naturally interested as well in securing wider markets for their exportable produce, like the landowners of Buenos Aires and Brazil, and cheaper and better sources of imported manufactures.

Far from being a revolutionary departure from the colonial policies of the Bourbon administrations, the decision to open the major Chilean ports to international trade represented rather a continuity, reinforced by dire necessity and unattractive alternatives. Thus, it should occasion no surprise to discover that it was supported by the most important groups of the colonial society, including the creole *letrados*. Consequently, after more than four months of discussion, the junta disregarded the views expressed by the mercantile interest and, invoking "our lord King Ferdinand VII in whose name the provisional government *Junta* rules this kingdom," proceeded to enact the decree that opened the four major ports of the country to world trade.[44]

There is ample evidence of the concern expressed by at least some members of the upper echelons of the civil service, notably Manuel de Salas, to protect and encourage the rudimentary industries of the country from the full impact of the inevitable increase in the importation of European manufactures; yet the only limitations and safeguards incorporated into the decree of 1811 were straightforward concessions to the non-

---

[44] The full text of this decree appears in Villalobos, *El comercio*, pp. 373–376. (author's translation.)

industrial traditional interests. The landowners, for example, secured the prohibition of the importation of wines and spirits not, as was oddly suggested by Martner, because of the desire to curb alcoholism,[45] but because some of the best land in central Chile was under vineyards, the wine industry was prosperous, and European wines and spirits were the only nontropical imports that could threaten the landed interest at the time, as imports of hides, wheat, tallow, and the like were most unlikely.[46]

The importation of tobacco and playing cards was also forbidden as these products were traditionally marketed through a government monopoly, the *estanco*, that produced considerable revenues and that, of course, was respected dutifully by the junta. Tradition was also meticulously observed in the important matter of the amount of duty levied on foreign imports. This was fixed at 28 percent *ad valorem* "plus or minus the amounts prescribed by article 21 of the free trade ordinance of 12 October 1778," plus 1½ percent of *subvención*,

[45] See Martner, *Historia económica*, I, 129. This does not mean that alcoholism was not a serious problem. In his *Informe* of 1803 Juan Egaña concluded that habitual drunkenness was a principal problem of the mining regions and recommended that the consumption of alcoholic beverages should be forbidden in those areas. However, it was not wine that was consumed in such vast quantities, but *chicha*, that is grape juice partially fermented. Egaña complained that landowners were putting some of their best lands under vineyards to manufacture *chicha*, which was easy to prepare and had a ready market in the mining districts. See Juan Egaña, *Informe anual que presenta la secretaría de este Real Tribunal . . .* (de minería) *. . . para el año de 1803*, ed. Diego Barros Arana, Santiago, 1894, pp. 119-120.

[46] Nevertheless, as early as November 1812, the tensions and uncertainties generated by the political situation and the imminence of war had resulted in widespread scarcity. An official report dated 6 November 1812 mentions the dearth of wheat in Santiago and points out that it was caused in part by muleteers afraid to bring farm produce into the city in case their animals were requisitioned by the army, *Boletín de Leyes y Decretos, 1810-1814*, pp. 184-185. During the next decade flour had to be imported on several occasions. In a report of 31 December 1825, C. R. Nugent, British consul in Valparaiso, explains that Chile had received imports of flour from the United States and France, "but during the last year great losses have been incurred on the importation . . . because the crops of Chile have been particularly good." *FO.* 16, vol. v, folios 70-72.

and ½ percent of *avería*.[47] All these were correctly described as "royal duties," as they were in fact determined by the regulations of the Bourbon legislation.

The only two industrial activities that had attained at least a modicum of success during the colonial period and could conceivably have developed further if protected were treated quite differently. Woolen textiles, for instance, were freely admitted on payment of the same duty as all other manufactured goods; the importation of rope and naval cordage, on the other hand, was prohibited. This difference reflected the degree of involvement of the traditional landed interest in these two activities; while sheep raising was of marginal importance and the weaving of cloth was done mostly by individual peasants or the inmates of some charitable or penal institutions, the manufacture of naval cordage and rope, in addition to its strategic value, created a growing demand for hemp, one of the successful cash crops of the central valley.

Of all the features of this decree of 1811, perhaps the most revealing in their orthodoxy were the limitations imposed on the commercial activities of foreigners. The local merchants, both creoles and Spaniards, justifiably feared that the opening of the ports would imperil their position, and therefore, accustomed as they were to benefiting from the complicated colonial system of privileges and exclusions, they insisted, no doubt as a straightforward compensation for the effects of freer trade, on the prohibition of retail trading by foreign merchants. However, the local merchants were allowed to associate legally with foreigners and thus play the passive but lucrative role of consignee or commission agents.

It was an unequal contest, for the merchants had little option when faced with the determination of the central government supported by mine proprietors and landowners; they knew they were ill-equipped to face foreign competition since

---

[47] Martner, *Historia económica*, I, 101. The *subvención* was a colonial import duty of 1½ percent ad valorem to cover the cost of unloading and storage, both functions performed by the state. The *avería* was also a traditional levy originally intended to provide for the cost of the convoys to the Indies, but later allocated to the payment of salaries of customs officials.

they were ignorant of international commercial practices, had no functional contacts with European financial centers, and no access to substantial international commercial credit or information.

The attitude of the merchants of Buenos Aires in 1809 and those of Chile in 1811 was not exceptional and cannot be attributed to the special political circumstances of the region.[48] At the same time that these debates were taking place in the southern extremity of the Spanish American empire, Mexican deputies were upholding a similar position before the Spanish Cortes that met between 1810-1813 to consider the means of defending the kingdom against the French usurpation. These Cortes included delegates from the American provinces as well as from the Spanish towns, the provincial juntas, and the population at large on the basis of one deputy per fifty thousand inhabitants. The record of the Mexican deputies at these Cortes has been studied in detail, and it does not suggest that they wanted trade liberalization as a policy for the empire.[49] Quite the opposite. When a proposal was made to allow the ships of neutral and allied nations free access to all Spanish American ports, two of the Mexican deputies actively helped to defeat the measure. One of them was Joaquín Maniau, deputy for Veracruz and closely associated with the city's merchant guild. Had the Mexican mercantile community favored liberalization, Maniau would have undoubtedly supported the measure, but instead, "[he] objected vigor-

---

[48] A similar situation obtained in Venezuela where "free trade was vigorously opposed by the merchants who realized that if the measure was approved, they would lose the benefits they derived from the subjection they had imposed on the farmers. . . . the merchants found the old system very advantageous and made every effort to stop the Spanish government from abandoning it. On the other hand the farmers . . . clamoured for freedom of trade to find buyers for their products in other colonies." See Eduardo Arcíla Farías, *Economía colonial de Venezuela*, México, 1946, pp. 262-365. (author's translation.)

[49] John H. Hann, "The Role of the Mexican Deputies in the Proposal and Enactment of Measures of Economic Reform Applicable to Mexico," in *Mexico and the Spanish Cortes*, ed. N. L. Benson, Austin, Tex., 1966.

ously to the concession of complete free trade."[50] The measure was defeated by forty-four votes. The striking feature of
this decision was that of the Mexican deputies present, eight
abstained, two, Maniau and Perez, voted against, and only
four voted in favor. Of the three deputies representing
Mexico City, Veracruz, and Acapulco, the major commercial
centers of the country, one voted against the measure (Joaquín Maniau from Veracruz), one abstained (José Ignacio
Beye de Cisneros from Mexico City) and only one voted in
favor (José Miguel Guridi Alcocer from Acapulco), and this
last was a parish priest, an eloquent orator, and a passionate
liberal who went into politics with some success and who had
no connection with the merchants of Acapulco.[51] A poor
record indeed for a commercial bourgeoisie supposedly engaged in a vigorous campaign to obtain the liberalization of
trade and the disruption of the Spanish empire.

As late as 1818, when the outcome of the wars of independence was still in the balance, the viceroy of Peru suggested
opening the ports to foreign trade in an attempt to procure
from customs duties the funds needed for the prosecution of
the military campaign, but the *Gremio de comercio*, the Lima
merchant guild, was opposed and offered to raise immediately the sum of 740,000 pesos (approximately 150,000
pounds sterling) requested by the viceroy rather than accept
the lifting of the colonial restriction.[52]

The uncomplicated, deterministic thesis implied by the two
assumptions examined in this chapter does not stand up to
scrutiny. The available evidence, which is not scant, would
suggest that it was not pressure from an incipient or rudimentary commercial bourgeoisie that forced the opening of the
ports on a reluctant administration. The reason why this policy was decided upon after 1808 was not the desire to destroy
the Spanish or Portuguese empires or even to depart from the
policies initiated by the reformers of the Enlightenment, but

---

[50] Hann, "The Role," p. 165.   [51] Hann, "The Role," p. 135.
[52] Humphreys, *British Consular Reports*, pp. 127-128.

simply the urgent need to secure funds to defend the empire against foreign enemies during the confused period after the Napoleonic usurpation.[53] The nature of this need changed as the movement for independence gathered momentum, but it was the local senior bureaucrats supported by the landed interest who insisted upon the freeing of trade for very practical reasons and against the opposition of the merchants. Both were proved right by subsequent events; the income from customs duties increased most satisfactorily, and the local merchants were all but wiped out by the fierce and perhaps unfair competition. Their disappearance created a vacuum that was quickly filled by foreign traders well-connected with firms based in Europe. By the end of the decade of 1830 the international commerce of the new republics was almost completely dominated by foreigners or foreign firms.

[53] This contradicts the interpretations of those historians who maintain that the opposition to the opening of the ports was motivated "by fear of the Spanish reaction against a measure of transcendental importance which definitely ended the Spanish commercial monopoly." Vitale, *Interpretación marxista*, III, 13. (author's translation.) In fact, as both Parry and Villalobos have pointed out, for all practical purposes that monopoly had ceased to function as early as 1797.

7

The Survival of Political Centralism

Strengthened and modernized by the reforms of the Enlightenment, the centralism of three hundred years of colonial rule survived into nineteenth-century Latin America, devolving on the leadership of the infant republics the task of adapting it to their needs of legitimacy and organization. During the years immediately following the Napoleonic invasion of Spain and the formation of governing juntas in the American colonies, this proved a most difficult and, at times, almost an impossible task. The outlying provinces were woefully unprepared for the swift collapse of the imperial center after it was torn by conflicting loyalties, pushed this way and that by developments in Europe, and generally unable to secure a consensus either for secession or for dynastic loyalty at any cost. Worse still, they were defeated by the viceregal military forces; by 1815 only the southern part of the old viceroyalty of the Río de la Plata had survived the successful counterattack of the royalist forces; Bolívar was exiled in Jamaica; in Mexico Hidalgo and Morelos were dead; O'Higgins had been forced to flee from Chile after the disastrous battle of Rancagua. It seemed then that it was only a matter of time before reinforcements would arrive from the peninsula to eliminate the remnants of armed resistance to colonial rule. At that moment Spain had the option of pursuing alternative policies that could perhaps have resulted in her retaining a measure of influence over the Indies, albeit under changed political arrangements. One such policy was to send military reinforcements and settle the issue on the field of battle, leaving the way open for a subsequent compromise. Another course, in the absence of troops and ships to transport them across the Atlantic, was to initiate negotiations immediately with a view to making conciliatory concessions.[1]

Bankrupt and virtually leaderless Spain did neither; though unable to reinforce the royal garrisons in the colonies, Ferdinand VII adopted the impolitic course of demanding a return to the status of the Indies before 1808, with full obedience to the crown and without the slightest face-saving concession to those who, at best, were hesitant supporters of secession and would have welcomed an opportunity to change their minds.[2] Five years later Major Rafael de Riego

[1] Captain James Hillyard, who spent some time in South America during 1813-1814 and met many of the leaders of the warring factions, had this to say in a dispatch addressed to the Foreign Office on 1 April 1814: "the troops [of the Viceroy of Peru] . . . I think will eventually be successful, and the Spaniards of course, regain their wanted ascendant; but unless a more liberal policy is adopted than heretofore, and they endeavour to conciliate instead of irritating and oppressing the Creoles; unless they allow them a fair proportion of the higher offices and all other employments of the State; and a real not nominal participation of the equal rights of all Spanish subjects; it will only last until the oppressed can find assistance to shake off the yoke." Cited in *Ideas and Politics of Chilean Independence* by Simon Collier, Cambridge, 1967, p. 120. Hillyard's reference to the creole complaint about exclusion from high office could be taken as interesting additional evidence about the sympathies of British officers. In fact, as is now well-known, those complaints were largely unfounded in the case of the viceroyalty of Peru, about which Captain Hillyard was writing; "the often cited exclusion of Americans from high office and of creoles from serving in their native province has now been disproven. Four of the six *oidores* of Lima in 1705 were *limeños*. Between 1740 and 1751 all fourteen judges appointed to that tribunal were creoles and eleven were *limeños*. When in 1777 royal investigator Antonio de Areche tried to reform the Lima High Court, he found that seven of the eight judges were creoles and five were natives of the city." Schwartz, "State and Society," p. 34.

[2] Raymond Carr has commented that it was "the refusal to concede that gives an obstinate glory to Spanish policy (that) conquered any thought of a negotiated settlement." The last gamble that, if successful, would have made concession unnecessary, was a new military expedition. In spite of its great financial difficulties, Ferdinand's unconvincing government started to organize an army that would cross the Atlantic to help Morillo. But the rot was far too advanced and this hastily assembled force rebelled against the regime in 1820 thus bringing down not the republican revolutionaries in America, but the monarchy itself. Carr, *Spain*, p. 124.

had rebelled in Spain; Bolívar had reconquered much of Venezuela and Colombia; O'Higgins and San Martín had crossed the Andes and defeated the Spanish forces at Chacabuco and Maipú and were actively preparing an expeditionary force to attack Peru. Perhaps more important, the republican consensus that had proved elusive before 1815 was there, at least in the regions that later became Argentina, Chile, Venezuela, Colombia, and Ecuador. In those imperial provinces, the powerful creole bureaucracy and the producers and exporters of agricultural and mineral products had tasted power and enjoyed the fleeting prosperity that followed the opening of the ports and the assumption of local controls; they were unwilling to return to the past. Moreover, during the short-lived military reconquest of most of those areas by the royalists, a violent repression was unleashed against those who had wavered in their loyalty to the crown, and this resulted in a growing opposition that made itself felt as soon as the revolutionary armies started to win fresh victories. Only the viceroyalties of Peru and New Spain held back; the former was invaded by outside revolutionary armies,[3] the latter effected the most paradoxical move of this turbulent period by seceding from Spain to avoid having to accept the imposition of the liberal constitution of 1812. Mexican independence was brought about by the creole and Spanish-born oligarchy as a reactionary move to stem the tide of liberal reform that appeared to be engulfing the metropolis after 1820.[4]

The unexpectedly bitter and protracted wars of independ-

[3] On this episode see Timothy E. Anna, "The Peruvian Declaration of Independence: Freedom by Coercion," *JLAS*, VII (November, 1975), 221-248.

[4] The Plan of Iguala, put forward by the Mexican revolutionaries under the leadership of Iturbide, included the offer of the vacant throne of New Spain to Ferdinand VII if he wished to take it, and if not, it named other members of the Spanish royal family. As it was Iturbide, who was commander of the Spanish forces, had himself elected Emperor Agustín I and was duly crowned in Mexico City on 25 July 1822. Less than a year later he was deposed and sent into exile by a liberal-republican revolt led by the commander of the Veracruz garrison, Antonio López de Santa Anna. As the Mexican historian Lucas Alamán described it, "independence was achieved by the same who until then [1820] had been opposing it." See Lucas Alamán, *Historia de Méjico*, México, 1849-1852, IV, 725. (author's translation.)

ence had important social sequels and, except in very few favored areas, a truly disastrous economic aftermath.[5] But possibly the most significant and obvious of these consequences was the militarization of the emerging republics. During the centuries of colonial rule established armies were few and small, central control emphatically civilian, and the military was clearly subordinate.[6] In less than a generation large numbers of civilians were obliged to bear arms; an officer corps had to be recruited from among the ablest, and, given the vicissitudes of such an extended war, an army career became one of the quickest avenues for moving up and across the traditional strata of society. Yesterday's *gaucho* or *llanero* could become the powerful senior officer of today; some were no doubt endowed as well with political talents; others were devoid of any appreciation of the responsibilities of office and aware solely of its privileges.[7] Those fortunate enough to secure power and occasionally prestige could, without undue

[5] Charles C. Griffin, "Economic and Social Aspects of the Era of Spanish American Independence," *HAHR*, xxix (1949), 174.

[6] This has been noted by Parry in his general study: "the Spanish Indies—reputedly so rich, so envied, so repeatedly attacked—possessed, until the Seven Years War, no standing army. . . . Land forces were negligible." Parry, *Seaborne Empire*, p. 325. A recent detailed study on the Peruvian military under the Bourbons reaches similar conclusions; "Despite the fact that the conquest of Spanish America had been primarily a military undertaking, during two centuries of Hapsburg rule the army played a secondary role, with real power and authority being vested in a pervasive civil bureaucracy." Leon G. Campbell, "The Changing Racial and Administrative Structure of the Peruvian Military Under the Later Bourbons," *TA*, xxxii (July, 1975), 117-133. This was true even in Chile, where the disastrous war raged against the Araucanians compelled the crown to establish a permanent military garrison on the southern frontier as early as 1600. This was financed directly by the crown through a special budget item called the *real situado*. Partly because they proved unequal to the demands of the bitter war, partly because their presence was needed in the agricultural and mining activities of the central region, the settlers were exempted from military service but they retained political control. This regular military establishment has remained in being, albeit under different guises, from the first year of the seventeenth century to this day and it may well be the oldest such entity continuously in existence in the Western Hemisphere. See Jara, *Guerra y sociedad*, pp. 129-143.

[7] Griffin, "Economic and Social Aspects," pp. 177-178.

difficulty, add the ownership of land to their achievements. After the wars were over, there was land to be had, not only in the vast expanse of virgin territory of the Latin American hinterland, but more importantly in valuable farms sequestered from those royalists who had died in the fighting or had been forced to emigrate to Spain abandoning their possessions. Revolutionary generals were unlikely to exchange swords for ledgers and become diligent merchants overnight; they possibly had even less inclination for bureaucratic pursuits and regarded land ownership as a more attractive gateway to affluence and permanent social prestige.

The landed military leadership that emerged after the wars tended, more often than not, to adopt a posture in political and economic matters that can fairly be described as "liberal."[8] This should not be exaggerated; it is enough to consider how tenuous such liberal commitments were for men like Santa Anna, who switched allegiance with ease from liberal to conservative and back. Their liberalism, moreover, was less the result of intellectual or moral conviction than of the peculiar circumstances that accompanied the militarization of the republics. With few exceptions, these men fought on the side of the revolutionaries and were therefore exposed to a stream of propaganda against the ultramontane and regalist Catholic establishment, the conservative aristocracy, and the central control that was readily identified with the viceregal administration and in favor of the rapid reform and liberalization of practically everything. Such views were given additional encouragement and prestige by the support of the significant number of European officers, many of them veterans of the Napoleonic Wars, who had joined the revolutionaries after 1815. A natural comradeship emerged between the survivors of countless armed encounters that was prolonged after the end of the hostilities. Such feelings did not extend to the civil bureaucracy of the young republics, especially as the bureaucracy, echoing the arrangements that

[8] See Frank Safford, "Bases of Political Alignment in Early Republican Spanish America," in *New Approaches to Latin American History*, ed. Richard Graham and Peter Smith, Austin, Tex., 1974, p. 71-111.

existed under the colonial administration, tried, not always without success, to retain administrative control and keep the military in what was considered a subordinate position. Relations between soldiers and civilians were often marred by bureaucratic delays in provisioning the troops and infrequent or insufficient payments exacerbated by the impatience of the military with the prolixity of bureaucrats reluctant to make exceptions, even in the case of distinguished foreign leaders fighting against Spain.[9] To these practical considerations must be added the inevitable awareness on the part of those military leaders who joined the ranks of the landed gentry that their immediate economic interest lay with a policy of liberalization of trade, as this promised access to wider and better markets for their products.

Behind the social-climbing swords were the revolutionary pens, the political writers, the *letrados*, lawyers, and civil servants who alone in such a legalistic society could bestow legitimacy and a minimum of efficiency to an administrative and political apparatus wrecked by a decade of civil war. The intelligentsia and the creole bureaucracy emerged with obviously enhanced influence and self-confidence after the defeat of Spain, united as well in the conviction that they were the bearers of the responsibility for guiding their countries into the postrevolutionary era. For them, the Enlightened *siglo de las luces* had been a gestation come to fruition in the Indies after the travail of the revolutionary war; they felt on the

---

[9] The difficulties between Lord Cochrane, one of the most eminent Europeans to fight with the rebels, and José Antonio Rodríguez Aldea, principal minister during the administration of Bernardo O'Higgins in Chile, were not exceptional; they reached such intensity that the noble lord wrote confidentially to O'Higgins, advising him to dismiss his controversial minister. See "Escritos y documentos del Ministro de O'Higgins Doctor don José Antonio Rodríguez Aldea," ed. Guillermo Feliú Cruz, *Colección de historiadores y de documentos relativos a la independencia de Chile*, Santiago, 1953, pp. 143-144, especially "Opiniones del Almirante Cochrane sobre el gobierno de O'Higgins y la influencia de Rodríguez Aldea." On the participation of European officers and soldiers in the wars of independence, see Alfred Hasbrouck, *Foreign Legionaries in the Liberation of Spanish America*, New York, 1928.

threshold of a new age and were prepared to transform the promise of that Enlightenment into an American reality. There were very few unbelievers in the Age of Reason among the intelligentsia of Spanish and Portuguese America; those who had access to the European writings of the period shared an overriding faith in the inevitability of progress through the exercise of liberalizing, republican rationality. One would have to search hard to find representatives of a sceptical, conservative intelligentsia; there were some, but these had very little, if any, contemporary influence. A reading of the contemporary literature, from poetry to epistolar outpourings and political tracts, leaves little doubt about the generalized acceptance among the intelligentsia of the broader assumptions underlying an optimistic belief in the dawning of a new era. This is not surprising if one recalls the importance of the dominant ideas of the Enlightenment on Caroline recentralization. Loyal Bourbon bureaucrats and rebellious republican intellectuals would have largely agreed on the theoretical conceptualizations of the Age of Reason had they been given the chance to discuss the subject around a seminar table. As it was, they parted ways when they came to consider the immediate and practical consequences of their shared understanding.

While the enthusiasm of the *letrados* and civil servants was tempered by three centuries of experience in the government of the Indies, the members of the intelligentsia outside the bureaucracy found it hard to resist the temptation of proclaiming themselves staunch liberals, federalists, opponents of absolutism in all its forms, republicans to a man, defenders of the laws of nature, and, at any rate, zealous upholders of decentralization at all costs. The ephemeral constitutions produced during this period were inevitably drawn up by these ingenious and industrious intellectuals who, in the midst of the struggles and uncertainties of the wars of Independence, found themselves suddenly elevated to the position of *éminences grises* by their military heroes. Often these provincial children of the French and Spanish Enlightenment knew as much about Europe or the United States as about their own hinterland.[10] Their responsiveness to developments in Paris, London, or Washington was usually prompt and keen while their interest in their own less fashionable literary and political tradition was seldom more than perfunctory. If there were *afrancesados* in Spain and Portugal, there most certainly was an abundance of *europeizados* in the Indies of Spain and Portugal. This fact must be borne in mind when considering the foundations on which the simplistic outward-looking nationalism of the post-Independence period was constructed: it rejected the Iberian past and sought models for emulation in the United States or in Europe beyond the Pyrenees.

The very special circumstances of the wars of independence and their aftermath, rather than any strongly held conviction, pushed the intelligentsia closer to the liberal military leadership than either would have thought possible a few years earlier; what the military lacked conspicuously, the intelligentsia provided abundantly, while their own evident weakness was more than compensated by their allies in uniform.

While the distinguishing feature of the intelligentsia outside the civil service was an almost engaging optimism and naiveté sustained by enthusiastic reading, the creole bureaucrats were essentially pragmatic in their attitude toward the problems of postrevolutionary America. Their pragmatism was sufficiently unimaginative to place them a good distance away from opportunism and very close to the minor but effective discipline of routine and continuity.

It is rare indeed to find instances when the telling dichotomy of Don Quixote and Sancho Panza does not express complex aspects of the Iberian character better than any lengthy explanation. This is not one of those exceptions. To understand the personality of Don Quixote is to take the first step toward an understanding of the Latin American intellectual while Sancho Panza is the quintessential bureaucrat of the

[10] See Roland D. Hussey, "Traces of French Enlightenment in Colonial Hispanic America," and John Tate Lanning, "The Reception of the Enlightenment in Latin America," in *Latin America and the Enlightenment*, ed. Arthur P. Whitaker, New York, 1942.

Iberian tradition. Ageing in the earthy heart of sixteenth-century Spain, Don Quixote nevertheless thought himself alive in an age of chivalry with enchanted castles, dragons, and damsels in distress. Likewise the postrevolutionary intelligentsia addressed itself to the problems of the Gran Colombia, Chile, or the United Provinces of the Río de la Plata as if these distant, vast, and underpopulated regions had been part of Europe, peopled by well-read, liberal Europeans. However, behind them repairing the damage and reconstructing the familiar shapes of practices and institutions came the Sancho Panzas of Latin America, the creole bureaucrats and *letrados*, heirs to centuries of dominance in the government of the Indies. Pragmatic and experienced, rich in the wisdom of the survivors, these creole bureaucrats felt that more than for any other comparable group, the victory of the movement for secession from Spain had been theirs. Whether justified or not, their discontent at the alleged denial of promotion to the higher posts in the imperial civil service had supplied the required momentum of dissent. Invariably steeped in a legalistic tradition of bureaucratic responsibility, they understood better than others the limitations and potentialities of reform as well as the advantages of prudence and continuity.[11] For many generations they had borne the main burden of the day-to-day administration of the colonies, and after independence they were the only ones who could implement the flood of reforms initiated by the victorious revolutionaries.[12]

[11] "All *Letrado* (that is, university trained civil servants) bureaucrats shared one common attribute, university training with a degree in canon or civil law." Graham and Smith, eds., *New Approaches*, p. 21. Parry has also observed that "a law degree and adequate seniority were the best qualifications for advancement in the Indies service." J. H. Parry, *The Audiencia of New Galicia in the Sixteenth Century*, Cambridge, 1948, p. 184. See also Javier Malagón-Barceló, "The Role of the *Letrado* in the Colonization of America," *TA*, xviii (July, 1961), 1-17.

[12] The participation of the creole bureaucracy in the republican administration was overwhelming. A study of the viceroyalty of New Granada indicates that of the 468 men who signed their names to the twenty constitutional charters promulgated during the first five years after independence, "no fewer than 303 had served in the Spanish colonial government before the wars of independence began. Among these were 92 lawyers, 100 members of

They were to prove indispensable; generals could come and go, but the permanence of an experienced bureaucracy was essential if the far-flung provinces were to retain any semblance of administration. It was through such expertise that they exercised their ubiquitous power, surviving innumerable despots, reforms, palace revolutions, conspiracies, and political intrigues, until gradually, and perhaps even unconsciously, they impressed on their respective societies the centralist arrangements they knew how to handle and for which no adequate substitute was found during the upheavals of the age. At the very center of the national stage, yet hidden by their bureaucratic anonymity, they persisted because they were necessary, as well as politically ambivalent and technically irreplaceable: it was far easier to hire mercenaries than to import well-trained civil servants. The reins released by the decaying monarchy in Madrid were seized by the local bureaucracies in Buenos Aires, Mexico, Santiago, and Bogotá, while in Brazil, reins and monarch were taken together, and Rio de Janeiro became an imperial capital overnight.[13]

The existence of this centuries-old bureaucratic establishment made many of the controversies respecting the administrative arrangements of the republics almost irrelevant, for, after varying periods of anarchy and violence, the centralist structure of government was retained under diverse authori-

---

cabildos and 107 in lesser bureaucratic positions." And the author adds a few lines further on, "Almost by definition lawyers were part of the political structure of Spanish colonial government." Glen Dealy, "Prolegomena on the Spanish American Political Tradition," *HAHR*, xlviii (1968), 49-51.

[13] The theoretical justification for this practical occurrence was an essential part of the prevailing ideology of liberalism in Spain as well as in America. Mariano Moreno, for instance, maintained that since Spain's "most beloved monarch" had been placed in captivity by the French emperor, the unique authority of the king had devolved to the people allowing for the legitimate establishment of governments, one of whose first functions was to take the reins of administration and prevent anarchy and civil strife. See Ricardo Levene, *El pensamiento vivo de Mariano Moreno*, Buenos Aires, 1942, pp. 66-67; for the Spanish background of this political philosophy, see Enrique De Gandía, *Mariano Moreno. Su pensamiento político*, Buenos Aires, 1968, pp. 299-311.

tarian guises because it was the only one known to the existing bureaucracy. Federalist administrative arrangements and federalism itself were exotic transplants from distant political climates,[14] rooted, moreover, in heretical religions. Liberalism was something learned from books, some of it from French books and some from English tracts reflecting the experience and aspirations of an island bourgeoisie whose views had been shaped, at least in part, by a religious nonconformism few Latin Americans had ever heard of, let alone understood. As for Spanish liberalism, given the opportunity, revolutionary Latin America rejected it, discovering in the process that the Spanish liberals had also rejected the independence movements in the Indies.[15]

The imaginative federal schemes, the audacious liberal constitutions, and courageous attempts at decentralization had one thing in common after the first few years of republican independence: they were all tried, but none worked. Some were disastrous; none survived. Among many other reasons was the fact that the economic base had been disrupted by war and was incapable of satisfying the new and often excessive

[14] Even somebody as responsive to European ideas as Esteban Echeverría was aware of the derivative nature of Argentine federalism at that time; in his well-known letters to de Angelis, Echeverría wrote, "the 'beau ideal' of a federal organization was . . . the constitution of North America; [Mariano] Moreno, the most doctrinaire mind of the opposition in Congress never ceased to invoke it. . . . For those men . . . the only federation possible was that of the North American type." Esteban Echeverría, *Cartas a Don Pedro de Angelis, editor del Archivo Americano*, Montevideo, 1847, p. 27. (author's translation.)

[15] The same would apply to the liberalism more directly associated with eighteenth-century western European thought; "Eighteenth century political liberalism was almost uniformly and overwhelmingly rejected by Spanish America's first statesmen. Though there is a wide variety in the form and content of the early charters, not one could be construed as embodying constitutional liberalism, however loosely that term may be defined." Dealy, "Prolegomena," p. 43. It is interesting to note that according to James Dealey, the sources of the Mexican federal constitution of 1824 are to be found in the Spanish liberal charter of 1812. Whether this is so or not, the fact remains that the Mexican experiment with federalism was also brief and disappointing. "The Spanish Sources of the Mexican Constitution of 1824," *TSAHQ*, iii (1900), 168.

demands made upon it.[16] Also, too many among the rising republican leaders appeared unwilling at first to accept the humdrum discipline of peacetime reconstruction while the people at large were confused, ill-informed about the new arrangements, or perhaps simply scared and disinclined to cooperate. These factors and many others contributed to the general disappointment, but two were crucial. First, the far-reaching administrative reforms made mandatory by the establishment of the new federal regimes were never implemented. At the very least for this reason, federalism was off to a poor start when hurriedly imposed on large countries that had always been ruled from capital cities where practically all the higher and middle-level civil servants had lived for generations. Poor communications and sheer reluctance to move to the provinces further inhibited the indispensable reallocation of human resources.

Secondly, there were at the time no social or economic groups with sufficient political weight, apart from a handful of intellectuals, committed to federalism, liberalism, or decentralizing schemes generally. There was no industrial bourgeoisie of any importance while the small domestic mercantile community was already crumbling under the thrust of the foreign competition after the opening of the ports. It is true that the traditional landed and mining interests wished to secure additional facilities to export their products, but this was more than overcome by their dislike of practically every other aspect of the federalist or liberal programs. Their support for the liberalization of trade was clearly specific and did not extend beyond commercial matters. Hence, during the early republican period, with the qualified exception of Argentina, federalism and liberal causes generally could count only on

[16] A detailed study of the financial aspects of the Central American Federation suggests that only a small part of the responsibility for its failure can be attributed to its "dismal record of financial maladministration and abortive economic development" and advances the view that "federal government failed because too many people did not want it to succeed." Robert T. Smith, "Financing the Central American Federation 1821-1838," *HAHR*, xliii (1963), 510.

the active support of sectors of the intelligentsia and the passive acceptance of a plurality, if not a majority, of the military leadership.[17] This last diminished visibly when the federal constitutions and liberal schemes proved unworkable in practice.

No doubt, as in other major regions, the closer one looks at the processes of social and economic development characteristic of each separate republic, the more one becomes aware of their distinctive features. Even so, there are enough similarities to warrant some cautious generalizations. In the history of Latin America during the past five centuries there are instances when such generalizations are justified, and this holds also for the remarkably parallel events that followed the conclusion of the wars of independence, perhaps with the exception of Paraguay.[18] The other republics underwent periods of disorder and anarchy eventually settling, with greater or lesser ease, under authoritarian regimes that represented at that time and under much changed circumstance the *sui generis* survival of Iberian centralism after the upheaval of the wars of independence and the deceptive promise of a liberal awakening. There are convincing factors that help to explain this sequel. The ideas of men like San Martin, O'Higgins, Santa Cruz, Bolívar, or Sucre were closer to the paternalism of the Spanish Enlightenment than to any of the new forms of west-

---

[17] The polarization of Argentine political life into *unitarios* and *federalistas* and the subsequent domination by the latter under the leadership of Juan Manuel de Rosas have, of course, little or nothing to do with federalism. In fact, the *unitarios* were closer to the liberal formulae than their rivals while the *federalistas* established an iron regime of absolute central control. Possibly the best comment on these issues comes from Rosas himself who, on the very day of attaining power said, "They think that I am a federalist, no Sir, I do not belong to any party, except that of the fatherland." Ricardo Levene, *El proceso histórico de Lavalle a Rosas*, La Plata, 1950, p. 147. (author's translation.)

[18] In Paraguay the enigmatic lawyer Dr. José Gaspar Rodríguez de Francia had little trouble with liberalism or federalism; he led his country's movement of independence against both Spain and Buenos Aires in 1811 and entrenched himself in power establishing an isolationist despotic regime that lasted without interruptions or major difficulties until his death of natural causes in 1840.

ern European liberalism. As Griffin has observed, the regimes led by these men "did not differ from frankly authoritarian governments and their behaviour stems more closely from the earlier enlightened despotism than from revolutionary ideology."[19] The rhetoric of revolution often clouds content and direction; the independence movements of Latin America are no exception. Their pronouncements and programs of reform are couched in the phraseology of European liberalism, but closer examination reveals that the proposed changes are deeply rooted in the Caroline reforms of the eighteenth century. It certainly does not require much imagination to accept that a man like Campomanes or Gálvez would have approved heartily of the vast majority of the policies advanced by O'Higgins or San Martin.

Even the most succinct description of those events in each independent republic that altogether justify the preceding generalizations would unavoidably splinter this chapter beyond repair. However, simply to let the matter rest here would be equally unhelpful. Possibly a reasonable selection of those cases that appear most representative will be of greater use in this explanation. I am therefore making a very brief reference to the key events of the postindependence period in Mexico, Argentina, Brazil, Uruguay, Chile, and the countries that emerged from the ruins of the Gran Colombia.

In Mexico, after the overthrow of Emperor Agustín I by General Santa Anna, a group of liberal intellectuals, with his aquiescence, prepared a federal constitution that divided the territory of the defunct viceroyalty of New Spain into nineteen states and a number of lesser regions. This project was strongly influenced by the experience of the United States. A summary of a federal constitution based entirely on that of the United States was presented to Miguel Ramos Arizpe by Stephen F. Austin in 1823, and there is little doubt that it was used in the eventual preparation of the federal constitution of Mexico.[20] The first president under this constitution and one

[19] Charles C. Griffin, "The Enlightenment and Latin American Independence," in *Latin America and the Enlightenment*, ed. Whitaker, p. 138.

[20] J. Lloyd Mecham, "The Origins of Federalism in Mexico," *HAHR*,

of its intellectual authors was Guadalupe Victoria who tried with all the zeal of the convert to make a success of the reform, but the federation proved unworkable. Mexico had been ruled for centuries from her viceregal capital and, not untypically, had no bureaucratic establishment of sufficient seniority, skill, or (possibly as important) social prestige at the local level that could possibly assume the responsibilities of regional government. After a few years of liberal rule marked by uncertainty and turmoil, General Santa Anna stepped in, took over the government, dismissed his intellectual friends, promulgated the conservative, centralist constitution of 1834, and became the dominant figure in Mexican politics, with brief interruptions, until finally ousted by another liberal revolt in 1855. Mexico today is a federal state, and has been for several generations, but as has often been pointed out: "Federalism has never existed in fact in Mexico. It is an indisputable commonplace that the Mexican nation is now and always has been federal in theory only; actually it has always been centralistic."[21]

In the United Provinces of the Río de la Plata, after the ex-

---

xviii (1938), 177-178. The echoes of the Mexican experiment in South America were also reinforced by references to its origins in the United States. Supporters of federalism in Chile, for instance, encouraged their compatriots to follow "the recent example of Mexico, whose rapid and extraordinary progress is due to the adoption of this system, which should serve to undeceive those who persuade themselves that a certain degree of education is necessary before the (federal) system can produce the salutary effects it has produced in North America." *Patriota chileno*, no. 14, ii, 13 May, 1826, quoted by Collier, *Ideas and Politics*, p. 313. As for the general influence of the United States on the thought of the first generation of republican political thinkers, perhaps it suffices to mention the case of Venezuela's first political theorist, who could write confidently that the progenitors of the Venezuelan system were Washington, Franklin, Lafayette, Paine, Madison, and Jefferson. See William Whatley Pierson, "Foreign Influences on Venezuelan Political Thought, 1830-1930," *HAHR*, xv (1934), 12.

[21] Lloyd Mecham, "The Origins," p. 164. Elsewhere in this article he adds, "Although there is emphatic and almost unanimous opposition to formal centralism in Mexico, yet, paradoxically, the Mexican Federal State has been from the beginning strongly centralistic in fact. The will of the centre has been consistently imposed upon the 'sovereign' states, by constitutional and extra-legal methods," p. 182.

pected sequence of paternalistic republicanism and anarchic dissolution, Juan Manuel de Rosas achieved power in 1830 on the strength of an unambiguous federalist program supported by the provinces in opposition to the presumably centralistic and despotic *unitarios* of Buenos Aires. He rapidly proceeded, however, to establish one of the most highly centralized, nationalistic, and long-lasting regimes Argentina has ever known, in the name of the *santa federación* and the Catholic Church and against the *salvajes unitarios*. The success of Rosas in constructing his centralist regime on a broad base of popular support was partly due to his skilful use of techniques of intimidation and mass propaganda that foreshadowed, over one hundred years ago, practices commonly associated with modern totalitarian regimes. As he himself commented, "I know and respect the talents of the gentlemen who have governed the country [before me], especially those of men like Rivadavia, Agüero, and others of their time; but in my opinion, they all incurred a serious error; their governments were very good for the upper, cultured classes, but despised the people of the lower classes, the men of the countryside . . . you know well the disposition against the rich of those who own nothing: I thought it important to gain an influence over the people of this class in order to restrain them and lead them, and I proposed to acquire this influence over them at all costs. For this . . . I found it necessary to become a *gaucho* like them, to speak with them, protect them and look after their interests."[22] This program worked so well that it is very hard to find a strongman in twentieth-century Argentina who has not tried, in one way or another, to emulate the cunning, populist chieftain.

[22] See, Levene, *El proceso*, p. 146. (author's translation.) This policy earned Rosas the odium of the intelligentsia who felt, correctly, that he had turned federalism upside down to serve his purposes, as Sarmiento complained, "before Rosas there was a federalist spirit in the provinces and the cities. . . . he obliterated it and organized to serve his ends the union which Rivadavia would have organized to serve everybody." Domingo Faustino Sarmiento, *Facundo*, Buenos Aires, 1921, p. 315. (author's translation.) See also Enoch F. Resnick, "Expresiones nacionalistas de Don Juan Manuel de Rosas," *TC*, no. 14 (1965), 164-188.

In Brazil, Dom Pedro I came to the throne on an upsurge of liberal and reformist sentiments that some Brazilian intellectuals took seriously enough to draft a liberal constitution. This the liberal monarch abolished forthwith replacing it with another more to his liking in which he reserved for himself what was described as a "moderating power," including a strong veto, the right to convene and disband parliament at will, and to appoint life senators. He thus transformed the office of the monarch into that of supreme arbiter of national political life—a role of which Pombal would have approved heartily. The constitution was promulgated in 1824 and lasted until the establishment of the republic of 1889. However, Dom Pedro was forced to abdicate in 1831, largely because of his undiplomatic conduct of affairs, and was replaced for a while by a regency. His eventual successor Dom Pedro II was more successful as a benevolent despot and retained power until the latter part of the century when the monarchy was finally replaced by a republican regime.[23] Though ostensibly federalist in spirit and again characteristically modelled after that of the United States, the constitution of 1891 did not necessarily mark the withering away of the centralist momentum in Brazil, and it was possible for a student of the period to write that "the President, by one means or another, has built up a new kind of centralization of power, infinitely greater than anything existing under the Empire."[24]

Uruguay achieved her independence in 1828, after seventeen years of struggle, first against Spain and Buenos Aires, and then from 1822 against the empire of Brazil. The domi-

[23] Dom Pedro II was also more attuned to the prevalent mood of his compatriots than some members of the liberal intelligentsia who, for instance, in 1834 introduced a bill in parliament providing for the creation of a federal union between Brazil and the United States and advancing this as the only solution to what they considered the otherwise intractable political problems of the country. Percy Alvin Martin, "Federalism in Brazil," *HAHR*, XVIII (1938), 149.

[24] Martin, "Federalism," p. 157. Martin lists among the shortcomings of the constitution of 1891 "the blameworthy intervention of the executive power in the states for the purpose of forcing upon them the rule of factions favoured by the authorities in Rio de Janeiro," p. 157.

nant political grouping at the time was the *Colorado* party of the guerrilla leader Fructuoso Rivera. This party had its main strength among the liberal-minded inhabitants of Montevideo while the *Blanco* party of Lavalleja found its supporters among the landowners from the interior of the country. After the characteristic period of confusion when there was a surfeit of high-sounding pronouncements in favor of popular representation as well as five unsuccessful constitutions,[25] the republic was actually organized under the watchful eye of Fructuoso Rivera and his *Colorados* on the basis of the unashamedly centralist constitution of 1830 that survived until 1919, despite the vicissitudes of Uruguayan politics during the nineteenth century: there were forty revolutions before it was over.

The independence of Chile was formally proclaimed in 1818 and the government entrusted to General Bernardo O'Higgins, styled *Director Supremo*. O'Higgins was the son of Ambrosio O'Higgins, the remarkable Irishman who, after a long career in the service of the king of Spain, was appointed viceroy of Peru. Ambrosio O'Higgins shared the reforming zeal of the Spanish Enlightenment and so did his son. During his term of office, Bernardo O'Higgins "attempted an ambitious programme of reforms, a programme reminiscent in some ways of an eighteenth century enlightened despotism."[26] Six years later he confidently announced that he had sanctioned a new constitution under which he intended to rule for another ten. This was too much for the landed aris-

---

[25] There were five constitutions before that of 1830: the Spanish one of 1812, one patterned after that of the State of Massachusetts and supported by Artigas, then one after the Portuguese constitution, the Brazilian one of 1824, and the one of the United Provinces in 1826. Juan E. Pivel Devoto and Alcira Ranieri de Pivel Devoto, *Historia de la República Oriental del Uruguay*, Montevideo, 1956, p. 30.

[26] Collier, *Ideas and Politics*, pp. 225-236. O'Higgins's reforms included the reorganization of the police under strong, central control, the abolition of cockfighting, bullfighting, religious processions, and games of dice. Church burials were forbidden and a Protestant cemetery founded in Valparaiso. In an attempt to curb the legal and the external attributes of aristocratic power, he abolished the titles of nobility and the entailed estates.

tocracy and the liberal elements among the military, and he was deposed and sent into permanent exile in 1823. A brief interlude of liberal-military rule ensued, in turn giving way to five years of chaos when governments came and went and a number of ineffectual constitutions were adopted, one being a federal constitution written by José Joaquín de Mora, a liberal intellectual who had earlier escaped from the conservative reaction in Spain. The federal constitution of 1828, according to the liberals, "contains all the precautions which the most ardent friends of liberty long for to calm the fears which the exercise of power might inspire in them."[27] This was probably so, but it failed to transform centralist Chile into a South American version of the much admired United States of North America; what it did achieve was to spark a powerful conservative centralist uprising that succeeded in taking power, inaugurating the longest period of stable government in any Latin American country. Although the first president of the conservative coalition was General Joaquín Prieto, the brain behind the revolution of 1829 and the subsequent institutional reforms was that of Diego Portales, an unsuccessful businessman with a notable political talent. Under his ministerial rule, a centralist constitution was promulgated in 1833 that remained effectively in force until 1925.[28]

Simón Bolívar attempted to construct one republic uniting three provinces of the old viceroyalty of Nueva Granada. The new entity the Republic of Gran Colombia included the *Audiencia* of Santa Fé, which later became Colombia, the captaincy general of Venezuela, and the presidency of Quito, now Ecuador. In 1822 following a series of military victories against the retreating Spaniards, Bolívar formally completed his master plan by proclaiming the annexation of the expresidency of Quito to his Gran Colombia. Five years later and after countless frustrated efforts to weld these old colonial

[27] This is a quotation from José Joaquín de Mora's paper, *El Mercurio Chileno*, 1 September 1828, cited by Collier, *Ideas and Politics*, pp. 321-322.

[28] For a study of the centralism of the constitution of 1833, see Alcibíades Roldán, "El centralismo de la constitutión de 1833," *RCHG*, LXXIV, no. 79, (1933), 410.

provinces into a new nation, he successfully led a centralist faction against his former federalist allies and had himself appointed dictator for life. After his death three years later his Republic of Gran Colombia dissolved into its constituent parts.

Bolívar's dream of a unified Gran Colombia did not fail simply because of centrifugal forces conspiring against federation, rather it was the case of one type of centralism defeating another, for he was a firm believer in central control. This is evident in the constitution he gave to Bolivia that for good measure formally established the office of life-president.[29] But, in attempting to impose a centralized regime on three old colonial administrative centers he was challenging a claim to legitimacy founded on centuries of centralist bureaucratic tenure in Caracas, Bogotá, and Quito. After the relaxation of power in Spain, central control devolved on those administrative centers through which it had been traditionally exercised. It was unlikely that a revolutionary leader, even one with the prestige of Bolívar, could undo in a few years the result of centuries of exacting bureaucratic practice. What destroyed the Republic of Gran Colombia was not federalism, a concept not really relevant to what was at stake, rather it was the centralism of Caracas, Bogotá, and Quito reasserting their respective claims after a momentary pause.[30] Further, it was not just a matter of bureaucratic continuity, in fact, the centralism of Quito, Bogotá, and Caracas reflected their different ways of life, traditions, and modes of political and social arrangements. As Bolívar himself explained, Caracas was an army barrack, Bogotá, a university, and Quito, a monastery. The

---

[29] Víctor Andrés Belaúnde defines Bolívar's political thought as "democratic, hierarchical, organic and technocratic" and contrasts it with that of "democratic individualism and monarchical reaction," Víctor Andrés Belaúnde, *Bolívar y el pensamiento político de la revolución hispano-americana*, Madrid, 1959, p. 19 (author's translation.)

[30] The centralism of Caracas was exercised internally as well as externally. As Sagarzazu noted in his constitutional study, "All Venezuelans know only too well that this autonomy [of the federal states] has never been practiced, but it is a myth written in all the constitutions." Luis Sagarzazu, *La constitución de 1901 y la reforma*, Caracas, 1904, p. 13. (author's translation.)

most symbolically appropriate man in Venezuela was probably the *llanero*, the cow-hand, in Colombia, the scholar, in
Ecuador, the monk.

And so it was after Bolívar's death. In Venezuela politics
was dominated for three decades by a *llanero* José Antonio
Páez, of humble origins, involved in murder before he was
seventeen, a cattle herder until the time he joined Bolívar's
army. Colombian political life was dominated by Francisco
de Paula Santander, a studious and meticulous lawyer who
fell out with Bolívar on questions of legal interpretation that
were of the greatest importance to him, but that the Liberator
thought trivial. Ecuador did not produce a Savonarola at
short notice and had to make do with an authoritarian
foreigner the Venezuelan Juan José Flores who, on and off,
occupied the center of the political stage for a generation. But
in time Ecuador too lived up to Bolívar's prophetic expectations; in 1860 after several years of anarchy a conservative
armed force led by Gabriel García Moreno, with the assistance of Flores, destroyed a liberal army led by a lesser chieftain called Guillermo Franco. This marked the beginning of
what Ecuadoreans call "the golden age of García Moreno."
There is little doubt that this was the first truly national
statesman the country had ever had. An austere, incorruptible
lawyer and journalist, he made great efforts to modernize
Ecuador: new roads were built; the fiscal system was overhauled, and a pitiless war against smuggling and speculation
was carried on with some success. Schools, all Church managed, increased three-fold. A deeply religious man, on Good
Fridays the president would march through the streets of
Quito carrying a heavy wooden cross, expecting his ministers
and higher officials also to participate in the ritual. He reor-
ganized the armed forces and gave new names to the crack
regiments such as Soldiers of the Infant Jesus, Guardians of
the Virgin, or Volunteers of the Cross. Having secured the
passage of a constitution that besides being centralistic transformed Ecuador into a virtual theocracy, in 1873 he obtained
from his docile congress an overwhelming vote approving
the consecration of the whole Ecuadorean nation to the Sa-

cred Heart of Jesus. In spite of his bizarre and disconcerting religiosity, García Moreno was also aware of the benefits that could result from more practical policies. In a mood reminiscent of the Pombaline reforms, he took a keen personal interest in the modernization of the School of Medicine, the foundation of an astronomical observatory, and the introduction of the Australian eucalyptus to help check the erosion of the Andean foothills.[31]

The first fifty years of independent life were not altogether encouraging for the federalist and liberal intelligentsia of the new republics. Time and again they tried to transplant European and North American political schemes to the republican Indies, but the soil proved inhospitable; their failure should not obscure the more important fact of the survival of the centralist style of politics into the second half of the nineteenth century.

[31] Manuel Gálvez, a biographer of García Moreno, compares him with Portales, Sarmiento, Rocafuerte, Francia, and Rafael Nuñez, adducing that all these share certain features such as being "European types of rulers, concerned principally with education, civilists and civilized, energetic and traditionalists . . . Catholic." Further on, the same distinguished Argentine author writes, "García Moreno has two great precursors; Philip II and Cardinal Jiménez de Cisneros with whom he shares a Roman and Catholic concept of the State, a counterrevolutionary spirit and an energy to defend the integrity of religious faith and the purity of morals." *Vida de don Gabriel García Moreno*, Madrid, 1945, pp. 339-342. (author's translation.) ·

8

Outward-Looking Nationalism
and the Liberal Pause

Nationalistic feelings are often, if not always, accompanied by a blossoming of intellectual and artistic curiosity about one's own historical traditions. Rising nationalism requires national explanations and justifications; it demands historical foundations on which to construct doctrines of purpose and certain destiny; it needs to define the aspirations of the national entity in terms rooted in a common understanding of cultural traits such as language, religion, and a shared historical experience that will bind a people together and distinguish them from others. Nationalism is about origins, and the intellectual demands it generates lead to introspection; they require a nationalistic scrutiny of the past that, though not necessarily critical, is usually quite specific and uninterested in general history except perhaps as a means of demonstrating the superior worth of a nation's past, future, or present. The criteria that nationalist movements normally use to justify or augment devotion for one national tradition and rejection of another need not be, indeed seldom are, rational, logical, or even civilized.

Nationalism is also associated with the populist voluntarism that is usually invoked by governments to bring forth from the citizenry exceptional exertions and a willingness to accept sacrifices for the sake of greater common goals. That such appeals have occasionally had impressive results is beyond dispute, regardless of the coherence or acceptability of those common goals or of the means proposed to attain them. It is now part of the popular view of nationalism to identify this phenomenon indiscriminately with notable political and economic achievement. Such a supposition is certainly discernible in the widespread acceptance of the interpretation that regards the great movements for Latin American independence as the direct consequence of a massive nationalist upsurge that, after the success of the initial struggle against the Iberian metropolis, retained its principal role as a political and social determinant throughout the nineteenth century.

A superficial examination of the sequence of events that preceded the secession of the Spanish Indies and the empire of Brazil would apparently reinforce such a commonly held view. First it was the American revolution, then the French one, accompanied by the rise of a romantic, modern nationalism that, by the early years of the nineteenth century, had achieved distinct expression in politics, military science, music, literature, and the arts. Then, apparently as the distant but direct consequence of these major political and intellectual developments, the Ibero-American colonies rose in revolt against their masters and after a prolonged struggle achieved their purpose, joining the United States and France in the front rank of progressive and enlightened republics.

It is easy to think in these terms, easy but erroneous. Indeed, in Latin America, the process was reversed; independence came first and nationalism followed, or rather a mood reminiscent of nationalism that when closely examined turns out to be different at least in one important respect from the phenomenon as it was known in Europe: instead of being introspective, the republican nationalism of nineteenth-century Latin America was uncompromisingly outward-looking, avid to learn and imitate anything coming from France and Britain and equally vehement in its rejection of everything related to its own Hispanic past.[1] José Victorino Lastarria, the eminent Chilean writer and man of affairs, calls the three hundred years elapsing between Columbus and Bolívar "a

---

[1] For a differing view, see Arthur P. Whitaker, *Nationalism in Latin America, Past and Present*, Gainesville, Fla., 1962. According to Whitaker, nineteenth-century nationalism in Latin America was "political, introspective, and liberal," p. 20.

black Winter."[2] The Argentine poet Esteban Echeverría, writing in the first half of the nineteenth century, is more explicit "we are independent but we are not free; the arms of Spain no longer oppress us, but her traditions weigh us down. . . . the social emancipation of Latin America can only be achieved by repudiating the heritage bequeathed by Spain." Had Echeverría written with complete candor, he would have added, "and by embracing the liberal heritage of France and Britain."[3]

Lastarria and Echeverría were not alone in their admiration for Europe beyond the Pyrenees. Their views reflected a general intellectual climate that negated the nexus with the Iberian metropolis and its traditions and nurtured the opaque myth of the Black Legend, the new obscurantism that turned Latin Americans against their own cultural heritage and led them readily to exchange three centuries of living history for the exotic novelties imported from Paris and London. Even the glorification of the conveniently distant symbols of pre-Columbian cultures, which some authors have regarded as symptoms of an incipient introspective nationalism, was largely motivated by the wish to lessen the relative importance of the Iberian participation in the making of the new nations. The phenomenon clearly was an echo of the European fad for the idea of the noble savage, which lent itself to a glorification of the Indian as he presumably was before the coming of the conquerors, and a vilification of the Iberians for having destroyed great civilizations and transformed those golden barbarians of the past into the melancholy and abulic indians of the present.

The Black Legend dates from the great controversies of the

[2] José Victorino Lastarria, *Recuerdos literarios*, Santiago, 1885, p. 22. Lastarria (1817-1888), eminent Chilean writer, staunch liberal, pioneer of Positivism in Latin America, claimed to have thought of Comte's system before the French philosopher. He was a great admirer of the United States and its "republican semecracy," or system of self-government, as he understood it.

[3] Stephen Clissold, *Latin America, A Cultural Outline*, London, 1965, pp. 85-86. On Echeverría and his literary and political activities see also, Alberto Palcos, "Echeverría y el credo de Mayo," *TC*, no. 9 (1960), 231-242.

sixteenth century about the theory and practice of the Spanish
conquest, but reappeared in a nineteenth-century guise. To all
the traditional accusations against Spain that accumulated during the preceding three centuries, it added a few more, the
product largely of the condescending opinions held by French
and British intellectuals and political leaders about a Spain so
obviously in decline and whose culture and institutions few
were prepared to defend. In Latin America, the great Venezuelan scholar Andrés Bello, founder and first rector of the
University of Chile and possibly the continent's most eminent intellectual figure, was one of very few men of standing
who tried, with characteristic moderation, to restore the balance, by calling on their contemporaries to pause before discarding everything Spanish in their impatience to become as
European as possible in the briefest time. He warned that
European models in the arts, philosophy and politics could
not instantly replace what was being repudiated and that
much of value in America was due to Spain, including the
courage and determination shown by the creoles in fighting
for their independence. Even his restraint and unassailable
erudition and prestige did not save him from the attacks of
writers like Lastarria who considered him hopelessly conservative and out of touch with the times.[4]

It was during the latter part of the decade of 1830 that
Echeverría, back in Buenos Aires after having spent five years
in his beloved Paris, became the intellectual leader of a notable
group of writers and political activists that used to meet at the
Librería Argentina, under the gaze of the poet's household
deities, Lord Byron and Victor Hugo, to discuss the latest
ideological and literary imports from Europe. There, in the
tense capital of the Rosas dictatorship, while Argentina and
Latin America were fumbling toward a definition of a viable

---

[4] See Lastarria, *Recuerdos*, pp. 222-249; for Bello's views see Clissold, *Cultural Outline*, pp. 86-88; for a study of the Black Legend before the nineteenth
century see Benjamin Keen, "The Black Legend Revisited: Assumptions and
Realities," *HAHR*, XLIX (1969), 709-719. See also Sverker Arnoldsson, *La
conquista española de América según el juicio de la posteridad; vestigios de la leyenda
negra*, Madrid, 1960.

national project, Echeverría and his friends feverishly conversed about the poetry of Byron, the newest pronouncements of Lammenais, the advanced views of Saint-Simon, Saint-Beuve, or Leroux, and the eclecticism of Cousin. It is difficult to exaggerate the influence that French ideas had on the liberal and radical youth of mid-nineteenth-century Latin America. The *Sociedad de la Igualdad*, founded in 1850 by a group of Chilean intellectuals, was directly motivated by the events of 1848 in France and adopted as its slogan, naturally, the words "liberty, equality and fraternity." Carried away with enthusiasm after reading Lamartine's *Histoire des Girondins*, the leading members of the society decided to exteriorize their ideological rebirth by changing their names for those of the revolutionary heroes featured in that work. Thus, Francisco Bilbao became Vergniaud; Santiago Arcos, son of a Chilean banker, and educated in France, chose Marat; Pedro Ugarte became Danton; Eusebio Lillo, Rouget de L'Isle; José Victorino Lastarria adopted the name of Brissot; Domingo Santa María that of Louvet and Manuel Recabarren, Barbaroux.[5]

It is possible to see in the repudiation of Spain and her culture one more lamentable result of the traumatic wars of independence, but such an apparently straightforward explanation suffers when applied to Brazil because there was no war and the transition to independent status was almost a joyful affair, conducted under the leadership of a prince of the blood.

[5] See Armando Donoso, *El pensamiento vivo de Francisco Bilbao*, Santiago, 1940, pp. 25-26. It should be pointed out that Lastarria, a key figure in these developments, was not just another young agitator, but a founder of the Chilean Liberal Party and coauthor, with Federico Errázuriz, of its famous manifesto *Bases para la reforma*. See Germán Urzúa, *Los partidos políticos chilenos*, Santiago, 1968, p. 37. Benjamín Vicuña Mackenna, hardly immune to the attractions of European culture and ideas, explained a few years later that Lamartine's *Histoire* "had in Chile, and especially in Santiago, an immense effect which no other book ever had nor probably ever could have in the future . . . Lamartine, from 1848 to 1858, was a semi-God like Moses." Cited by Thomas Bader, "Early Positivistic Thought and Ideological Conflict in Chile," *TA*, xxvi (April, 1970), 379. The actual quotation comes from Vicuña Mackenna's *Los girondinos chilenos*, Santiago, 1902, p. 8.

Yet, as Cruz Costa has observed, "when we [Brazilians] separated ourselves from Portugal, we turned toward France." Mainly toward France, no doubt, but not exclusively, for "the Brazilian mind turned toward the different European markets which supplied it. It was felt that within the tomes of European wisdom must lie concealed some ideal and miraculous formula. The surrounding reality was completely forgotten by the majority of the [Brazilian] intellectuals of the nineteenth century to whom it seemed that the literary and philosophical moulds of Europe fitted Brazil perfectly. France provided literary and philosophical patterns; England, proud possessor of a model monarchy, furnished the ritual of parliamentary government; and Germany, especially after 1870, sent us not only her traditional metaphysics, but also her new scientific orientation."[6]

Europe was this and more throughout the regions newly won for republican liberty. There was a breathless desire to be like the French and the British, to dress like the fashionable Europeans, to write and paint like them, to imitate their architecture, their manners and affectations, and the suspicion arises whether this was not also partly the reaction of the vanquished before the victor.[7] In less than a generation, the

---

[6] Cruz Costa, *History of Ideas*, pp. 48–49. In the decades of 1820 and 1830 Rio de Janeiro achieved a reputation in Latin America as a fledgling artistic center. This was principally due to the presence in the imperial capital of a number of French artists who, having had close relations with the Bonapartist regime chose to flee their country after Waterloo. Among those who are still remembered either for their works or their teaching are Le Breton, Debret, the brothers Taunay, and the architect Grandjean de Montigny. See Arminda D'Onofrío, *La época y el arte de Prilidiano Pueyrredón*, Buenos Aires, 1944, p. 21.

[7] It is not easy to exaggerate how importantly France loomed on the cultural horizon of Latin America during the mid-nineteenth century. A glimpse can be had from the lines written by Benjamín Vicuña Mackenna on his arrival in Paris for the first time, in 1853: "I was in Paris. . . . I was in the capital of the world, the heart of humanity which beats with the gigantic pulsations that the spirit of all the peoples of the earth send to this centre of life and intelligence. Miniature of the Universe, everything that has ever been created exists here; intelligence, virtue, the dregs of human misery, the most sublime epic of history; nature, genius, heroism, pleasure; frenetic passion, vice,

Spanish Empire had been humbled by the French; those who in viceregal Lima, Mexico, and Buenos Aires had pitied the lot of the French monarchy after 1789 and lamented the eclipse of France from the constellation of the powers lived to see French armies overrunning Europe. It is worth asking to what extent the almost irrational admiration for France of the nineteenth-century Latin American intelligentsia was not prompted by the scarcely conscious awareness that from Paris had issued the orders resulting in the undoing of the Spanish Empire. And the French were in turn vanquished by the British. Although glory rested with the stubborn Corsican, the number of Latin Americans who appreciated the fact that they were witnessing the beginning of a British century was not small. France and Britain were worthy models indeed; it was not difficult—indeed it was true—to think of these two nations as standing in the vanguard of mankind in the arts, in politics, in technical achievement, in fashion, in everything.[8] Even at their most reactionary, these rich cultures could equally harbor in them the most attractive and progressive

refinement." Several paragraphs further he writes, "Three cities are said to have symbolized the world in which they existed; Athens, Rome, and Paris. But Paris has assumed the mantle of all; son of Minerva, Paris illumines the earth; son of Mars, Paris has subjugated the Universe; Paris is the daguerreotype of humanity, the epitome of history, the foundation and the peak of modern civilization. Paris is unique; although today he is the slave of an adventurer, he is still master of Europe and the world." The reference, of course, is to Napoleon III. See Benjamín Vicuña Mackenna, *Páginas de mi diario durante tres años de viaje, 1853-1854-1855*, Santiago, 1936, I, 281-282. (author's translation.)

[8] The uncritical appreciation of all things French extended to the great country's military establishment; Vicuña Mackenna's views, which were echoed throughout the new Latin American republics, are illustrative, "on several occasions I saw this French army, the first in history without any doubt whatsoever, in matters of valour, skill and genius. . . . 'La France est un soldat' has been the magnificent expression of Chateaubriand." Vicuña Mackenna, *Páginas*, p. 298. (author's translation.) Eventually, France was defeated by the rising might of Germany, and this was also echoed in Latin America; the republics that had almost to a man adopted the French uniform for their new armed forces swiftly changed over to the Prussian style, and by the eve of the First World War there were few, if any, red pantaloons to be seen from Mexico to Cape Horn.

challenge; the opposition to conservative France or Britain did not come from elsewhere, but from within; there was in France and Britain sufficient complexity and richness of detail to satisfy the extremes of radical and conservative opinion in Latin America.

On the other hand, Spain had little to offer, at least to the members of the novel republican intelligentsia; the liberalism of Cádiz and Madrid was twice removed from the same sources—be it London or Paris—used by liberals in Caracas, Lima, and Buenos Aires. There was little that was original in Spanish liberalism, save the special and robust tradition of municipal autonomy always resurrected to justify or explain any challenge to the central authority.[9] At any rate, this appeal to an historical precedent of sorts, and a most distinguished one, made Spanish liberalism different in quality from the one that eventually flourished in nineteenth-century Latin America and that, as a result of the Black Legend, was severed from an Hispanic tradition that could, perhaps, have given it some claim to being autochthonous. The Spanish liberals failed tragically to bring down the old regime; the revolution was put down with the help of French arms, and the voices that could conceivably have elicited a sympathetic echo from the emancipated Indies were stilled. It was, however, most unlikely that the Peruvian or Chilean revolutionaries who defeated the viceregal forces at Ayacucho would have appreciated the fact that in Spain herself there were forces fighting to achieve liberal, constitutional ends, though not necessarily to dissolve the empire and grant republican au-

[9] It is difficult to disagree with Raymond Carr when he maintains that Spanish liberalism lacks any originality of thought, and that there is little in it that cannot be derived from French doctrinaires and their opponents, or, less frequently, from English radicalism. According to Carr, what gives Spanish liberalism its characteristic flavor is "its use of a unique system of historical references, while its significance lies in its attempt to apply, by means of military sedition, the politics of interest and the machinery of parliamentary government to an under-developed society." Carr, *Spain*, p. 130. For a dissenting view see Sánchez Agesta, *Historia del constitucionalismo español*, Madrid, 1964, especially pp. 45-112.

tonomy to the rebellious provinces.[10] There may have been contemporary merits in such an enlightened attitude, but now, *a posteriori*, one can only record that Latin America was apparently doomed to ignore the Spain of Goya and passionately, to admire the France of Ingres and Delacroix.

It was no mean feat to negate a cultural history as robust and well-represented in painting and architecture as that flourishing in the great imperial cities during the heyday of the Spanish and Portuguese baroque, but Latin America accepted the challenge with zest. In some instances, the skills that for generations had nourished distinguished artistic traditions, like the Quito school of painting, were deflected into more progressive and acceptable directions. On the occasion of the 1861 Paris Universal Exhibition, the government of Ecuador proudly sponsored the presentation of a number of copies of European paintings cleverly done by Ecuadorean artists who, according to the careful prose of the official catalogue, enjoyed a great reputation in Ecuador not because of their originality, but because of the fidelity with which they could imitate the European masters.[11] The transition was all the more marked in architecture as the new regimes disowned the creations of the despised colonial period and did their very best to remedy what they could. In Buenos Aires, the cathedral, which had been started in 1734, was still unfinished at the time of independence. The task of completing it was naturally entrusted to a French architect, M. Prosper Catelin, who

[10] The Cortes of Cádiz, which marked the brief moment of Spanish constitutional liberalism at the beginning of the century, have been described, with some justification, as a bloodless replica of the French Revolution. Whole articles of the revolutionary constitution of 1791 were faithfully translated and incorporated without significant alterations into the Spanish Constitution of 1812, affording good grounds for suspecting that their authors were possibly too eager to imitate their French mentors. This was certainly the opinion of that most severe and formidable critic of the Spanish Francophile intelligentsia (*afrancesados*), the eminent historian Marcelino Menéndez y Pelayo. See Sánchez Agesta, *Constitucionalismo*, p. 46.

[11] Gustavo Beyhaut, *Raíces contemporáneas de América Latina*, Buenos Aires, 1964, p. 70.

promptly discarded the original design and gave the building a fashionable neo-classic façade inspired by the Parisian Madeleine.[12] In the field of education a French passport was as good as a university degree; to justify the claim that the *Colegio Histórico del Uruguay* was the very best school in the region, it sufficed to mention the fact that no less than three of its teachers were French: M. Pasquier ("a graduate of the University of Paris"), M. Lavergne ("a disciple of l'École Centrale de Paris"), and M. Peyret ("a Frenchman and a man of letters").[13] This respect and admiration for everything French, British, or generally European became at times almost obsessive. Lastarria, who in his dealings with his Latin American colleagues could be arrogant and overbearing, betrayed an infantile joy when he received a courteous note from Edgar Quinet thanking him for some books the Chilean writer had sent to him. Lastarria actually had the complete eleven line text of the note, including the date, reproduced in his literary memoirs adding that this was for him "a word of encouragement from Old Europe . . . and an unexpected prize."

The admiration of these earnest liberals and radicals for France and Britain was occasionally made extensive to the United States. Lastarria, for instance, eventually came to the conclusion that although liberalism had originated in Europe, the Old World had been incapable of realizing its potential, and it had been left to America to witness its full flowering, and also that "the first duty of the statesmen of Latin America is to imitate the United States, to quicken, as they had done, the beneficial effects of the natural laws that rule humanity," and so on, and so forth, at great length, in the same vein.[14]

José Vasconcelos, the controversial Mexican thinker and political leader, writing in his later years when he was con-

[12] Leopoldo Castedo, *A History of Latin American Art and Architecture*, New York, 1969, pp. 204-205.

[13] Manuel E. Macchi, "Urquiza en la instrucción pública," *TC*, no. 14 (1965), 147-148. (author's translation.)

[14] Lastarria, *Recuerdos*, p. 252. See also Luis Oyarzún, *El pensamiento de Lastarria*, Santiago, 1953, p. 103. et seq. (author's translation).

vinced that the only hope for the advancement of Latin America lay in her European roots, stated nonetheless that during the nineteenth century Mexican statesmen "were only lackeys of English thought, lackeys who kept repeating the ostensible doctrines of 'The English Speaking Peoples of the World.' "[15] In this he touched on a contradictory, possibly even a paradoxical aspect of the problem, for it is perfectly obvious that with remarkably few exceptions the intelligentsia of nineteenth-century Latin America, whose attitude toward the Iberian cultural heritage was directly based on a strong rejection of colonialism and all it implied, was nevertheless quite blind to the imperial exploits of France, Britain, and the United States. It is worth pointing out that the ink was hardly dry on Lastarria's condemnation of Spanish and Portuguese colonialism and his warm endorsement of the "semecracy" of the United States when the semecrats marched into Mexico and annexed a considerable part of her territory. The France so sincerely admired by Echeverría, Vicuña Mackenna, and Sarmiento was guilty of one of the crudest attempts to establish an imperial presence in Mexico using the ill-fated Maximilian. The Great Britain whose liberal attitudes were celebrated in countless elegant salons from Bogotá to Santiago and Rio de Janeiro was at the time successfully constructing the greatest empire of the century and in ways that were not particularly humane or enlightened.

The rejection of what is Spanish in Latin America and the parallel glorification of contemporary French, British, and generally European values possibly achieved their best ex-

---

[15] José Vasconcelos, *A Mexican Ulysses, The Autobiography of José Vasconcelos*, trans. and abridged by W. Rex Crawford, Bloomington, Indiana, 1963, pp. 81-82. Whether "lackey of English thought" is a fair description is, of course, at the very least questionable, but it is interesting to note that when Vicuña Mackenna was searching for the highest praise he could convey as he prepared his biography of Sucre, he finally chose as an adequate title for his work, "El Washington del Sur"—The Washington of the South. Vasconcelos would have probably observed that it was highly unlikely that an English biographer of Washington would have chosen "The Sucre of the North" as a title for his work. Benjamín Vicuña Mackenna, *El Washington del Sur, Cuadros de la Vida del Mariscal Antonio José de Sucre*, Madrid, 1893.

pression in the work of Domingo Faustino Sarmiento, the Argentine writer and political leader. Sarmiento's best known book *Facundo* was originally published with the telling subtitle *Civilization and Barbarism*. To the author the issue was clear; Europe was civilized, Latin America, barbarous. Inasmuch as the new republics were able to free themselves from the limitations imposed by the Hispanic tradition, they would become civilized. A strong opponent of the Rosas regime, he lived many years in exile, mostly in Chile, where he wrote *Facundo*. From a Paris he found absolutely fascinating on his first visit in 1846, he tried to explain why France led humanity in everything related to the intellect and the arts, "the ideas, the fashions, the literary production [of France] are a model and a goal for all the other nations; I believe that this which we regard as a desire to imitate, is in reality the aspiration of human beings to approach a type of perfection which is inside all of us but which develops with more or less success according to the circumstances which affect each nation."[16]

This seat of perfection, most worthy of imitation, came into direct conflict with the despotic regime of Juan Manuel de Rosas when French warships blockaded the River Plate. Naturally this confrontation sparked a tremendous xenophobic popular reaction in Argentina skillfully encouraged by Rosas in the name of Americanist sentiments outraged at the imperialistic pretensions of the French. To this situation Sarmiento addressed himself in one of the latter chapters of *Facundo*, and it is worth noting how delicate and difficult it was for somebody like him to persist in his attacks on Rosas even when the strongman was also being attacked by European military forces. At any rate, considering the fact that he eventually became president of Argentina, it can be safely as-

[16] D'Onofrío, *Pueyrredón*, p. 23. (author's translation). The idea of Europe as the model the nations of Latin America ought to imitate has proved remarkably persistent; half a century after Sarmiento, the Bolivian poet Franz Tamayo wrote from Paris, "the only way in which the countries of South America can hasten their development is through close contact with the thought and achievement of Europe." Fernando Diez de Medina, *Franz Tamayo*, Buenos Aires, 1944, p. 67. (author's translation.)

sumed that his views did him less harm a century ago than they would today. Sarmiento wrote as follows, and he is worth quoting at length: "The French blockade brought to the surface a sentiment that we appropriately called 'Americanism,' everything that is barbarous in ourselves; everything that separates us from cultivated Europe came to the fore at that moment in Argentina, organized systematically to try and construct in our country an entity distinct and separate from the peoples of Europe. The institutions that we had so carefully and diligently copied from Europe were being destroyed; a persecution was unleashed against the use of European dress, against fashion, against trimmed sideburns, against the shape of trousers and lapels, against the French style of coiffure; and to oppose these exterior signs of European influence, the regime forcibly encouraged the use of the wide and loose creole trousers, the red waistcoat, the short jacket, the *poncho*—all in the guise of a national dress, eminently 'American' . . . and the *Gaceta* [Rosas' official newspaper] agitated and encouraged its readers to hate the Europeans, to despise the Europeans who want to conquer us; Frenchmen are called lousy clowns; Louis Philippe, pig-keeper, and generally European politics are described as barbarous, disgusting, brutal, sanguinary, cruel and inhuman."[17] Against this, according to Sarmiento, the educated youth of the country rebelled, for they understood that the better and higher interests of humanity were being defended by the European powers in their struggle against Rosas: "The youth of Buenos Aires shared the generous idea of a community of interests between Argentina, France and Britain; their love for civilization, for the institutions and the knowledge which Europe had bequeathed to us and that Rosas was destroying invoking the name of America, substituting another way of dressing for the European dress; other laws for the laws of Europe; another government for the European type of government. This youth, imbued with the civilizing ideas of

---

[17] Sarmiento, *Facundo*, p. 297. (author's translation.) The first edition of *Facundo* was published in Santiago in 1845; the fourth edition, published in Paris in 1874, had the complete title, *Facundo o civilización y barbarie*.

European literature recognized in the European enemies of
Rosas their own noble ancestry and models for emulation;
their true allies in the struggle against America represented by
Rosas; barbarous like Asia; despotic and bloodthirsty like
Turkey, persecuting and despising intelligence like Islam."[18]
Sarmiento's blind love for Europe was only equalled by his
contempt for Spain; "I feel called to struggle against the
Spanish race, so incapable of understanding freedom, here as
well as in Spain. The Spanish language is an insurmountable
obstacle to the transmission of culture. . . . Spain has never
had a thinker, not one notable writer, not a single philosopher. . . . Spain has condemned to backwardness the descendants of Europeans in America."[19] Such views reflect a silli-
ness, ignorance, and pettiness that is hard to associate with a
man of Sarmiento's stature, and it is fair to say that when
carefully considered against the contemporary background,
they would look less extreme. Certainly the opinions about
Islam, Turkey, and Asia in general are those of liberal Europe
and can hardly be original with the Argentine writer; his
views on Spain and her cultural heritage are merely a violent
restatement of the Black Legend, and his admiration for everything European, even fashion, was characteristic of an intelligentsia whose patriotism could not be faulted, but whose
nationalism was positively outward-looking rather than introspective.

This is an important difference even if only considered
comparatively. When the United States gained its independence from Great Britain, there was no simultaneous secession
from English literature or from the mainstream of cultural
and political traditions that use the English language as their
vehicle. The revolutionary institutions of the United States,
its political philosophies, its attitudes toward freedom and
despotism, its style of life, and the aspirations of its people all
had roots that went deep into the history of the English-

[18] Sarmiento, *Facundo*, pp. 306-307. (author's translation.)

[19] Pedro de Paoli, *Sarmiento, su gravitación en el desarrollo nacional*, Buenos
Aires, 1964, p. 68 n. (author's translation.)

speaking peoples.[20] In 1776 and after, and despite the war of 1812, the United States did not reject its British ancestry in favor of other cultural models. Far from it, the introspective mood of the nationalism of the emancipated North American colonies was so emphatic as to reach the very boundaries of quaint and unashamed provincialism. This was not so in the Iberian regions of the New World where the imitation of Europe, and occasionally of the United States as well, became the dominant style of the century. The process of imitation was heterogeneous, variously modified by regional differences, geographical as well as cultural. Before the days of the British Council, the *Alliance Française* or the *Goethe Institut*, what passed for an English school, a French *lycée*, or a German *gymnasium* in Caracas, Tegucigalpa, Temuco, or Petrópolis could be disconcertingly different from the original model. Such variations were sometimes tempered, others

---

[20] The cultural continuity of the English-speaking world was well appreciated by Lastarria who contrasted it with the dramatic interruption that, according to him, marked the Hispanic world since colonial days; see Lastarria, *Recuerdos*, p. 49, et seq. During the latter years of the eighteenth century a number of reliable observers described what they considered symptoms of a growing creole nationalism in the Spanish Indies. Alexander von Humboldt, for instance, reporting on his visit to New Spain explains that "since the Peace of Versailles, and, in particular, since the year 1789, we frequently hear proudly declared: 'I am not a Spaniard, I am an American,' words which betray the workings of a long resentment." There is little doubt that notwithstanding the muted impact of European events—possibly their influence was greater on Humboldt than on the creoles he was meeting in New Spain—the first stirrings of American nationalism in the Spanish Indies must have followed closely the classical introspective pattern; at least there is little evidence on which to base the supposition that it could have been necessarily as outward-looking as it in fact turned out to be following the events of 1810. After all, whatever the ultimate direction of the juntas of 1810, they were in fact formed with popular approval to defend the king of Spain against the usurpation of Napoleon; there is certainly no contemporary indication to suggest that in about 1800 feelings of admiration for Britain, France and the United States were as prevalent among the creole intelligentsia as they became a generation later.

For Humboldt's report on the Americanist feelings amongst the creoles of New Spain, see Humphreys and Lynch, *The Origins*, pp. 269-274.

exacerbated, by the complex effect of folkloric symbolism.[21] It suffices here to note that the acceptance of what Europe had to offer was not absolute, but as varied and as capable of departing from its models as allowed by the characteristics of each host culture.

The public approval of practically everything that Europe had to offer greatly eased the way for the early introduction and acceptance of the liberal economic ideas and concepts then prevailing in the academic and administrative centers of the Old World. Such an acceptance was already apparent by the middle of the century, but it became overwhelming during the decade of 1860 when the twin centers of the civilized world, as seen from Latin America, formally embraced the principles of free trade and institutionalized their endorsement in the treaty that bound the France of the Second Empire to the Britain of Victoria according to terms laid down by the archpriest of free trade Richard Cobden himself. In one of his comments on the differing characters of Paris and London, Vicuña Mackenna suggests that these two cities together dominated the modern world: "Paris because of her intelligence and social influence; London because of her wealth and material power. I think that if by magic these two empires could be United, Rome would be resurrected."[22] In fact they were united in their espousal of liberal economic policy, and the effect on the Latin American republics was momentous. For the liberal concepts that gained such dramatic sponsorship from the two leading nations of Europe coincided with the

---

[21] Opera houses, for instance, were constructed in practically every major urban center; very different the one from the other, they ranged from sumptuous elegance to insufferable pretentiousness but they shared, and many still do, the disconcerting popular reputation of being, each of them, no matter how different, faithful replicas of the much admired Second Empire Parisian model. The explanation of this oddity has nothing to do with ignorance, but much with the expectations of a relatively prosperous and culturally ambitious urban middle sector. Even today, the information that the *Teatro Municipal* of Santiago, or the *Teatro Colón* of Buenos Aires are not modelled on the Paris Opera would be received with disbelief by the average inhabitants of those capitals.

[22] Vicuña Mackenna, *Páginas*, p. 392. (author's translation.)

interests of the principal economic pressure groups in Latin America and considerably reinforced their claims to represent the general interest of their respective nations. They also coincided with the economic aspects of the liberal doctrines supported by the intelligentsia. Thus, pragmatic exporters, idealistic writers, and politicians were of one mind in upholding the doctrines of economic liberalism; at the same time they shared the satisfying feeling that their position was also that of the leaders of civilization and progress.

If a single cause has to be assigned for the failure to develop a significant industrial sector in Latin America during the nineteenth century, this formidable coalition of interests, convictions, and aspirations would be the most acceptable. It was extremely difficult for a central government, faced with such an array of powerful interests, to implement the type of protectionist economic policy necessary for the development of a nascent industrial sector. The outward-looking nationalism of the early decades after independence opened the way for the liberal pause that characterized the history of Latin America during the hundred years between the mid-nineteenth and the mid-twentieth centuries.[23] Obviously such

---

[23] Some authors, notably Osvaldo Sunkel in *El subdesarrollo latinoamericano y la teoría del desarrollo*, would date the liberal period from 1750 onward. Although this view can certainly be defended, I am happier thinking that the "liberalization" associated with the Spanish and Portuguese Enlightenment had less to do with liberalism than with a traditional centralism characteristic of Iberian political practice and distant from the British institutions that at the same time were blossoming into what we have later come to associate with economic liberalism. Harold Laski traces the principal components of European liberalism to the seventeenth century, and even further back, but mainly to that century when Europe saw "the victory for utilitarianism in morals, for toleration in religion, for constitutional government in the sphere of politics. In the economic realm, the state becomes the handmaid of commerce," and so on. Surely this is correct when applied to Britain, but it will simply not do for Latin America, not even with respect to the movements for independence that, I would suggest, are better interpreted as the result of factors other than the rise of liberalism in the Indies. See Osvaldo Sunkel y Pedro Paz, *El subdesarrollo latinoamericano y la teoría del desarrollo*, México, 1970, pp. 297-321; Harold J. Laski, *The Rise of European Liberalism*, London, 1962, p. 59.

dates are not exact and need not be, but it can be said that roughly between 1850 and 1870 practically all the countries of Latin America entered a period that can fairly be described as a "liberal pause" when, without discarding their centralist structure and institutions, they embraced the libertarian economic doctrines emanating from radical Paris and liberal London.[24]

The spirit of imitation of things European did not extend to the European manner of production, but remained solely and most significantly an imitation of the ways in which Europeans consumed.[25] The enthusiasm of those who were ready to accept everything that France and Britain had to offer moved them to emulate the way the French and British spent their wealth: their style of dressing, architecture and literary fashions, their music, their manners, their affectations and exotic habits, and, almost inevitably, their social, economic, and political ideas. They did not copy the way Europeans produced because there was no need for them to do so. The ruling groups, the intelligentsia, the upper social strata; the people whose views were significant; more, the inhabitants of the great cities, the tertiary sector of the economy, the bureaucrats, and the members of the professions—all these people had direct or indirect access to the wealth and prosper-

[24] There was open agreement between the intelligentsia, the exporters of primary commodities, and the artisans when it was a question of supporting economic freedom; this agreement did not hold, however, in matters related to political freedom. The same commercial, mining, and agricultural interests that loudly proclaimed themselves to be supporters of economic liberalism were hesitant to support any extension of political liberty and in pursuing an authoritarian policy found it easy to side with the central government against the radical intelligentsia and their urban followers.

[25] For purposes of comparison it is useful to consider the case of Japan during the Meiji period when she evidently tried systematically to imitate the modern European modes of productions, but not their manner of consumption, or the way in which they organized the family, or their scales of values. Turkey under Kemal Ataturk, on the other hand, would provide an instance closer to the Latin American experience during the nineteenth century for the main thrust of Ataturk's modernizing reforms was in the direction of social habits, mode of dress and the like, rather than toward modern industrial or agricultural production.

ity that became characteristic of the economy of Latin America during the greater part of the century of the "liberal pause." It was this affluence that facilitated the imitation of European fashions so impressively achieved by the dominant urban groups of the new republics; it also made it unnecessary to change the manner of production because the traditional systems of mining and agriculture, even if only slightly modified by the improvements periodically introduced by foreign enterprises, were sufficient to supply a growing international market with the mineral and agricultural exports that Latin America appeared to produce almost effortlessly.[26] The needed wealth came from the sale of sugar, rubber, copper, wool, hides, wheat, nitrate of soda, cotton, and other such products for the most part to the major industrial countries of Europe whose processes of industrialization had generated apparently inexhaustible demands. The income from the sale of these products was used to pay for the importation of English clothes and furniture, French wines and porcelain, Italian glassware and textiles, Flemish lace, and generally the fabrics and other manufactures needed to house and clothe the ambitious urban inhabitants of Latin America in a manner befitting their condition as diligent apprentice Europeans. It was also used to smooth the introduction of liberal economic ideas and to palliate the misgivings of reluctant central governments. Had times been hard financially, it is most improbable that free-trading Manchesterian liberalism would have been so widely and enthusiastically adopted. As it was, the wealth pouring in from the sale of exportable commodities played a decisive role in convincing, or minimizing the resistance, of the central governments. The traditional central bureaucracy and a handful of nationalist and, perhaps, far-seeing, political

[26] An interesting instance of the early introduction of technological innovations into a traditional activity is that of the reverberatory furnaces for copper smelting introduced into Chile by Charles Lambert during the decade of 1820. The extended use of these furnaces was largely responsible for the expansion of Chilean copper exports during the first half of the century. See Claudio Véliz, "Egaña, Lambert, and the Chilean Mining Associations of 1825," *HAHR*, LV (1975), 647-655.

leaders were the only ones prepared to oppose the trend. Their resistance was unimpressive against the tide of prosperity associated with the freeing of trade barriers and the indiscriminate encouragement of primary commodity exports. The most responsive sectors to the lure of European culture and manners were naturally those in the middle and upper reaches of urban society who were in a position to test and accept the validity of the concepts outlined by men like Echeverría, Sarmiento, or Lastarria and who were likely to appreciate the intrinsic worth of the way in which Europeans went about the business of building houses, educating the young, or spending their leisure. There were, however, other urban groups, placed lower in the social scale, whose incomes were a fraction of the incomes earned by the average middle class family and whose political significance was notoriously circumscribed. These groups were mostly made up of independent artisans and manual workers of the tertiary sector. They constituted an urban working class in a nonindustrial society that drew most of its income from mining and agriculture; they were the nearest Latin American equivalent to the Parisian masses, and it is not surprising to note that the liberal and radical intellectuals who returned to the southern hemisphere after receiving an education in Europe addressed themselves to them. Hence it turned out that although the urban artisan or manual worker was unlikely to drink tea from English silver or eat his meals from French porcelain, he did nevertheless think French political ideas and espouse English economic principles. Liberty was the aim, applied to the realms of politics and economics; the great enemy was the central state with its interventionist bias, its tendency toward greater bureaucratic control, its traditional economic ideas, and its outmoded demands that adequate protection be given to the infant industries of the new republics.

No doubt with the welfare of the people at large primarily in mind, the apostles of European radical and liberal ideas in Latin America maintained that it was absurd for the new nations to attempt to compete in the international markets with the industrial producers of Europe, that it was cheaper and certainly more rational to accept the logic of international specialization. Even Sarmiento concerned himself with the problem and summarized the "progressive" view by explaining that, "we are neither industrialists nor navigators, so, for centuries to come, Europe will supply us with manufactures in exchange for our primary commodities; and we will both profit from such an exchange."[27] Presented in this way the issue appeared abundantly clear; to protect local industries was simply to subsidize inefficient producers at the expense of the mass of the people who would have to pay higher prices for their everyday necessities. Moreover, to impose a protectionist policy would have extended the power of the central government and this was anathema to those who, like the Europeanized intelligentsia of the time, identified a strong central government with the Bourbon colonial administration in particular or with monarchical institutions in general. To defend the concept of strong central administration became tantamount to defending the restoration of the monarchy, and therefore no great effort was required to convince popular opinion to resist such tendencies. Thus the urban working class and their radical and liberal mentors, acting in pursuit of straightforward progressive ends, adopted a position against the augmentation of central government power, against limitations on freedom, political or economic, and consequently against measures of protection for the infant industries of the new republics.

Simultaneously, but for different reasons, the most important economic pressure groups arrived at the same conclusion. The exporters of primary commodities and the importers of manufactured goods were almost by definition ardent supporters of *laissez-faire* liberalism because, unless they completely misunderstood their own immediate interest, they had no option but to oppose any tax or restriction on the free movement of goods across international frontiers.[28] In

[27] Sarmiento, *Facundo*, pp. 312-313. (author's translation.)

[28] Farmers may or may not support the tenets of free-trading liberalism; exporters of farm products have no such choice open to them. Throughout the second half of the nineteenth century, Chilean farm products continued to

this position, which they defended with zeal, they found themselves in the paradoxical company of the intelligentsia and the better organized radical working class groups of the times.

On the occasion of the reform of the Chilean customs ordinance, early in the decade of 1860, precisely such a coalition of interests became active in support of a lowering of tariffs. A number of historians have unfairly accused a French economist Jean Gustave Courcelle-Seneuil of influencing the Chilean government and generally the ruling circles of the country and convincing them of the need to establish what amounted to a regime of absolute free trade thereby severely damaging the few industries of the country and actually destroying the Chilean merchant marine.[29] However, an

---

find profitable outlets overseas, and the Chilean farming interest was unwavering in its support of free trade. The affluence characteristic of the period plus a reasonable rate of population growth resulted in a considerable increase of domestic consumption toward the end of the century. This change in market conditions as well as the threat of an important influx of cheaper farm products from Argentina forced the farming interest to change its stance and move toward an acceptance of fully-fledged protectionism. See Thomas C. Wright, "Agriculture and Protectionism in Chile, 1880-1930," *JLAS*, VII (May, 1975), 46-47; also Claudio Véliz, "La mesa de tres patas," *DE*, III, no. 1-2 (April-September, 1963), 231-247.

[29] According to Francisco Encina, for instance, "during the ten year period between 1860 and 1870, the Chilean merchant marine was obliterated. . . . Following faithfully the economic postulates of Courcelle-Seneuil, the Customs Ordinance of 1864 had abolished the national monopoly for the coasting trade replacing it with an absolute freedom to enter it for ships flying any foreign flag. . . . The folly of the President and the ruling aristocracy which though honest and sane, was also short-sighted, led to the destruction of the only chance that Chile had of retaining the principal place that years of orderly and wise government had earned for her amongst the nations of America." *Historia de Chile desde la prehistoria hasta 1891*, Santiago, 1942-1952, XIV, pp. 642-643. (author's translation.) According to Julio César Jobet, "the preaching of Courcelle-Seneuil helps to bring about the triumph of 'laissez-faire' at the expense of the national wealth. . . . The ideas of Courcelle-Seneuil inspired the Customs Ordinance of 31 October 1864, that eliminated the possibility of making an industrial nation out of Chile." *Ensayo crítico del desarrollo económico-social de Chile*, Santiago, 1955, pp. 44-45. (author's translation.) Other authors who have echoed the same views are, Martner, *Historia económica*, pp. 320-321; Guillermo Subercaseaux, "La protección de la marina

examination of the available evidence leads to different conclusions. In the first place, the initiative eventually leading to the reform of the customs ordinance was that of the government and not of the French economist. When consulted, Courcelle-Seneuil made a careful comparative study of the Chilean legislation and that of France, Great Britain, and the United States. The results of this study he published in a paper whose main conclusion was that no reform was needed "because I believe that when laws are adequate, it is best to keep them as they are. . . . Far from suggesting a reform of the Chilean Customs Ordinance, I think that it is superior to that of the other three countries studied, both from an economic point of view, from the point of view of commercial relations, and of the simplicity of procedure. It could very well serve as a model to the other countries when they decide to reform their legislation."[30] This was in 1856. Four years later, after Courcelle-Seneuil had travelled to France and returned to Chile once again, the government insisted on reforming the ordinances and formally instructed the French economist, who at the time was teaching political economy at the National Institute, to prepare a new customs ordinance for the country incorporating the most modern ideas on the subject. Pressed in this manner, the economist agreed and eventually completed a project of law that after some delay was discussed by Congress in 1864.

---

mercante nacional ante el Honorable Senado," *El Mercurio*, Santiago, 29 November 1916; Aníbal Pinto, *Chile, un caso de desarrollo frustrado*, Santiago, 1959, pp. 34-36; and especially the biographer of Courcelle-Seneuil, Leonardo Fuentealba, who concludes that "the influence of the French economist, considered within the general development of the national economy, was pernicious for Chile. With his admirable erudition he ensured the predominance of liberal and free trading doctrines at the time when the great imperialisms were trying to establish their universal hegemony. Shielded behind such wise theories, the Chilean oligarchy was able to hand over to foreign capitalists the principal sources of our national wealth in exchange for the undisturbed enjoyment of political power." "Courcelle-Seneuil en Chile, Errores del liberalismo económico," *AUCH*, series 4a, nos. 55 and 56, (1944), 101-206. (author's translation.)

[30] Claudio Véliz, *Historia de la Marina Mercante de Chile*, Santiago, 1961, p. 134. (author's translation.)

Courcelle-Seneuil was correctly regarded, in Europe as well as in South America, as one of the most ardent defenders of free trade and hence a man attentive to every possibility of extending this system that could arise in a country such as Chile. And yet, the project reaching Congress retained a number of mild protectionist features that were undoubtedly considered to be fully justified by this principal exponent of free-trading liberalism, but that nonetheless were bitterly denounced by the Radical and Liberal parties.

The suggestion that a small duty should be levied on the export of silver, copper, guano, and nitrate of soda included in the project of the law was attacked as "erroneous and pernicious" by a liberal deputy who thought that such duties should simply be eliminated.[31] Manuel Antonio Matta, one of the founders of the Radical party, objecting to the retention of some minor duties on the importation of manufactured goods, commented that, "such conduct on the part of the government would be shameful for our country; now that all the nations of the world are turning their backs on the old system we cannot return to the past abandoning the liberal system accepted by Britain, France, Germany, Italy, etc."[32] The project prepared by the French economist actually retained the monopoly of the coastal trade for vessels carrying the Chilean flag, but this privilege was abolished by the minister of finance who proudly justified his decision on grounds that would have made Richard Cobden cheer loudly indeed. The cheers were loud enough from the radical and liberal benches when this was known; Matta expressed his approbation of the ministerial decision, but added that the best solution to the problem of customs was not to reform the existing ordinance, but to abolish tariff barriers altogether and open the frontiers of Chile to the unimpeded flow of international trade. These views were warmly endorsed by the most influential daily newspaper of the country and a loyal supporter of the com-

[31] These were the views of Ambrosio Montt, liberal author and friend of Lastarria, who represented the agricultural province of Talca in Congress. *El Ferrocarril*, 26 September 1862. (author's translation.)

[32] Véliz, *Historia*, pp. 140-141. (author's translation.)

mercial interests at stake; *El Mercurio* commented editorially opposing a proposed duty of 25 percent on the importation of ready-made European clothing and footwear, "instead of taking a long step forward, we will move backwards if we are to accept what the government has proposed. Instead of listening to the people who are studying ways of abolishing customs altogether, the government is trying to increase the tariff barriers. . . . the abolition of the national monopoly in the coasting trade . . . is an idea we applaud without reserve."[33]

So the ill-used French economist was very far from being the villain of the story; although a convinced free-trading liberal, he produced a reformed tariff that the Chilean radicals and liberals considered too protectionist by half. Here again, the fiery reformers and the pragmatic commercial pressure groups coincided in opposing the protectionist measures and enthusiastically espousing the total abolition of customs.

A few hundred miles east and twenty-five years later, *El Obrero*, an important left-wing newspaper of Buenos Aires, published an article in which it explained to its working class readers that the protectionist system was a "tremendous capitalist barbarity, that capriciously raises the prices of the most essential products with the following objectives: (1) To free the upper classes from paying taxes by shifting these to the shoulders of the workers. (2) To create a special class of industrialists. (3) To expropriate the independent workers and artisans. (4) To accumulate capital. (5) To exploit the labour force as much as possible."[34]

Almost diametrically opposed to what *El Obrero* stood for, *La Prensa*, one of the most august defenders of the commercial interests, offered its readers a similar fare stating that,

[33] Véliz, *Historia*, p. 143. (author's translation.) *El Mercurio*, Valparaiso, 20 July 1864.

[34] José Panettieri, *Los trabajadores en tiempos de la inmigración masiva en Argentina 1870-1910*, Buenos Aires, 1966, pp. 62-63. (author's translation.) The article quoted appeared in the issue no. 9 of 21 February 1891. In issue no. 4 of 17 January 1891 another article appeared entitled "Abolition of the pernicious protectionist system."

"our protectionism has resulted in tariff barriers, in prohibitive and aggressive [import] duties which invariably have greater effects on the most popular consumer goods. All this so that one or very few rudimentary industries can sell their inferior goods at prices which at best are the same as the ones for the imported products. In other words, this is the exploitation of the consumer."[35]

Such examples abound and indicate that although there is little doubt the liberalization of Latin American trade generally was to the advantage of foreign commercial and industrial interests, it would be a mistake to think that these interests had to exert exceptional efforts to impose their liberal policies on a reluctant Latin America. It was quite the contrary; their task was easy as they could hardly improve on the performance of local merchants and radical intellectuals.

The "liberal pause" lasted as long as the prosperity on which it was founded. Its first major setback came with the Great Depression of 1929; its end with the economic malaise of the sixties that forced the countries of Latin America, some with greater ease than others, to accept the challenge of returning to their own centralist mainstream.

[35] The article appeared in *La Prensa* of 20 June 1910. See Panettieri, *Los trabajadores*, pp. 64-65. The author notes the coincidence of views between the working-class leaders and organs of opinion and those of the well-to-do commercial interests and explains that in Argentina, during the last decades of the nineteenth century and the first of the twentieth, the worker regarded the industrialist as a man after quick profits who, enjoying the support of the central state, could secure huge gains producing merchandise of inferior quality that he sold at inflated prices.

9

Latitudinarian Religious Centralism

Hobsbawm has described the transition to a more secular society in nineteenth-century Europe as the most profound of all contemporary ideological changes. Religion, he explains, "from being something like the sky, from which no man can escape and which contains all that is above the earth, became something like a bank of clouds, a large but limited and changing feature of the human firmament."[1] It should do no violence to the inner meaning of this metaphor to use it to explain that in Latin America the sky has remained cloudless for almost five centuries. There have been no transformations, no dissidence, or nonconformity comparable to those that so dramatically altered the European firmament. This is significant in the context of this study because of the role religious nonconformity played in shaping the western European historical moment that proved such a bountiful source of models deemed worthy of imitation by Latin Americans. The bank of clouds modified not only itself, but the whole western European sky; its presence was inescapable and it would take a brave student of the period to try and discover a principal aspect of social and political life totally unaffected by it. Morcover, even a cursory examination of the changes implied in Hobsbawm's metaphor will immediately trace the origins of these processes beyond the frontiers of the nineteenth century at least to the Reformation and the English Revolution of 1640 and onward to the struggles associated with social reform, religious toleration, political freedom, and the rise of the modern liberal and radical movements—Marxism and so-

[1] Hobsbawm, *Revolution*, p. 217.

cial democracy. It is not possible to study the gestation of any of these momentous concepts and ideologies without encountering along the way the vigorous influence of religious nonconformity or its near relation, political dissidence.[2]

One of the consequences, perhaps unintended, of these processes was the growth of a concept of liberty and toleration commonly associated with English liberalism. There are many explanations of this phenomenon, but one that may have received less attention than it deserves postulates that toleration in England became a necessity after the attempt to impose religious uniformity had failed.[3] Toleration, seen in this way, was the result of the pragmatic acceptance of diversity after all efforts to eliminate it had proved unsuccessful. If this is true even in part, and if, as it appears to be well-established, there is a functional relationship between religious dissidence and the principal libertarian movements of the last three centuries, it would be tempting to speculate on what would have been the political consequences of the achievement in the sixteenth century of that elusive uniformity so fervently desired by the Tudor monarchs and the established church. Of course, this being an ahistorical proposition, for which I apologize, anything could have happened, or nothing at all; we simply do not know and have no way of knowing. Yet, fully conscious of the limitations of an hypothesis contrary to a fact, I would nevertheless like to suggest that had religious uniformity been achieved in the sixteenth century the political history of England and Europe would have been completely different, so different as to re-

---

[2] As Walzer has argued, the methodical, impersonal, disciplined political activity characteristic of modern revolutionary parties dates from Calvin and not from Machiavelli; "it was the Calvinists who first switched the emphasis of political thought from the prince to the saint (or the band of saints. . . . what Calvinists said of the saint, other men would later say of the citizen; the same sense of civic virtue, of discipline and duty lies behind the two names. . . . the diligent activism of the saints—Genevan, Huguenot, Dutch, Scottish and Puritan—marked the transformation of politics into work," and, perhaps most important of all, "in politics as in religion, the saints were oppositional men and their primary task was the destruction of traditional order." Michael Walzer, *The Revolution of the Saints*, London, 1966, pp. 2-3.

semble what actually occurred in Latin America, where religious uniformity was effectively secured and institutionalized from the sixteenth century through the regalist administration of the Indies.

The centralism of Latin Americans is as evident in the style and practice of their religion as it is in more worldy matters; their Catholicism has survived virtually unchallenged for almost five centuries and retains to this day its overwhelming dominance.[4] This fact is not unique in the modern world, but taken together with other manifestations of a pervasive centralist tradition, it invites a number of related observations: first, that Latin America has never had the formative historical experience of religious nonconformity; second, that the vigorous anticlericalism that flourished from the nineteenth century onward cannot be considered a substitute for it; third, that Latin America is the most extensive and populous region of the world never to have generated a systematic, "exportable" religion as distinct from cults of restricted local significance; fourth, that the absence of nonconformity is an additional manifestation of the centralist temper of society; the

---

[3] Ursula Henriques, *Religious Toleration in England, 1787-1833*, London, 1961. Henriques opens her study with the statement that "The development of religious toleration in England was an ultimate and wholly unintended consequence of the Reformation." According to her, it was the existence of relatively powerful or stubborn, or sufficiently numerous, groups that made the acceptance of diversity ultimately necessary. Certainly there were voices raised in favor of toleration all along, and Dr. Henriques mentions them, but the existence of those groups that so blatantly disrupted the desired uniformity under an established church highlighted the political advantages of toleration.

[4] It would be difficult to overlook such an overwhelmingly obvious fact, and this has not happened in the past. More recently, Paul Johnson, in his ambitious study of Christianity, has written about Latin America that "this huge continent, where paganism was quickly expunged, where great cities, universities and sub-cultures were soon established, where Christianity was united and monopolistic, carefully protected by the State from any hint of heresy, schism or rival, and where the clergy were innumerable, rich and privileged, made virtually no distinctive contribution to the Christian message and insight in over four centuries. Latin America exuded a long, conformist silence." Johnson, *Christianity*, p. 407.

centralism of Latin Americans is mirrored in their religious habits and institutions as faithfully as their social, economic, and political arrangements.

The hundred years following independence from Spain were marked by the emergence of a vigorous anticlericalism that drew strength and inspiration from Iberian and European sources as well as from local irritants. But this Latin American anticlericalism from its very beginnings exhibited an emphatic juridical and political character; it never quite developed as a religious phenomenon. Rather, as a careful student of this problem has noted, it showed itself "an 'anticlericalism' which was not anti-religious, but merely sought to deprive the Church of those means and privileges which enabled it to exercise political power."[5]

There was no dearth of conflictive issues to encourage this politically colored view of the established Church; during the struggle for independence the Vatican and the ecclesiastical hierarchy in the Indies supported the royalist cause, and after the ousting of the Spanish forces they found themselves subjected to the unpopularity reserved for the vanquished.[6] The

[5] Lloyd Mecham, *Church and State*, p. 417. Luis Pereira Barreto, a well-known anticlerical thinker, proposed the "suppression of theology," but took care to remind his readers of the eminent services that the Church had accomplished adding that this elimination—in the best Comtian manner—could be effected "without offending the priests." Cruz Costa, *History of Ideas*, p. 92.

[6] In an encyclical of 24 September 1824, less than three months before the decisive battle of Ayacucho, Pope Leo XII made a statement of his position with respect to the movement for independence. This began by lamenting "the impunity with which malevolent revolutionaries are allowed to indulge in unbridled licence . . . and the propagation of incendiary books and pamphlets which has accompanied the formation of those *juntas* which have emerged like locusts and in which everything that is most sacrilegeous and blasphemous of all the heretical sects . . . is concentrated." In order to remedy such a situation, His Holiness instructed the archbishops and bishops of America to "describe and explain the august and distinguished qualities that characterize my well-beloved son Ferdinand, Catholic King of Spain, whose sublime virtue has moved him to place the lustre of religion and the happiness of his people before the splendour of his own grandeur." See Miguel Luis Amunátegui, "Encíclicas de los Papas Pío VII y León XII contra la independencia de la América Española," in *La iglesia frente a la emancipación americana*,

understandable enmity of the new regimes was further augmented by the problems arising from the exercise of the *Patronato real* to which the republican rulers considered themselves entitled as heirs of the imperial administration. There were also difficulties with ecclesiastical property, the control of education, and the civil status of churchmen. As the century advanced, and despite the political and juridical character of the anticlericalism of governments, the clashes between church and state and, at a more general level, between the emerging radical and liberal movements and the Catholic groups became increasingly bitter, occasionally leading to armed conflict in which both sides indulged in reprisals and counterreprisals of indescribable ferocity, either in the name of progress and reason or for the sake of one of the more accessible Christian virtues. After a century of anticlerical activity, the Catholic Church was disestablished in Ecuador, Cuba, Brazil, Chile, Mexico, Honduras, Uruguay, Panama, and Nicaragua; in most countries the state assumed control of the educational system; lay cemeteries were established everywhere; fees were abolished for religious ceremonies, and civil marriage was universally instituted.

The central state and its power were anathema for the liberal and radical reformers who espoused the anticlerical laws, and yet, the passage of those laws resulted in a considerable augmentation of that central power. The control of marriages, births, and deaths; the control of education and many beneficent institutions, hospitals, and the like were taken from the Church and handed over to the central state with the resulting increase in bureaucratic control. This paradox was

ed. Hernan Ramírez Necochea, Santiago, 1960, pp. 18-19. (author's translation.) Considering that everybody in Europe, except Ferdinand VII, knew by 1824 that the American colonies had been lost, the decision by Pope Leo XII to issue such a forthright declaration precisely at that moment is inexplicable. Mecham has noted that "because of the very absurdity of the action, the encyclical was declared by some to be apocryphal. . . . Yet, the Cardinal Secretary when questioned did not deny the authenticity of the encyclical. But whatever the reason for its issuance, its publication certainly did not facilitate the establishment of a working agreement between Rome and America." See Lloyd Mecham, *Church and State*, pp. 77-78.

noticed by contemporaries. Lastarria, for instance, thought that "education was an extension of individual responsibility, and thus ought to be free of state control," but he also believed that the state had the specific obligation of "removing obstacles to progress and thus must intervene to revolutionize the ineffectual Catholic school system. Thus, by reasoning markedly 'Jesuitical'—although Lastarria would have hated such a description—the leading Chilean Positivist tried to explain away the apparent paradox of laissez-faire reformers working for state control of education."[7]

By the middle of the twentieth century the major political and juridical objectives of the anticlerical movement had all been accomplished, and yet in each of the countries that had so dramatically experienced the full impact of victorious anticlericalism, the Catholic Church remained without a shadow of doubt the central and dominant religious institution; the only *de facto* national religion.[8] In spite of their evident success, liberalism, radicalism, and anticlericalism had not eroded the religious supremacy of Catholicism. There are some, no doubt, who may see in this rather obvious fact a reflection of spiritual virtues of one type or another, but it would seem more plausible to regard it as a consequence, first, of the essentially nonreligious character of the anticlerical challenge and, second, of the pervasive centralism of Latin American society. Latin American anticlericalism did not challenge Catholicism *qua* religion, and it did not *per se* ad-

---

[7] Thomas Bader, "Positivistic Thought," pp. 385-386.

[8] The Catholic Church occupies this dominant position even in countries such as Chile, which has the largest non-Catholic minority in the region. In fact, Chile also has the most favorable ratio of inhabitants to priests with 3,443 Chileans per priest, while in neighboring Argentina the proportion is 4,772 inhabitants per priest, in Mexico, 5,947 per priest, and in Cuba, the opposite extreme, only one priest per 38,003 inhabitants. If one considers that in the Irish Republic there is one priest per 551 inhabitants, the idea could be entertained that Latin American Catholicism is less dependent on a numerous clergy, or that the relative scarcity of priests, as compared with Ireland, is a distant result of the secularization following the success of the anticlerical movements. The figures are for 1969 and have been taken from Frederick C. Turner, *Catholicism and Political Development in Latin America*, Chapel Hill, N.C., 1971, pp. 15-17.

vance alternative doctrinal or philosophical solutions to religious problems. Of course there was a surfeit of humanist, rationalist, and other related groupings that tried to fill the vacuum they hoped would be left after the demise of institutionalized Catholicism, but these were marginal to the main thrust of Latin American anticlericalism and their influence was slight. There were no Latin American Cromwells or Wesleys; anticlericalism proved to be more of a political than a religious challenge. It was unlikely therefore to evolve into a militant dissidence organized around a hard core of doctrinal belief precisely because it originated from a fundamental rejection of such concepts as valid foundations for political action.

The absence of a doctrinal commitment or a coherent and well-defined ideology characteristic of the diffuse, populist, and successful anticlericalism of Latin Americans would certainly not apply to the upholders of the positivist "Religion of Humanity." During the second half of the nineteenth century and until the First World War, faithful followers of Comte entertained the hope that their creed would replace both Catholicism and anticlericalism.[9] The Religion of Humanity, as is well-known, was the result of Auguste Comte's later years when, though rejecting the traditional religions based on dogma and revelation, he constructed a positivist one with humanity occupying the place of the deity and with an organization and ritual patterned after that of the Catholic Church. Humanity was symbolized by a statue of a woman "of about thirty years of age," according to the precise instructions of the master, with a child in her arms. The whole effect was reminiscent of the cult of the Virgin Mary although

---

[9] Miguel Lemos, the leader of the Brazilian positivists at the end of the nineteenth century, was convinced that Catholicism was dead as a social force in his country and this partly explained why the clergy looked upon positivism "as a usurping rival, growing in strength and influence among those destined to predominate in a more or less near future." Quoted by Cruz Costa, *History of Ideas*, pp. 166-167. Luis Pereira Barreto also thought that positivism was a doctrine "capable of replacing to advantage the tutelage that the Church exercised over the Brazilian intellect." Cruz Costa, *History of Ideas*, pp. 95-96.

the expression on the face of Humanity was intended to be different from that usually found in Catholic statuary.[10] Strongly influenced by Catholic writers such as Bonald and De Maistre who believed that a religious framework for society was absolutely indispensable, Comte was nevertheless unwilling to accept any of the existing "unscientific" religions and proceeded to invent his own, retaining from Catholicism the universality, structure, and flexibility he so much admired and substituting his own positive dogma for "superstitious theological belief."

Positivism in various forms was a major influence in practically every major Latin American country during the half century before the First World War, but this influence was most clearly seen in Brazil, Chile, Mexico, and Argentina. Certainly the positivists in these countries exerted an influence out of all proportion to their numbers, which never exceeded a few thousand. In Chile and Argentina their adherents constituted for a while a plurality among the intelligentsia and helped to shape the policies of the radical movement. In Mexico the positivists played an important role during the "Porfiriato," while in Brazil they were involved crucially in the overthrow of the monarchy, the politicization of the military, and the establishment of the republic.[11]

That Comte should have had followers in Latin America is perhaps not surprising considering the sway that European and notably French culture had over the new republics, but that his Brazilian disciples should have embraced the positivist faith with the ardor they did is astonishing even to this day.[12] Their enthusiasm led them at times to share a sincere

[10] See Alexander J. Ellis, *Auguste Comte's Religion of Humanity*, London, 1880, pp. 60-62.

[11] See Leopoldo Zea, *El positivismo en México*, México, 1943; William D. Raat, "Leopoldo Zea and Mexican Positivism: A Reappraisal," *HAHR*, XLVIII (1968), 1-18; Ricaurte Soler, *El positivismo argentino*, Buenos Aires, 1968; for a study of one of Chile's principal positivists, Oyarzún, *Lastarria*; for a critical view, Pedro Nolasco Cruz, *Bilbao y Lastarria*, Santiago, 1944; João C. de Oliveira Torres, *O positivismo no Brasil*, Petrópolis, 1943; Ivan Monteiro de Barros Lins, *Historia no positivismo no Brasil*, São Paulo, 1964.

[12] Benjamin Constant wrote to his wife from the Paraguayan battlefields

concern for what they correctly regarded as the indifferent development of the Religion of Humanity in its birthplace. "Paris remains almost alien to the new faith," complained Miguel Lemos, adding that the Parisian proletariat "increasingly subjected to the influence of communist aberrations and anarchist hatreds" did not seem aware of the fact that a French philosopher had "resolved all the great problems on which depend the integration of the working class into modern society."[13] It was an unequal contest; Catholicism and communism prospered while the Brazilian Church of Humanity or, as it was called locally, the *Igreja Positiva Brasileira* just managed to survive into the twentieth century. The last time its adherents were listed separately in the national census was in 1940, and they numbered 1,299, a decline of 28 from the membership reported half a century earlier. Nine years later in 1949, the number of Protestants in Brazil was well over one million and a half while altogether just under 95 percent of the total population described itself as members of the Catholic Church.[14]

Positivism undoubtedly had a determining influence on Brazilian political life during the years at the turn of the century; it inscribed its magnificent motto, "Order and Progress" on the national flag; it gave the military academies a scientific justification, almost a mandate, to intervene in politics,

---

of 1867: "you mean more to me—much more—than did Clotilde de Vaux to the wise and honoured Auguste Comte. . . . I am a follower of his doctrines, I accept his principles and beliefs: the Religion of Humanity is my religion. I believe in it with all my heart," while Miguel Lemos, who became a positivist in Paris together with the Chilean Jorge Lagarrigue, described his experience exultantly; "Blessed the day I decided to come to Paris . . . the holy city . . . and enter into the first temple of the new religion, to hear the word of the Master's disciple and to become a convert." The master's disciple was Emile Littré. Cruz Costa, *History of Ideas*, pp. 87, 103.

[13] Cruz Costa, *History of Ideas*, pp. 151-152.

[14] T. Lynn Smith, *Brazil, People and Institutions*, Baton Rouge, 1963, p. 513. Between 1925 and 1961, the number of Protestants in Brazil increased from 101,454 to 4,071,643, or 6.06 percent of the total population. See Thomas C. Bruneau, *The Political Transformation of the Brazilian Catholic Church*, Cambridge, 1974, p. 62.

and it helped to rationalize and make respectable the idea of an enlightened dictatorship aimed at the attainment of the common good. Much could be written about the nature of this complex influence, but for the purposes of this explanation, there are three aspects that must be highlighted. First, positivism failed absolutely to overshadow, let alone replace the Catholic Church. Like anticlericalism generally, the Religion of Humanity was embraced by an elite drawn from the cultured and prosperous urban middle sectors, and it never succeeded in obtaining the type of popular support usually associated with the generation and growth of new religions. A list of the anticlerical and positivist leadership in Brazil, and elsewhere in Latin America, would go a considerable way toward the making of a bourgeois-rationalist Almanack de Gotha; the characteristic populist dimension of religious nonconformity is absent from the Brazilian and the Latin American experience of the Religion of Humanity.

Secondly, the Religion of Humanity was not a Latin American, but a French creation, and it retained its Parisian, Comtian character all along. As Leopoldo Zea observed, the positivist *científicos* of the Díaz period "sought to Europeanize the natives without taking into account Mexico's conditions."[15] Comte, of course, had no doubts whatsoever about the appropriateness of such a policy, and although he claimed universality for the new religion, he did nothing to dilute its strong French character. For instance, in his detailed instructions for the building of the temples of the Religion of Humanity, he specified that the grand avenue spanning the distance between the entrance lodge and the main nave should "in every country . . . be directed towards Paris."[16]

[15] Raat, *Mexican Positivism*, pp. 15-16.

[16] Commenting on this, one of his followers wrote that this might create difficulties at first "on account of the shape of the earth, for temples in Australia, for example, which would probably be overcome by drawing a great circle between the given place and Paris, and taking the direction of a tangent to it at the place." See Ellis, *Religion of Humanity*, p. 62. The dependent, Francophile character of Brazilian positivism remained throughout a feature of the movement. Outlining a plan of action that they hoped would revive their fortunes in Brazil, Teixeira Mendes and Lemos ended it with the statement "we

The Brazilian disciples did not improve on the master's idea, and toward the end of the century they found themselves reduced to the rather sorry plight of hoping that Boulangism would succeed in establishing a "dictatorial republic" in France and thus rescue the movement from the doldrums. The Religion of Humanity had little chance of spreading outside a restricted circle; it was emphatically a European transplant, unintelligible to the majority of the population and regarded with suspicion even by the politicians who profited from its disconcerting support.

Thirdly, a feature of the Religion of Humanity that may have had a more lasting and pervasive influence was the encouragement it gave to the idea that intractable social and economic problems could be solved by establishing an enlightened positivist dictatorship. Such a regime would of necessity reflect the "intellectual integrity and historical homogeneity" of Brazil, successfully preserved from the contagion of Protestantism and the dangers of anarchic dissolution by the resilience of Catholicism during the revolutionary upheavals. The positivist leaders thought that conditions in Brazil during the closing years of the century were specially favorable because they detected "a great need for political unity" and concluded this could only be achieved under a centralist dictatorship that was for Brazilians "as inevitable as the air we breathe." These were the opinions of Lemos, Teixeira Mendes, and their friends who were convinced that "only the adoption without delay, of the dictatorial policy counselled by Auguste Comte . . . could forestall the terrible social struggles in store." They went on to describe the positivist dictatorship as one based on the establishment of "scientific-industrial republics; in other words, nations completely free of theology and militarism. In these republics, faith will be replaced by science, not supported by privilege, but by its own prestige; industry will not be in the hands of monopolies; universal brotherhood will permit armies and

---

hope that our progress will have its effects on Paris, on whose regeneration depends the regeneration of the whole world." Cruz Costa, *History of Ideas*, p. 162.

navies to be dispensed with." It is not difficult to find Comtian sources for such views. After all, it was the French thinker who maintained that the only temporal leader of any eminence in his time was "the noble Czar, who, whilst he gives the immense empire of Russia all the progress compatible with its actual condition, preserves it by his energy and prudence from useless ferment."[17] This aspect of Comte's thought must have received moral nourishment during the time he served as private secretary to the count of Saint-Simon whose particular brand of utopian socialism was permeated with a faith in the effectiveness of authoritarian paternalism. As Hobsbawm has pointed out, the Saint-Simonians never ceased in their search for "an enlightened despot who might carry out their proposals," and at one time they thought they had finally discovered him in the improbable figure of Mohammed Ali, the Egyptian ruler.[18] At first Egypt under Mohammed Ali may appear as unlikely a setting for Saint-Simonian socialism as Latin America for the establishment of a positivist dictatorship, but in fact, as early as 1854, Comte writes in his *Système de politique positive* that in the new republics of Latin America conditions are particularly favorable for the transition to what he describes as a "Positive polity." He then predicts that even before France is able to rid herself of parliamentarism, the new republics will move "directly towards sociocracy," their armies easily changing themselves into *gendarmeries* as soon as the anxieties about foreign invasions disappear.[19] As it is now obvious, this prophecy has been fulfilled, though in ways that the distinguished thinker did not envision. The majority of the countries of Latin America live today under diverse types of dictatorship or single-party systems while France still retains her

---

[17] See Miguel Lemos and Raimundo Teixeira Mendes, *A ultima crise*, Rio de Janeiro, 1891, quoted by Cruz Costa, *History of Ideas*, pp. 172-173, and Auguste Comte, *The Catechism of Positive Religion*, trans. by Richard Congreve, London, 1858, p. 3.

[18] Hobsbawm, *Revolution*, p. 244.

[19] Auguste Comte, *Système de politique positive*, Paris, 1851-1854, IV, 489-490. (author's translation.)

parliamentary regime albeit often modified by constitutional reforms. Also, perhaps with the qualified exception of Brazil, it would be bizarre to attribute the proliferation of authoritarian governments to the teachings of Comte and his Latin American followers.

If victorious anticlericalism and ardent positivism failed signally to dismantle the religious foundations of Catholic centralism, the syncretisms of the hinterland and the colorful messianic cults and folkloric religions could hardly be expected to do better. Most of these have to be excluded from consideration simply because they are virtually unknown outside those parts of Latin America where they may have achieved a degree of significance.[20] Many cults and movements of this type exist and have existed in the past in Latin America, but none has succeeded in projecting an influence beyond their immediate locality,[21] and most certainly none could possibly be regarded as even the precursor of a serious religious challenge to Catholicism. By far the most important of these cults have been the messianic movements of the Bra-

[20] These cults of considerable local importance appear to be more frequently found outside the Iberian tradition in Latin America. The Ras Tafari cult in Jamaica, for instance, has been the object of academic interest. At least until the death of Haile Selassie, Rastafarians shared only two beliefs, that the Emperor of Ethiopia was the living God and that salvation for Jamaican negroes would only come through repatriation to Africa; "on all other matters the opinion of the brethren vary widely. . . . they are also very disorganized and lacking in leadership." Roy Augier and others, *Report on the Ras Tafari Movement in Kingston, Jamaica*, Kingston, 1960, pp. 17-18. See also Leonard E. Barrett, *The Rastafarians*, London, 1977.

[21] Although the reverse situation is encountered occasionally, as was the case with the millenarist ideas of Father Manuel Lacunza, a Chilean Jesuit who, after the expulsion of his order by Charles III, lived for over 30 years in Imola in the papal states where he wrote the three volumes of his *La venida del Mesías en gloria y majestad*. This work was published posthumously and went through several editions in many languages attaining notable popularity in European circles while remaining virtually unknown in America. One of the commentators of Lacunza's work considers the Jesuit's eschatological bent places him in the mainstream of an intellectual tradition that includes authors such as Campanella, Postel, Jurieu, Vieyra, Bengel, Bloy, and Soloviev. See Manuel Lacunza, *La venida del Mesías en gloria y majestad*, ed. by Mario Góngora, Santiago, 1969.

zilian hinterland, and these have characteristics that are difficult, if not impossible, to reconcile with those associated with European religious nonconformity. Their followers were not, as the Calvinists were, for instance, "oppositional men" in religion or politics; on the contrary, the messianic cults have been fundamentally conservative in politics as well as religion although their loyalty and piety were occasionally expressed in unorthodox ways.[22]

Among the numerous messianic movements of the Brazilian hinterland, those of Antonio Conselheiro and Father Cicero have undoubtedly been the most significant. Conselheiro, who was not an ordained priest, gained international fame during the last decades of the nineteenth century as the messiah of Canudos, his "Holy City." For many years he carried on activities largely regarded as beneficial by the authorities as they consisted mainly of the organization of voluntary labor for the repair and reconstruction of churches, cemeteries, and the like. He was "a wandering servant of the Church, eagerly encouraged by local priests," but hardly a Jan Hus or a Martin Luther. According to those who knew him well, Conselheiro "never questioned the doctrines of the Church, the efficacy of her sacraments, or the spiritual authority of her virtuous priests,"[23] but he did question the doctrines, efficacy, and spiritual authority of the republican government of Brazil that he thought impious and sinful. He especially objected to the republican policy of separation of Church and state that had annulled the Church's traditional jurisdiction over births, marriages, and burials. The conflict worsened in 1893 when

[22] The blessed Lourenço, a disciple of Father Cicero, appears to be the one well-known exception, as he advocated forms of communal ownership to which the conservative label could not possibly be applied. However, the rest of the Brazilian messiahs have not attacked private property nor the privileges of the rich, "they only condemn the use to which rich people put their money, and their lack of charity . . . (the messianic movements) do not propose the modification of the existing social order." María Isaura Pereira de Queiroz, *Historia y etnología de los movimientos mesiánicos*, México, 1969, pp. 117-119. (author's translation.)

[23] Ralph Della Cava, "Brazilian Messianism and National Institutions: A Reappraisal of Canudos and Joaseiro," *HAHR*, xlviii (1968), 407-408.

Conselheiro advised his many followers not to pay taxes to the central government, and the government responded by sending a military force against Canudos. Four military expeditions had to be sent before the Holy City was finally destroyed, and this was after all its defenders had been killed. Conselheiro himself died of wounds a few days before the final collapse.[24]

Among the leaders of Brazilian messianic movements, Father Cicero was the only ordained priest. A loyal supporter of the ecclesiastical establishment, his difficulties with the Church arose from his having allegedly witnessed a miracle in his Holy City of Joaseiro. At first this was received enthusiastically by members of the clergy who even organized pilgrimages to Joaseiro and bombarded the Brazilian press with news of the extraordinary event. The alleged miracle was that the host that Father Cicero was administering to a woman turned to blood, presumably Christ's blood. At first the local priests, with the knowledge of the ecclesiastical authorities

[24] The epic history of Antonio Conselheiro forms the plot of one of the great works of Latin American literature *Os sertões* by Euclydes da Cunha, first published in 1902. Euclydes da Cunha was a positivist reporter accompanying the expeditionary force sent by the republic against the Holy City of Canudos. See Pereira de Queiroz, *Movimientos mesiánicos*, pp. 101-103. Under the monarchy, Conselheiro had no difficulty in establishing a flourishing community, the Holy City of Good Jesus of Itapicuru, where he resided for twelve years. The monarchical regime was satisfied to let him be, knowing that he was a stabilizing, even a moral, influence in those distant territories. The republic was less amenable and Conselheiro's attitude also hardened. Popular resistance to republicanism and the survival of strong monarchical feelings could be ingredients of an as yet unwritten chapter in the history of nineteenth-century Latin America. There are numerous incidents that liberal and republican historians have tended to dismiss and that may, taken together, reflect a significant phenomenon of monarchical survivals. For instance, in 1860, an otherwise obscure Frenchman walked into the Indian controlled territory of southern Chile and had himself proclaimed King Orllie-Antoine I of Araucanía and Patagonia. He was eventually arrested by the Chilean authorities, declared insane, and expelled from the country. During his brief reign, however, he managed to secure considerable support from Araucanian tribes, which even half a century after independence still appear to have nurtured a loyalty for the monarchical institutions. See Armando Braun Menéndez, *El reino de Araucanía y Patagonia*, Buenos Aires, 1967.

and no doubt impelled by their hostility toward the spread of Protestantism and rationalism, readily championed the miracle of Joaseiro hoping that this would help in their struggle against these rivals. They found their earliest and staunchest supporters among the local Catholic landowners, merchants, and professional men, and only much later among laborers and peasants. The movement of Joaseiro originated and evolved within the established ecclesiastical structure.[25] It was only some years later, after waves of pilgrims had given it a distinctly populist character, that Father Cicero found himself the undisputed leader of a movement that virtually controlled the State of Ceará; his Holy City of Joaseiro had well over 30,000 inhabitants, and his followers numbered at least three times as many. It was partly this popularity that threatened to get out of hand, and partly the influence of the republican government, oversensitive to this type of movement after the tragic experience with Conselheiro, that prompted the Catholic Church officially to condemn the alleged miracle of Joaseiro and to suspend Father Cicero. The messianic leader

[25] Della Cava, *Brazilian Messianism*, p. 410. The nationalistic mood of the Brazilian clergy and the consequent rejection of the excessive Europeanization of the middle decades of the nineteenth century, may have played an important role in the evolution of the Brazilian messianic movements, especially with respect to their acceptance by the ecclesiastical establishment. Graduates from local seminaries in the decades of 1870 and 1880 reflected this nationalistic spiritual revival. They were, as one student of the period has put it, "zealous, perhaps overzealous men. Educated at a time when the Church of Rome was defensive and apologetic, this new Brazilian secular clergy also reflected western European Catholicism's unflagging hostility towards Masonry, Positivism, and Protestantism." As these locally trained priests increased in numbers, the scarcely veiled criticisms against the Europeans who staffed the seminaries and controlled the missions of the backlands became more evident. The Brazilian messianic movements at the end of the nineteenth century can be better understood if considered against this background of growing nationalism bound with an open commitment to this special kind of spiritual revival. The heartiness with which the clergy first supported Conselheiro and Father Cicero was probably a consequence of this nationalistic mood that saw in the otherwise simplistic efforts of these self-styled prophets, a truly Brazilian "populist" brand of religion that could be of help to the local inhabitants while not challenging doctrinal orthodoxy. See Della Cava, *Brazilian Messianism*, p. 406.

responded, not by rebelling against this decision but by humbly addressing himself to the ecclesiastical hierarchy in Rio de Janeiro and Rome, eventually travelling to Rome himself in 1898 to place his case before the pope in an effort to secure his reinstatement as a priest. This was not granted, but he was allowed to return to Joaseiro and live in his Holy City where he died in 1934, revered to the point of veneration by his many thousands of followers.

It needs a special type of bias to see either in Conselheiro or Father Cicero the leaders of a religious challenge to the Catholic Church.[26] No doubt these movements are of the greatest interest and importance; they may even reflect anomalies in the social arrangements of the regions where they appeared, but it is unrealistic to see in them the Latin American equivalent of western European religious nonconformity. They have been almost without exception conservative in religion and reactionary in politics. None of them was able, indeed, never tried, to construct a systematic ideological framework; in fact, none of them has survived the disappearance of their founders.[27] Furthermore, they have never had more than local significance, and their leaders have never claimed, even when at the zenith of their popularity, to be laying the foundations for a new religion or for a dissenting sect that could be remotely construed as a threat to the dominance of the Catholic Church.

This last consideration is of particular significance seen

[26] Vittorio Lanternari, in his book *The Religions of the Oppressed*, New York, 1963, adduces that although these messianic movements "profess strict adherence to Catholic doctrine and to the papacy, as in the case of the cult led by Father Cicero, in practice, however, they oppose both official Christianity and the present structure of society, with its class oppression and its political leaders, who are also powerful land-owners and wield despotic and arbitrary authority," p. 186.

[27] Some residual manifestations are worth mentioning. In Brazil, especially, where the "Sebastianism" of Portugal has taken roots, there are many people in the interior who still hope for a return to life of Father Cicero and João Maria, another local prophet, contemporary with Conselheiro. These revivalist cults, however, are but the shadow of the original messianic movement. Lanternari, *Religions*, p. 187.

against the notion that sects have played a crucial role in the shaping of Western religious and political society.[28] Commenting on a remark by Montesquieu on the frequency with which piety, tolerance, and commerce are found in close association, a keen student of these problems has written that the piety may be considered, partially at least, a sectarian phenomenon and that tolerance was a condition "which only the emergence of strategically influential, but socially deviant, religious interest-groups—namely sects—made necessary."[29] This view would coincide with that of Henriques, mentioned earlier, on the historical development of religious toleration in England. If uniformity proves impossible, toleration may well become an unavoidable virtue. The growth and prosperity of militant sectarianism would then be a necessary condition for toleration to emerge. And if not sects, then some other form of nonconformist grouping, "strategically influential but socially deviant." Conversely, in the absence of a meaningful challenge, be it religious nonconformity or political dissidence, toleration would appear to be unnecessary. These observations are made, of course, from a western European vantage point, and their applicability rests on the assumption that the European sequence must be repeated with the same protagonists, or as nearly as possible, if similar results are to be obtained elsewhere. Moreover, this process would be regarded as a dynamic one, the outcome of the interaction of many factors, a process that begins with the uniformity of a Catholic Europe and becomes diversified through a series of successful challenges to that central dominance. It proceeds from one Church to many, and these in turn are the mature results of the evolution of sectarian militancy and dissent into many modes of conformity and toleration.

A mechanical application of these experiences and assumptions to the modern history of Latin America would lead to

---

[28] See Bryan Wilson, *Religion in Secular Society*, London, 1966, pt. 4, "The Sectarian and Denominational Alternative"; also Henriques, *Religious Toleration*, p. 263.

[29] Wilson, *Religion*, p. 227.

serious errors, for while it is true that Latin Americans have
not invented sects, denominations, or churches able to pose
an effective challenge to the dominance of the centralist religion, this does not necessarily mean that the Catholic Church
in Latin America is an absolutely intolerant and monolithic
institution. It also does not follow that Latin American
Catholicism must have remained fundamentally unchanged
for five centuries. On the contrary, the nature of the Catholic
dominance suggests that there are other ways of achieving
toleration than that suggested by the English experience.
Perhaps toleration is not the best word to use in this context
and something closer to latitudinarianism, to an acceptance of
diversity under a broad mantle of formal allegiance, would be
a more appropriate concept to apply.[30] For it is not possible to
ignore the fact that under the mantle of Latin American
Catholicism are found varieties of ritual practice and doctrinal
belief that would strain the proverbial flexibility of a Church
of England. The ideological, spiritual, and ritualistic latitude
that separates a prince of the Church officiating in the Cathedral of Buenos Aires from his Catholic brethren engaged in
quasi-pagan ceremonies in a rural church in the north of
Brazil, from an ordained priest armed with a machine gun
and fighting with guerrilla bands in the Andes, or from a
learned Jesuit intellectual actively collaborating with the
socialist and communist parties in Mexico is not matched by
any other major western church. Would tolerance or latitude
be the right term to describe this situation? At any rate, it
exists today, and it existed in the early centuries of the con-

---

[30] "What is toleration? It is the prerogative of humanity. We are all steeped
in weaknesses and errors: let us forgive one another's follies, it is the first law
of nature." Thus Voltaire declares in his *Dictionnaire Philosophique*, and he
continues, "The Romans permitted all cults, even those of the Jews and
Egyptians, for which they had so much contempt. Why did Rome tolerate
these cults? It was because neither the Egyptians, nor even the Jews, tried to
exterminate the ancient religion of the empire. They did not run up and
down the earth to make proselytes." Notwithstanding additional arguments,
perhaps this one would explain why the Catholic Church in the Indies was
tolerant with respect to the pre-Columbian rites as long as their practitioners
agreed to call themselves Catholics and swear allegiance to king and empire.

quest and settlement although it did undergo a marked decline during the nineteenth century for reasons that will be
examined. That Latin American Catholicism was intolerant
of European heresies is not in the slightest doubt, but this was
a direct inheritance, more, a reflection of what was happening
in Europe; it was not a Latin American development. Lu-
theranism and Judaism were persecuted in the Indies because
the Church persecuted them in the peninsula; the intolerance
of Catholicism in Spain was thus projected across the Atlantic.

A different case altogether was that of the relationship between the Church and the pre-Columbian cults and rites. If it
is accepted, even in the guise of a working hypothesis, that
the growth of religious toleration in western Europe was
causally related to the proliferation of sects and denominations, then it can be stated that in Latin America there was no
need to wait for the emergence of new sects to break the
Catholic uniformity into a comparable diversity, for in the
Indies the diversity was already there before the arrival of the
Iberians. The differences between the religion of the Aztecs
and that of the Tupis, or of the Quechuas, or the Araucanians,
or the Siboneys were at least as great as, if not greater, than
those between Methodists and Presbyterians, Anglicans, and
Catholics. Moreover, had the cults and religions of the
greatly varied pre-Columbian cultures all been exposed simultaneously to the same European Catholicism, and in the
same manner, it is conceivable that a degree of uniformity
would have been achieved. But this did not happen. To the
diversity existing in the vast region before the arrival of the
conquerors was added that of intent, of style, even of skill,
with which different parts of the empire were brought to a
knowledge and a formal acceptance of the new religion.[31]

---

[31] The spiritual conquest of New Spain was carried on by "picked men,
daring religious radicals" whose extraordinary zeal in destroying ancient
idolatries and replacing them with the stern and militant Catholicism in the
early years of the sixteenth century resulted in "a new theocracy, a new
priesthood and a hybrid religion. The cult of the Virgin was superimposed
upon, and confused with, the cults of the earth-mother and corn-goddess . . .

The results were consequently different, adding yet another dimension to the richness of the pre-Columbian cultural texture, ill-disguised under the nominal uniformity suggested by a shared allegiance to the established religion of the conquering state.

The Church that crossed to the Indies was led by the king and not by the pope. The nominal allegiance lay with Rome, but the overwhelming political fact was that it was obedient to Madrid.[32] The Catholic fervor of the Spanish monarchy is not to be doubted, but when faced with the problem of extending administrative and military control over a whole new

---

with all its inevitable mixtures and dilutions." There is no doubt that out of the ruthless destruction and reconstruction, "a new living Church has been created." But this was in Mexico; several years later and thousands of miles to the south, in Peru, the experience was not the same, "events in Peru pursued a different course, Peru was more distant, less accessible; its physical obstacles more formidable, its native peoples more resistant. . . . Spanish and Indian communities remained widely separate. Moreover, the Peruvian enterprise began later. Whereas New Spain had been settled initially during a decade of humanist ascendancy in Spain, Peru was conquered in a decade of anti humanist reaction." Parry, *Seaborne Empire*, pp. 161-165. A comparable, if not greater diversity, can be found in modern Latin American countries. See Frederick B. Pike, "South America's Multifaceted Catholicism: Glimpses of Twentieth Century Argentina, Chile, and Peru," in *The Church and Social Change in Latin America*, ed. Henry A. Landsberger, Notre Dame, Ind., 1970, pp. 53-75.

[32] On this point, see Shiels, *King and Church*, p. 17. "The establishment of the Spanish *Patronato real* and the Portuguese *Padroado real* in the fifteenth century marks a sudden and decided break in [the] long established beneficiary pathway to Rome. Instead of holding firm to full papal appeal and reservation, the popes now in two outright grants handed over to the crowns of these nations the fullness of presentation, tithe and reservation." The consequence of this, according to John A. Mackay, was that the patronage exercised by the Spanish and Portuguese states over the Church in America "was much more absolute than that obtaining in the Peninsula. While in the mother lands the Church was independent of the civil power in economic matters, in the Indies it was subordinate to the state in this respect." And further, "until the birth of independent nations, the Pope occupied a secondary mission in the religious affairs of Ibero-America. A Christian Caesar was supreme, whose title was his 'Royal, Sacred, Catholic and Caesarian majesty.' " *The Other Spanish Christ, A Study in the Spiritual History of Spain and South America*, London, 1932, p. 43.

world, its devotion became tempered with a pragmatism that perhaps would have been unnecessary had the task been limited, for instance, to the pacification of Granada. The problem was less to ensure that the Indians understood the essence of the Catholic doctrine and became true believers than to make certain that they declared themselves to be loyal Catholics and obedient subjects of the crown, with the emphasis on the latter part of the proposition.[33]

Many good Englishmen were closer in doctrinal matters to the Archbishop of Toledo than were millions of Quechuas converted formally to the new and often misunderstood faith, but in the Spanish Indies the Englishman would have had a better chance to burn for heresy, and this as much because of his Englishness as because of his religious beliefs.

The cultural diversity of the Indies, the geographical vastness, the strangeness of everything the conquerors encountered, the distance from Europe—all these factors combined to force the Church into a well-nigh unavoidable latitudinarian attitude. Given the conditions under which a handful of friars had to convert millions of Indians to Catholicism, there was scarcely room for anything more demanding. They

---

[33] The conquering Church was undoubtedly filled with religious zeal, but it was also the religion of a modern state ruled by modern monarchs who, though greatly devout, were at least equally conscious of their temporal responsibilities. Perhaps on this subject as well, it is best to go to Voltaire's *Dictionnaire Philosophique* where, under "religion" we find the following: "Should not state religion and theological religion be carefully distinguished? The former requires imams to maintain registers of the circumcised, and priests or ministers registers of the baptized; that there be mosques, churches, temples, days devoted to worship and rest, rites established by law; that the ministers of these rites be given respect without power; that they teach good behaviour to the people; and that the ministers of the law watch over the behaviour of the ministers of the temples. Such a state religion can never make trouble. This is not true of theological religion. This is the source of all imaginable follies and disorders; it is the mother of fanaticism and civil discord." Even though this caricatured picture was not penned with the sixteenth-century Catholic Church of the Indies in mind, the description of state religion certainly does apply to the extension of the Catholic faith to the overseas empire of Ferdinand of Aragon and Philip II.

were unlikely to postpone conversion until the knowledge of doctrine was letter perfect, and it was unrealistic to imagine that they could afford to be punctilious when confronted with the evident goodwill and sincerity of Indians who were happy to call themselves Catholics for reasons that were perhaps unrelated to matters of faith or doctrinal understanding.[34] These and other considerations made the Church particularly sensitive to local needs and conditions and led to the institutionalization of a pragmatic attitude that would have been almost unthinkable in western Europe. This response was further encouraged by the bureaucratic diligence of a central administration so conscientious in the discharge of its imperial pastoral responsibilities that it even circulated questionnaires to discover what the local rites and customs were in order to improve missionary methods. The authority and intention of the crown were sufficiently clear to force the missionaries, regardless of their own inclinations, to accept without protest

[34] The ritual aspects of the Catholic faith may have had a great importance in this process. As Mariátegui points out, "Because of its sumptuous ritual and cult of pathos, Catholicism was uniquely well endowed to capture the allegiance of a people who could not suddenly come to an understanding of the spiritual and abstract aspects of religion. Catholicism could count, moreover, on its remarkable capacity of adaptation to any epoch or historical climate. The task began many years earlier in western Europe, through the absorption of ancient rites and the appropriation of the pagan calendar continued in Peru in the cult of the Virgin found on the shores of Lake Titicaca, whence originated the Inca theocracy." Further on he quotes Emilio Romero "the Indians were deeply moved by the Catholic rites. They would discover the image of the Sun God in the brilliant embroidery of the chasuble and vestments of the priests. . . . It was the paganism of the Indians that rose and responded to the call of the religious festivals, that is why they took their finest offerings to church. . . . Later they themselves would construct elaborate altars for the celebration of the Corpus Christi, covered with mirrors and framed with silver gilt, and at the feet of the sacred images, the first fruits of the harvest. . . . They would drink *jora* before the saints with the same unction with which they had done it in front of *Capac Raymi*. . . . then amidst shrill shouts which the priests interpreted as cries of penitence, they danced the strident *cachampas* and plunged into the athletic feats of the *kashuas* before the petrified smiles and glassy stares of the grotesque saints." Mariátegui, *Siete ensayos*, pp. 127-128. (author's translation.)

the royal decision to respect the indigenous culture of the people they were trying to convert to Christianity.[35] It was not unusual to find both the authority of the crown and of the Vatican invoked to justify decisions that in other latitudes and circumstances would have been unacceptable. Writing toward the close of the sixteenth century, Father José de Acosta, the Jesuit historian of the Indies noted that "generally it is better to leave the customs and uses of the Indians as they are and, in accordance with the advice of Saint Gregory, the Pope, to try and direct their own feasts and celebrations in such a way that they can be used to honour God."[36] Charles V, who so meticulously concerned himself with the imperial administration, also devoted attention to these problems and when instructing bishop Zumárraga before his first visit to New Spain encouraged him to explain to the Indians that the sun and the moon "which they revere, are ministers of God, created to execute his will, for the better governance and conservation of this world."[37] Pope Paul IV went further in the same direction and ordered that "the days which the Indians, in accordance with their ancient rites, devote to the sun . . . be used to honour the true Sun, which is Jesus Christ, and His Holy mother."[38]

Few things illustrate better the disparity between Catholic policy in Europe and the Indies than the way in which the dreaded institution of the Inquisition functioned in Spanish America. After the decision of Philip II in 1569, the Holy Office was extended to the Indies ostensibly to "maintain purity of faith and dogma." It is only natural to assume that the

[35] Fernando de Armas Medina, *Cristianización del Perú*, Sevilla, 1953, p. 77, quoted by Gabriel Guarda, O.S.B., "Itinerario del Paganismo en la cristianización de America," *TV*, VIII, no. 2 (April-June, 1967), 112. (author's translation.)

[36] José de Acosta, S. J., *Historia natural y moral de las Indias*, Seville, 1590, cited by Guarda, "Itinerario," p. 117. (author's translation.)

[37] Diego de Encinas, *Cedulario indiano recopilado por Diego de Encinas*, Madrid, 1945, IV, 222, quoted by Guarda, "Itinerario," p. 117. (author's translation.)

[38] Balthasar de Tobar, *Bulario índico*, ed. M. Gutierrez de Arce, Seville, 1954, I, 325, quoted by Guarda, "Itinerario," p. 118. (author's translation.)

inhumanity and cruelty so rightly associated with the activities of this fearsome institution in Europe crossed the Atlantic with it and accompanied it during its two and a half centuries of existence. In his *Dictionnaire philosophique*, under the entry "Inquisition," Voltaire quotes Ludovicus de Paramo's boast that 100,000 people had been put to death by the Inquisition in Europe, and this claim was made in 1598, early in the life of the institution. Surely greater horrors would follow the arrival of such a destructive instrument in a new world peopled almost entirely by heretics. Surely the most diligent and legalistic bureaucracy would tremble when faced with the obscure and tremendous power of a holy inquisitor. If an institution were needed to bring about the desired uniformity, the required zeal, observance of ritual, and regard to doctrine to the faith of the Indies, this was such an institution, for who could defy it? Who could possibly afford not to obey its dictates?

Such have been the popular views regarding the work of the Holy Office in the Indies. They are horrifying and mistaken. The jurisdiction of the Inquisition in America extended over Spanish Catholics accused of heresy and schism, over foreigners, and Protestants. It did not extend over the Indians as is made plain in the instructions drafted by the king for the inquisitors in Spanish America.[39] It was not possible, partly, no doubt, because of the obsessive legalism of the colonial re-

---

[39] The instructions read: "Item, you are forewarned that by virtue of our power you are not to proceed against the Indians in your district, because for the time being, and until we order differently, it is our will that you should only proceed against old Christians and their descendants and other persons and against whom proceedings are entered in the kingdom of Spain, and in those cases when you will enter proceedings, you are to act with moderation and with much consideration, because it is good to act in this way so that the Inquisition will be greatly feared and respected and there will be no reason for anybody to hate it." (author's translation.) This exception in favor of the Indians was not universally popular, and there were many complaints, especially in Peru, where Viceroy Toledo, for instance, appealed to the king to revoke it to help him in his struggle to eradicate the use of the *coca* leaf among the Indians and to prevent them from teaching Spaniards, notably women, how to use it. See José Toribio Medina, *Historia del Tribunal del Santo Oficio de la Inquisición en Chile*, Santiago, 1890, I, 201-203.

gime, for an Indian to be brought to trial before the Holy Office. Although distance from Spain and the natural laxity of procedure during those early decades of conquest could explain numerous departures from such a law, there is only one known case of an Indian having been arraigned before this tribunal.[40]

No doubt the activities of the Inquisition deserve the condemnation they have received involving as they did the use of torture and the sentencing of people to the stake for their religious convictions. They will in no way be less blameworthy if the instances of injustice are few. In ethical problems, quantity is a dubious factor; to kill ten human beings is not ten times worse than killing one, to murder one, as bad as to murder a dozen. But considering the ways of that world in the sixteenth, seventeenth, and eighteenth centuries, noting the manner in which Elizabethan England went about its religious problems, or the religious persecutions in the rest of Europe, there is room to doubt whether the Holy Office in the Indies was as horrible, as inhuman, as exceptionally ferocious as has been popularly depicted. It was established in the middle of the sixteenth century and abolished early in the nineteenth century. It had therefore a duration of just over two and a half centuries. In this period the total number of victims who died as a result of the activities of the Inquisition in the Indies, including those who were driven to commit suicide or went insane under torture, did not exceed ninety.[41] This is ninety too many. But ninety victims—all of them Spaniards, foreigners, or Protestants, with only one exception—means one execution every three years in the whole of

[40] This was the case of don Carlos de Mendoza, a noble Indian condemned in 1538 before the establishment of the Holy Office when the affairs of the Inquisition were handled through the episcopal offices. José Toribio Medina, *La primitiva inquisición americana (1493-1569)*, Santiago, 1914, I, 141-175; also, Henry Charles Lea, *The Inquisition in the Spanish Dependencies*, New York, 1908, p. 196.

[41] Salvador de Madariaga, *El auge del imperio español en América*, Buenos Aires, 1959, p. 207 et seq. The figure given by Madariaga is an approximation; actually it is known that in all the centuries of colonial rule, only 30 heretics were executed in Lima and 41 in Mexico City.

the Indies. Comparisons are odious in this respect, but it should be permissible to note that very few political conflicts of the past three decades, most of which have not been particularly edifying, have claimed less victims than the Inquisition in three hundred years in the Indies.

For as long as the Church in the Indies was under the control of the monarchy, the style of the Catholic dominance was pragmatic, flexible, and political. Better still, it was latitudinarian. It did not require the Indian to accept the Catholic faith absolutely. It endeavored to learn about the local customs and rites and tried to adapt the Catholic ritual to the usages of the indigenous inhabitants. Such latitude would not necessarily satisfy an English dissenter's definition of what constitutes toleration, for it was not the result of a successful challenge, or a dialogue, or a confrontation between independent holders of power. None of these descriptions would apply to the rise of latitudinarian religious centralism in the Indies: there was no dialogue between the conquering Catholic establishment and the pre-Columbian cultures. The Europeans invaded and emerged almost immediately victorious from all but one of their military confrontations, but were then forced by the very size and diversity of the world they had conquered into a pragmatic acceptance of much of the indigenous orthodoxy, albeit under different names.[42] This latitude did not reflect a proliferation of dissidence, but a coming to terms with a diversity so rich and complex and so spread out over a world several times larger than the whole of the Iberian peninsula that it was in fact impossible to absorb completely.

Until the outbreak of the movement of independence, the dominance of the established Church largely retained those characteristics of pragmatism, regalism, and flexibility that, in this interpretation, amounted to virtual latitudinarianism. After independence the situation changed. Separated from Madrid, blind to the aspirations and interests of the newly es-

---

[42] The one exception was the war on the Araucanían frontier that went on intermittently for over three hundred years, the final battles being fought between the Indians and Chilean republican troops in 1883.

tablished republican regimes, unable to understand, let alone support, the transformations that were wrecking the imperial orthodoxy, the Church of the Indies was left without leadership and found itself forced by circumstances to accept the rule of Rome.[43] The virtues, political and religious, that accrued as a result of its association with a conquering, imperial state, its acceptance of regalism, its identification with an almost populist missionary spirit, its learning rooted in Spain and the Indies, its progressive outlook, and robust humanistic acceptance of diversity—all these traits that played a positive role in the centuries of imperial responsibility—disappeared overnight to be replaced with an illiberal, frightened, Italian dogmatism permanently on the alert against the incursions of the European enemies of orthodoxy, ignorant of Latin America, and unforgiving toward those who had severed the regal ties.[44] The bold stroke of chisel on stone, the proud

[43] This lack of understanding has not passed unnoticed by religious scholars. Father Arturo Gaete, a Chilean Jesuit who has devoted much attention to the general problem of the relationship between Christianity and Marxism, observed in one of his articles, that the nineteenth-century Christians, as well as those of today, "found it difficult to conceive of a revolution. . . . Then and now Christians have arrived too late to an understanding of revolutionary change. There are various reasons for this. One was the fear that the idea of revolution would compel them to revise their idea of God and His relationship with human history. Another has to do with the personal contacts of the Church; in the French Revolution, it was nearer to the nobility; in the socialist revolutions it found itself nearer to the bourgeoisie. Such proximity to those who were about to be defeated naturally spread the contagion of their fears to the Church." But Father Gaete ends this article with a statement reflecting the contemporary latitudinarian mood of the Catholic Church in Latin America: "finally I will indicate under what conditions, from both sides, a reconciliation (between Christians and Marxists) can develop into a stable and profound collaboration." (author's translation.) See "Socialismo y comunismo, historia de una problemática condenación," *Mensaje*, xx, no. 200 (July, 1971), 301-302. This is the first article of a series published in xx, no. 205 (December, 1971); and xxi, no. 209 (June, 1972).

[44] As Rubén Vargas Ugarte, a Jesuit historian explains, "emancipation [from Spain] brought about close relations with Rome, with which the South American Church had not been able to maintain a stable relationship during the colonial period, the contacts that existed then [were] always through the cabinet in Madrid." *El episcopado en los tiempos de la emancipación sudamericana*, Lima, 1962, p. 8. (author's translation.)

baroque of the Indian craftsmen who built the lofty towers of a truly unique Catholic American culture were replaced by the plaster saints and flimsy devotional postcards of a religion that was losing its way overwhelmed with fear and bereft of inspiration. The sturdy faith of the missionaries who learned the Indian languages and helped to build a new civilization on the frontiers of mankind was replaced with the syrupy ritualistic sentimentality of unconvincing nineteenth-century miracle workers. At the risk of gross unfairness, the situation can be summarized thus: on one side was Juarez with his people building a nation, on the other panic-stricken priests hiding behind the bayonets of Napoleon III. There is no doubt that las Casas, Zumárraga, and Sahagún would have been closer to Juarez than to his adversaries.

And yet weak in heart and weaker in imagination but profiting from the momentum of a centralist tradition that favored its claim to exclusiveness, nineteenth-century Latin American Catholicism survived the successive onslaughts of anticlericalism, positivism, and Messianism. On the losing side in practically every important political confrontation, it nonetheless retained the allegiance of the immense majority of the people, even if by default, and remains to this day virtually unchallenged in its central position within Latin American society.

10

A Preindustrial Urban Culture

In the advanced countries of the Northern Hemisphere, urbanization and industrialization proceeded along parallel courses; the overwhelming majority of the peoples of these countries lived away from the cities before the advent of industrialization, and it was factors such as the rise in agricultural productivity, improvements in communications, and the spread of the factory system that were mostly responsible for the rural exodus and the corresponding growth of modern urban centers. Inextricably bound together, industrialization and urbanization have modified and reacted on each other, their interaction resulting in the proliferation of modern cities that bear the mark of the machine age; growing spontaneously rather than in a planned way, they are, in the jargon of urban sociologists, agglomerative and nonnucleated.

This has not been the case in Latin America where large planned cities formally structured around powerful bureaucratic nuclei preceded the coming of industry by many generations. Long before the Great Depression, when massive industrialization was a thing of the future, the main cities of Latin America were already impressively populated and occupied a dominant position in their countries.[1] In the decade

[1] In a study of eight Latin American capital cities, Richard M. Morse has indicated that if a rule of thumb "primacy" criterion is used, namely, that the largest city in a national system should be at least double the size of the next largest, only 4 of the 8 capitals studied were "indisputably primate [sic] throughout the period 1800-1920." However, the figures produced by Morse show that in 1850, six of the capitals, one of them "barely," occupied a position of primacy; all eight were in this position in 1900 and seven in 1920. This must surely be quite without parallel in the history of urbanization, and the

of 1890 Rome had a population of just over four hundred thousand and Madrid a few thousand less. It would not have been possible at that time to describe either Buenos Aires or Mexico City as industrial centers nor Argentina and Mexico as industrial countries, and yet, there were then more than half a million people living in Buenos Aires and nearer to six hundred thousand in the Mexico City of the "Porfiriato."[2] At the same time, the United States was the principal steel producer and major world industrial power, and New York, her most important commercial outlet, had only one million inhabitants, not a vast difference from preindustrial Mexico City. Eighty years later, Toynbee singled out the United States as a good illustration of "the overwhelming preponderance of the numbers of the urban population" and predicted that this would become a worldwide phenomenon before long. This may well be so, but in the meantime it is interesting to note that the United States is less urbanized than at least four Latin American countries: Venezuela, Chile, Uruguay, and Argentina.[3]

In that same closing decade of the nineteenth century, Japan was well on its way to becoming one of the great industrial powers and one out of every forty Japanese lived in Tokyo,

---

fact that only four capitals remained "primate" throughout is again an exceptionally high record compared to what obtained in any comparable region of the world at the time. The capitals studied by Morse were Buenos Aires, Rio de Janeiro, Santiago, Bogotá, Havana, México, Lima, and Caracas. The only capital not to qualify for primacy in 1920 was Bogotá that, for special political and geographical reasons, has always been untypically close to her nearest competitors: Cali, Medellín, Cartagena, and Barranquilla. See Richard M. Morse, *The Urban Development of Latin America, 1750-1920*, Stanford, Calif., 1971, p. 7.

[2] One hundred years earlier, at the beginning of the nineteenth century, Mexico City was the largest city in the Western Hemisphere. See Norman S. Hayner, "Mexico City: Its Growth and Configuration," *TAJS*, L, no. 1 (January, 1945), 298; also Moisés González Navarro, *Estadísticas sociales del Porfiriato*, México, 1956. On the social and political implications of population movements in Argentina, see Sergio Bagú, *Evolución histórica de la estratificación social argentina*, Buenos Aires, 1961; also Panettieri, *Los trabajadores*, especially on aspects of the urbanization of Buenos Aires, pp. 27-35.

[3] Arnold Toynbee, *Cities on the Move*, London, 1970, p. 36.

but one in every twenty Mexicans lived in preindustrial Mexico City, and one in every eight Argentines lived in Buenos Aires.[4] The Buenos Aires they inhabited was not an agglomeration of villages or a simple accumulation of human beings pushed together by fear, hunger, or incapacity to find shelter elsewhere, but a vital and prosperous capital city run by an ambitious municipal government intent on programs of improvement and adornment that would have taxed the treasury of any of the smaller European nations. The magnificent Avenida de Mayo, which even today remains one of the impressive boulevards of the world with its carefully studied perspectives and handsome Second Empire buildings, is a worthy monument to those prosperous and self-confident times. The luxurious building of the Jockey Club of Argentina, eventually burned to the ground by a Peronist mob in 1953, was erected in 1881, the same year of the Club Naval y Militar, which still flaunts its *fin de siècle* magnificence from its fashionable setting.[5] Many of the more sumptuous buildings of Buenos Aires date from those years; the post office, the law courts, the Congress building which provides a stunning climax to the Avenida de Mayo, as well as the elegant residences of the *Barrio norte*. The fervent wish to improve on what the great European capitals had to offer went beyond architectural splendor: Buenos Aires was one of the first cities to develop a comprehensive electric tramway system and by 1880 already boasted 146 kilometers of lines, in contrast to London with only 91 kilometres for its three and a half million inhabitants, or New York with 121 kilometers, or Vienna with only 22 kilometres. Street lighting was introduced in 1899; a running water supply system was in operation by 1868, while before the memorable inauguration of the Avenida de Mayo, in 1894, the whole central sector of the huge city had been carefully and expensively paved with cobblestones laid down according to elaborate Parisian designs.[6]

---

[4] Ricardo M. Ortíz, *Historia económica de la Argentina, 1850-1930*, Buenos Aires, 1955, I, 106-109.

[5] James R. Scobie, *Buenos Aires: Plaza to Suburb, 1870-1910*, New York, 1974, p. 119.

[6] Panettieri, *Los trabajadores*, pp. 29-30.

The general importance of immigration as a determining factor in these processes of urban growth has not been as great as it is usually supposed. As is well known, massive immigration from Europe swelled the urban population of Uruguay and Argentina during the years immediately preceding the First World War, but even there, it was not the decisive factor. Immigration into Chile during the same period was negligible, but during the ninety years preceding 1920, the total population increased threefold while urban population went up twenty times. Bolivia, a country where European immigration has been even less important than in Chile, had at that time one in every seven inhabitants living in the capital.

Uruguay to this day depends on the export of agricultural products, but for generations has had about half of its population living in the capital, and of late this proportion has increased. Ten years ago, when their respective levels of industrialization were hardly comparable, the degree or urban concentration in centers of 100,000 and more was still greater in Latin America than in Europe or the Union of Soviet Socialist Republics.[7] In 1880 when Britain was still the leading industrial nation, 67.9 percent of her population was classified as urban; in 1970 Uruguay was not one of the most industrialized countries on earth, but 78.6 percent of its population was urban. In 1880 43 percent of the population of highly industrialized Belgium was urbanized, but ninety years later 49.2 percent of the population of Peru, certainly not an industrial country, was living in cities. Even more illustrative is the contrast between the obviously advanced industrial economy of Sweden in 1945 with 42.3 percent of her population in cities and Argentina in 1895 with the same proportion inhabiting urban centers. Moreover, although the economy of Mexico has industrialized rapidly during the past few decades, it cannot be compared with that of Germany or France of even a few years ago, but in 1933 56.6 percent of the population of Germany was classified as urban, and the percentage

[7] David V. Glass, "Population Growth and Structure: A Socio-Demographic Study," in *Social Aspects of Economic Development in Latin America*, edited at UNESCO, Paris, 1963, I, 95.

for France in 1946 was 53.2 percent while in 1970 61.8 percent of the Mexican population was in cities. Great Britain, one of the most highly urbanized among industrial nations, reached the telling record of 80 percent of her population living in cities in the months before the Great Depression of 1929; the percentage for Venezuela today is 75 percent, but less than a quarter are engaged in industrial activities.[8]

The urbanization of Latin America is not a recent phenomenon, the consequence of the rapid industrialization of the past few decades. As early as the middle of the sixteenth century, when Tokyo with 150,000 inhabitants was one of the largest cities in Asia and Seville astonished Europeans with a population that exceeded 80,000, Mexico City had over 160,000 people living within its boundaries, and a century later Potosí had reached a similar figure.[9] These colonial cities were worthy precursors of what was to come in the nineteenth and twentieth centuries. Impressive in scale and conception, they afford an interesting contrast to the urban centers of British North America; as Parry indicates: "urban magnificence was characteristic, in colonial times, of Spanish America, not of the Americas in general. British America produced nothing of the kind. Its towns grew up as local markets or as modest harbours."[10] It is possible that these differences reflect cultural traits that may have received less attention than they deserve.[11] It is, for instance, fairly obvious

[8] Sergio Bagú, "Industrialización, sociedad y dependencia," *RLACS*, I (June-December, 1971), 172-197. Generalization is unavoidable when discussing these aspects of Latin America. This is partly the consequence of the scarcity of detailed monographic studies. Fortunately, some of these are now beginning to appear, and they augur well for the future. On the urban problems of Venezuela and Mexico, for instance, see D. J. Robinson, "The City as Centre of Change in Modern Venezuela," and David J. Fox, "Urbanization and Economic Development in Mexico," both papers published under the title *Cities in Changing Latin America*, London, 1969.

[9] Erwin Walter Palm, *Los monumentos arquitectónicos de La Española, Ciudad Trujillo*, Santo Domingo, 1955, I, 110; Lewis Hanke, *The Imperial City of Potosí*, The Hague, 1956, p. 1.

[10] J. H. Parry, *The Cities of the Conquistadores*, London, 1961, pp. 1-2.

[11] Although at least two national histories—of Peru and Argentina—have been written around the main theme of the influence of the capital city on the

to anybody who has ever lived in London and Buenos Aires that there are more people in the British capital who have patted a horse or a cow in their lives than in Buenos Aires. There are more people in Paris who have slept under canvas than in Caracas or Montevideo, more people who go sailing for sport in land-locked Hungary or Switzerland than in Peru or Chile, more people, without doubt, in Manchester or Stuttgart who have climbed mountains or gone skiing in their lives than in cities like Quito or Santiago that nestle against the foothills of the high Andes.

The people of the Iberian tradition share an appreciation of urban life and a disinclination to appreciate fully the virtues of an intimacy with nature that are uncommon in the English-speaking world or in northwestern Europe generally.[12] Most of the inhabitants of Chile live in the Central Valley, a narrow strip of level land hemmed in between the second highest mountain massif on earth and the greatest ocean, and yet Chile has never developed a mountain culture nor a seafaring tradition of importance. Chileans avoid the sea and the mountains and have traditionally settled in cities built on the flat, fertile, amiable, and well-watered valley. Their capital—founded in 1541—is in the middle of that valley, distant from the sea, and today contains almost one third of the total population of the country. Today many Chileans and Argentinians practice skiing and mountaineering, but this is a recent development, largely the result of the efforts of foreign residents aided by improvements in air transportation that allow sportsmen from Europe and the United States to visit the Andes during the northern summer.

---

life of the nation. James R. Scobie, *Argentina: A City and a Nation*, New York, 1964, and Jorge Basadre, *La multitud, la ciudad y el campo en la historia del Perú*, Lima, 1947.

[12] There are some interesting differences between the Portuguese and Spanish experiences of colonization, but, as Morse has indicated, one of their common features is that "colonization was in large part an urban venture, carried out by urban-minded people. The municipal nucleus was the point of departure for settlement of the land." Richard M. Morse, "Recent Research on Latin American Urbanization: A Selective Survey with Commentary," *LARR*, I, no. 1 (Fall, 1965), 38.

The urban bent of Latin Americans, and Iberians generally, affects virtually all aspects of social activity and underlies a style of life that contrasts sharply with that of the British colonizing culture. For when the British explored Africa, Asia, and the islands of the tropics, when they navigated the Congo and the Zambesi and hacked their way through impenetrable bush, when they climbed Kilimanjaro and sighted Everest and lived for months and years away from urban civilization, they loved it and transformed their experiences into sport. They invented and perfected skiing and mountaineering, camping and sailing and canoeing, not as unavoidable and cumbersome techniques of transportation—as they probably appear to the pragmatic Lapps, Swiss villagers, or Pacific islanders who have to do these things whether they want to or not—but as delightful, expensive, and socially acceptable sports. It is not an accident that such an august feature of the world's skiing calendar as the Kandahar competition should be named after an English peer. The English-speaking peoples share a characteristic appreciation of nature; they tolerate their cities grudgingly, and given the slightest excuse they leave them, if not to retire, at least for their hallowed weekends.

The Spanish conquerors also had to endure the travail of pioneering exploration; they crossed huge jungles and deserts, navigated the Amazon and the Orinoco; they climbed the Andes and survived the Atacama desert and hated every minute of it, never stopped complaining, and at the first opportunity unfurled their flags, donned their finery, and, with all the pomp that circumstances allowed, founded cities in which to take refuge from the barbaric, harsh, uncivilized, and rural world outside. They did not settle out-stations or trading posts, but major cities ambitiously planned from their very beginnings according to the precise royal instructions issued from the imperial center. Once the city was founded, its straight streets drawn at right angles, the site of the church determined, a gibbet—the inevitable symbol of authority—planted in the middle of the portalled square and the blocks of land apportioned among the participants in the expedition,

the Iberian conqueror, no matter how uncouth, understood
that he was at home and that the flickering light of civilization
would survive in that distant urban setting, diligently and
painfully transplanted from the Mediterranean to the Indies.
For those men civilization was strictly and uniquely a function
of well-ordered city life; what lurked outside the boundaries,
rural, rustic, and barbarous nature, was to be avoided. This
was clearly reflected in their attitude toward farming and life
in the country. In contrast with their English counterparts,
the Iberian landowners of the Indies did not, as Parry has indicated, "settle as farmers, and did not develop a resident
squirearchy." Their estates provided them with income and
diversion, but "they were by preference town dwellers and
town builders."[13]

Few of the cities of the Old World—and most of the exceptions were founded by Romans—were actually established in
accordance with a systematic program of urban settlement;
most developed as convenient market places or strategic
strongholds, or both, and their survival and prosperity has
usually been a function of their capacity to retain their usefulness either as markets or fortresses in the face of changing circumstances. Improvements in military technology, notably
the development of artillery, led to a gradual decline in the
importance of strategic considerations in the establishment or
maintenance of urban centers. On the other hand, the significance of undiluted commercial or economic factors has
tended to increase greatly. The effects of this secular change of
emphasis can be seen quite distinctly in the case of settlements
like those of Gibraltar, Valetta, Singapore, or Hong Kong, all
of which owe their origins to the requirements of an imperial
policy, but only those have prospered that in spite of the decline of their military importance have managed to become
major commercial and industrial centers in their own right.[14]

[13] Parry, *The Cities*, pp. 6–7.

[14] Toynbee has explained that "all but a handful of the host of cities that
rose and fell or rose and survived during those seven or eight millennia before
the Industrial Revolution were market-towns serving a surrounding countryside with a radius that was short enough to allow the rural food producer

The settlement of Australia and the United States was strongly influenced by this flexible, pragmatic attitude based on ancient traditions: cities happened when and where they were needed, and there was no juridical requirement to inform a central authority of their foundation, or to plan and build them in any special way, or to fulfil elaborate formal prerequisites. There were no fixed and centrally enforceable procedures for the setting up of municipal authorities or for the choice of sites; a site was good as long as its usefulness lasted, and this was principally a function of the viability of trading routes and the availability of food supplies. In the United States and Australia very few major cities were formally founded; most of them simply grew until they became important enough for the central authorities to notice their existence and bless them with some minimal type of recognition and control. Moreover, these early settlers and squatters initially dispersed over the vast territory recreating with their homesteads and small villages and townships the pattern of rural dispersion typical of their places of origin. Germany, Britain, the Low Countries—all have village civilizations; even their major cities are sometimes secular agglomerations of villages; social, cultural, and political life begins, and often ends, at the village level. Certainly in Britain for the past three centuries the village church, pub, shop, and social relations have had a formative influence on the national culture and mores. It took an industrial revolution to force the British out of their villages and into the cities they so much dislike.

In Latin America the process of urbanization has been entirely different. The only parts of the region where village culture has any importance are those that inherited it from pre-

---

to bring his product into the city, sell it there, and get back to his rural home again between daybreak and nightfall." He also points out, quoting Thucydides, that the Greek city-states were pulled in opposite directions by the conflicting requirements of trade and defense, for trade called for the city to be located close to good land and water transport while defense called for a location "out of reach of pirates, brigands, and invading armies," regardless of the fertility of the surrounding territory or the accessibility of waterways. See Toynbee, *Cities*, pp. 19, 29.

Columbian times, notably Mexico, parts of Central America, and the Andean countries. Elsewhere village communities are relatively unimportant; it is the city that dominates the social and cultural horizon. The conquerors were founders of cities, formally, with all the required, elaborate ceremony, the ritual, and solemnity, invoking the name and authority of the distant monarch. With few exceptions,[15] cities were founded on a particular site not because it was well positioned for trade—there were scarcely any trade routes in pre-Columbian America and the existing ones were irrelevant to the imperial commercial arrangements—or because it was easy to defend, or possessed other important military or strategic advantages,[16] but because according to the careful guidelines that the conquerors were ordered to apply, it was considered to be a good place for the monarch's subjects to live and prosper in peace, a good setting for the church to conduct its evangelical work, a satisfactory center from which the vast outlying ter-

[15] Mining settlements such as those of Taxco and Potosí would be exceptions, although they were also centrally regulated and grew into large and well-administered cities; another would be the towns founded on the Isthmus of Panama, whose sites were mainly determined by trade and defense, and when either or both of these needs disappeared, those towns fell into decline and, at least in two interesting cases, disappeared altogether. See David Howarth, *The Golden Isthmus*, London, 1966, pp. 12-13, on the vanished cities of Acla and Santa María.

[16] "Spanish American cities were, for the most part, unfortified. Only coastal cities, such as Cartagena and Havana, which might be attacked from the sea, possessed extensive formal fortifications. Most of the major cities were inland, safe from foreign invaders. . . . The cities of Spanish America, unlike those of Europe, were untrammelled in their growth by the encumbrance of massive encircling walls. They developed as modern cities, seats of government and industry, undefended and open to commerce and travel." Parry, *The Cities*, pp. 4-5. Possibly the largest number of inland cities originally founded as military strongholds is found in the southern regions of Chile, as a consequence of the long war with the Araucanians. According to Father Gabriel Guarda, of the 104 foundations made by the Spaniards in Chile between 1541 and 1810, 52 had fortifications, either immediately upon being founded, or later on. Almost all of these were founded during the sixteenth century and in the war zone of the southern frontier. See Gabriel Guarda O.S.B., "Influencia militar en las ciudades del reino de Chile," *BACH*, XXXIII (1966), 6-7.

ritories could be well and efficiently administered for the crown.[17]

In a political climate as legalistic and bureaucratic as that of Spain in the sixteenth century, such objectives could not but be translated into formal rules and regulations. In this instance, dispersed enactments that had been used during the first decades of the conquest were codified under the personal supervision of Philip II into the now famous *Instrucción* of 1573.[18] The first ten articles refer to the choice of sites for the new settlements and direct the conqueror to observe the indigenous inhabitants of the region where it is proposed to found the city in order to discover if they are "of good complexion, colour, disposition, and without illness." Also the conqueror was to examine animals and trees, paying special attention to their size and health and make certain that the soil does not contain "poisonous and nasty things" and that the sky is "of good and happy constellation . . . clean and benign, the air pure and soft, without impediment or alteration . . . and tempered, without excessive heat or cold."[19] The new cities are not to be built too high for such places are difficult to reach with heavy loads and are often buffeted by winds nor too low, for these are usually unhealthy. If the city is to be built by a river bank, it should be on the eastern side "so that the sun shines first on the city and then on the water." And so on, at length and with infinite detail, the Castilian bureaucrats

[17] Basadre, the distinguished Peruvian historian, has explained this well by noting that the Latin American cities were not born, like those ancient cities studied by Fustel de Coulanges "from the sacred fire of the home, but were created so that homes could be born from within them." Basadre, *La multitud*, p. 36. (author's translation.)

[18] Father Guarda lists the following regulations and enactments including directives for the foundation of urban settlements dating from before the *Instrucción* of 1573: the instructions issued by Ferdinand of Aragon in 1513 for the use of Pedrárias Dávila; the instructions given to Hernán Cortés in 1523 that also included those issued for Diego Velázquez in 1518; the imperial provisions of Granada of 1526, and the detailed instructions of 1568 prepared by Philip II for the use of the viceroy of Peru, Francisco de Toledo. See Gabriel Guarda, O.S.B., *Santo Tomás de Aquino y las fuentes del urbanismo indiano*, Santiago, 1965, p. 11 n.

[19] Guarda, *Santo Tomás*, p. 30. (author's translation.)

guided the judgment of those hardened captains of men who so unexpectedly found themselves charged with the responsibility of extending Mediterranean urban civilization to the Indies. The methods they used to select a site and plan the city may seem amusing to us, but it cannot be denied that they were eminently successful as well as simple. Modern environmental studies have not improved, conceptually, very much on Philip II's advice to observe carefully the local inhabitants, the sky, the water, the forests, the animals, the soil, before drafting the plans for the new settlement.

This good advice was followed attentively and of the many hundreds of cities founded by the conquering Spaniards and Portuguese, only a handful proved disappointing and none of the capital cities are among these. Thus the site of Bogotá was chosen in 1538 not because it was particularly accessible to trade or easily defensible, but because of the great number of healthy inhabitants it contained, "and the good sky and the temperament of the land." Of Caracas, the king was informed that it had been founded after much reconnoitering, in a valley "famous, fertile and amiable." When Pedro de Valdivia reported to Charles V on his decision to found Santiago in the Chilean Central Valley, he wrote, "and those people who would like to come and live here, let them come, because this land is such, that to live in it and procreate there is none better in the whole world . . . level, very healthy and full of contentment."[20] The reports on the foundations contain page after page of observations worthy of a mid-twentieth-century ecologist, florid perhaps, but astonishingly free of error. The enduring monuments to their success, those cities all over Latin America after four and five centuries show in their different characters and virtues as human habitat the ability of their enterprising founders. Never in the annals of colonization has a metropolitan power—not even Rome—founded as many cities as Spain, and, of course, the vast majority of those cities are still enjoying a busy existence.

[20] Pedro de Valdivia, *Cartas de relación de la conquista de Chile*, Santiago, 1970, pp. 43-44. (author's translation.)

Once a convenient site had been selected, the task of planning the future city demanded at least as much attention and was equally regulated. The remarkable uniformity in the basic plans for the cities of the Indies—there are exceptions, but they are not numerous—has been the subject of much discussion.[21] The characteristic quadrangular grid plan has been attributed by some to a direct influence of the Renaissance; others have seen in it a summing up of ancient Iberian practices somewhat modified by contemporary trends.[22] No mat-

[21] It is virtually impossible to determine precisely how the grid plan of the cities of the Indies originated. It may have been inspired on the neoclassical books on town planning that were fashionable at the time, and the great majority of these came from Italy. As Parry observes, there is little doubt that the cities of America "approximated much more closely to Italian Renaissance ideas of what cities ought to be like, than to actual Spanish cities of the time." *The Cities*, p. 4. On the other hand, Father Guarda defends the thesis that there was little, if any, influence from Italian town planners, but that the one important and hitherto disregarded influence in the urbanization of the Indies is that of St. Thomas Aquinas, especially through the precepts contained in the first part of *De regimini principum ad regem Cypri*. Guarda, *Santo Tomás*, pp. 33-47. Leopoldo Torres Balbas maintains that the grid was a feudal survival uncommon in Spain though found often in Navarre. Leopoldo Torres Balbas and Fernando Chueca Goitia, *Planos de ciudades iberoamericanas y filipinas*, Madrid, 1951, p. xiii.

[22] Although there are some interesting differences in the physical plan of Portuguese and Spanish cities in the Indies, this does not mean that the urban component is less important in Brazilian society, only that its origins are not the same. The typical Portuguese township of late-medieval times was an agro-commercial, maritime one, usually sited on the coast "in response to economic possibilities rather than to politico-military design," as would have been the case with the typical Castilian settlement. The Brazilian townships appear to reproduce the Portuguese pattern. Most towns in Brazil are coastal settlements with a "natural" layout that contrasts with the quadrangular, planned layout of the Spanish towns. The centralist mood of Spanish town planning is also reflected in the relation between dwellings and the *Plaza Mayor*, or central square. The Spanish American city is normally "a *Plaza Mayor* surrounded by streets and houses, rather than an assemblage of houses and streets around a *Plaza Mayor*." The few departures from this norm found in Spanish America, in places such as Nacimiento, Trujillo, Cuzco, or Valparaíso, are usually explained by the difficult terrain, the existence of major pre-Columbian settlements, or the need for exceptional military fortifications. See Morse, "Recent Research," p. 37. The reference to the *Plaza Mayor* is quoted by Morse from Robert Ricard, "La *Plaza Mayor* en Espagne et en

ter what the merits of different explanations, what is most significant is that all these cities were planned and built in strict accordance with instructions issued by the imperial center. At times these had intriguing political overtones. The conquerors were advised that the shape and size of houses must be such that would be regarded with awe and admiration by the Indians and would convince them that the Spaniards intended to remain forever in these places and would move them "to fear and respect [them], to seek their friendship and avoid giving them offence."[23] In addition to the physical plan for the settlements, the instructions also covered bureaucratic and administrative arrangements in considerable detail; herein possibly lies the main clue for an understanding of the unvarying enthusiasm with which the rugged conquerors approached the task of founding cities in the Indies. For it was only through the setting up of valid municipal offices, sanctioned by the crown, that these warriors could transform their *de facto* military power into *de jure* political authority and prestige. Cities were needed to change their informal bands of followers into municipal councils with authority, precisely and efficiently delegated by the Iberian metropolis, to act in the name of the distant crown.[24] This was therefore the complete antithesis of the haphazard, pragmatic urban development characteristic of the western expansion of the United States or the settlement of Australia.

Amérique Espagnole," *AESC*, II, no. 4 (October-December, 1947), 433-438; see also Jorge E. Hardoy, "El modelo clásico de la ciudad colonial hispanoamericana," *Actas del XXXVIII Congreso Internacional de Americanistas*, Stuttgart-Munich, 1968, IV, 143-181.

[23] Torres Balbas, *Planos de ciudades*, pp. xii-xiii. (author's translation.)

[24] After rewarding his associates with land grants or *encomiendas*, or both, the main preoccupation of the commander of a conquering expedition was "to provide a legal method whereby the temporary and informal organization of the army could be transformed into an official and permanent organization for local government. The normal method was that of municipal incorporation. Every leader of a conquering army made it his care to establish towns, to get them legally incorporated by the Crown, and to install his immediate followers as the officers of the municipal government." Parry, *The Cities*, p. 8.

Before the first building went up, a fully-fledged, meticulously legal, and most solemnly formal municipal, political, and administrative structure was established that assumed responsibility for the city and its surrounding territory; in Latin America the urban bureaucracy preceded the actual construction of the cities. The capital cities of the Indies, moreover, had no reason to encourage or tolerate any dispersal of their authority and normally retained their dominant position throughout the colonial period. No way was left open in which a rural periphery could wrest power from the city. From its very beginnings, the cities of the Indies "assumed the direction of political affairs," and possibly the weightiest evidence of their achievement is that none of the rural rebellions was ever successful. The political authority of those cities derived from the Iberian metropolis. It should not be forgotten that the monarchs had earlier deprived the traditional municipalities of their ancient privileges and immunities; the colonial dominance of the cities of Latin America was a faithful reflection of the central control exercised by the crown.[25]

It should not be necessary to insist that the modern European and North American urban centers owe much to industrialization in their demographic composition, the types of employment they offer, and their processes of growth. No doubt, there were great cities in Europe and Asia before the advent of industry, and they harbored impressive urban cultures, but their absolute size was limited by technological and health factors. The provision of adequate drainage for urban centers with hundreds of thousands of inhabitants was an obstacle that only cities such as Venice, Potosí, or Tokyo were partially able to surmount.[26] The absolute predominance of a labor-intensive agriculture as the basic economic activity necessarily resulted in the greater portion of the population

[25] See Basadre, *La multitud*, p. 259-260. (author's translation.)

[26] Regular tides and an altitude of 16,000 feet that all but stops decomposition respectively eased the problem for Venice and Potosí while Tokyo was helped by the Japanese practice of using nightsoil as a fertilizer in the intensive agriculture of the region surrounding the capital.

living dispersed in rural villages. The lack of cheap and efficient means of transportation made this rural dispersal permanent as well as mandatory. Of course, numbers of farmers and peasants visited the principal cities, but a massive, peacetime migration did not take place until the stresses caused by the Industrial Revolution and, in Britain, the enclosure movement made such changes unavoidable regardless of the transportation facilities available or the cost in human suffering. Within a few years of these large-scale migrations into the growing urban industrial areas, general technological advancement and the resulting improvements in sanitation and other municipal arrangements allowed for the solution of many of the problems that had earlier limited the absolute size of the cities. This was the time—roughly during the one hundred years preceding the Great Depression of 1929—when the modern cities of the world were built or rebuilt and when the correlation between industrialization and urbanization was most meaningful.

This was also the time when the middle and upper circles of the new Latin American republics, flushed with the confidence based on their easy prosperity, the result of massive sales of primary commodities in the European market, vied with each other in their efforts to become as European as possible in the briefest time possible. As it has been explained earlier, much of that wealth was used to pay for the importation of luxury consumer goods, but a far greater proportion was devoted to the construction of monumental boulevards, opera houses and theatres, public buildings, and private mansions—all slavishly and lavishly patterned after the prevailing fashions in Europe. It was French architectural fashion in particular that reigned supreme. As Castedo has noted, "in Brazil the process of Frenchification was absolute," and what Grandjean de Montigny was invited to do in Rio de Janeiro, Alejandro Christophersen did in Buenos Aires and Francois Brunet de Baines in Santiago. Brunet was appointed to the first chair of architecture in the newly reopened University of Chile and soon his influence was felt in the reconstruction of the capital. Santiago's famous *Alameda* acquired the airs and style of a modest French boulevard "less elegant than the *Paseo de la Reforma* in Mexico City and considerably less elegant than the grand boulevards laid in Buenos Aires," but French nonetheless. The Haussmann of Santiago was the distinguished writer Benjamín Vicuña Mackenna, a keen admirer of everything French, and since there was no native architecture of any note, the urban improvement of the city was, naturally, in the French style.[27] There were differences, of course, in the way different urban centers accepted the neoclassic revival, and it is correct to assume that those cities that had experienced prosperity and urban affluence during the preceding two centuries and were thus able to develop a vigorous Baroque architecture could resist the French neoclassic onslaught better than the lesser capitals where the native Baroque had a more restrained influence.[28]

Fashionable, ambitiously conceived and constructed, prosperous, organized concentrically around a concept of bureaucratic authority that preceded their very physical existence, the cities of Latin America emerged into the mid-nineteenth century politicized to the core. The institutions, civic habits, and mores were shaped, after centuries of experience, by a practical understanding of the uses, prerogatives, and responsibilities of authority and of the prestige it bestows on those who wield it. These cities were primarily conceived as bureaucratic centers; commerce and industry had almost no part in their formative period; very few of them bear the military imprint. Almost without exception they developed and reached maturity as centers for the exercise of civilian, bureaucratic, and legal authority, and for a long time before the coming of industry they harbored relatively large populations

[27] See Castedo, *Art and Architecture*, pp. 204-206, and also Adolfo Morales de los Ríos Filho, *Grandjean de Montigny*, Rio de Janeiro, 1941.

[28] As Parry has explained, the modern buildings being constructed in Lima today are not replacing the adobe houses of a provincial town, but "an eighteenth century stone-built city of size and distinction." In Mexico, he adds, "the continuity of scale is still more striking, since the seventeenth and eighteenth century splendour of the *Zócalo* and the surrounding streets stands in its entirety within easy distance of some of the boldest and most interesting buildings of this century in the world." Parry, *The Cities*, p. 3.

out of all proportion to the development of their manufactures. These urban inhabitants were obviously not farmers or peasants: neither were they industrial workers. What were they? How did they earn their living? The answer is simple: they served each other; they were employed in the service, or tertiary, sector of the economy and included domestic servants as well as lawyers, teachers, dentists, civil servants, salesmen, politicians, soldiers, janitors, accountants, and cooks.[29] The funds to pay their wages and salaries, gratuities and emoluments, fees and bills also came from the sale of primary commodities—from the proceeds of the sale of wool, wheat, rubber, sugar, copper, tin, coffee, and the like in the international markets.

The workers who produced these commodities very seldom lived in or near the capital cities. Hundreds, sometimes thousands of miles separated these cities from the mines and plantations where the wealth was generated that financed the extravagant plans of urban renewal. Whatever political weight those distant miners and plantation workers could have had was largely dissipated by distance and isolation. On the other hand, the tertiary sector workers and employees who constituted such an important part of the urban population were politically aware, mostly literate and sensitive to the reformist ideas so enthusiastically espoused by the intelligentsia.

A noteworthy consequence of this was the formation, during the second half of the nineteenth century, of a number of reformist, urban-based political parties that took to heart the anticlerical radicalism of the French, the free-trading liberalism of the English, and, generally, the romantic, revolutionary postures and ideas characteristic of the European mid-century avant-garde; they prospered in their urban settings and became an efficient vehicle for the importation of many European institutions generated or revived by the impact of an Industrial Revolution that had not yet arrived in Latin

[29] On urbanization and the expansion of the tertiary sector, see Morse, "Recent Research," pp. 44-46.

America. Thus, industrial trade unionism and schemes for social reform reached Latin America many years before industrialization.

By the turn of the century, at the height of the liberal pause there existed in the dominant cities of the region a lively, almost buoyant, pretentious and dependent urban intelligentsia. For reasons that had evidently nothing to do with the development of industry, this intelligentsia had grown side by side with a remarkably large tertiary sector many of whose members were ready to accept the leadership of their local intellectuals. This intelligentsia, as explained earlier, was responsive to European ideological developments and eager to organize itself and its followers into reformist political parties, liberal, radical, or both, that were to have a decisive influence during the following decades.

Human society shapes its environment in many different ways. Its style, its purpose, and limitations can be ascertained from the writings of poets and scholars as well as from the paintings, the sculptures, the music, and the drama produced by artists, or by the nature of dwellings, one by one, or collectively, as in cities. If care is exercised by a man who purchases a book, greater care is exercised by he who buys a painting and yet even more by a person who orders a house to be built. Possibly this is a function of the relative expense of each of these things, perhaps more important and transcendental considerations are involved, but it can be safely said that few material aspects of the environment portray the taste, the quality, the hopes, ambitions, and generally, the cultural tone of societies better than the cities they inhabit. If this is true, then it can be affirmed that the cities of Latin America, with their preindustrial urban culture are yet another faithful reflection of her essential centralist temper.[30]

[30] For a dissenting view, see Rodolfo Quintero, *Antropología de las ciudades latinoamericanas*, Caracas, 1964, especially Ch. 4, "Ciudades artificiales," pp. 157-208.

11

The British Model of Industrialization

The centralism that so forcefully shaped the political and religious arrangements of Latin Americans during four centuries has not been absent from the sphere of economic activity. The question of whether it was a centralist economy that forced political centralization on Latin American society or whether the persistent centralist bias in all other aspects of Latin American life also influenced economic arrangements is an important one and deserves scrutiny if only to satisfy intellectual curiosity. However, the following examination of the process of centralist industrialization is based on the acceptance of the latter view as a valid and useful functional hypothesis.[1]

---

[1] There is an alternative way of putting this question that should be borne in mind. There appears to be no *a priori* considerations convincing enough to deter somebody so inclined, for instance, from entertaining the view that by necessity it must have been the centralist relations of production of the Castilian economy that imposed their rationale on the political attitudes of Ferdinand and Isabella and that through Fonseca and Conchillos, and then again later, through Charles and Philip and a long line of kings and ministers, projected such centralist arrangements on to the Indies. Furthermore, it could then be argued that because of the nature of the relations of production within the empire, and especially between Spain and the Indies, and the mode of central control exercised by the metropolis, a highly centralized imperial economy was the only viable alternative. This argument is farfetched and a trifle circular, but not bad enough to be discarded. At any rate, it is rather difficult to escape the "chicken and egg" trap when considering such questions and perhaps allowances should be made. But even after such allowances, the basic problem would remain of explaining in a satisfactory way why the Castilian economy of the fifteenth and sixteenth centuries should be considered centralist at all within the framework of the concept of "relations of production," and, if so, how it was that, in such a brief period between the accession

The phenomenon of industrialization that elsewhere, principally in Britain, marked a sequence of peripheral challenges and a relative attenuation of central power in Latin America has been associated with the strengthening of the political center. During the decades that followed the Great Depression and the Second World War, the centers of decision and responsibility for the economies of Latin America were controlled not by the private, but by the public sector. This has little or nothing to do with the position of the ruling political parties in the classical spectrum: the governments of Cuba and Mexico; Chile and Peru; Brazil and Argentina are centralist not because they are left-wing, right-wing, capitalist, or socialist, but because they are Latin American.

The circumstances that preceded and accompanied the industrialization of Latin America are different from those associated with the Industrial Revolution in the nations of the Northern Hemisphere at least in the following: first, large-scale modern industry came to Latin America not as the result of domestic decisions, but in response to an exceptional, external stimulus; second, industrialization was neither the consequence of the exertions of an industrial bourgeoisie, nor did it generate an industrial proletariat; third, the technology imported into Latin America during the process of industrialization of the decades following the Great Depression was, by definition, capital-intensive rather than labor-intensive; fourth, the central state has played the principal role in the Latin American process, either through timely political decisions or directly through the channelling of resources into centrally controlled, sponsored, encouraged or protected industrial ventures. Last, and perhaps most important, industrialization has not been "revolutionary" in that it has not brought about the substantial social, political, and cultural changes associated with the nineteenth-century European phenomenon. Latin America is indeed industrializing, and rapidly, but she appears to have been by-passed by the Euro-

---

of the Catholic monarchs and the institutionalization of the imperial arrangements for the Indies, the centralist character was impressed on the whole body politic of the kingdom as well as on its vast imperial domain.

pean type of Industrial Revolution. This does not mean, of course, that the Latin American phenomenon has not proved disturbing to the existing cultural, social, and political structure, but the resulting changes are quite unlike those commonly linked with the European experience.[2]

To present these differences in their appropriate perspective it is necessary to consider them in relation to the principal features of the classic instance of industrialization afforded by the Industrial Revolution in Britain.

Writing almost a century ago, Cunningham explained that "the History of industry does not describe a series of remodellings made from without, but a slow and continuous growth that takes place from within."[3] This is a convincing and helpful concept to apply to the task of interpreting the British industrial experience. The great social and economic changes associated with the Industrial Revolution in Britain were rooted in that country; the accumulation of industrial capital proceeded over many years, perhaps generations, not as the direct response to outside stimuli, but almost as a marginal product of a way of life; technological innovation flowed from large numbers of provincial scientific societies[4] as well as from the shops of hard-working artisans, engineers, and

---

[2] There is one other reason that would justify a closer examination of these processes, and this is that a number of important political interpretations and plans for action in contemporary Latin America have been based on the assumption that the general sequence, the stages of economic growth, characteristic of the industrialization of the European nations would somehow be reproduced in the New World. Hence, if one could discover the "stage" at which any given Latin American nation found itself, it would be easy to diagnose the "changes" necessary before that nation could move on to the next "stage." Such a belief is evidently behind schemes as different in their political inspiration as the Alliance for Progress, launched by the Kennedy administration in the early 1960's, the National Liberation Front program of the orthodox Communist Parties of the region, and the Worker's Front policy of the more extreme left-wing movements, at one time vaguely associated with the position of Maoist China and usually quite active as urban or rural terrorist groups.

[3] William Cunningham, *The Growth of English Industry and Commerce*, Cambridge, 1885, p. 2.

[4] See A. E. Musson and Eric Robinson, "Science and Industry in the late Eighteenth Century," *EHR*, XIII (December, 1960), 222-224.

craftsmen fired with an energy and curiosity perhaps uncomfortably linked to a desire for private gain or disconcertingly influenced by the wish to live a pious Christian life. As Bergier has pointed out in his study of the industrial bourgeoisie, the basic technological innovations of that time were almost invariably simple and comparatively inexpensive, the work of amateurs or artisans of modest financial resources. With few exceptions, the successful entrepreneurs had small plants they built themselves. Their capital was also modest and was usually put together with contributions from their circle of relatives and friends; their only resources for expansion or renewal came from the reinvestment of their profits; "Self financing was the rule at the start of industrialization."[5]

Those people who later became members of an affluent and almost arrogant industrial bourgeoisie, lived their everyday lives in ways that were functionally and purposefully linked with technological advancement, the accumulation of industrial, as distinct from financial, capital, the development of rational business methods, and an expansionist disposition; their frugality, faith, zeal, and ambition were part of a cultural totality and developed within it. Further, they lived and prospered away from the centers of traditional power and prestige; they owed little or nothing to Westminster; their success was their own, and at first they showed little inclination to participate in national and political and economic affairs.[6] The industrial challenge surged in the periphery, away in the Midlands and the Border Country; many of the innovators and

[5] Jean-Francois Bergier, *The Industrial Bourgeoisie and the Rise of the Working Class, 1700-1914*, London, 1971, pp. 20-21.

[6] Apparently this was also true of the bourgeoisie of prerevolutionary France. A study making extensive use of the diary of E. J. F. Barbier, *Chronique de la régence et du regne du Louis XV, 1718-1763*, Paris, 1857-75, indicates that, according to the observations of the author, a prominent lawyer, "in general the bourgeoisie took very little interest in the world of politics in which they had no legitimate share." Barbier himself sums up this attitude when he stated, "I think one should do one's job honourably, without interfering in the affairs of State over which one has neither power nor authority." Elinor G. Barber, *The Bourgeoisie in 18th Century France*, Princeton, N.J., 1955, p. 70.

early investors had never even been to London, and they most certainly did not feel that official protection, encouragement, or straightforward favoritism were essential for the success of their initiatives. Undoubtedly there was industrial development before the accession of George III, and much of it, especially in the textile and metallurgical industries, directly related to national policy, but such growth was eventually overshadowed by the immense proliferation of manufacturing activity at the periphery, characteristic of the Industrial Revolution.

By the time the leaders of the rising industrial bourgeoisie felt the need to challenge the established political order and secure the participation they felt was owed to them in the conduct of national affairs, they also found themselves at the head of a vast popular movement. According to Trevelyan's hearty description, "from squire to postilion, from cotton-lord to mill-hand, everyone was talking of the need for reform. . . . There was . . . general agreement that the new industrial and the old rural districts ought to obtain a representation more in proportion to their wealth and the number of their inhabitants."[7] Confident in the righteousness of their political stance, they also shared cultural inclinations that, though not easily defined in those areas where they blended with the prevailing tastes of the bourgeoisie elsewhere in

---

[7] Trevelyan, *A Shortened History of England*, London, 1962, pp. 473-474. The reform movement of 1832 was not the first such development. Much earlier, when the cohesion among the members of the industrial bourgeoisie was very tenuous, the need to overcome some important obstacles forced them to act with at least a semblance of unity, "The first obstacles were political ones. . . . the entrepreneurs were reluctant to get involved in politics. But it was important to them that government policy should suit their interest. When necessary, they managed to agree among themselves and put forward proposals, indeed demands, as early as 1784, for instance. Boulton was not merely speaking for himself but clearly for the whole group when he protested at the government bill for a duty on raw materials: 'Let taxes be paid upon luxuries, upon vices, and if you like upon property; tax riches when got, and the expenditure of them, but not the means of getting them.' . . . The puritanical, 'class-conscious' overtones in these words tell a story in themselves." See Bergier, *Industrial Bourgeoisie*, pp. 24-25.

Europe, had a distinctness, an originality, and a richness that impress to this day and that we have learned to identify as the culture of the triumphant industrial bourgeoisie. From the reform of 1832 until the First World War, the history of Britain is their history. More than any other comparable segment of European society they were prepared to depart from the accustomed behavior of social climbing groups by their reluctance to accept uncritically the culture, the habits, and tastes of their predecessors in the enjoyment of power. A principal factor in the sense of cohesion among them was precisely "the development of an ethos, a culture peculiar to the industrial bourgeoisie."[8]

Within this vigorous cultural awareness, religious feeling played a principal role. It provided a firm foundation for the supreme confidence with which the Victorian bourgeoisie disapproved of the customs, habits, and beliefs of those who had preceded them as political rulers and arbiters of taste and manners. In this context, piety most certainly transcended sectarian limitations; it was as important in Pugin's enthusiasm for a Gothic revival as an aspect of his Catholicism as it was in the Earl of Shaftesbury's evangelical fervor or Ruskin's Gothic Protestantism.[9] Bergier notes that the members of the industrial bourgeoisie "kept to themselves," and

[8] Bergier, *Industrial Bourgeoisie*, p. 23.

[9] Ruskin and Pugin were united by their architectural taste, but most interestingly divided by their religious feelings. Ruskin's attack on Pugin's Gothic revivalism could not have been fiercer. Referring to the aesthetic inducements to Catholicism, Ruskin wrote, "of all these fatuities, the basest is the being lured into the Romanist Church by the glitter of it, like larks into a trap by broken glass; to be blown into a change of religion by the whine of an organ-pipe; stitched into a new creed by the gold threads on priest's petticoats; jangled into a change of conscience by the chimes of a belfry. I know nothing in the shape of error so dark as this, no imbecility so absolute, no treachery so contemptible." Ruskin, John, *The Stones of Venice*, London, 1851, Appendix 12, p. 371. As Kenneth Clark has indicated in his celebrated study, "Ruskin's Protestant eloquence achieved its end. Had he not salted his description of Italian Gothic with attacks on Rome, he would certainly have been considered a Roman Catholic. . . . The dissociation of Gothic architecture and Rome was, perhaps, Ruskin's most complete success." *The Gothic Revival*, London, 1974, pp. 195-196.

this he attributes to their tendency to religious dissent; "many entrepreneurs in England were adherents of nonconformist sects and a number of the French entrepreneurs were Protestants. From this religious and social dissent they derived vigour and, ultimately, cohesion."[10] They did indeed and were as united and vehement in their dissent from the amiable latitude of the established Church as they were in their rejection of the manners, morals, and taste of the established aristocracy. This striking feature, common to nonconformist groups, is well-illustrated by the activities of early nineteenth-century evangelicals. In a recent study of their impact on Victorian society, Ian Bradley observes that the positions on which the evangelicals concentrated their attacks "were essentially aristocratic and the values which they exalted were predominantly bourgeois."[11] They complained persistently

[10] Bergier, *Industrial Bourgeoisie*, p. 25. "By the middle of the century the industrialist was universally hailed as the modern Prometheus, the begetter of a new society. Economists, philosophers, and social reformers (Saint-Simon, Enfantin, and Constantin Pecqueur) all gave him their blessing. 'The time has come' wrote Isoard in 1834, 'for our industrialists to occupy the positions held since 1789 by successively, the priests, the soldiers, the lawyers, and the men of letters.' " That the rise of a different class of people to the higher reaches of power and prestige did not pass unnoticed by contemporaries is also quite evident. Disraeli, in *Endymion*, makes the point clearly enough contrasting precisely the dominance of the landed aristocracy with what was to follow. Before the rise of the middle class, he wrote "the great world . . . was limited in its proportions, and composed of elements more refined, though far less various. It consisted mainly of the great landed aristocracy. . . . Occasionally an eminent banker or merchant invested a large portion of his accumulations in land, and in the purchase of parliamentary influence, and was in time duly admitted into the sanctuary. But those vast and successful invasions of society by new classes which have since occurred, though impending, had not yet commenced." *Endymion*, London, 1881, p. 23.

[11] William Wilberforce put the matter succinctly when he complained that a man could call himself a Christian, "and if he be not habitually guilty of any of the grosser vices against his fellow creatures, we have no great reason to be dissatisfied with him, or to question the validity of his claim to the name and privileges of a Christian." *A Practical View of the Prevailing Religious System of Professed Christians in the Higher and Middle Classes in this Country contrasted with Real Christianity*, 7th ed., London, 1798, p. 91. Cited by Ian Bradley, *The Call to Seriousness, The Evangelical Impact on the Victorians*. London, 1976, p. 19.

about the influence throughout society of the values and habits of the aristocracy, "their great aim was to secure the triumph of the virtues of hard work, plain living and moral propriety which characterized the middle classes." That they emerged victorious, is beyond doubt, "the middle classes did not just cease to emulate the behaviour of the aristocracy . . . they came positively to despise it." Moreover, the standard of behavior they wanted their contemporaries to accept "was very largely taken up and followed in nineteenth century England." A principal reason for this was "that it provided a useful and timely ethic for the emerging middle class."[12]

Court and courtiers they held in very low esteem; they detested the affectations and mannerisms of the traditional landed aristocracy; they strongly disapproved of their lack of religiosity and considered their educational practices, their art, music, and architecture equally abhorrent. Even such an unlikely supporter of egalitarian causes as Pugin could write with feeling about the upper orders of contemporary society. When referring to "the wretched state of architecture at the present day," he singled out Brighton as "abominable," describing it further as "the favoured residence of royalty, and the sojourn of all triflers who wait upon the motions of the court."[13] To the then fashionable neoclassic vogue in architecture, the rising industrial bourgeoisie opposed their very special preference for an indigenous, almost "nationalistic," Gothic revival; an "English" style, *sui generis* in conception and execution; the disciples of Andrea Palladio and other less august foreign architects found their match in Ruskin, Scott, Pugin, Barry, and their followers and imitators. In this respect, the reconstruction of the Houses of Parliament posed an architectural problem that could most properly be resolved by ascertaining the national mood, and it was the challengers who won the day, their victory fittingly commemorated by the charming anachronism that adorns the banks of the

[12] Bradley, *Seriousness*, pp. 145, 153-154.

[13] A. Welby Pugin, *Contrasts: or, A Parallel Between the Noble Edifices of the Middle Ages and Corresponding Buildings of the Present Day: Shewing the Present Decay of Taste*, Victorian Library Edition, Leicester, 1969, p. 15.

Thames by Westminster Bridge.[14] As Kenneth Clark has pointed out, in the eighteenth century most of the gentlemen who undertook building had a knowledge of architecture and together with the professional architects they dictated style. And he adds that with a few exceptions we may say that "the more they knew about architecture the less likely they were to build Gothic," because although popular and fashionable as early as 1830, Gothic was still considered a nonprofessional style. "No architect of talent had used it with conviction." This amateurishness, however, was unimportant, for after 1830 "we meet with the belief that neither knowledge nor experience is necessary to criticize a work of art, and the 'impartial' middle class, with no tradition of culture, becomes final arbiter of taste."[15]

Was the revived Gothic the taste of the rising industrial leaders or better, is there a significant relation between the art that flourished in England during the reign of Victoria and the social groups that dominated the political and economic life of the nation? Obviously, there was neo-Gothic architecture before the turn of the century. That the Gothic survived in England between the thirteenth and the eighteenth centuries is beyond doubt, but, as Kenneth Clark indicates, a clear division must be established "between survival and revival."[16] However, the peculiar mood that is so rightly identified with the climax of Victorian industrial society in England includes an extension, a usage, and an emphasis on the Gothic linked not only with the other arts, but with social and moral attitudes that are bound distinctly and intimately with the changes brought about by the rise of industry. Ruskin was

[14] It should not be forgotten that the main reason why Gothic was chosen for the new Houses of Parliament was "the important belief that Gothic was essentially an English style. . . . how could a few pedants, who insisted that Gothic originated in France, stand against the flood of romantic nationalism? Gothic must be used because it was the national style. Everyone liked an argument which could be put so clearly, so shortly and with so few technicalities." Clark, *Gothic Revival*, pp. 114-115.

[15] Clark, *Gothic Revival*, p. 117.

[16] See Clark, *Gothic Revival*, especially chapter one on the survival of the Gothic.

convinced that the art of any country reflects its social and political virtues; "The art, or general productive and formative energy of any country, is the exact exponent of its ethical life."[17] More than a century later, confirmation of such a view comes from the pen of a French sociologist who proposes that the relationship between artistic creation and external reality is constantly confirmed by experience. If this were not so, one would have to look on art as no more than nostalgic dreaming; "nature as the artist describes it cannot be nature 'as it really is' because it has been twice transformed—once by society and again by the artist."[18] If we assume this to be true, it is then legitimate to think that the art of Victorian England reflected the tastes, moods, and aspirations of the triumphant industrial bourgeoisie. The various doctrines, techniques, feelings, and fashions identified not only with the Gothic revival and the Pre-Raphaelite brotherhood, their friends and disciples, but with the whole cultural complex of the time, including the poetry, the music, and the prose, altogether afford a convincing portrait of the essential features of that historical moment. One could argue that there was scarcely an English painter active during the second half of the century that was not influenced significantly, for instance, by the Pre-Raphaelite brotherhood, and this influence went far beyond painting, into printing, furniture, clothes, architec-

---

[17] There have, indeed, been periods in history when an essential identification of art and society is simply not to be discovered, but I find it difficult not to accept that this hypothesis is tenable when applied to nineteenth-century Europe and those parts of the world, especially the Americas, which were colonized from Europe. In developing this concept to apply it to a comparative study of the rise of industry in Britain and Latin America, I have made extensive use of Raymond Williams' important work, *Culture and Society*, London, 1961, especially chapter seven. The basic concept is best expressed by Williams: "An essential hypothesis in the development of the idea of culture is that the art of a period is closely and necessarily related to the generally prevalent 'way of life,' and further that, in consequence, aesthetic, moral and social judgements are closely interrelated," pp. 137, 142.

[18] Jean Duvigneaud, *The Sociology of Art*, London, 1972, p. 29. For a more restricted study of the relationship between industry and art, see Francis D. Klingender, *Art and the Industrial Revolution*, London, 1972.

ture, and the design of practically every conceivable household good, no matter how trivial.[19] Obviously it would be excessive to identify Pre-Raphaelitism and its influence directly with the tastes and moods of the industrial leadership of Britain, but a loose and nonetheless useful correlation could be established between the art that proved fashionable at the time and the people whose continuing patronage afforded principal and substantial evidence of that acceptance.

The class of people who stood in the vanguard of the Industrial Revolution and who profited from it were not blind to the fruits of their victorious enterprise, and this had a direct and important consequence for the arts. Writing about Victorian artists, Quentin Bell indicated that he could not examine the English contribution to painting during the second half of the century without first attempting some generalizations about the social context, mainly referring to the effects of the Industrial Revolution. After noting that "Capitalism produced dividends," he adds; "There was a striking increase in the number of people who could afford to live in Islington. . . . Great fortunes were amassed by industrialists in Liverpool, Manchester, and Leeds—a few of whom were ready to buy Pre-Raphaelite pictures."[20] More than a few did precisely that, and also had their homes built and decorated in the fashionable styles; these styles were as Clark has explained, "organically connected with society, something which springs inevitably from a way of life." Industrial technology was only one aspect of the cultural complex; the people who invented those modern techniques and those who used them and profited from them did so because they lived their lives in distinct and novel ways. There was indeed a great gulf between them and their immediate predecessors. That conceptual chasm so clearly separating the pleasure-loving Regency from the earnestness of Prince Albert's times is one that no Latin American urban bourgeoisie has ever bridged. Here lies perhaps the most signal difference between the industrial experience as

[19] Jeremy Maas, *Victorian Painters*, London, 1969, p. 125.
[20] Quentin Bell, *Victorian Artists*, London, 1967, p. 5.

it affected Britain and western Europe during the nineteenth century and Latin America during the decades after the Great Depression.

The process whereby the British industrial bourgeoisie attained this position can be summarized in this way; first, economic power was acquired, laboriously, gradually over many years, perhaps generations, of hard work, technological innovation, and expansion. During this time, a cultural pattern emerged associated with industrial activity. Secondly, based firmly on a position of economic strength, the bourgeoisie knocked on the doors of Parliament to demand, successfully, their share of political power. Thirdly, having created their own cultural values and institutions, instead of embracing those of the displaced land-owning aristocracy, they imposed their own on the nation, and, because of Britain's preponderant position in world affairs, their industrial culture followed the British flag throughout the globe. For the British bourgeoisie, first came economic power, then, political power, and finally, social prestige and cultural preponderance.

The expansion of industrialization also gave rise to an industrial proletariat. Again this is a difficult concept to define. A recent historian of the English working class has affirmed that "the working class presence was in 1832, the most significant fact in British political life." And then explains that "most English working class people came to feel an identity of interests as between themselves, and as against their rulers and employers."[21] Observers of the contemporary scene, Marx and Engels among others, arrived at the same conclusion. Regardless of whether an accurate definition is needed of what constitutes the "industrial proletariat," what should be beyond dispute is that, given the levels of labor-intensive

[21] R. Currie and R. M. Hartwell, "The Making of the English Working Class?" *EHR*, XVII (December, 1965), 634. The actual quotation is from E. P. Thompson, *The Making of the English Working Class*, London, 1963, pp. 11-12. It must be pointed out that the essay cited above is a most useful complement to the actual book in pointing out the difficulties that beset the scholar who attempts too circumscribed a definition of, for instance, the concept of "class."

technology in the eighteenth and early nineteenth centuries, the development of industry ran parallel with the formation of a large industrial labor force. People emigrated from the countryside during the second half of the eighteenth century for a variety of reasons, among them the attraction of employment in industry and the effects of the enclosure movement; they seldom returned. Agricultural production rose rapidly, and manufacturing industry absorbed an important proportion of the displaced rural workers. Grouped together in factories, earning low wages for long hours of work, living in subhuman conditions in the teeming slums that proliferated around the new industrial centers, these were the first victims of the Industrial Revolution. Whether their class-consciousness was as well-defined as Thompson suggests is again a matter for debate, and yet it is undeniable that the industrial working class, to differentiate it from the peasantry or the tertiary sector of a later period in the industrial evolution of western Europe, provided the mass support, the committed rank and file, the social momentum behind the reformist and revolutionary movements of that period.

Against the perspective afforded by the time elapsed between the first Elizabeth and the Victorian consolidation of industrial society, the rise of both an industrial bourgeoisie and proletariat appear as processes that necessarily must have led to an attenuation of central power. Without paying excessive attention to the constitutional implications of such a trend, it should nevertheless be clear that whatever measure of effective power was attained by the industrial bourgeoisie by virtue of their economic preponderance or by the industrial working classes because of their militancy, representativeness, or organization that power was either wrested from the central authority or it generated restraints and limitations qualifying its exercise. In this sense it can be affirmed that one of the early results of the growth of modern industry was a relative dispersal of power from a preindustrial center toward an industrial periphery in which the new bourgeoisie and proletariat played principal roles. As the proletariat was unable to secure political control throughout the great century of the

Industrial Revolution, it was the bourgeoisie—no doubt tempered or hindered by a militant and progressively politicized working class—that had the opportunity of influencing public affairs.[22] And yet, precisely because of their characteristic liberal inclinations, they were the least likely to augment willingly the power of the central state at the expense of peripheral interest groups. Of course, during this century and especially since the Second World War, other factors have developed suggesting that the enhanced importance of the central state in the economic life of most nations is not going to decline in the foreseeable future. But this is clearly a later stage of the process. What is important now is to note that the British Industrial Revolution had a peripheral rather than a central origin; it resulted not from the planned and conscious exertions of successive Hanoverian regimes, but from factors not directly related to government policy. Moreover, once under way, it was associated either as cause or effect or both with the formation of two social groupings—the industrial bourgeoisie and the proletariat—whose influence increased at the expense of that traditionally wielded by the preindustrial centers of political authority.

[22] The extension of the electoral franchise through three successive reforms was symbolic of the increased political importance of the working class; the first Reform Bill of 1832 enfranchised most of the middle class, but left the working class out absolutely; the Second Reform Bill of 1867 gave the vote to most of the factory workers doubling the size of the electorate; the third bill of 1885 finally extended the vote to those workers who had been excluded by the two previous bills.

12

The Latin American Experience
of Industrialization

In less than a generation, the countries of Latin America adopted the industrial technology that took Europeans centuries to create. It has been tempting, for many of those who lived through this process, to hope that the wholesale introduction of this advanced technology would somehow turn Latin Americans into Europeans or force on Latin American society the changes experienced by Europe during the time modern industrial technology was developed and applied. Those who felt that what had actually happened in the Europe of the nineteenth century was worth having made sincere efforts to use the opportunity to transform this or that Latin American economy and society into a twentieth-century replica of mid-nineteenth-century Britain. Others felt that the rapid industrialization of Latin America offered a second chance to those political and economic expectations that for good or bad reasons had been frustrated in nineteenth-century Europe; the political revolutions that did not follow the European Industrial Revolution would, perhaps, painlessly follow the coming of industry to Latin America.[1]

Such hopes and expectations have been reflected in the generalized adoption of European ideological models, economic programs, doctrines for improvement, and recipes for progress as adequate means for understanding and guiding the changes that have accompanied the industrialization of the re-

[1] On this point, see Philippe C. Schmitter, "Desarrollo retrasado, dependencia externa y cambio político en América Latina," *FI*, xi (October-December, 1971), 135-137.

gion. It requires, however, more than stubbornness to maintain that their belated application in the Southern Hemisphere has been an unqualified success. To understand why they did not succeed, it would appear reasonable to suggest that a necessary first step should be a comparison of the process of industrialization in Latin America with the European experience.

Industrialization did not come to Latin America as the result of an indigenous process of growth, but as a complex response to an external stimulus. If in Britain the growth of industry was, as Cunningham explained, "a slow and continuous growth . . . from within," in Latin America it was a relatively rapid response to an outside stimulus. An exhaustive analysis of this process would have to mention both world wars and the Great Depression of 1929 as the crucial external events that, taken together, created the circumstances responsible for industrialization. Until 1929, however, with the qualified exception of Argentina, there had been no significant industrial advances in the five most industrialized countries. In 1929 the percentage share of industrial production within the gross national production was 22.8 percent for Argentina, 14.2 percent for Mexico, 11.7 percent for Brazil, 7.9 percent for Chile, and 6.2 percent for Colombia.[2]

This limited industrial growth was a secondary result of the expansion of the traditional export sector of the economy and not of a consciously pursued industrializing effort; its dynamism was as minimal as its capacity for endogenous growth. A second look at these pioneering efforts, shows them to be more modest than the nationalistic rhetoric would have us believe. As Farley has noted, most of the industrial efforts prior to the First World War were variations on the cottage industry theme. A few isolated industries, mainly financed by foreign interests and producing exportable goods appeared in some urban locations, "But the majority of local factories were engaged in simple acts of transforming local

---

[2] Celso Furtado, *La economía latinoamericana desde la conquista ibérica hasta la revolución cubana*, Santiago, 1969, p. 111.

raw materials, and their activities bore little dynamic relation to the local economy." At this early stage, industrialization was helped by urban concentration that offered internal markets in addition to the normal export outlets and by massive immigration that created an important nucleus of entrepreneurial and technical talent.[3] What is possibly most important about this type of industrialization is that even as early as the 1920s it showed symptoms of exhaustion. In Argentina, for instance, when the share of industrial production in the gross national product reached 20 percent in 1910, this proportion was maintained until after 1920; by 1925 it increased to 23.6 percent and then it declined to 22.8 percent in 1929. But during the same period, the volume of Argentine exports increased by over 140 percent highlighting the extraordinary contrast between the rapid overall growth of the economy and the relative immobility of the industrial sector. Figures for Brazil and Mexico suggest similar trends. In Mexico during the first decade of the century, the overall rate of growth was of 4.2 percent but industrial production increased only by 3.6 percent. In Brazil, after a period of relatively rapid growth before 1914, the share of industrial production in the gross national product remained stationary until the Great Depression.[4]

Argentina is the exception. Her volume of industrial production was almost proportionately double that of Mex-

[3] Rawle Farley, *The Economics of Latin America*, New York, 1972, p. 206. It is conceivable that in the absence of the dramatic external stimulus of crisis and wars, the economies of Latin America would have gradually developed an important industrial sector through the process Albert O. Hirschman has described as "import swallowing"; he writes "industrialization has not only been the response to sudden deprivation of imports: it has taken place in many erstwhile nonindustrial countries as a result of the gradual expansion of an economy that grows along the export-propelled path. As incomes and markets expand in such a country and some thresholds at which domestic production becomes profitable are crossed, industries come into being without the need of external shocks or government intervention." "The Political Economy of Import-Substituting Industrialization in Latin America," in *Latin America; Problems in Economic Development*, ed. Charles T. Nisbet, New York, 1969, p. 240 et seq.

[4] Furtado, *La economía*, p. 107.

ico, the second most industrialized nation in the region, but this was to a considerable degree the result of the exertions of European immigrants who tended almost exclusively to associate with the more modern establishments within the industrial sector.[5] It was not, therefore, a domestic development comparable to the early stages of the Industrial Revolution in Britain or northwestern Europe; that industrial activity that managed to prosper in the country during the decades before 1929 was the fruit of the endeavors of people who had acquired their industrious habits and inclinations elsewhere and who, moreover, found it extraordinarily difficult to obtain official encouragement or support. As Cornblit has indicated, "the apparent passiveness of the industrialists is one of the most conspicuous aspects of the contemporary struggle for power in Argentina."[6]

Large-scale, modern industrialization came to Latin America after 1929. The experience of each country varies considerably both in the rapidity with which the new technology was incorporated and the success with which the industrial development programs were implemented, but, in

[5] In a study of the role played by European immigrants in Argentine industry, Oscar Cornblit observes that "in 1895 there were almost four and a half times as many foreigners than native born Argentines engaged in manufacturing industry. Twenty years later the situation had not changed very much; three times as many foreigners as Argentines were still engaged in secondary activities." Oscar Cornblit, "European Immigrants in Argentine Industry and Politics," in *The Politics of Conformity in Latin America*, ed. Claudio Véliz, London, 1967, p. 227. According to Cornblit's study, in 1914 foreign proprietors of industrial firms represented 66 percent of the total for Argentina.

[6] Looking further into the reasons for this situation Cornblit presents the following preliminary considerations: "first, that by the end of the first world war there were industrial entrepreneur groups in some parts of the country—chiefly in the Buenos Aires and Rosario areas—sufficiently mature to try to influence the central government's economic policy; secondly, that the tenuous influence they actually exerted resulted from their lack of contact with the political élite, especially with the Radical Party, which remained in power between 1916 and 1930; and lastly, that this failure of communication occurred because the system of selection of the political élite discriminated against the immigrants, who promoted the great majority of the industrial undertakings." Cornblit, "European Immigrants," p. 221.

general, it is true to say that it was after the Great Depression that Latin America entered decisively into the era of modern industry. Brazilian industrial production increased by 42 percent between 1929 and 1937, but in the following decade it went up by 82 percent, and between 1947 and 1957 by 123 percent, totalling an increase of 475 percent for the period 1929-1957. Argentina was off to a relatively slow start with a 23 percent rise between 1929 and 1937, but industrial production accelerated to 73 percent in the next decade, reaching a total of 220 percent for the period 1929-1957. Colombia registered an initial increase of 90 percent for 1929-1937, rose to 110 percent for the next decade and 130 percent for the following one, adding up an impressive total of 830 percent rise in industrial production for the whole period. The figures for Mexico show an increase of 46 percent between 1929 and 1937, of 86 percent between 1937 and 1947, and of 98 percent between 1947 and 1957, giving a total of 407 percent for the twenty-eight year period.[7]

Such rates of growth were not unusual in the region and were in part the consequence of a rapid process of industrialization through import-substitution. This was realized most successfully in those countries that having attained a measure of industrial diversification before 1929 allowed for a more intensive utilization of existing plant and entrepreneurial capacity. Hence the upward trend noticeable in the major countries of the region is not necessarily paralleled in those unable, for a variety of reasons, to develop significant infrastructural facilities or the beginnings of a domestic industrial establishment. Moreover, it is possible to differentiate between those countries able to profit from the opportunity afforded by the depression by bringing about changes in their internal economic structure as well as in their relations with the international

[7] Furtado, *La economía*, p. 112. The figures for net per capita output of manufactured goods are equally impressive: from 1938 to 1947 Argentine output increased from 24 to 105 constant dollars per capita, Brazilian output increased from 9 to 52 constant dollars, Chilean output from 18 to 93 constant dollars and Mexican output of manufactured goods increased from 8 to 38 constant dollars per capita. Farley, *The Economics*, p. 208.

economy and those unable to do so. Countries such as Brazil, Argentina, Uruguay, Chile, Mexico, and Colombia should be listed among the former and the rest among the latter.[8] This is not the place for a more detailed examination of these processes. It suffices to affirm that this was a major industrializing effort in response to external circumstances. The catastrophic effects of the Great Depression on the exporting economies of Latin America with the sequel of unemployment and severe reductions in import capacity virtually forced governments to adopt protectionist policies that in turn made the rapid development of an import-substituting industry almost mandatory.[9]

After a century of independent life when most of these countries lived from the export of primary commodities to the industrial markets of the northern hemisphere, a diversified urban demand had been generated at home for imported manufactured products. The needs of this local market had been traditionally supplied from the industrialized centers of Europe and North America, but the interruption of normal commercial relations to a limited degree first during 1914-1918 and massively after 1929 and again in 1939-1945 resulted in exceptionally favorable conditions for the development of import-substitution industries through the region. As Baltra has pointed out, after 1929 the decision to industrialize was not a matter of choice, "it was not even one among several alternative courses of action; it was an unavoidable necessity, the only solution to the development problems of Latin America."[10] The central state responded to this challenge by

[8] See Sunkel y Paz, *El subdesarrollo*, pp. 349-355.

[9] During the crisis years, "the prices of primary products fell and export earnings went so low that Latin America's capacity to import dropped some 50 percent in the period 1914-1945." Farley, *The Economics*, p. 207. In the specific case of Chile—perhaps the most severely affected by the Great Crisis—the import coefficient fell from 31.2 in 1929 to 13.8 in 1937; similarly, in this country, the coefficient of industrialization rose during the same period from 7.9 to 11.3. See Furtado, *La economía*, p. 111.

[10] Alberto Baltra, *Crecimiento económico de América Latina*, Santiago, 1959, p. 83. (author's translation.) This type of industrial development carried its

promptly assuming the initiative in redirecting resources toward the development of new industrial ventures and their
requisite infrastructure. It was, of course, eminently well-
placed to do this, for, as Wythe indicated in his pioneering
study published more than thirty years ago, "despite brief in-
terludes when the liberal and free-trade doctrines . . . have
been popular, in the Latin American republics the philosophy
of interventionism has held sway." and "mercantilism in

---

own problems that became critical during the decades of 1960 and 1970. As
Sunkel has indicated, the export sector that initiated the process later became
its principal limiting factor. See especially, pp 355-380, *El subdesarrollo*. It is
tempting, nonetheless, to suggest that the essence of the problem in many of
the countries of the region may have been best described by the West Indian
novelist V. S. Naipaul when he wrote that "Industrialization, in territories
like ours, seems to be a process of filling imported tubes and tins with various
imported substances. Whenever we went beyond this we were likely to get
into trouble." *The Mimic Men*, London, 1969, p. 216. Latin America, of
course, went beyond this and did get into trouble. As Hirschman has explained, a high tariff protection for the infant industries combined with very
low tariffs, or even preferential treatment for those industries' imported inputs can lead, and has led, to situations in which "the greater the difference
between the level of protection accorded to the import-substituting industry
and that applying to its imported inputs, the more will the profit margin of
the industry depend *on preventing* domestic production of the inputs. For it is
a fair assumption that the backward linkage industries would, once established, be eligible for a level of protection similar to that benefiting the initial
import-substituting industry. . . . [therefore] the newly established industries
may not act at all as the entering wedge of a broad industrialization drive.
The high customs duties on their outputs, combined with low duties on their
inputs, could almost be seen as a plot on the part of the existing powerholders
to corrupt or buy off the new industrialists, to reduce them to a sinecured,
inefficient and unenterprising group that can in no way threaten the existing
social structure. Indeed, like the worker's aristocracy in Lenin's theory of im-
perialism, these pampered, industrialists might go over to the enemy—that
is, make common cause with agrarian and trading interests which had long
been opposed to the introduction of 'exotic' industries." In the face of this
structural passivity on the part of the private industrial sector, only decisive
action by the central state could overcome this impasse. It is thus legitimate
to conclude, with Hirschman, that "the resistance of the initial industrialists
to backward linkage" contributed importantly to enhancing "the potential
contribution of public policy to the process." Hirschman, "Political Economy," pp. 254-255.

Latin America has never died."[11] Perhaps not quite mercantilism, but certainly a prolix, meticulous bureaucratic concern with the health of the economy has been a persistent characteristic of the political arrangements in the region. Even during the years of the "liberal pause," the central governments did not entirely abdicate their responsibilities, but simply abstained from tampering with decisions that resulted in satisfactory gains for the exporting sectors.

Most of the policies implemented by the central governments after 1929 were mainly designed to cushion the economies against the rigors of the depression and included such orthodox measures as restrictions on imports, the acquisition of primary commodity surpluses, exchange controls, and the like.[12] However, the magnitude of the collapse generated understandable nationalistic reactions that reinforced the industrializing momentum making it unlikely that even in the event of a rapid recovery, which did not take place anyway, the governments of the region could retreat easily and adopt a more passive stance. The decade of 1930 was not over when the Second World War reaffirmed the conviction, even among those who had earlier profited from the external dependence of the export economies, that the old days were gone forever and the countries of Latin America had to find their own way to survival in a competitive and increasingly industrial world.

The persistence of the external conditions favoring Latin American industrialization and the nationalistic mood contributed significantly to the enhanced role of the central state in the promotion of industrial activity. In very few years the protectionist devices and other emergency measures that had been originally adopted as a direct response to the crisis were institutionalized into official government programs for the advancement of industry. Moreover, the strategic position of

[11] George Wythe, *Industry in Latin America*, New York, 1945, p. 65.

[12] In the case of Brazil, for instance, the recovery of the economy from 1933 onwards was principally due to "the pump-priming unconsciously adopted . . . as a by-product of the protection of the coffee interests by the central government." See Furtado, *Economic Growth*, 1963, pp. 203-213.

the central state as main comptroller of the flow of resources generated by the export sector permitted successive governments to play a principal role in directing these funds into industrial promotion. Hence, within the space of one generation, the central state consolidated its key position at least with respect to three of the principal aspects of modern economic policy: it became the main financial entity able to supply capital to private industrial ventures; it assumed the function of arbiter in the process of income redistribution through the implementation of a variety of social policies; and it assigned a dynamic role to the public sector directing toward it the financial resources required for the development of an adequate industrial infrastructure and the creation of the basic sectors of the new industrial economy.[13]

In different nations of Latin America, under varying political regimes, a number of semiautonomous public corporations were created that through the crucial decades after 1939, when the first one was established in Chile, played a principal role in the industrialization of the region.[14] Largely through

---

[13] Sunkel, *El subdesarrollo*, p. 377. According to a senior Mexican economist and civil servant, the new role of the state in the development of industry includes four types of policy: first, measures to protect domestic industry from foreign competition; second, measures to regulate and stimulate industry; third, direct government promotion of industrial activity, and last, government provision of technical assistance to industry. See Plácido García Reynoso, "Government Policy and Business Responsibility in the Process of Industrial Development and Economic Integration in Latin America," in *IADB* (1969), 3-29.

[14] *The Corporación de Fomento de la Producción* or Chilean Development Corporation, otherwise known as CORFO, was founded in 1939 under the Popular Front administration of President Pedro Aguirre Cerda; "as the basic agent in the government's development effort, CORFO has acted as financier, entrepreneur, investor, innovator and researcher, and frontierman. As such it has dominated economic life since 1939. CORFO controlled the lion's share of the country's investment in machinery and equipment (in ten years during the period 1940-1954 it controlled more than 30 per cent); it also controlled an average of more than 25 per cent of public investment . . . and as much as 18 per cent (in 1954) of gross domestic investment." Markos Mamalakis and Clark W. Reynolds, eds. *Essays on the Chilean Economy*, New Haven, Conn., 1965, pp. 18-19. On CORFO, see also Herman Finer, *The Chilean Development Corporation*, Montreal, 1947.

their action, the key sectors of the national economies came early under the responsibility of the state or, often enough, were in fact created from the center with public capital controlled by managers working either directly for the government as civil servants or indirectly in autonomous state corporations. Although it would be futile to disregard the importance of nationalization policies when considering the involvement of the central state in the economic life of the region, it would be equally mistaken not to consider the creative role these state agencies played in the launching of the early industrial ventures assisting and sustaining private investment and generally working for the implementation of long-term programs that were quite beyond the capacity of the region's unimpressive private sector. In the absence of these state initiatives, very few of the major industries of the region would exist. Petroleum and oil refineries in Mexico, Chile, and Argentina, steel in Chile and Brazil, electricity almost everywhere, as well as banking and transportation, fisheries, and technologically complex new developments in agriculture and mining—all owe much or everything to such initiatives. Even today, when a nation like Brazil is paraded outside Latin America as an example of what dynamic private enterprise can accomplish, there is the risk of overlooking the fact that well over 60 percent of the country's banking and financial activities are run by the state, or that 73.5 percent of the industrial infrastructure is state-contiolled as well as 52.5 percent of the production of intermediate manufactured products. In Chile, in 1969, two years before the *Unidad Popular* regime assumed power, over 70 percent of total investment was public investment; in Mexico, which can hardly be described as a socialist country, well over a third of total direct industrial investment is public investment. It is unnecessary to continue illustrating what should be abundantly clear; the central state played the principal role in the industrialization of the region.

A major difference therefore between the Industrial Revolution as it took place in Britain and the process of industrialization of Latin America is that, while the former had a peripheral origin and eventually resulted in a relative attenuation of central power, in the latter case the main impetus came from the center and, far from weakening it, considerably strengthened it. A corollary of this would be that, while in Britain the industrializing effort was associated with the activities and manner of life of a rising industrial bourgeoisie, in the case of Latin America, the coming of modern industry has been neither preceded nor accompanied by the formation of such a group.

Having said this, it must be added that it is untenable to consider those Latin American urban groups that played a protagonic role in the development of industry as the counterpart of the British industrial bourgeoisie. With some hesitation, I would suggest that a better parallel, though not an entirely satisfactory one, could be drawn between the Latin American industrial managers, bureaucrats, and civil servants who guided the growth of industry and the French *bourgeoisie d'affaires*, those men who, as Bergier has observed, "held all the reins at the close of the *ancien régime*" and whose incomes were frequently higher than those of the declining nobility. Moreover, this group produced by far the best officials and "where the nobility was lightweight . . . it *was* the State."[15] If the sequence suggested earlier as a summary of the stages whereby the British industrial bourgeoisie reached its dominant position were to be compared to what happened in Latin America, one would have to note that this Latin American *bourgeoisie d'affaires* attained political power before the coming of industry, and that it was as bureaucratic managers that it acquired direct or indirect control of the process of industrialization. Subsequently it supported enthusiastically corporate industrial growth; it allocated tenders, granted licenses, encouraged doubtful ventures, and channelled foreign exchange and public credit in the direction of their friends, relatives, and political supporters. To the evident gratification of these

---

[15] Bergier, *Industrial Bourgeoisie*, p. 10.

managers, industry prospered and so did their friends. By the decade of 1960, they were not only politically powerful as a group, but wealthy as well.

In the absence of a diversified and independent industrial bourgeoisie, and given the well-established clientelistic traditions of *compadrazgo*, nepotism, and the like that have been part of the political history of many of these countries, it was almost unavoidable that when the need arose to delegate responsibility for developing new projects, to manage state supported industrial ventures, or simply to represent loyally and efficiently the best interests of the central state in crucial posts connected with industry these tasks should be allocated to people who were linked to those already in positions of responsibility.

There is an unavoidable parallel here with the Japanese experience of the *zaibatsu*. At the stage of industrial foundation, the allocation of responsibility for the management of the new enterprises was largely determined by the pattern of the family relationships, allegiance to clan, and the like. While in Japan, however, these enterprises emerged as private ventures, albeit closely associated with the general policies of the state, in Latin America they resulted in the creation of strategic public enterprises and a host of lesser entities dependent on state assistance. In fact, perhaps the only truly "private" enterprises, in that their centers of decision were almost wholly independent from state guidance, control, or critical support, were the subsidiaries of major foreign corporations that later evolved into what are now known as multinational corporations.[16]

[16] On this last point, see Osvaldo Sunkel, "Big Business and *dependencia*, a Latin American View," *FA*, 1 (1972), 517-531. The particular circumstances that accompanied the extension of private foreign investment into industrial ventures eventually leading to the elaboration of a "theory of dependence" were noted early in the process. It is interesting to see, for instance, that Pedro Aguirre Cerda, the victorious Chilean Popular Front candidate in the presidential elections of 1938, wrote a book in 1933 on the general problem of industrial development in which he states that, "the great European or North American enterprises come to our countries to establish subsidiaries, and with the use of their privileges and patents and the pretext that they must

The flow of state capital into industry was thus guided by people who belonged largely to the same social groupings of those who occupied key posts in the administrative and political structure. The wealth they acquired resulted almost inevitably from their holding strategic positions in the critical sectors of economic and political decision at a time that, from their personal point of view, must have been both fortunate and fortuitous. Together with their friends, relatives, and associates, they soon constituted a kind of industrial clientele deeply conscious of the fact that their well-being depended in large measure on their remaining a loyal and cooperative extension of the central state apparatus. Their newly acquired wealth was not industrial capital resulting marginally from a style of life; there was no cultural or religious infrastructure behind their association with industrial ventures; there had been no commitment to austerity or general reforms and improvements in the educational system leading to substantial technological innovation; but most important of all, there was no cultural ethos associated with the task of industrialization.

The growth of modern industry during the decades following the Great Depression proceeded without undue risks, and the people who adopted the decisions, those who managed the new enterprises and chose alternative ways of development, were largely the same people who had lived quite pleasantly without industry only a few years earlier. For them industrialization and industrial technology were external phe-

---

maintain standards, bring . . . all the factors they need for the elaboration of their products and thereby, utilizing the prestige of a foreign trade mark they impose on us the consumption of their merchandise without compensation or benefit to the national economy. It is easily understood that these investments if adequately regulated could become a means whereby our governments could bring into our countries new industrial activities and technicians ready to instruct us in these matters as well as new sources of just taxation. But without adequate legislation to force these subsidiaries into close cooperation with nascent national industries, after a short time, and having received only minimal benefits, our countries will be exposed to an indefinite outward flow of resources." Pedro Aguirre Cerda, *El problema industrial*, Santiago, 1933, p. 107. (author's translation.)

nomena, not integral parts of a way of life. To its manipulation and control, they brought the attitudes and habits formed during a century of meticulous imitation of the ways in which the upper strata of western European society went about their political, social, and cultural affairs.

These managers, bureaucrats, and civil servants were mostly members of the intelligentsia that prospered under the shelter of Latin America's preindustrial urban civilization. Since their early ascent to positions of influence, they had shown themselves to be acutely sensitive to the intellectual and political developments in western Europe. They naturally aspired to be in the vanguard of things, and, as has been explained elsewhere in this study, they proceeded with enthusiasm to adopt the ideas and aspirations then current in the major capitals of the Northern Hemisphere. Thus they became early advocates of the fashionable European reformist ideologies and, by the second decade of this century, constituted an enlightened reformist urban sector, well-disposed toward changing many traditional features of the existing social structure, moved often by a sincere concern for the lot of the less privileged, but also, no doubt, conscious that such reforms successfully implemented would contribute to ensure the popular support necessary for their continuing in positions of power and influence. Many, if not most, of these groups had organized themselves into reformist political parties before the First World War and, through various means, had reached power, or at the very least had moved closer to the centers of decision during the years between the two world wars.

Their first experiences in office were not entirely successful. For a number of reasons, not excluding the disastrous consequences of the Great Depression as well as their lack of power sufficient to overcome conservative resistance, they were unable to implement many of their projected reforms. They were hence additionally interested in industrialization because they hoped that its development would bring about the desired social transformations. Industry became a gigantic *deus ex machina* expected to solve social and political problems, change attitudes, and bring about reform. As it was, and no doubt partly as the result of the essentially fortuitous relationship that existed between industry and its novel setting, the growth of manufactures proceeded apace with only slight effects on the traditional structure of society. More will be said about this in the light of the experiences with the introduction of a capital-intensive technology into the region, but here it should be noted that the momentous changes that many thought would follow the introduction of modern industry simply did not occur.[17] Again it must be repeated, changes did take place, but they were not necessarily the expected ones.

The cultural isolation of industrial activity was even more noticeable. That explosion of creativity in mechanical craftsmanship, industrial design, technical innovation, and the arts accompanying the British Industrial Revolution was not repeated in Latin America. It would not be possible in 1979 to write a book on the art of Latin American industrialization because there is none that is not unashamedly derivative or a straightforward imitation of foreign industrial designs. Francis Klingender could list with ease the diverse shapes of fixtures used for gas lighting as a feature of the industrial art of Britain. Nothing comparable could be attempted in the case of Latin America, for practically all the designs produced during the last four or five decades are of direct foreign origin. The point can possibly be better expressed by stating that while Scandinavian and Japanese designs have made a significant mark on modern tastes, there is yet to appear one Latin American industrial design to secure international recognition.

This apparent lack of interest or passive acceptance of

[17] As Hirschman has indicated in his study of the process of import-substituting industrialization in Latin America, "it has become possible for industrialization to penetrate into Latin America and elsewhere among the latecomers without requiring the fundamental social and political changes which it wrought among the pioneer industrial countries. . . . Industrialization was expected to change the social order and all it did was to supply manufactures." Hirschman, "Political Economy," pp. 265-266.

foreign models ought not to be regarded as a general condition of society. During these same years, Latin America produced towering figures in the arts, literature, music, and architecture, but none who could without hesitation be identified with a "culture of a rising industrial bourgeoisie." The poetry of Gabriela Mistral, Antonio Machado, or Pablo Neruda; the prose of Mario Vargas Llosa, Gabriel García Márquez, or Ernesto Sábato; the architecture of Costa, Niemeyer, or Candela; the music of Chávez, Villalobos, or Ginastera—all are distant from the experiences of industrialization. And this isolation is not a deception induced by their choice of subject matter; the very full analytical index of Neruda's complete works, for example, does not include the word "industry."[18] It is rather that neither a positive nor a negative reaction to industrialism is found in the work of these Latin American artists. Duvigneaud has indicated that one of the responses to the impact of industrialization on western European and Japanese society took the form of "a nostalgia for a lost communion, an impossible dream kept alive by man's undying wish for emotional unity. . . . this attitude is expressed by the visions of Schiller, Goethe, Hölderlin, Nietzsche (all dreaming of the lost world of Greece), of Hugo and Wagner (inspired by the legends of the Middle Ages); and by the nostalgia among the Japanese artists who looked back to 'the great past.' . . . This attitude is romantic in the real sense of the word." And then he adds, "we stress the fact that this nostalgia is not caused by recognizing that even in an industrial society, whether developing or established, there is a possibility of achieving reconciliation. It is provoked by the atomization of man's life which is the irreversible outcome of man's commitment to a technological world."[19] Hence, a romantic, nostalgic vision, a longing for a

---

[18] Pablo Neruda, who was awarded the Nobel prize for literature in 1971, was an active and most important member of the Chilean Communist Party for most of his adult life, and this makes it doubly significant that his voluminous poetical production hardly refers to industrial activity at all. Many of his poems are on themes related to the life of the miners and agricultural workers, but none are precisely about industrial labor or reflect the impact of industrial technology on Latin American society.

[19] Duvigneaud, *Sociology of Art*, pp. 69–70.

lost order, imaginary or not, a backward glance that does not need to justify itself even by the slightest mention of industrialism can be nurtured from the very depths of industrial society. The Gothic revival can certainly be explained in such terms and so can the music of Elgar or the poetry of Browning or Rosetti; there is no need for the culture of the industrial bourgeoisie to refer to industry at all. It is not because it ignores the industrial experience altogether that the vigorous, imaginative, artistic and cultural life of contemporary Latin America can be said to be isolated from it, but because it is so completely untouched by it, that it does not even reject it through nostalgia for a preindustrial order.[20] Contemporary Latin American society has simply not accepted this "commitment to a technological world" and persists in considering industry as basically instrumental, a tool to be used for purposes that transcend both its demands and consequences.

But if the artistic and literary creators have mostly ignored the fact of industrialization, those associated with industry have not ignored the arts, either because of genuine interest and concern or because such a preoccupation was almost a natural consequence of their rapid enrichment. For there was much wealth to be had from industry during those decades after 1929, and more often than not it was used to raise the levels of consumption of the protagonists in the industrializing process. Private domestic investment remained low throughout the period, the bulk of industrial capital coming either from the agencies of the central state or from foreign sources; private industrial wealth was conspicuously channelled into spending, and nowhere was this more vividly reflected than in the impressive growth of the sumptuous residential districts constructed in the outskirts of the Latin American capitals during the period.

The choice of styles for their private dwellings mirrors

[20] There are some apparent exceptions to this generalization. Neruda's masterpiece, *Alturas de Macchu Picchu*, could be wrongly considered a nostalgic glance backward to the pre-Columbian past by those who have not read it, or that having done so, have not fully understood the tremendous question posed by the poet, *"Piedra en la piedra el hombre, donde estuvo?"* Pablo Neruda, *Obras completas*, Buenos Aires, 1967, I, 345, line 1.

those who have profited from industrial growth better than they would have supposed. Notwithstanding the distinction and originality of many public edifices in the region, notably in Mexico and Brazil, what appears most striking about the proclaimed taste of these managers, bureaucrats, and dependent industrialists is the absence of a discernible style, the sheer banality of their ecclecticism.[21] Their efforts, geographically dispersed over a whole continent, are not even graced by identifiable bad taste. There are those who have maintained forcefully that the Gothic revival in Britain was in awful taste, and nobody would pretend that the monumental architecture of the Stalinist period in the Soviet Union is in very good taste, but these styles are distinct and reflect the confidence of their patrons in a manner of life embraced with dedication. This is not so in Latin America where the exclusive residential districts of the major cities are veritable architectural zoos with at least one specimen of every conceivable style ever associated with power, wealth, and prestige somewhere in Europe or the United States. The district of Vitacura in Santiago possibly contains more local versions of the Petit Trianon than exist in the whole of France, and if a count were taken of the half-timbered Tudor mansions in the residential districts of Buenos Aires, Lima, or Bogotá, the total figure would surely be comparable to that for England with Normandy thrown in for good measure. Perhaps nowhere in the world have the modern styles featured in the popular architecture journals of the Northern Hemisphere been more slavishly imitated than in the newer residential districts of

[21] This is understandable. Considering that monumentality has been a key feature of public architecture during the period and that multistoried structures do not quite lend themselves to Tudor, Baroque, or Second Empire treatment, good architecture flourished under the direct patronage of state authorities happy to leave matters to the specialists as long as the results were impressive and internationally acceptable. It was another thing altogether when it came to the design of private homes. What was wanted in this case was a direct and flattering symbolic association with a period of history or a way of life that would devolve added prestige on the owner, thus the proliferation of replicas of sprawling "Hollywood" style bungalows, English manorial houses, French chateaux, and the like.

these Latin American cities. Such examples can be multiplied and the conclusion is inescapable that while neither in their managerial role, nor as investors of capital, let alone as technological innovators, can these urban middle groups be considered to have played a role comparable to that of the British industrial bourgeoisie, it is in their failure to generate from within a cultural ethos in some way related to the development of industry that they have clearly shown that they are not a latter day industrial bourgeoisie.

Industrialization is a contemporary fact of Latin American life, but it was neither preceded nor accompanied by the formation of an industrial bourgeoisie. Neither has it created an industrial proletariat comparable to the massive working class that played such a signal role in the political and social history of nineteenth-century Europe. Whatever other characteristics could be ascribed to the vast social group loosely referred to as "industrial proletariat," it is clear that it was large in numbers, badly paid, and politically disorganized. The influence of trade unions was minimal; only a small number of workers were organized in any way at all. This differs essentially from what has occurred in Latin America. Here the process has made use of an emphatically capital-intensive technology, not a matter of choice, but of necessity. If industrial technology has progressed at all during the last century, it has done so in this respect: it needs a smaller labor force to produce the same, or more often, a larger amount of goods. When in the decade of 1870 Great Britain became the first nation in history to produce one million tons of steel, almost four hundred thousand men were directly behind that achievement; today, only ten to twelve thousand men are required to produce one million tons of steel in any of the several Latin American countries that have surpassed that symbolic figure.

It is not necessary, or possible, to recapitulate the process of technological advance in order to make use of the most modern techniques. If Ghana or Paraguay decide today to establish major electronic industries, they need not begin with the techniques used by Edison, but must, if they wish to be of significance in the market, endeavor to use the most advanced level of available technology. This is the reason why the industrial technology introduced into Latin America is by necessity capital-intensive and the labor force it requires relatively small.[22] In addition, because of the complexity of the equipment it uses, it is relatively skilled, and because of the peculiar character of the preindustrial urban setting within which it was formed, it enjoys the benefits of early trade unionization.[23] Hence, the Latin American industrial labor force has tended to be from its very inception, small, relatively skilled, relatively well organized, and, perhaps most important, relatively well paid.

But possibly the most important feature of this industrial labor force has been its acceptance of the primacy of the central state. This pragmatic attitude has been helped by the unashamed secondary role played by private domestic firms throughout the process of industrialization. The Latin American entrepreneurs have normally behaved more like politicians than independent industrialists; at all times they are attentive to secure and retain that state protection they consider, correctly, as it happens, essential for their interests. The business firm therefore has seldom been able or inclined to negotiate directly with the trade unions since it is not truly autonomous, but part of a complex network of pressure groups

[22] The Latin American labor force grew at an annual rate of 2.6 percent during the period from 1950 to 1965, when rapid industrialization should have resulted in important changes in its composition. However, the agricultural labor force grew at only 1.6 percent and the nonagricultural at 3.5 percent. It would be understandable to expect that employment would increase more rapidly in industry than in the tertiary sector, but, as Farley has indicated, the evidence shows exactly the opposite trend; agricultural labor as a percentage of the total labor force declined while the percentage of the nonagricultural labor engaged in services rose and that in industry went down. Farley, *The Economics*, pp. 133-134.

[23] Most Latin American trade unions can trace their origins to the mutual aid and friendly societies of the second half of the nineteenth century, but their political features derive mostly from the years immediately before the First World War when many of them came under the influence of socialist or anarchist immigrant workers. Jorge Barría, "The Trade Union Movement" in *Latin America and the Caribbean: A Handbook*, ed. Claudio Véliz, p. 736 et seq.

aimed at obtaining the support of the central state. This is why trade union action is overwhelmingly, and possibly unavoidably, directed toward the higher government circles where decisions are actually made. As Pecaut indicates, "it is no accident that in most Latin American countries trade union demands are in fact discussed at the Ministry of Labour much more than within the firm."[24] This necessary tendency to seek the protection, if not the guidance, of the central state has been further facilitated by the composition of the unionized labor force which is drawn overwhelmingly from the large-scale modern industrial sector of the cities. Only a small proportion of the membership comes from the traditional crafts or the rural areas.[25] This helps in part to explain the important role played by organized labor in urban populist movements such as those associated with Getulio Vargas in Brazil, Carlos Ibáñez in Chile, Juan Perón in Argentina, Lázaro Cárdenas in Mexico, or Víctor Paz Estenssoro in Bolivia. Far from constituting, as was the case in nineteenth-century Britain, a peripheral locus of effective power posing an actual or potential threat to the central state, the Latin American industrial labor force can well be described as a clientelistic labor aristocracy

[24] Daniel Pecaut, "The Urban Working Class," in *Latin America and the Caribbean: A Handbook*, ed. Claudio Véliz, pp. 678-679. Each Brazilian regime since 1930 has taken a special interest in representing trade union concerns through official and closely controlled channels. This system was consolidated by Getulio Vargas in 1942 through the passage of an exceptionally paternalistic labor legislation that has remained the basic labor law of Brazil to the present day. See Roett, *Brazil*, pp. 130-131. Even in Chile, where Angell suggests that unions remained distant from the established centers of political decision "they were always taken into account" and had some representation, as corporate interests, on the boards of the Central Bank, the State Bank and the Development Corporation. However, Angell adds, "the hand of the state lies heavily on the labour movement." Alan Angell, *Politics and the Labour Movement in Chile*, London, 1972, pp. 79-81.

[25] According to official figures quoted by González Casanova, only 1.9 percent of Mexico's agricultural workers are unionized while for the electronic industry the figure is just under 90 percent. Pablo González Casanova, *La democracia en México*, México, 1969, p. 145. In Chile in 1967, manufacturing accounted for 18 percent of the active population with a level of unionization of 62 percent while agriculture had 27.7 percent of the active population of which only 14 percent were in unions. Angell, *Labour Movement*, p. 46.

that has almost invariably pursued pragmatic policies based on the primacy of the state. These policies have in turn resulted in a strengthening and extension of the power of that central state.

The attitude of those associated with the management of industrial ventures underwent a comparable development. Identified conspicuously by the rest of the community with the aspirations of the urban middle sectors as reflected in the pronouncements of their political parties, the views of the majority of the press, and, generally, the style of life prevailing in the preindustrial cities, they found themselves in the vanguard of a process of social ascent and economic betterment that had almost universal value within their society. This generalized acceptance was facilitated by the inflationary pressures unleashed during the process of industrialization, for these acted as a formidable social solvent permitting hopes and ambitions to go well beyond the limits of the possible. The constant change in the price of goods and the resulting wage and salary increases voted by governments increasingly sensitive to populist demands blurred the frontier between illusion and reality. Many people did amass well-publicized fortunes in short periods of time and the popular imagination did the rest. There was, moreover, a real process of redistribution that encouraged such expectations, and the proliferation of available consumer goods profusely marketed through popular outlets added a material dimension to the feeling of increased social mobility.

From top to bottom, the urban middle sectors viewed industrialization from a consumer's point of view; it did not mean an industrial way of life, nor an industrial ethos. While the wealthier managers were able to build half-timbered Tudor mansions, the wives of industrial workers shopped in vast supermarkets and their husbands went into debt to buy motorcycles, refrigerators, television sets, or, occasionally, motorcars. That expectations were often frustrated is beyond doubt, but they were more often revived with the powerful help of a relentless inflationary spiral. Latin American urban society in the decades of 1950 and 1960 appeared to be decisively on the road to better things. But the leaders of this movement, the managers and bureaucrats of the new industrial enterprises and their clientele, had only an accidental connection with industrialization. Their interest in its development was not part of a larger commitment; they did not share a novel cultural complex that could possibly afford a foundation from which to challenge the established cultural, social, and economic arrangements. Whatever their individual reformist protestations—more frequent as the first thrust of import-substituting industrialization lost its momentum—they had no viable alternate social architecture.[26] On the contrary, having reached the centers of political decision and having also acquired significant economic power, they found themselves at this time advantageously poised to take the final step in their ascent, the one that would give them the social prestige they hungered for, and this one, far from demanding a challenge to the established order, required of them the more attractive course of amiable acceptance of things as they were.

This vanguard of the Latin American urban middle sectors could not, as the Victorian bourgeoisie had done effortlessly, impose their own values on a traditional, nonindustrial society for they had no Dr. Arnold to rationalize their ideas about education, no heroes to symbolize their feelings of moral superiority, no Ruskin, or Morris, Dickens, or George Eliot to tell them what they wanted to know about themselves and

[26] And it should be added that they were certainly not looking for one. At the time there were, and still are, dozens of anarchist, socialist, communist alternative schemes, and variations thereof available to choose from, but the problem of the so-called rising industrial bourgeoisie was not one of contrivance, but one of conviction and commitment, and they could hardly be expected to embrace doctrines that justified and actively supported their undoing. For other reasons, however, perhaps related to similar developments in Europe and the United States, a sizeable proportion of their younger members did join extremist movements and eventually played an important role in the terrorist campaigns of the Peruvian, Colombian, Venezuelan, and Mexican guerrillas, as well as with the Uruguayan *Tupamaros*, the Argentine *Ejército Revolucionario del Pueblo* and *Montoneros*, the Chilean *Movimiento de Izquierda Revolucionaria* and other organizations of this type.

the world they wished to create. There was then no culture of the Latin American industrial bourgeoisie, no set of values to replace those that reigned supreme before the coming of industrialization, no cultural bastions from which to launch a challenge against the remnants of preindustrial society. Unable to impose their own standards of social worth, they had of necessity to seek the prestige they so much wanted where they could find it; they were obliged, therefore, to embrace the culture of the traditional upper classes.

The upper classes of different Latin American countries have little in common save for their powers of survival. They originate from different parts of the Iberian peninsula and were formed at different times between the sixteenth and the early nineteenth centuries.[27] Nevertheless, for a long time, and with few exceptions, the same families have tended to be near the sources of political power, have enjoyed great wealth, and have had a virtual monopoly of social prestige. Even in those countries, like Bolivia and Mexico, where they were almost exterminated in violent revolutions, the survivors retained their prestige, and, most important, they eventually regained positions of responsibility in national affairs.[28]

---

[27] The experiences of Cuba, and Puerto Rico, for instance, are so different from those of the rest of the region that perhaps it would be wiser to treat them separately. While the rest of the region gained independence from Spain early in the nineteenth century, Cuba and Puerto Rico had to wait until the beginning of the twentieth; while Latin America lived through a crucial period of adaptation of western European ideas and institutions throughout the nineteenth century, Cuba and Puerto Rico became little more than cultural and political satellites of the United States after securing their independence from Spain. While the rest of Latin America was able to build on the institutional inheritance received from the three centuries of Iberian dominance, the principal efforts of the administrators of Cuba and Puerto Rico were directed toward the dismantling of their traditional administrative and political arrangements. In short, if the present status of Puerto Rico as an "associated free state" of the United States can be justly considered a political freak, in the sense of mutation, or a biological sport, the same can be said of the Cuban Revolution: it provides a chapter in a trans-Atlantic saga, rather than in the history of Latin America.

[28] The Mexican Revolution affords an interesting example. As Edmundo Flores has indicated, the revolution eventually resulted in the formation of a

Elsewhere in Latin America their persistence as influential groups in society is almost without parallel. If a list were compiled of one thousand families that two or three centuries ago were near the centers of political and economic power and monopolized social prestige, and the same list were examined today, it would probably be discovered that a large proportion of those names are still prominent in the ruling circles of their respective countries. No doubt many new names would have been added to such a list, but the number of those that survived the wars of independence, the political disorders of the republican period, and the economic crises of this century would be high indeed. This is in part due to the fact that for generation after generation these families have been active participants in public affairs exhibiting, over time, a capacity to adapt to changing circumstances that compares favorably with that of the more resilient European aristocracies. It is a rare case for a traditional upper class family in Latin America never to have had a member in the civil service: in some cases a family association with the bureaucracy has been so frequent as to amount to a lineage of public servants.[29] Undoubtedly

---

new middle class and a new elite; "the latter was formed by the coalescence of the first and second generation of the *revolucionarios* with the avowedly conservative, but adaptable remains of the aristocracy. . . . the *revolucionarios* now appear in the guise of elder statesmen, bankers, industrialists, top bureaucrats, and intellectuals while the old aristocracy that salvaged and later increased its urban real estate wealth has merged with the newer families bringing to them the patina of old family names." "The Significance of Land-Use Changes in the Economic Development of Mexico," *LE*, xxxv, no. 2 (May, 1959), 115.

[29] Even in regimes as committed to far-reaching changes as that of the *Unidad Popular* in Chile, a significant proportion of the leadership could claim such a lineage. Among President Allende's ministers at least three: Clodomiro Almeyda, minister for foreign affairs; Luis Matte, minister of housing; and Gonzalo Martner, minister of planning belong to families with a distinguished record of participation in public affairs. To these must be added Senator Carlos Altamirano Orrego, then secretary-general of the Socialist party, who can claim ancient aristocratic origins on both sides of his family in addition to a notable record of involvement in public life and President Allende himself, scion of a family that has produced many important civil servants. Argentina is one of the few major countries where the upper class has

much of this would apply to the *bourgeoisie d'affaires* of eighteenth-century France, and there is also an intimation of what James Burnham has described as a managerial class. With the coming of industrialization and the gradual extension of the public sector into the economic life of these nations, many of the strategic posts in the civil hierarchy with responsibility for industry were occupied by members of the upper classes. Without entirely abandoning their claim to sizeable areas of the shrinking private sector, especially in agriculture, finance, and commerce, the upper classes showed a perceptible tendency to participate in the more dynamic state initiatives. This trend certainly brings to mind the description put forward by Burnham: "The managers will exercise their control over the instruments of production and gain preference in the distribution of the products, not directly, through property rights vested in them as individuals, but indirectly, through their control of the state which in turn will own and control the instruments of production."[30] This led to a situation whereby the leadership of the urban middle groups linked with industrialization became closely associated with the managerial sector of the traditional upper classes. Whether the beginnings of a "managerial revolution," as suggested by Burnham, could possibly follow from there is debatable, but the association of these groups in their guise of a bureaucratic, industrial clientele of the central state is of significance. The least that can be said about its political implications is that far from becoming the protagonists of a confrontation, these two groups have cooperated in the advancement of what they consider their mutual interests.

Since the rising managerial middle classes proved unable to create alternate symbols of prestige, the only way open to obtain the measure of social prestige they felt due to them was

almost completely withdrawn from active politics during the past decades. After Marcelo Torcuato de Alvear, who was president of the country in 1922-1928, very few members of the Argentine aristocracy (an interesting exception being that of José Martínez de Hoz) have been prepared to accept political responsibilities of any significance.

[30] James Burnham, *The Managerial Revolution*, New York, 1941, p. 72.

by associating with the traditional upper classes. This the leading groups of those urban middle classes proceeded to do with persistence and success. Their children were entered in the schools patronized by the aristocracy so that they could start making useful contacts at an early age. They bought land and horses and earnestly learned to practice upper class sports. They made every effort to join aristocratic clubs and endeavored to imitate the manner of dress and speech of their members. They built and furnished their homes in the districts and styles presumably approved by the aristocracy and actually succeeded in becoming very much like their models, thinking like them and defending their interests with the zeal of the newly converted. The upper classes did not view this process with distaste as all they needed to do was to bestow minimal social favors in exchange for impressive financial and political support. Consequently, those who prospered with the coming of industry did not become a "round-head" vanguard of forward-looking, antiaristocratic, bourgeois reformers, but are likely to go down into the history of Latin America as the group responsible for the institutionalization of social climbing.

It would be difficult to find a great amount of dissent from the suggestion that most of the major political and social changes that took place in the advanced industrial nations had either the industrial bourgeoisie or the industrial proletariat as protagonists or supporters. Without these two groups, classes, or whatever term one chooses to describe them, nineteenth-century European history would become quite unintelligible. The temptation is there for many students of Latin American contemporary history to assume that because industrialization has come to this region, both these groups will also assume their protagonic roles largely in the European manner. The simple observation of what has happened in Latin America during the past decades will indicate that this is not so. The industrialization of Latin America has been neither the result of the exertions of a classic industrial bourgeoisie nor has it resulted in the formation of a classic industrial proletariat. These two social groupings are not to be found in modern

Latin America except in forms so modified as to nullify the usefulness of the concepts altogether.

There are other regions where such considerations may possibly also apply, but no group of countries entering the path of industrialization during the postwar years has had the centralist tradition of Latin America nor the preindustrial urban development that taken together so effectively reinforce the power and influence of the central state. Although the political and religious centralism of Latin Americans has survived centuries of change it would have been understandable to expect, *a priori*, that the effects of widespread industrialization would have led to the undermining of that tradition for largely the same reasons that applied in the case of the British and European Industrial Revolutions. This has not happened. On the contrary, the process of industrialization centrally guided and encouraged has led to a strengthening of the power of the central state without generating peripheral challengers of importance.

13

Authoritarian Recentralization

Seventeen governments were overthrown by force in twelve Latin American countries during the three years that followed the Great Depression of 1929.[1] Twenty-five years later, the pendulum swung in the opposite direction, and the mood was distinctly social democratic and populist. Another twenty-odd years bring us to the present when all but three countries are under authoritarian centralist regimes, most of them military, but some civilian as well. These changes and counter changes reflect the fluctuations of the closing years of the liberal pause and the prosperity that sustained it.[2] After what

[1] These were the following: Argentina in September 1930; Bolivia, June 1930; Brazil, October 1930 and July 1932; Chile, July 1931, June and October 1932; Dominican Republic, February 1930; Ecuador, August and October 1931 and August 1932; El Salvador, December 1931; Guatemala, December 1930 and February 1931; Panama, January 1931; Peru, August 1930 and March 1931.

[2] It can easily be argued, however, that no major region of the world has changed as little as Latin America during this century. Elsewhere vast empires have collapsed and countries that played a minimal role in world affairs have surged forward and taken a place among the great powers while scores of new ones have been born from the imperial debris; things have changed greatly in the world, but they have changed least in Latin America. This is all the more surprising because in the past few decades a preoccupation with the apparent need to bring about major transformations, be it through gradual or violent means, has dominated political activity. There has been a persistent use of the rhetoric of reform, development, and revolution, and behind the barrage of words, a commitment to rapid change ostensibly shared by the most articulate members of society. This has found a sympathetic echo on the part of many foreign observers interested in Latin America. It is now abundantly clear, however, that Latin Americans have not behaved in the way that these people thought they should. Seldom have so many well publicized

appeared like an auspicious mid-nineteenth-century beginning, followed by several decades of success, both the prosperity and the liberalism started to crumble with the Great
Depression. There was a hesitant revival during the Second
World War and its aftermath, followed by a fitful end during
the economic malaise of the late sixties and seventies. Today,
only three countries—Costa Rica, Colombia, and Venezuela—are not under single-party systems or one or another
variant military and civilian, authoritarian rule. Venezuela
may well owe this to its fabulous oil wealth; Colombia is
finding the maintenance of a social democratic government
increasingly difficult while Costa Rica is the proverbial exception that highlights the direction taken by the rest of the region.

During the affluent years of the liberal pause the countries
of Latin America were able to imitate, some more thoroughly
than others, what they admired best in Europe and the United
States in the arts and literature as well as in social and economic policies. Flourishing export economies and abundant
foreign investments provided an ample cushion insulating the
intelligentsia, the ruling groups, and their extended clientele
from the need to consider seriously their own cultural and
political traditions in the making of policy. Eager apprentices,
they felt it was only a matter of time before their countries
became acceptable imitations of their admirable north Atlantic models; their economic well-being allowed them to indulge, within understandable limits, in practices that otherwise would have been misplaced or beyond their means and
that, in the event, affected directly only a small part of the
population. At the risk of trivializing what at the time were
matters of deep-seated conviction, it could be said that European political party labels, social legislation, economic policies, military arrangements, and sartorial fashions were
copied by some with the same seriousness and care with

domestic revolutionaries and foreign prophets had so little to show for their
Byronic efforts, and this is despite the pseudoacademic clamor about shaky
institutions, frustrated expectations, and the imminent danger of massive social convulsions lest profound reforms are implemented.

which others founded English "public schools" in Lima, Buenos Aires, or Valparaiso, or French "Lycees" in Caracas and Rio de Janeiro, or learned the intricacies of golf and polo, or established the local "Derby" as the crowning social event of the season.

All this required funds that were not forthcoming after the Great Depression. The economies of Latin America were all but ruined. Countries that for some years had been inching forward with ambitious and well-intentioned programs of modernization and cultural and social improvement based on the returns from rising exports were faced overnight with massive unemployment and empty treasuries. The effects of the crisis were more catastrophic for Latin America than for any other peripheral region of the international economy. Discontent was rife and political tensions reached critical levels under the constraints of a fairly flexible institutional framework. More important still, for the first time since the conquest, Latin Americans found themselves alone, without immaculate models to imitate. For almost five centuries the peoples of Hispanic and Portuguese America lived in the shadow of Europe and the United States either receiving commands from an imperial center or deriving moral and cultural sustenance from those northern countries they chose to copy. After 1929 the sources for this support appeared to have gone dry. In Britain and Germany, France and the United States, the edifice of prosperous complacency seemed to be in ruins. Unable to import explanations, let alone solutions, from Europe or the United States, Latin Americans turned inwardly and sought support in those cultural and institutional continuities that appeared to have survived unscathed by the economic collapse. The unpremeditated introspection of the thirties produced in the first instance a crude and excessively assertive version of the traditional centralism modified by a nationalism that was substantially different from the outward-looking mood of the liberal pause.

This early return to centralism took the form of a sudden and relatively short-lived swerve toward outright military rule, almost a panic response to the unprecedented crisis. Of the seventeen *de facto* governments that took power during the period from 1930 to 1933, fourteen were military regimes. The cry was for a firm hand at the helm with few bothering about the precise direction to be followed apart from wishing that authoritarian control would eliminate partisan dissension and somehow restore economic prosperity. This first military recentralization proved unpopular and mostly ephemeral. The urban middle sectors, whose support was necessary then, as it is today, for the survival of any government, did not feel sufficiently threatened or despondent to accept the sacrifice of their freedom for what soon looked like an ineffective and excessive remedy. The military did not help their cause with their woeful inexperience and their ignorance of public administration and economic management; at best, they produced inefficient government, at worst, senseless tyrannical regimes. The international climate was also increasingly adverse to undisguised dictatorial rule, and before long most of the *de facto* regimes that had sprouted in the immediate aftermath of the Great Depression were replaced.

The new nationalism also had inauspicious beginnings. It was prompted mainly by a disillusionment and resentment akin to that of the loyal disciple betrayed by an admired master; the northern gods had indeed failed their faithful Latin American followers; nowhere had Europe and the United States been so keenly imitated and their advice so devotedly followed, and yet, the countries of Latin America were utterly helpless to prevent or to protect themselves against the economic disaster of 1929. This was a crisis for which they believed themselves clearly blameless no matter how current at the time the myths about lack of enterprise, technological backwardness, and dearth of capital.[3] The responsibility lay entirely beyond the frontiers of Latin America, in Europe, and the United States. It was felt therefore that reconstruction could only take place from within, and a policy of self-sufficiency at all costs appeared to many as the most appropri-

---

[3] Foreign investment in Latin America increased from 320 million dollars in 1897 to 1,680 million in 1914 and over 5,000 million in 1930. Sunkel, *El subdesarrollo*, p. 345.

ate solution. But regardless of the economic merits of a strict nationalistic posture, it proved very difficult to translate immediately into a viable alternative policy; trade sensitive countries that had for generations been closely linked to the international economy found it impossible to improvise at short notice a convincing autarkic development program. Moreover, the old habits of cultural dependence were hard to break, and it was not long before the intelligentsia and sectors of the political elite discovered that it was easier and more prestigious to embrace those European creeds that attributed the responsibility for the depression and its consequences to a supposedly declining democratic and capitalistic order. By the mid-thirties the ideas of European fascism, communism, socialism, anarcho-syndicalism, and even national-socialism had strong or growing support.[4] Although claims to political universality are not a novelty and occasionally may have some legitimate basis, the rapture was striking with which in the name of nationalism and national revival so many Latin American intellectuals and politicians devoured and publicized the latest translations of the writings and pronouncements of German nazis, Russian communists, Italian fascists, and French socialists, offering to them an allegiance as intense and uncritical as that their predecessors had given to English liberalism, French radicalism, or American federalism. However, it should also be said that this alacrity reflected the fact that many members of the intelligentsia thought the new autarkic nationalism a crude, oversimple, and unconvincing alternative to the fashionable European political philosophies of the time.

Mexico was not an exception although its robust cultural

[4] Revolutionary organizations copied from Europe existed in practically every Latin American country for some years before the Great Depression, but before 1929 popular response to their activities had been minimal. It is a moot point whether these early movements would have been as influential in the thirties if there had been no crisis, but it is clear that until 1930 the leadership and rank and file support for these groups had come from fairly small sectors of the intelligentsia with a limited echo from among the urban labor force. Also, before 1930 the most important among these groups were emphatically internationalist in outlook.

nationalism antedates the Great Depression by a few years. Between the fall of Porfirio Díaz in 1910 and the assumption of power by Plutarco Elías Calles in 1925, a break took place with the dependent cultural mood of the liberal pause, and by the late twenties an imaginative leadership helped by a generation of remarkable artists and writers convincingly established the credentials of modern Mexican cultural nationalism. This, however, did not extend to economic policy, and Mexico had to wait with the rest of Latin America for the traumatic effects of the Great Depression to generate that "wave of nationalistic radicalism that undermined the faith of post-revolutionary intellectuals in the feasibility of building [the] economy along liberal lines."[5] The famous article twenty-seven of the Constitution of 1917 in which the revolutionaries declared that subsoil wealth was inalienable national property was not enforced before 1925, and after this date, under the presidency of Calles, its implementation was so watered down by exceptions and qualifications that it was rendered largely ineffective. Calles's nationalism was not mere rhetoric, but he did share with the Mexican middle sectors the hope "that a new liberal society could be built on the ruins of the past, on the basis of the country's rich potential resources."[6] It was only in the thirties, under the rule of Lázaro Cárdenas, that a nationalist economic policy was carried out culminating with the expropriation in 1938 of the foreign-owned oil industry whereby, at one stroke, "the foreigner was put in his place and Mexican sovereignty assured."[7]

The military recentralization of the early thirties failed to last, but this did not put an end to the reemergence of cen-

[5] James W. Wilkie, *The Mexican Revolution*, Berkeley and Los Angeles, Calif., 1960, p. 66.

[6] Miguel Wionczek, "Electric Power: The Uneasy Partnership" in *Public Policy and Private Enterprise in Mexico*, ed. Raymond Vernon, Cambridge, Mass., 1964, p. 40.

[7] Wilkie, *Mexican Revolution*, p. 79. The Cárdenas regime had already completed the nationalization of the railways by 1937 and even before he assumed power, the legal foundations had been laid for the direct intervention of the central state in the petroleum industry and in electric power generation and distribution.

tralism. Nor did the dependent attitude of the intelligentsia smother the rising tide of nationalism. After the men on horseback returned to their barracks and the intellectuals resumed their briefly interrupted European apprenticeship, the centralism and nationalism they had discarded, combined with social democratic rhetoric and generous welfare and redistributive schemes, became the standard policy of the numerous urban populist movements that emerged from the chaos and disenchantment of the thirties. Ideologically amorphous and, with few exceptions, bereft of intellectual support, these populist movements nonetheless dominated the political spectrum during the postwar years either from positions of power associated with the personalist leadership of their initiators, or, more importantly, through the generalized adoption of their populist programs by practically all the major parties and coalitions of the region.[8] These programs had many shortcomings and some virtues, but only their nationalistic and redistributive policies need detain us here because it was as a direct consequence of their implementation that the populist movements and their imitators contributed so significantly to the recentralizing momentum of the past half century.

In the absence of more elaborate frameworks within which to fit day-to-day political actions there is a certain attraction in

[8] This is not the place to introduce a typology of Latin American political parties and movements with all its problems of semantic and conceptual folklore. Just to list the populist movements would present some interesting difficulties once the obvious cases of Getulio Vargas in Brazil and Juan Perón in Argentina have been mentioned. The argument can possibly be made clearer simply by stating in the first place that there are more similarities than differences between regimes such as those of President Carlos Andrés Pérez in Venezuela, Presidents Eduardo Frei and Salvador Allende in Chile, President Arturo Frondizi in Argentina, President João Goulart in Brazil, President Fernando Belaúnde Terry in Peru, and President Hernán Siles Suazo in Bolivia and secondly that these similarities owe more to earlier populist regimes throughout the region than to any common extra-Latin American ideological factor. I should add that one of the most useful brief descriptions of the Latin American political parties—not a typology—is found in Simon Collier, *From Cortés to Castro, An Introduction to the History of Latin America, 1492-1973*, London, 1974, pp. 340-371.

falling back to the inner ramparts of elemental, unquestioned loyalties. Tribal and national loyalties have often proved efficient substitutes for ideology. Their defenders are well aware that in times of crisis they are in a good position to demand the uncritical support of the whole population regardless of other supposedly lesser and conflicting interests. In such circumstances a nationalistic commitment can help to bridge the chasm between a confused and uncertain present and a more satisfactory future, the transition, moreover, to be effected by a united people, their only enemies foreigners distant and unknown or traitors. Once the national interest, as defined by the rulers, is accepted or imposed as the yardstick to measure the worth of policy and achievement, only the central state will be considered legitimately able to represent it. Nationalism is therefore a driving force behind the quest for recentralizing power in preparation for what is invariably seen as a confrontation with an external enemy, be it a neighboring country, the CIA, international communism, or even the ultramontane groupings within the Catholic Church. This relationship between nation and state was expressed in Latin America in statements that were predictably simple and repetitive. The manifesto of the Brazilian Revolutionary Movement in 1930 indicated that its principal aim was "to face up to the specific problems of Brazil, finding Brazilian answers, solving them *brasileiramente* [without] relying on foreign . . . political systems;" therefore, the manifesto continued, "the State must intervene in the economic life of the nation to stimulate and control initiative, direct and coordinate production and see to the needs of labour."[9] In Mexico,

[9] Peter Flynn, "The Revolutionary Legion and the Brazilian Revolution of 1930" in *Latin American Affairs*, ed. Raymond Carr, St. Antony's Papers, no. 22, Oxford, 1970, p. 86. The Revolutionary Legion, of course, failed, but the principles embodied in its manifesto remained important features of Brazilian political thinking. Only a few years later in 1937, Getulio Vargas proclaimed his *Estado novo* in terms strongly reminiscent of the Manifesto of 1930 stating that "among the profound changes brought about by the new regime are . . . the substitution of the principle of independence of powers by the supremacy of the Executive, . . . the effective and efficient participation of the economy . . . in the constructive and integrating work of the government. . . . The

"nationalism created a consensus in favour of *mexicanidad*. . . . This nationalism based on the principles of patriotism and *mexicanidad* made it harder to challenge the centralism [of the government]."[10] Sentiments similar to these are found in the pronouncements of populist movements throughout the region; they reflect the generalized adoption of a simple nationalistic idea as a badly needed unifying social cement in time of crisis.

However, it was the redistributive bent of populism and social democracy that contributed most to the recentralizing trend. Social justice became a general aspiration (Perón even named his official doctrine *Justicialismo*) that in practice was taken to mean the incorporation of as many people as possible in the central state's vast concentric system of patronage and clientelistic relations that promised protection from economic uncertainty as well as from the vagaries of political change. Far from representing a revolutionary posture, these demands for social justice reflected the conservative anxieties of a predominantly urban population that, having been badly shaken by the Great Depression, wanted above all guaranteed employment and generous social security arrangements within the existing system. Neither industrial nor revolutionary, the prevailing ethos was distinctly bureaucratic. The aspiration common to the urban middle and lower sectors as well as to the children of industrial workers was to secure regular tenured employment, preferably wearing collar and tie and sitting behind a desk, in other words, to join the bureaucracy. Not all achieved this goal, but enough did to transform the central bureaucracy into one of the growth sectors of the regional economy. More important, bureaucratized even before they were employed, the newcomers added the weight of

Estado novo embodies . . . the will and ideas which oppose and work against all those factors tending to weaken and dissolve the Fatherland." W. Raymond Duncan and J. Nelson Goodsell, eds., *The Quest for Change in Latin America*, New York, 1970, pp. 149-150. The quotation is from Getulio Vargas, *A nova política do Brasil*, Rio de Janeiro, 1938, v, 188-189 and 259-260.

[10] Leopoldo Solís, "La política económica y el nacionalismo mexicano" *FI*, IX (January-March, 1969), 241. (author's translation.)

clientelistic commitment as well as numbers to a hard-core establishment that had retained its centralist attitudes throughout the period of the liberal pause and into the decades of the mid-twentieth century, confirming the Weberian thesis that once established a bureaucracy "is among those social structures which are the hardest to destroy."[11]

The Latin American centralist bureaucracies did more than survive. When during the liberal pause all the major pressure groups were agreed on the wisdom of dismantling the state apparatus and minimizing its role, these centralist bureaucracies were able, with remarkable success, to retain prestige and influence and exercise them on behalf of what they considered the better interests of the state that often, no doubt, coincided with those of their office. When the liberal revolutions of the nineteenth century opened the way to dozens of petty military chieftains (mostly keen imitators of Napoleon) who gave international currency to the word *caudillo*, it was the impersonal machinery of the surviving bureaucracy that kept those countries functioning in a more or less acceptable manner, playing a role that brings to mind Weber's comment on the French experience when he wrote that "with all the changes of masters in France since the time of the First Empire, the power machine has remained essentially the same. Such a machine makes 'revolution' in the sense of a forceful creation of entirely new formations of authority, technically more and more impossible."[12] Substantially the same can be affirmed about the performance of the centralist bureaucracies of Latin America. Perhaps with the arguable exception of Cuba, none of the other bureaucratic establishments of the region has been dismantled in ways that would prove the Weberian thesis wrong.[13]

---

[11] Gerth and Mills, *Weber*, pp. 228-229.

[12] Gerth and Mills, *Weber*, p. 228.

[13] And in Cuba there was not much to dismantle, for this country had been unable in the relatively short time since gaining independence from Spain to create an institutional structure even remotely comparable to the one existing elsewhere in the region. A contributing factor was clearly the overwhelming dominance of the United States during the decades that followed independence. After half a century of nominally free republican existence, Cuba was

When the populist movements of the thirties and forties clamored for the intervention of the state in the economic life of their countries, the traditional bureaucracy found itself willingly in the vanguard of the process. During the following decades it presided over the formation and, in some ways, the administration, of a large and politically significant clientele that developed around the central state's system of patronage. For instance, as was explained in the previous chapter, the centralist industrialization of Latin America resulted in the creation of a managerial group that, whether operating directly under state control or in association with the private sector, depended on the good will of the state. Even excluding the unavoidable factor of corruption, this meant, in fact, the good will of individual civil servants.

Another important clientelistic sector developed as a consequence of the special relationship that existed between the state and the industrial labor movement. But by far the largest clientele emerged from those urban sectors that benefited from the rapid extension of welfare and social security programs during the years of populist dominance. There is no doubt that such programs were needed; poverty and deprivation were then and still are important regional problems and many political leaders were moved by considerations of humanity and social justice to support policies that would ameliorate suffering. It is also very clear that the populist leadership was not blind to the political advantages implicit in such a course of action. At a time when their movement's most urgent need was to secure a broad basis of political support, their enthusiastic advocacy of these measures together with strongly redistributive wages and fiscal policies proved a most effective means of attracting it. The redistributive strategy was an immediate political success, although in the long-term it proved economically disastrous. However, it was this short-term political effectiveness that prompted the major social democratic parties of the region to vie with each other and with their populist rivals in their offers of public generosity.

---

still trying to graft institutions of United States provenance to the withering trunk of its Hispanic past.

Popularity and largesse were mutually reinforced in a seemingly vicious circle that, as long as the economy maintained its upward trend, few questioned and fewer were prepared to break. This was further emphasized by the theoretical outpourings of economic popularizers who, with undeniable force and cogency, maintained that the steady increase in domestic demand was an essential and Keynesian condition for the sustained growth of the new industrial economy of the region. Every quantitative increase of real wages, the provision of social services, the improvement of educational facilities, hospitals, and the like was accompanied by a corresponding expansion of the bureaucratic machinery required to administer it, and this in turn further expanded the central state's system of clientelistic patronage. Changes of government did not necessarily, in fact, seldom did, reverse the trend. Incoming regimes rewarded their supporters with additional posts not daring to dismiss those members of the bureaucracy who had acquired the hallowed tenure or *inamovilidad administrativa* and thus leave their own clientele exposed to the dangers of retaliation by the next tenants at the government palace.

By the early sixties, the populist and social democratic cornucopia had consolidated huge pressure groups that regarded their better interests as identical with those of a prosperous central state. The hard core of these groups remained the established bureaucracies of predepression days, but the outer fringes encompassed almost the whole of an urban social ambit that had accepted as valid the minimal bureaucratic aspirations of political survival, economic security, and steady promotion—all reasonable goals as long as sufficient funds were forthcoming.

As is well known, the capacity of any population to consume public funds is inexhaustible while the sources for such funds are painfully restricted. The wealth that the early populist and social democratic administrations utilized to enlarge their bureaucratic establishments and finance ambitious and public-spirited programs was part of the accumulated product of more than a century of investment by individuals and institutions that had at one time or another chosen to postpone immediate consumption for the sake of greater future rewards. By disbursing these funds the populist administrations were not entirely out of line with the consumption habits of the liberal pause except that in this case they were used to finance badly needed schools, hospitals, pensions, and other social services to be used by the many, instead of luxury constructions and imports for the enjoyment of very few. But a more important difference affected the continued availability of investment capital. In the nineteenth century the ruling groups in Latin America shared the liberal outlook of those who provided the investment for the region, while in the mid-twentieth century the changed international economic climate and the outspoken nationalistic attitudes of the populist regimes conspired against the investment of new capital. This problem was not so urgent during the early years of import-substitution industrialization because either through taxation or other means governments were able to acquire an increasing share of the income generated by what was at the time a growing and profitable activity. In fact it appeared during the mid-fifties that the countries of Latin America would be able in the near future to complete without undue difficulty the transition from a dependence on foreign private investments principally directed at the production of exportable primary commodities to principally domestic or state-controlled investment directed at the production of manufactured or semimanufactured products.[14] This was also a time when the general price level of primary commodities in the international market was relatively high, partly because of the accelerating process of postwar reconstruction in Europe and also as a consequence of the Korean War.

Ten years later this situation had changed ominously. The price of primary commodities deteriorated steadily reducing the income received by the Latin American governments. At

[14] Although by the late fifties, as has been pointed out by the main theorists of *dependencia*, there was a distinct trend on the part of foreign private investment to move into the production of manufactured products for domestic consumption. See Sunkel, "Big Business."

the same time, the populist political strategy of "mobilizing the people" proved so effective that the demand for higher incomes and better and more extensive social services was continuously outstripping each country's capacity to satisfy it. As the populist and social democratic regimes were unlikely, either because of humanitarian concern or political astuteness, to cut substantially the level of public expenditure in these services, the first to be curtailed were the long-term investment programs whose postponement had no immediate political consequences and that could be explained away as a temporary measure to last until the return of better days. But the better days did not return, and to the ills of empty treasuries were added those of unemployment and inflation, largely of domestic origin, but exacerbated in the late sixties and seventies by the malaise that was affecting the international economy.[15]

Unable to continue providing the services and real income to which the urban population had grown accustomed, the social democratic regimes had to face growing discontent, especially among the middle sectors whose expectations had risen highest during the decades of largesse and were consequently more vulnerable to rising inflation and declining economic fortunes. Their appeals, however, were not for a revolutionary change of the social and economic system, but for more state intervention along the same lines as before, in the hope that a reinvigorated domestic demand would restore the economic health of their respective countries.

Of all the important groups in Latin American society that dissented significantly from this position, possibly the most

[15] Each Latin American country experienced these general processes in special ways, and there are many important factors that affected some and not others. Technological advancement, for instance, contributed to the rapid loss of income by countries that exported products for which cheaper substitutes had been discovered. One dramatic case is that of Uruguay whose economy depended mainly on the export of certain types of wool that were literally swept off the market by the general introduction of artificial fibers into the world economy. There is less exaggeration than it would appear at first reading in stating that the distant cause of the terrorist outrages of the Tupamaros was the invention of rayon and nylon.

influential was the radical intelligentsia. Its political response to the unfolding crisis was quasi-catalytic; for while it remained virtually unchanged in its views, it contributed crucially to those changes in attitude on the part of the urban middle sectors that appear finally to have brought to an end the liberal pause and opened the door to the current process of authoritarian recentralization.

With very few exceptions the Latin American intelligentsia continued in the sixties and seventies to tread the path of dependent orthodoxy, loyally echoing the views they found most congenial from among those current in Europe, the United States, or even the Far East.[16] Familiar with European and American publications, they seldom read anything published in Latin America outside their own capital cities; academic achievement was rarely measured in terms of the approval bestowed by Latin American peers, but by university centers elsewhere. The average Latin American intellectual would have had no difficulty in listing European and American scholars prominent in his field of interest but would have been hard put to do likewise, regardless of merit, with his Latin American colleagues. In short, the Latin American intellectuals of the sixties and seventies were the willing and inevitable victims of the process of cultural dependence they so forcefully impugned in their writings and utterances.[17] Feel-

---

[16] The exceptions are few but distinguished. Just to mention the names of Celso Furtado, Osvaldo Sunkel, Victor Urquídi, Raúl Prebisch makes the point in the field of political economy while in the richer vein of literature, the works of Mario Vargas Llosa, José Donoso, Ernesto Sábato, Gabriel García Márquez, Julio Cortázar offer convincing evidence of renewal and originality, for they owe little or nothing in style or subject-matter to the prevailing fashions of Europe or the United States. It is interesting, however, to note that most of the outstanding Latin American writers of the so-called "boom" of the past few years either live in Europe, publish in Europe, or wrote their most important works while residing in Europe.

[17] No doubt there are good reasons that explain why this is so. Regardless of the many merits of a national stance in such matters, it is beyond dispute that centers such as the Sorbonne, Harvard, Princeton, the London School of Economics, or Heidelberg amply justify their international prestige and attraction. Learning was with us before national frontiers came into being and remains an uneasy applicant for national passports, visas, or citizenship

ing able to regard the problems of Latin America from a global vantage point, they were particularly sensitive to the effects of external factors on domestic issues; theirs was the grand perspective, the wide historical stage where events could be understood as pieces in a great design, clear to them, but obscure to those limited by the obtuse parochialism of the homeland. Life in Asunción, or Lima, or Potosí, seen from within, through the eyes of the unenlightened, monolingual, mean-spirited petty bourgeoisie, was to them boringly meaningless. True significance could only be a function of the larger conception of things. What was actually felt by haberdashers in Montevideo, bank clerks in Santiago, or dentists in Medellín had a small meaning, important only to those who experienced it, and a greater, infinitely more important meaning susceptible of being understood by those, like the internationally-minded radical intellectuals, who could see it against the canvas of global history written very large indeed.

The Cuban Revolution, for instance, attracted little attention while it remained basically a middle class libertarian struggle half-heartedly supported by the United States and equally vaguely opposed by the Cuban communists. But when Fidel Castro's victory was rapturously received by the radical intelligentsia in Paris, London, and New York, the Latin American intelligentsia immediately accepted it as a portent of an inevitable and most desirable future for the region. In a world grown unaccustomed to romantic endeavors, the epic prowess of Castro and his companions revived the hopes of those who believed in the possibilities of direct revolutionary action. Latin America was sufficiently distant and unknown to afford an undemanding field for the released Byronic imagination of European and American radical intellectuals who knew that a successful revolution in France, the Netherlands, or the United States was unthinkable. Latin America became the revolutionary frontier, the

---

rights. Many Latin American publications enjoy a deserved reputation for excellence, but how can one fail to notice that they tend to be better known in European universities than in Latin America?

wilder shore of politics, where the good fight could still be fought and with better prospects of success than in Stuttgart, Manchester, or Lyon.

To this notoriety the Latin American radical intelligentsia answered enthusiastically. In a frenzied spiral of encouragement and response radical intellectuals, North and South, read each others' writings and rose to ever higher levels of commitment. When Régis Debray and Ernesto Guevara tendered their revolutionary advice in the form of the *foco* theory, the radical intelligentsia of Latin America felt on the threshold of history. The jaded platitudes about "the continent of the future" at long last began to have a realistic sound. With their minds loyally attuned to a Parisian or Californian radical version of world affairs, they gladly embraced a theory that maintained that, if conditions were not ready for revolution, it was their historical responsibility to make them ready. If the people—the vast majority of the people—were clearly disinclined to go to the barricades, this was evidence of the need to strengthen the process of *concientización* to help them rectify what was obviously a distorted appreciation of their true interests. More important, *foci* of revolutionary violence had to be created to draw the already vacillating and frightened social democratic regimes into the morass of endless repression punctuated with increasingly daring exploits by the dashing urban terrorists. With a kidnapping here, an assassination there, a well-placed bomb somewhere else, they would strike where least expected and would evade the action of the police, like a fish in water, making full use of the excellent organizational resources provided by a well-educated and fanatically inspired minority as well as of their growing popularity. The expectation was that the fumbling central governments would be forced into increasingly repressive measures that would further alienate domestic support until they crumbled under a mighty revolutionary upsurge, presumably like the one that toppled Batista, although his regime cannot possibly be described as a social democracy.

That this has not happened is historical fact. The terrorist outrages did force the central governments to adopt repressive policies, and at the beginning the spectacular character of some of the terrorist exploits did elicit a measure of amusement, if not support, but as time went on and the shootings, kidnappings, and bombings increasingly disrupted the normal life of the major cities, public opinion hardened not against the central government, but against the perpetrators.

The middle sectors believed they had good reasons to throw their lot on the side of institutional stability. The growth of the clientelistic central state during the postdepression period had given many of them a stake in the conservation of things as they were. Their concern was not with the destruction of the state or its replacement with another state apparatus, but with the solution of the economic problems besetting the existing one. They still retained the feeling, or hope, that they had a foot in the door of the edifice of the established order and were reluctant to help with the work of demolition. They were not inclined to regard economic decline, runaway inflation, and political terrorism mainly as threats to landowners and capitalists, but as dangers to their own position in a social arrangement that still offered viable possibilities for advancement.

A tragic escalation followed in which every legal measure against terrorism, laboriously obtained from parliaments where precarious social democratic majorities were already eroded by the deepening economic crisis, was answered by even more daring attacks. Hesitant or unable to resort to extreme policies, the central governments gave an impression of impotence while demands for the restoration of order became vociferous.

The members of the middle sectors of Latin America do not enjoy a reputation for collective physical valor or daring acts of violence. Their past successes have been the reward of prudence and caution rather than audacity. In this they are unlike the intellectual elite who with their affluent backgrounds, international connections, and universalist views find it easier to indulge in the implementation of violent prescriptions. Instead they are the parochial, pusillanimous, and vulnerable shopkeepers, salesmen, clerks, aspiring provincial lawyers, and doctors. They have, however, armed friends and relatives, for in Latin America the military have traditionally been drawn not from the upper strata of society, but from the middle and, increasingly, from the lower middle sectors. Whenever in the past few decades the middle sectors have felt critically threatened, they have appealed to the professional manipulators of official violence for help. As José Nun has abundantly demonstrated, the intervention of the military in Latin American politics during the last half century has almost invariably been at the behest of the beleaguered middle sector.[18] At this opportunity, the sequence of challenge and response was played in strict accordance with precedent. To the violent revolutionary action of the extreme leftwing terrorists, the middle sectors responded first with legal repressive measures administered by social democratic regimes. When these appeared insufficient to stem the tide of violence or when the parallel economic deterioration threatened a general institutional collapse, the middle sectors appealed to the military for help.[19]

[18] José Nun, "The Middle Class Military Coup in Latin America," in *Politics of Conformity in Latin America*, ed. Claudio Véliz, London, 1967, pp. 66-118.

[19] The immediate reasons why each military establishment was invited by the middle sectors to assume power understandably vary from country to country. In Uruguay it was outright terrorism that brought about the collapse while in Argentina it was a combination of government corruption and inefficiency as well as an escalation of armed attacks by urban terrorists. In Chile it was the inability, or unwillingness, of President Allende to curb the illegal activities of an increasingly violent and defiant extreme Left that prompted first the comptroller-general of the republic, then the Supreme Court, and finally Parliament itself to declare officially that the president had placed himself outside the law, thus opening the way for the intervention of the armed forces. In Brazil it was a combination of economic mismanagement and a last hour failed attempt by President Goulart to subvert noncommissioned officers that brought about military intervention. The loss of freedom, the severe, often brutal repressive measures taken by the military, the awareness that the restoration of parliamentary democracy is very much in the future cannot have pleased many members of the middle sectors, but by the time the military assumed virtually absolute power it was too late to complain, and the middle sectors have no alternative but to accept, grudgingly perhaps, an order of things they were glad to condone when truly frightened by what appeared a precipitous descent into revolutionary chaos, or worse, revolutionary order.

Despite the fact that since the beginning of the seventeenth century small contingents of professional soldiers receiving regular pay and serving under contract were a feature of the colonial frontier, Latin America never evolved an aristocratic military tradition. The Prussian Junkers or the elite British regiments have no Latin American counterpart. Notwithstanding their successes in the field or their occasional incursions into politics, the military never succeeded in securing the social recognition and prestige they felt was their due. In times of peace, they were relegated to provincial regiments after receiving their commissions, often married early into unpretentious local families so that by the time promotion and posting to the capital were achieved, their accents, demeanour, and connections proved liabilities in their quest for social acceptance. No matter how senior their postings, professional distinction alone did not erase the outward marks of their social origin. Unknown in fashionable urban circles and hard put to keep up appearances on what, contrary to prevailing beliefs, was almost without exception modest pay,[20] their frustration was not a solitary grudge, for the military shared then, and still do, the aspirations, fears, and prejudices of the middle sector. They felt the threat of revolutionary dissolution as keenly as their civilian relations; inflation affected their income as acutely. Conversely, the attitude of the middle sectors generally also found a faithful echo among the military. Their hesitant performance during the aftermath of the Great Depression of 1929, for instance, reflected the indifferent support of a middle sector that mostly regarded them as unimpressive and uncalled-for usurpers of offices traditionally and legitimately occupied by civilians.[21]

[20] This economic factor, though important, was certainly not decisive or even mainly responsible for bringing about military intervention. It is enough to recall the fact that President Salvador Allende's government in Chile granted substantial salary increases to the armed forces.

[21] A less sharply defined but comparable feeling of insecurity affected the military who intervened against some populist regimes during the fifties. In Argentina, for instance, after the overthrow of President Juan Perón, the government of General Juan José Aramburu spent much time apologizing to everyone for being in power at all and giving assurances that as soon as the

This time, however, they enjoy considerable and indispensable support from civilians, even if by default, and in the same way that the radical intelligentsia fancies itself the vanguard of the proletariat, the military regard themselves as the vanguard of the middle sector. The claim is not without justification, for they are indeed the middle sector in arms; at least as bureaucratic as their friends and relations, equally hostile to what they consider a dangerously cosmopolitan and antinational intelligentsia, similarly preoccupied with the desire to rise in the existing social scale, and utterly disillusioned with the populist and social democratic arrangements of the closing years of the liberal pause.

There is nevertheless a paradox in this relationship because partly as a reflection of their undeniable anticommunism and also because of their wish not to displease their new upperclass friends who hold the key to their social advancement (their wives' and families' as well as their own), the military are enmeshed in a pseudoliberal rhetoric that attributes all the economic ills of their countries to the interventionist policies of their predecessors in office.[22] But as it was precisely those policies that greatly enlarged and consolidated the vast urban clientele that called them to power, to dismantle the public sector built over the past three or four decades would risk their disaffection. However, the military also belong to the

---

situation was back to normal they would return power to a democratically-elected civilian administration. Such protests, of course, ensured minimal civilian cooperation for few were prepared to jeopardize their political future for the sake of a military regime voluntarily condemned to an ephemeral and unpopular existence.

[22] The bastions of Latin American cultural dependence are well-manned by the radical intelligentsia and the upper-class business and landowning groups. The loyalty that the former have demonstrated to the doctrines of violent revolutionary action, the latter have shown to the tenets of free-trading liberalism their forefathers embraced during the prosperous days of the liberal pause. Although their survival in business or agriculture has almost without exception been the result of successful adaptation to the demands of a state-controlled clientelistic system, whenever they have a chance of voicing their intimate thoughts about policy, they revert to the undiluted free-trade gospel of the nineteenth century.

most nationalistic or patriotic organization in society, and the most minutely and strictly bureaucratized. Their view of administration is that of the conscientious and reliable bureaucrat, albeit in uniform, who obeys orders efficiently and without questions.[23] Their criterion to measure the worth of policy is to ask whether it accords with their superior officer's definition of the national interest. They are therefore unlikely to reverse the process of recentralization; on the contrary, their policies since taking office suggest that they will intensify it. For instance, in their frequent and increasingly acrimonious confrontations with the more politically committed sectors of the Catholic Church they have acted in ways entirely consistent with a regalist tradition that will be as important as their professional stubbornness in their eventual success in maintaining the political subordination of the Church. In the universities their policies have been almost a caricature of those reforms introduced two centuries ago by Pombal when he wanted to impress a more practical, less speculative direction to Portuguese universities that he felt would be essential for his nationalistic and recentralizing program.

But possibly the most revealing indication that the recentralizing process has acquired a momentum that will not be deflected easily comes from the field of economic policy. Some authoritarian regimes that have decided to advance measures of economic decentralization that they hope will prove attractive to private investors have no alternative but to

---

[23] The bureaucratic disposition of the middle sectors may have had an influence on the formal organization of the new military regimes that differ markedly from those of the *caudillos* of earlier times. The traditional military chieftains have now been replaced with colorless chairmen who are little more than the executors of the collective decisions adopted by the committees or *juntas* over which they preside. The style of these committees or *juntas* can well be described as managerial and even technocratic, a far cry from the dependence on personal loyalty or charismatic appeal characteristic of the rule of the *caudillos*. In fact, it is quite possible that the last two *caudillos* of the old school will be President Alfredo Stroessner of Paraguay and Prime Minister Fidel Castro of Cuba, and as Castro is a young man, he may still achieve the distinction of being the last and the longest-lived *caudillo* of them all.

order summarily that these should be obeyed, thus indulging in the ultimate paradox of decentralization under severe central control. The formal requirements of a free market economy are satisfied by ordering economic units to act freely, as long as their decisions are in accordance with government directives.[24] Absolute central power is exercised absolutely in the name of liberal economic theories and schemes whose obvious prerequisites are diversity and freedom of choice.

Although there is more than a little Orwellian newspeak in this, there is also the confusion resulting from the fact that centralism remains a pragmatic tradition devoid of ideology, a style of ordering society perceptible in practice, not in theory, and as much the consequence of accidental external circumstances as of deliberate choice.[25] Indeed, Latin America may well feel now the need for a theoretical statement of what she has been doing for the past five centuries. This would be in line with Oakeshott's explanation of the origins of ideology in which he maintains that far from a political ideology being "the quasi-divine parent of political activity, it turns out to be its earthly stepchild. Instead of an independently

[24] There are, of course, precedents of the successful implementation of this type of policy. The case of Japan during the industrializing effort of the Meiji Restoration and after is an interesting one, for there the *zaibatzu*, though under private ownership and control, in fact tended to operate almost as informal state corporations, never departing significantly from the long-term policies of the central government. The economic development of Japan has always been a popular subject in the Latin American military academies and perhaps there are more instances of sympathetic imitation along these lines than have been discovered thus far.

[25] By this I mean the effects of successive world-wide economic crises, not the conspiratorial activities of intelligence agencies serving the Great Powers. A surprising amount of nonsense has been written about the supposedly decisive influence of Soviet and American political agencies on Latin American events. I think that these agencies are efficient and ubiquitous and tend to cancel each other out. There are instances when these spies and counter-spies may assist a process that is already under way, but generally their importance is less than marginal. It would be as absurd to maintain that, for example, João Goulart or Salvador Allende reached power because of Soviet involvement as to think that if the United States had refrained from intervening they would not have been ousted.

premeditated scheme of ends to be pursued, it is a system of ideas abstracted from the manner in which people have been accustomed to go about the business of attending to the arrangements of their societies. The pedigree of every political ideology shows it to be the creatures, not of premeditation in advance of political activity, but of meditation upon a manner of politics. In short, political activity comes first and a political ideology follows after."[26]

The centralist disposition of Latin Americans ought not to be confused with an ideology. Rather, it can be taken to be a more or less felicitous description of the ways in which Latin Americans have gone about attending to their economic, social, and political arrangements. That a theoretical or even an ideological statement could be constructed on such a foundation is by no means impossible, but for this to happen there must be meditation upon the centralist continuities that underline the development of Latin American society. This is unlikely to be encouraged under military rule. Authoritarian regimes rarely welcome speculation about social or political matters, and since the current tendency in Latin American universities is to foment practical studies after the Pombaline fashion, there are scant grounds for expecting that most of those in power today will take kindly to Oakeshott's prescription and encourage or permit "meditation upon their manner of politics."

Until now the centralist tradition has been latitudinarian, legalistic, and emphatically civilian. Throughout the long period during which it shaped Latin American society, the political role of the military was of small importance: in the three centuries of colonial rule there is one brief instance of outright military domination and that ended with Pizarro's public execution. Military intervention in politics is a nineteenth-century, post-Napoleonic phenomenon characteristic of the liberal pause; its reappearance today may well be judged by future historians to have been an exceptional departure prompted by an unprecedented challenge. It would be idle to

[26] Michael Oakeshott, *Political Education*, Cambridge, 1951, p. 14.

speculate on how long the military will remain in power, but it is safe to conclude that only a very lengthy and successful tenure of office will allow them the opportunity, which they may not feel disposed to use, of impressing upon the process or recentralization a style radically different from the legalistic, latitudinarian, and civilian style associated with the centralist tradition. In the past, as the old joke suggests, it has proved easier to civilize the military than to militarize a stubbornly civilian Latin American society; there appear to be no convincing arguments to suggest that this will change in the near future.

Plato wisely prescribed that philosopher-kings should "wipe the slate of human society and human habits clean" before starting on their work of social reconstruction: it is far more pleasant to "sketch the outline of the social system" on a *tabula rasa* than on one messy with the vestiges of earlier tracings.[27] Unhappily this cannot be done in the real world where reformers are inescapably bound by the limitations and potentialities of existing societies, complex, often intractable, perhaps vitiated by injustices and shortcomings and inhabited by human beings with memories, anxieties, fears, and dispositions, even undesirable habits of the type Plato wished eliminated at the outset. This, of course, is a truism for which there are no exceptions in Latin America where the only available slate is cluttered with designs, some unfinished, others partially erased and still others clear and distinct despite much scrubbing and wiping, as is the case with the imprint left by five centuries of centralist experience.

This should not be taken to mean that the centralism of Latin America will never be altered, but merely that since it has survived the liberal onslaught of the nineteenth century when economic, political, and cultural conditions favored its obliteration, it is difficult to imagine it withering away in the last quarter of our century when practically every domestic factor as well as the trend of affairs elsewhere in the world ap-

---

[27] *The Republic*, trans. Desmond Lee, London, 1974, p. 297; pt. 7, bk. 6; Stephanus 501 a.

pear to point in the direction of greater centralization. Reformers of the social order may make additions, deletions, and modifications, but the viability of these changes will depend on their compatibility with the basic centralist structure. Not even the atomization of traditional community and institutional arrangements brought about by the formidable social solvent of military defeat need necessarily result in departures from centralism, as shown by the historical experience of the Bolivian, Cuban, and Mexican revolutions.[28]

The extension to Latin America of the universalist tenets of various exotic political schemes rests on the absurd assumption that Latin America can be extricated from its historical context and treated as if it were a *tabula rasa*, its social and historical dimensions regarded either as irrelevant or as sufficiently similar to those of the societies whence the models originate. There have been two major reformist challenges based on this considerable error; first it was the affluent and Europeanized intelligentsia of the nineteenth century that, impelled by the political climate of the period, tried to transform Latin Americans into passable imitations of English liberals or French radicals. Their fragile achievement, to a great extent sustained by the prosperity of expanding export economies, did not survive the Great Depression.

The second challenge came in the mid-twentieth century, again led by a strongly motivated upper-class intelligentsia committed to a variety of Marxist creeds tried in Asia or parts of eastern Europe. Their failure was swifter still, for in their partisan enthusiasm they frightened and antagonized the crucially important urban middle sectors that called the military to defend what they considered to be their better interests as well as those of their respective countries. In the wake of this

---

[28] The left-wing revolutionary movements active in Latin America would, if victorious, substitute an even more severe form of centralism for the existing one. The main difference would be that while the actual centralism reflects the aspirations—just or not—of the dominant urban middle sectors, the new regimes would presumably advance the interests of an ideal or abstract industrial and rural proletariat in accordance with the classical requirements of their respective doctrines.

frustrated attempt, the traditional centralist arrangements have emerged stronger than before, this time under undisguised authoritarian control.

These experiences are not without precedent in the Hispanic political tradition. Goya, Iriarte, Meléndez Valdes, Moratín, and most of the Spanish intelligentsia of the turn of the century were happy to equate civilization and progress with the France of the Enlightenment and the aftermath of revolution, and when Napoleon placed Joseph Bonaparte on the Spanish throne, they were far from displeased.[29] The people of Spain, however, perhaps ignorant of their better interests, no doubt superstitious and unenlightened, rose up in arms against what they considered simply a foreign invasion and wrote one of the heroic pages of Spanish history with their stubborn resistance.

There must be some virtue in being able to take things as they ought to be and not as they are. It appears to be, nonetheless, an impractical way of proceeding. Perhaps it would have been better, more conducive to progress and the general improvement of society, for a declining Spain to be governed by the uniformed children of the French Enlightenment, but this was not possible because the immense majority of the Spanish people, unlike the intelligentsia, did not wish to live under French rule, no matter how benevolent or enlightened.

If there are precedents for failure, there are also reformist experiences that afford grounds for a modicum of optimism. After the sanguinary dismantling of the liberal edifice constructed by Porfirio Díaz, the heirs of the Mexican Revolution were able to graft a variety of democracy to a robust cen-

[29] The case of Goya is intriguing and characteristic. That he was an *afrancesado*, a Francophile, is beyond doubt, in spite of Hugh Thomas's prudent reservations ("About Goya's political views in May, 1808, it is impossible to be precise") but then, his disillusionment with the French was equally evident. Perhaps Malraux's comment on the *Disasters of War* is the most illuminating; they not only bring to mind the work of an embittered patriot, but also that of a betrayed friend, "the sketchbook of a communist after the occupation of his country by Russian troops." See Hugh Thomas, *Goya, The Third of May 1808*, London, 1972, pp. 63-65; also André Malraux, *Saturne*, Paris, 1950, p. 110; and F. J. Sánchez-Cantón, *Goya*, Paris, 1930, pp. 61-63.

tralist root. Under a one-party system of government, they retained some of the more attractive features of liberal democracy, with limitations, and this has been achieved without the benefit of ideology, rather in the manner characteristic of an essentially pragmatic and bureaucratic tradition.[30]

There have been important changes in the past in Latin America, and there will undoubtedly be more in the future, but they are unlikely to be understood or even accepted by those who insist in considering the countries of the region as incipient western European countries, or overdeveloped parts of the so-called third world. Despite the expectations encouraged by extraneous political creeds, modern Latin America has been clearly unresponsive to the imposition of reforms that ignore the historical dimension of its social and political arrangements. It is improbable that the general disposition responsible for this in the past will change very much in the foreseeable future.

---

[30] For a country as strongly anticlerical as Mexico, it is paradoxical that possibly the nearest parallel to its peculiar latitudinarian centralism will be found in the Latin American Catholic Church, which is at least as centralized and equally tolerant of diversity. It is probably as difficult to be expelled from Mexico's ruling *Partido Revolucionario Institucional* as it is to be thrown out of the Latin American Catholic Church.

Selected Bibliography

Acosta, José de, S. J. *Historia natural y moral de las Indias*. Seville, 1590.

Aguirre Cerda, Pedro. *El problema industrial*. Santiago, 1933.

Alamán, Lucas. *Historia de Méjico*. México, 1849-1852.

Alden, Dauril. *Royal Government in Colonial Brazil*. Berkeley and Los Angeles, Calif., 1968.

———, ed. *Colonial Roots of Modern Brazil*. Berkeley and Los Angeles, Calif., 1973.

Alemparte, Julio. *El cabildo en Chile colonial*. Santiago, 1966.

Alvarez de Morales, Antonio. *Las Hermandades, expresión del movimiento comunitario en España*. Valladolid, 1974.

Amunátegui, Miguel Luis. "Encíclicas de los Papas Pío VII y León XII contra la independencia de la América Española." In *La iglesia frente a la emancipación americana*, edited by Hernán Ramírez Necochea. Santiago, 1960.

Angell, Alan. *Politics and the Labour Movement in Chile*. London, 1972.

Anna, Timothy E. "The Peruvian Declaration of Independence: Freedom by Coercion." *JLAS* vii (November, 1975), 221-248.

Arcila Farías, Eduardo. "Commercial Reform in New Spain." In *The Origins of Latin American Revolutions, 1808-1826*, edited by Humphreys and Lynch.

———. *Economía Colonial de Venezuela*. México, 1946.

Armas Medina, Fernando de. *Cristianización del Perú*. Seville, 1953.

Arnoldsson, Sverker. *La conquista española de América según el juicio de la posteridad; vestigios de la leyenda negra*. Madrid, 1960.

Ashton, Robert. "Puritanism and Progress." *EHR* n.s. xvii (April, 1965), 582.

Augier, Roy and others. *Report on the Ras-tafari Movement in Kingston, Jamaica.* Kingston, 1960.

Azcona, Tarsicio de. *Isabel la Católica.* Madrid, 1964.

Azevedo, João Luzio. *O Marquez de Pombal e sua época.* Lisbon, 1922.

Bader, Thomas. "Early Positivistic Thought and Ideological Conflict in Chile." *TA* xxvi (April, 1970), 379, 385-386.

Bagú, Sergio. *Evolución histórica de la estratificación social argentina.* Buenos Aires, 1961.

——. "Industrialización, sociedad y dependencia." *RLACS*, i (June-December, 1971), 172-192.

Baltra, Alberto. *Crecimiento económico de América Latina.* Santiago, 1959.

Barber, Elinor G. *The Bourgeoisie in 18th Century France.* Princeton, N.J., 1955.

Barbier, E. J. F. *Chronique de la régence et du regne du Louis XV, 1718-1763.* Paris, 1857-1875.

Barrett, Leonard E. *The Rastafarians.* London, 1977.

Barría, Jorge. "The Trade Union Movement." In *Latin America and the Caribbean, A Handbook*, edited by Véliz.

Barros Arana, Diego. *Historia de Chile.* 16 vols. Santiago, 1884-1902.

Basadre, Jorge. *La multitud, la ciudad y el campo en la historia del Perú.* Lima, 1947.

Belaúnde, Víctor Andrés. *Bolívar y el pensamiento político de la revolución hispano-americana.* Madrid, 1959.

Bell, Quentin. *Victorian Artists.* London, 1967.

Beloff, Max. *The Age of Absolutism, 1660-1815.* London, 1954.

Beltrán y Rozpide, Ricardo. *América en tiempo de Felipe II según el cosmógrafocronista Juan López de Velasco.* Madrid, 1927.

Benson, N. L., ed. *Mexico and the Spanish Cortes.* Austin, Tex., 1966.

Bergier, Jean-Francois. *The Industrial Bourgeoisie and the Rise of the Working Class, 1700-1914.* London, 1971.

Berlin, Isaiah. *The Hedgehog and the Fox, An Essay on Tolstoy's View of History*. London, 1953.

Beyhaut, Gustavo. *Raíces contemporáneas de América Latina*. Buenos Aires, 1964.

Blackburn, Robin, ed. *Régis Debray, Strategy for Revolution*. London, 1970.

Bliss, Horacio William. *Del Virreinato a Rosas. Ensayo de historia económica argentina, 1776-1829*. Tucumán, 1959.

Boxer, Charles R. *The Golden Age of Brazil, 1695-1750*. Berkeley and Los Angeles, Calif., 1964.

———. "Padre Antonio Vieira, S. J. and the Institution of the Brazil Company in 1649." *HAHR* xxix (1949), 474-479.

———. *The Portuguese Seaborne Empire, 1415-1825*. London, 1969.

Brading, D. A. *Miners and Merchants in Bourbon Mexico 1763-1810*. Cambridge, 1971.

Bradley, Ian. *The Call to Seriousness: The Evangelical Impact on the Victorians*. London, 1976.

Braudel, Fernand. *The Mediterranean and the Mediterranean World in the Age of Philip II*. London, 1975.

Braun Menéndez, Armando. *El reino de Araucanía y Patagonia*. Buenos Aires, 1967.

Brito Figueroa, Federico. *Historia económica y social de Venezuela*. Caracas, 1966.

Britto, Lemos. *Pontos de partida para a história económica do Brasil*. Rio de Janeiro, 1923.

Bruneau, Thomas C. *The Political Transformation of the Brazilian Catholic Church*. Cambridge, 1974.

Burgin, Miron. *Aspectos económicos del federalismo argentino*. Buenos Aires, 1960.

Burnham, James. *The Managerial Revolution*. New York, 1941.

Butterfield, Herbert. *The Statecraft of Machiavelli*. London, 1955.

Camara, Helder. *The Church and Colonialism: The Betrayal of the Third World*. London, 1969.

Campbell, Leon G. "The Changing Racial and Administra-

310   *Bibliography*

tive Structure of the Peruvian Military Under the Later Bourbons." *TA* xxxii (July, 1975), 117-133.

Carr, Raymond. *Spain, 1808-1939.* Oxford, 1966.

————, ed. *Latin American Affairs.* St. Anthony's Papers. Oxford, 1970.

Casas, Fray Bartolomé de las. *Historia de las Indias.* Colección de documentos inéditos para la Historia de España, edited by Marqués de la Fuensanta del Valle and José Sancho Rayón. 5 vols. Madrid, 1876.

Castagnino, Raúl H. *Rosas y los jesuítas.* Buenos Aires, 1970.

Castedo, Leopoldo. *A History of Latin American Art and Architecture.* New York, 1969.

Chiappelli, Fred, ed. *First Images of America: The Impact of the New World on the Old.* Berkeley and Los Angeles, Calif., 1976.

Chueca Goitia, Fernando. See Torres Balbas, Leopoldo.

Clark, Kenneth. *The Gothic Revival.* London, 1974.

Clarke, H. Butler. "The Catholic Kings." In *The Cambridge Modern History,* edited by A. W. Ward, G. W. Prothero, and Stanley Leathes. vol. 1. Cambridge, 1904.

Clissold, Stephen. *Latin America, A Cultural Outline.* London, 1965.

Collier, Simon. *From Cortés to Castro, An Introduction to the History of Latin America, 1492-1973.* London, 1974.

————. *Ideas and Politics of Chilean Independence.* Cambridge, 1967.

Comte, Auguste. *The Catechism of Positive Religion,* translated by Richard Congreve. London, 1858.

————. *Système de politique positive.* Paris, 1851-1854.

Cornblit, Oscar. "European Immigrants in Argentine Industry and Politics." In *The Politics of Conformity in Latin America,* edited by Véliz.

————. "Society and Mass Rebellion." In *Latin American Affairs,* edited by Carr.

Crawford, W. Rex, trans. and ed. *A Mexican Ulysses: The Autobiography of José Vasconcelos.* Bloomington, Ind., 1963.

Cruz Costa, João. *A History of Ideas in Brazil: The Develop-*

ment of Philosophy in Brazil and the Evolution of National History. Berkeley and Los Angeles, Calif., 1964.

Cruz, Pedro Nolasco. *Bilbao y Lastarria*. Santiago, 1944.

Cuevas, Mariano, S. J. *Historia de la Iglesia en México*. México, 1921.

Cunha, Euclydes da. *Os sertões*. Rio de Janeiro, 1902.

Cunningham, William. *The Growth of English Industry and Commerce*. Cambridge, 1885.

Currie, R. and Hartwell, R. M. "The Making of the English Working Class?" *EHR* xvii (December, 1965), 634.

Dealey, James Q. "The Spanish Sources of the Mexican Constitution of 1824." *TSAHQ* iii (1900), 168.

Dealy, Glen. "Prolegomena on the Spanish American Political Tradition." *HAHR* xlviii (1968), 49–51.

De Gandía, Enrique. *Mariano Moreno. Su pensamiento político*. Buenos Aires, 1968.

De Kadt, Emanuel. *Catholic Radicals in Brazil*. London, 1970.

Della Cava, Ralph. "Brazilian Messianism and National Institutions: A Reappraisal of Canudos and Joaseiro." *HAHR* xlviii (1968), 407–408.

Diez de Medina, Fernando. *Franz Tamayo*. Buenos Aires, 1944.

Disraeli, Benjamin. *Endymion*. London, 1881.

Dobb, Maurice. *Studies in the Development of Capitalism*. London, 1946.

———. See Sweezy, Paul M.

Domínguez Ortíz, Antonio. *Crisis y decadencia de la España de los Austrias*. Barcelona, 1969.

———. *La sociedad española en el siglo XVIII*. Madrid, 1955.

D'Onofrío, Arminda. *La época y el arte de Prilidiano Pueyrredón*. Buenos Aires, 1944.

Donoso, Armando. *El pensamiento vivo de Francisco Bilbao*. Santiago, 1940.

Duarte Rodríguez, Alfredo. *O Marquez de Pombal e os seus biógrafos*. Lisbon, 1947.

Duncan, W. Raymond and Goodsell, J. Nelson, eds. *The Quest for Change in Latin America*. New York, 1970.

312   Bibliography

Dutra, Francis A. "Centralization versus Donatorial Privilege: Pernambuco, 1602-1630." In *Colonial Roots of Modern Brazil*, edited by Alden.

Duvigneaud, Jean. *The Sociology of Art*. London, 1972.

Echeverría, Estéban. *Cartas a Don Pedro de Angelis, editor del Archivo Americano*. Montevideo, 1847.

Egaña, Juan, *Informe anual que presenta la secretaría de este Real Tribunal . . . (de minería) . . . para el año de 1803*, edited by Diego Barros Arana. Santiago, 1894.

Elliott, J. H. *Imperial Spain, 1469-1716*. New York, 1966.

Ellis, Alexander J. *Auguste Comte's Religion of Humanity*. London, 1880.

Emmet, Dorothy. See Gellner, Ernest.

Encina, Francisco Antonio. *Historia de Chile desde la prehistoria hasta 1891*. 20 vols. Santiago, 1942-1952.

Encinas, Diego de. *Cedulario indiano recopilado por Diego de Encinas*. Madrid, 1945.

Eyzaguirre, Jaime. "El alcance político del decreto de libertad de comercio de 1811." *BACH* XXXIII, no. 75 (1966), 115-161.

──────. *Ideario y ruta de la emancipación chilena*. Santiago, 1957.

Faoro, Raymundo. *Os donos do poder, formação do patronato político brasileiro*. 3rd ed. rev. Porto Alegre, 1976.

Farley, Rawle. *The Economics of Latin America*. New York, 1972.

Farriss, N. M. *Crown and Clergy in Colonial Mexico, 1759-1821: The Crisis of Ecclesiastical Privilege*. London, 1968.

Feliú Cruz, Guillermo, ed. "Escritos y documentos del Ministro de O'Higgins Doctor don José Antonio Rodríguez Aldea." *Colección de historiadores y de documentos relativos a la independencia de Chile*. Santiago, 1953.

Filho, Morales de los Ríos. *Grandjean de Montigny*. Rio de Janeiro, 1941.

Finer, Herman. *The Chilean Development Corporation*. Montreal, 1947.

Finot, Enrique. *Nueva Historia de Bolivia*. La Paz, 1954.

Fisher, J. R. *Government and Society in Colonial Peru. The Intendant System 1784-1814*. London, 1970.

Fisher, Lillian Estelle. *Viceregal Administration in the Spanish-American Colonies*. New York, 1926.

Flores, Edmundo. "The Significance of Land-Use Changes in the Economic Development of Mexico." *LE* xxxv, no. 2 (May, 1959), 115.

Floyd, T. S., ed. *The Bourbon Reforms and Spanish Civilization*. Boston, 1966.

Flynn, Peter. "The Revolutionary Legion and the Brazilian Revolution of 1930." In *Latin American Affairs*, edited by Carr.

Fox, David J. "Urbanization and Economic Development in Mexico." In *Cities in Changing Latin America*. London, 1969.

Frank, A. G. *Capitalism and Underdevelopment in Latin America*. New York, 1967.

Freyre, Gilberto. *Casa-grande e senzala*. 14th ed. Rio de Janeiro, 1966.

Fuentealba, Leonardo. "Courcelle-Seneuil en Chile, Errores del liberalismo económico." *AUCH* series 4a, nos. 55 and 56 (1944), 101-206.

Fuentes, Carlos. "The Argument of Latin America: Words for the North Americans." In *Whither Latin America?*, edited by Sweezy and Huberman.

Furtado, Celso. *La economía latinoamericana desde la conquista ibérica hasta la revolución cubana*. Santiago, 1969.

―――. *The Economic Growth of Brazil*. Berkeley and Los Angeles, Calif., 1963.

Gaete, Arturo S. J. "Socialismo y comunismo, historia de una problemática condenación." *Mensaje* xx, no. 200 (July, 1971), 301-302.

Galtung, Johan. *Feudal Systems, Structural Violence, and Structural Theory of Revolutions*. Oslo, 1969.

Gálvez, Manuel. *Vida de don Gabriel García Moreno*, Madrid, 1945.

García Gallo, Alfonso. "El encomendero indiano." *REP* xxxv (1951), 141-161.

García Icazbalceta, Joaquín. *Don Fray Juan de Zumárraga*. México, 1881.

García Icazbalceta, Joaquín, ed. *Colección de documentos para la historia de México*. México, 1858-1866.

García Reynoso, Plácido. "Government Policy and Business Responsibility in the Process of Industrial Development and Economic Integration in Latin America." *IADB* (1969), 3-29.

Gellner, Ernest. "Concepts and Society." In *Sociological Theory and Philosophical Analysis*, edited by Dorothy Emmet and Alasdair MacIntyre. London, 1970.

Gerth, H. H. and Mills, C. Wright, trans. and ed. *From Max Weber: Essays in Sociology*. New York, 1958.

Gibson, Charles. *The Spanish Tradition in America*. New York, 1968.

Glass, David V. "Population Growth and Structure: A Socio-Demographic Study." In *Social Aspects of Economic Development in Latin America*, edited at UNESCO. vol. I, Paris, 1963.

Góngora, Mario. *Encomenderos y estancieros, 1580-1660*. Santiago, 1970.

González Casanova, Pablo. *La democracia en México*. México, 1969.

González Navarro, Moisés. *Estadísticas sociales del Porfiriato*. México, 1956.

Goodsell, J. Nelson. See Duncan, W. Raymond.

Graham, Richard and Smith, Peter H., eds. *New Approaches to Latin American History*. Austin, Tex., 1974.

Griffin, Charles C. "Economic and Social Aspects of the Era of Spanish American Independence." *HAHR* XXIX (1949), 174.

―――. "The Enlightenment and Latin American Independence." In *Latin America and the Enlightenment*, edited by Whitaker.

Guarda, Gabriel, O.S.B. "Influencia militar en las ciudades del reino de Chile." *BACH* XXXIII, (1966), 6-7.

―――. "Itinerario del paganismo en la cristianización de América." *TV* VIII, no. 2 (April-June, 1967), 112.

―――. *Santo Tomás de Aquino y las fuentes del urbanismo indiano*. Santiago, 1965.

Halperin Donghi, Tulio. *Historia contemporánea de América Latina*. Madrid, 1969.

Hanish, Walter S.J. *Itinerario y pensamiento de los jesuítas expulsos de Chile 1767-1815*. Santiago, 1972.

Hanke, Lewis. *The First Social Experiments in America*. Cambridge, 1935.

———. *The Imperial City of Potosí*. The Hague, 1956.

———. "Pope Paul III and the American Indians." *HTR* III, no. 2 (April, 1937), 77.

———. *The Spanish Struggle for Justice in the Conquest of America*. Philadelphia, 1949.

Hann, John H. "The Role of the Mexican Deputies in the Proposal and Enactment of Measures of Economic Reform Applicable to Mexico." In *Mexico and the Spanish Cortes*, edited by Benson.

Hardoy, Jorge Enrique. "El modelo clásico de la ciudad colonial hispanoamericana." In *Actas del XXXVIII Congreso Internacional de Americanistas*. Stuttgart-Munich, vol. 4, 1968, 143-181.

Haring, Clarence H. *The Spanish Empire in America*. New York, 1963.

Hartwell, R. M. See Currie, R.

Hartz, Louis. See Morse, Richard M.

Hasbrouck, Alfred. *Foreign Legionaries in the Liberation of Spanish South America*. New York, 1928.

Hayner, Norman S. "Mexico City: Its Growth and Configuration." *TAJS* L, no. 1 (January, 1945), 298.

Heaton, Herbert. "A Merchant Adventurer in Brazil, 1808-1818." *JEH* VI (May, 1946), 5-6.

Henriques, Ursula. *Religious Toleration in England 1787-1833*. London, 1961.

Herr, Richard. *The Eighteenth Century Revolution in Spain*. Princeton, N.J., 1958.

Herrmann, Albert. *La producción en Chile de los metales y minerales más importantes . . . desde la conquista hasta el año 1902*. Santiago, 1903.

Hill, Christopher. See Sweezy, P. M.

Hilton, Rodney. See Sweezy, P. M.

Hirschman, Albert O. "The Political Economy of Import-Substituting Industrialization in Latin America." In *Latin America; Problems in Economic Development*, edited by Nisbet.

Hobbes, Thomas. *Leviathan, or the Matter, Forme and Power of a Commonwealth Ecclesiasticall and Civil*, edited by Michael Oakeshott. Oxford, 1960.

Hobsbawm, Eric J. *The Age of Revolution: Europe from 1789 to 1848.* London, 1962.

Howarth, David. *The Golden Isthmus.* London, 1966.

Huberman, Leo. See Sweezy, P. M.

Humphreys, R. A. *British Consular Reports on the Trade and Politics of Latin America, 1824-1826.* London, 1940.

────── and Lynch, John, eds. *The Origins of Latin American Revolutions, 1808-1826.* New York, 1965.

Hussey, Roland D. "Traces of French Enlightenment in Colonial Hispanic America." In *Latin America and the Enlightenment*, edited by Whitaker.

Ildefonso, Luciano. "Primeras negociaciones de Carlos V, rey de España, con la Santa Sede." *Cuadernos de Trabajo de la Escuela Española de Arqueología e Historia en Roma.* II (1914), 68.

Ireland, Rowan. "The Catholic Church and Social Change in Brazil: An Evaluation." In *Brazil and the Sixties*, edited by Roett.

Jara, Alvaro. *Guerra y sociedad en Chile.* Santiago, 1971.

──────. *El salario de los indios y los sesmos del oro en la Tasa de Santillán.* Santiago, 1960.

Jobet, Julio César. *Ensayo crítico del desarrollo económico-social de Chile.* Santiago, 1955.

Johnson, H. B., Jr. "The Donatory Captaincy in Perspective: Portuguese Backgrounds to the Settlement of Brazil." *HAHR* LII (1972), 203-214.

Johnson, Paul. *A History of Christianity.* London, 1976.

Kagan, Richard L. *Students and Society in Early Modern Spain.* Baltimore, 1974.

Keen, Benjamin. "The Black Legend Revisited; Assumptions and Realities." *HAHR* XLIX (1969), 709-719.

Klingender, Francis D. *Art and the Industrial Revolution*. London, 1972.

Krebs Wilckens, Ricardo. *El pensamiento histórico, político y económico del Conde de Campomanes*. Santiago, 1960.

Kroeber, Clifton B. "El Consulado de Buenos Aires en el proceso de la revolución de Mayo." *TC* no. 9 (1960), 130.

Lacunza, Manuel, S.J. *La venida del Mesías en gloria y majestad*, edited by Mario Góngora. Santiago, 1969.

Lafaye, Jacques. *Los conquistadores*. México, 1970.

Lahmeyer Lobo, Eulalia María. *Processo administrativo ibero-americano*. Rio de Janeiro, 1962.

Landsberger, Henry A., ed. *The Church and Social Change in Latin America*. Notre Dame, Ind., 1970.

Lanning, John Tate. "The Reception of the Enlightenment in Latin America." In *Latin America and the Enlightenment*, edited by Whitaker.

Lanternari, Vittorio. *The Religion of the Oppressed*. New York, 1963.

Laski, Harold J. *The Rise of European Liberalism*. London, 1962.

Lastarria, José Victorino. *Recuerdos literarios*. Santiago, 1885.

Lea, Henry Charles. *The Inquisition in the Spanish Dependencies*. New York, 1908.

Lemos, Miguel and Teixeira Mendes, Raimundo. *A ultima crise*. Rio de Janeiro, 1891.

León Pinelo, Antonio de. *Tratado de confirmaciones reales*. 1630; facsimile rpt. Buenos Aires, 1922.

Levene, Ricardo. *El pensamiento vivo de Mariano Moreno*. Buenos Aires, 1942.

————. *El proceso histórico de Lavalle a Rosas*. La Plata, 1950.

Lord, Robert Howard. "The Parliaments of the Middle Ages and Early Modern Period." *CHR* xvi (1930), 125-144.

Lynch, John. *Spanish Colonial Administration, 1782-1810: The Intendant System in the Viceroyalty of the Rio de la Plata*. London, 1958.

———— and Humphreys, R. A., eds. *The Origins of Latin American Revolutions, 1808-1826*. New York, 1965.

Maas, Jeremy. *Victorian Painters*. London, 1969.

Macchi, Manuel E. "Urquiza en la instrucción pública." *TC* no. 14 (1965), 147-148.

Macedo, Jorge. *Situação econômica do tempo de Pombal*. Oporto, 1951.

Machado Ribas, L. *Movimientos revolucionarios en las colonias españolas de América*. Montevideo, 1940.

MacIntyre, Alasdair. See Gellner, Ernest.

Mackay, John A. *The Other Spanish Christ, A Study in the Spiritual History of Spain and South America*. London, 1932.

MacLeod, Murdo J. "Las Casas, Guatemala, and the Sad but Inevitable Case of Antonio de Remesal." *Topic*, Washington and Jefferson College, no. 20 (Fall, 1970), 54.

Madariaga, Salvador de. *El auge del imperio español en América*. Buenos Aires, 1959.

————. *The Fall of the Spanish American Empire*. London, 1947.

Malagón-Barceló, Javier. "The Role of the *letrado* in the Colonization of America." *TA* xviii (July, 1961), 1-17.

Malheiro Dias, Carlos. "O regímen feudal das donatárias." In *História de colonização portuguesa no Brasil,* edited by Carlos Malheiro Dias. Oporto, 1924.

Malraux, Andre. *Saturne*. Paris, 1950.

Mamalakis, Markos and Reynolds, Clark W., eds. *Essays on the Chilean Economy*. New Haven, Conn., 1965.

Manchester, Alan K. "The Growth of Bureaucracy in Brazil, 1808-1821." *JLAS* iv (May, 1972), 80.

Maravall, José Antonio. *Estado moderno y mentalidad social*. Madrid, 1972.

Mariátegui, José Carlos. *Siete ensayos de interpretación de la realidad peruana*. Santiago, 1955.

Martin, Percy Alvin. "Federalism in Brazil." *HAHR* xviii (1938), 149.

Martner, Daniel. *Estudio de política comercial chilena e historia económica nacional*. Santiago, 1923.

Marx, Karl. "Der achtzehnte Brumaire des Louis Napoleon." In *Karl Marx Friedrich Engels Werke*, vol. 8. Berlin, 1960.

Maxwell, Kenneth R. *Conflicts and Conspiracies: Brazil and Portugal, 1750-1808.* Cambridge, 1973.

———. "Pombal and the Nationalization of the Luso-Brasilian Economy." *HAHR* xlviii (1968), 609.

Mecham, J. Lloyd. *Church and State in Latin America: A History of Politico-Ecclesiastical Relations.* Chapel Hill, N.C., 1966.

———. "The Origins of Federalism in Mexico." *HAHR* xviii (1938), 177-178.

Medina, José Toribio. *Historia del Tribunal del Santo Oficio de la Inquisición en Chile.* Santiago, 1890.

———. *La primitiva inquisición americana (1493-1569).* Santiago, 1914.

Mendes, Cándido. *Memento dos vivos: A esquerda católica no Brasil.* Rio de Janeiro, 1966.

Menéndez Pidal, Ramón. *El Padre Las Casas. Su doble personalidad.* Madrid, 1963.

Mills, C. Wright. See Gerth, H. H.

Molinari, Diego Luis. *La representación de los hacendados de Mariano Moreno.* Buenos Aires, 1939.

Monteiro de Barros Lins, Ivan. *Historia no positivismo no Brasil.* São Paulo, 1964.

Morales de los Rios Filho, Adolfo. *Grandjean de Montigny.* Rio de Janeiro, 1941.

Moreno, Mariano. *Representación que el apoderado de los hacendados de las campañas del Río de la Plata dirigió al Excelentísimo Sr. Virrey Don Baltasar Hidalgo de Cisneros.* Buenos Aires, 1874.

Morse, Richard M. "The Heritage of Latin America." In *The Founding of New Societies*, edited by Louis Hartz. New York, 1964.

———. "Recent Research on Latin American Urbanization: A Selective Survey with Commentary." *LARR* i, no. 1 (Fall, 1965), 38.

———. *The Urban Development of Latin America, 1750-1920.* Stanford, Calif., 1971.

Musson, A. E. and Robinson, Eric. "Science and Industry in

the late Eighteenth Century." *EHR* xiii (December, 1960), 222-224.

Naipaul, V. S. *The Mimic Men.* London, 1969.

Neasham, Aubrey V. "Spain's Emigrants to the New World, 1492-1592." *HAHR* xix (1939), 147-160.

Neruda, Pablo. *Obras completas.* Buenos Aires, 1967.

Nisbet, Charles T., ed. *Latin America; Problems in Economic Development.* New York, 1969.

Nisbet, R. A. *The Sociological Tradition.* London, 1972.

Nun, José. "The Middle Class Military Coup in Latin America." In *The Politics of Conformity in Latin America*, edited by Véliz.

Oakeshott, Michael. *Political Education.* Cambridge, 1951.

———, ed. Hobbes, Thomas. *Leviathan, or the Matter, Forme and Power of a Commonwealth Ecclesiasticall and Civil.* Oxford, 1960.

Oliveira Lima, Manoel de. *Dom João VI no Brasil, 1808-1821.* Rio de Janeiro, 1908.

Oliveira Torres, João C. de. *O positivismo no Brasil.* Petrópolis, 1943.

Ortíz, Ricardo. *Historia económica de la Argentina, 1850-1930.* Buenos Aires, 1955.

Oyarzún, Luis. *El pensamiento de Lastarria.* Santiago, 1953.

Palacio, Ernesto. *Historia de la Argentina.* Buenos Aires, 1954.

Palcos, Alberto. "Echeverría y el credo de Mayo." *TC* no. 9 (1960), 231-242.

Palm, Erwin Walter. *Los monumentos arquitectónicos de La Española.* Ciudad Trujillo, Santo Domingo, 1955.

Panettieri, José. *Los trabajadores en tiempos de la inmigración masiva en Argentina.* Buenos Aires, 1966.

Paoli, Pedro de. *Sarmiento, su gravitación en el desarrollo nacional.* Buenos Aires, 1964.

Parry, J. H. *The Audiencia of New Galicia in the Sixteenth Century.* Cambridge, 1948.

———. *The Cities of the Conquistadores.* London, 1961.

———. "A Secular Sense of Responsibility." In *First Images of America, The Impact of the New World on the Old*, edited by Chiapelli.

————. *The Spanish Seaborne Empire*. London, 1966.

————. *The Spanish Theory of Empire in the Sixteenth Century*. Cambridge, 1940.

Parsons, Talcott. *The System of Modern Societies*. Englewood Cliffs, N.J., 1971.

Paz, Octavio. *The Labyrinth of Solitude*. New York, 1961.

Paz, Pedro. See Sunkel, O.

Pecaut, Daniel. "The Urban Working Class." In *Latin America and the Caribbean: A Handbook*, edited by Véliz.

Peñaloza, Luis. *Historia económica de Bolivia*. La Paz, 1953.

Pereira de Queiroz, María Isaura. *Historia y etnología de los movimientos mesiánicos*. México, 1969.

Peters, Richards. *Hobbes*. London. 1956.

Pierson, William Whatley. "Foreign Influences on Venezuelan Political Thought, 1830-1930." *HAHR* xv (1934), 12.

Pike, Frederick B. "South America's Multifaceted Catholicism: Glimpses of Twentieth Century Argentina, Chile, and Peru." In *The Church and Social Change in Latin America*, edited by Landsberger.

Pinto, Aníbal. *Chile, un caso de desarrollo frustrado*. Santiago, 1959.

Pivel Devoto, Alcira Ranieri de and Pivel Devoto, Juan E., eds. *Historia de la República Oriental del Uruguay*. Montevideo, 1956.

Plato. *The Republic*, translated by Desmond Lee. London, 1974.

Poblete Troncoso, Moisés. *La reforma agraria en América Latina*. Santiago, 1961.

Prado Junior, Caio. *Historia económica del Brasil*. Buenos Aires, 1960.

Prescott, William H. *History of the Conquest of Peru*. London, 1847.

————. *History of the Reign of Ferdinand and Isabella the Catholic*. London, 1885.

————. *History of the Reign of Philip II, King of Spain*. London, 1855-1859.

Pugin, A. Welby. *Contrasts: or, A Parallel Between the Noble Edifices of the Middle Ages and Corresponding Buildings of the*

322   Bibliography

Present Day: Shewing the Present Decay of Taste. Victorian Library Edition, Leicester, 1969.

Puiggros, Rodolfo. *Historia económica del Río de la Plata.* Buenos Aires, 1948.

Pulgar, Fernando del. *Crónica de los Reyes Católicos.* Madrid, 1943.

Quintero, Rodolfo. *Antropología de las ciudades latinoamericanas.* Caracas, 1964.

Raat, William D. "Leopoldo Zea and Mexican Positivism: A Reappraisal." *HAHR* xlviii (1968), 1-18.

Ramírez Necochea, Hernán. *Antecedentes económicos de la independencia de Chile.* Santiago, 1959.

———. "The Economic Origins of Independence." In *The Origins of Latin American Revolutions, 1808-1826*, edited by Humphreys and Lynch.

———. *Historia del movimiento obrero en Chile.* Santiago, 1956.

Ramsay, John Fraser. *Spain: The Rise of the First World Power.* University, Ala., 1973.

Ranke, Leopold von. *La monarquía española de los siglos XVI y XVII.* México, 1946.

Resnick, Enoch F. "Expresiones nacionalistas de Don Juan Manuel de Rosas." *TC* no. 14 (1965), 164-183.

Reynolds, Clark W. See Mamalakis, Markos.

Ribeiro, Darcy. *The Civilizational Process.* Washington, D.C., 1968.

Ricard, Robert. "La *Plaza mayor* en Espagne et en Amérique espagnole." *AESC* ii, no. 4 (October-December, 1947), 433-438.

Rivas, Angel César. "Prosperity—the Fruit of Generous Reforms. In *The Bourbon Reforms and Spanish Civilization*, edited by Floyd.

Robertson, William. *History of the Reign of Charles V.* London, 1774.

Robinson, D. J. "The City as Centre of Change in Modern Venezuela." In *Cities in Changing Latin America*, London, 1969.

Robinson, Eric and Musson, A. E. "Science and Industry in the late Eighteenth Century." *EHR* 13 (December, 1960), 222-224.

Rodríguez Casado, Vicente. *Iglesia y estado en el reinado de Carlos III*. Seville, 1948.

Roel, Virgilio. *Historia social y económica de la colonia*. Lima, 1970.

Roett, Riordan, ed. *Brazil in the Sixties*. Nashville, Tenn., 1972.

————. *Brazil: Politics in a Patrimonial Society*. Boston, 1972.

Roldan, Alcibíades. "El centralismo de la constitución de 1833." *RCHG* LXXIV, no. 79 (1933), 410.

Ruskin, John. *The Stones of Venice*. London, 1851.

Saco, José Antonio. *Historia de la esclavitud de la raza africana en el Nuevo Mundo*. Barcelona, 1879.

Safford, Frank. "Bases of Political Alignment in Early Republican Spanish America." In *New Approaches to Latin American History*, edited by Graham and Smith.

Sagarzazu, Luis. *La constitución de 1901 y la reforma*. Caracas, 1904.

Sánchez Agesta, Luis. *El concepto del Estado en el pensamiento español del siglo XVI*. Madrid, 1959.

————. *Historia del constitucionalismo español*. Madrid, 1964.

Sánchez-Albornoz, Claudio. *Estudios sobre las instituciones medioevales españolas*. México, 1965.

Sánchez-Cantón, F. J. *Goya*. Paris, 1930.

Santos Martínez, Pedro. *Las industrias durante el virreinato, 1776-1810*. Buenos Aires, 1969.

Sarfatti, Magali. *Spanish Bureaucratic Patrimonialism in America*. Politics of Modernization Series, No. 1, Berkeley, Calif., 1966.

Sarmiento, Domingo Faustino. *Facundo*. Buenos Aires, 1921.

Sarrailh, Jean. *L'Espagne Éclairée*. Paris, 1954.

Schmitter, Philippe C. "Desarrollo retrasado, dependencia externa y cambio político en América Latina." *FI* XI (October-December, 1971), 135-137.

Schwartz, Stuart B. "State and Society in Colonial Spanish America: An Opportunity for Prosopography." In *New Approaches to Latin American History*, edited by Graham and Smith.

Scobie, James R. *Argentina: A City and a Nation*. New York, 1964.

324 *Bibliography*

Scobie, James A., *Buenos Aires: Plaza to Suburb, 1870-1910.* New York, 1974.

Shiels, W. Eugene, S.J. *King and Church: The Rise and Fall of the Patronato Real.* Chicago, 1961.

Simpson, Lesley Byrd. *The encomienda in New Spain.* Los Angeles and Berkeley, Calif., 1929.

Smith, Peter H. See Graham, Richard.

Smith, Robert T. "Financing the Central American Federation, 1821-1838." *HAHR* XLIII (1963), 510.

Smith, T. Lynn. *Brazil: People and Institutions.* Baton Rouge, La., 1963.

Soler, Ricaurte. *El positivismo argentino.* Buenos Aires, 1968.

Solís, Leopoldo. "La política económica y el nacionalismo mexicano." *FI* IX (January-March, 1969), 241.

Solórzano y Pereyra, Juan de. *Política indiana: antología*, edited by Luis García Arias. Madrid, 1947.

Sousa Pedroso, Antonio de, Visconde de Carnaxide. *O Brasil na administração pombalina.* Rio de Janeiro, 1940.

Stein, Stanley J. and Stein, Barbara. *The Colonial Heritage of Latin America.* New York, 1970.

Stoetzer, Carlos O. *El pensamiento político en la América española durante el período de la emancipación, 1789-1825.* Madrid, 1966.

Subercaseaux, Guillermo. *Monetary and Banking Policy in Chile.* Oxford, 1922.

———. "La protección de la marina mercante nacional ante el Honorable Senado." *El Mercurio* de Santiago, 29 November, 1916.

Sunkel, Osvaldo. "Big Business and *dependencia*." *FA* LI (April, 1972).

——— and Paz, Pedro. *El subdesarrollo latinoamericano y la teoría del desarrollo.* México, 1970.

Sweezy, Paul M. and Huberman, Leo, eds. *Whither Latin America?* New York, 1963.

———, Dobb, Maurice, Takahashi, H. K., Hilton, Rodney, and Hill, Christopher. *The Transition from Feudalism to Capitalism, A Symposium.* New York, 1963.

Takahashi, H. K. See Sweezy.

Teixeira Mendes, Raimundo. See Lemos, Miguel.

Thomas, Hugh. *Cuba, or the Pursuit of Freedom*. London, 1971.

———. *Goya, The Third of May 1808*. London, 1972.

Thompson, E. P. *The Making of the English Working Class*. London, 1963.

Tobar, Balthasar de. *Bulario índico*, edited by M. Gutierrez de Arce. Seville, 1954.

Tocqueville, Alexis de. *Democracy in America*, translated by Henry Reeve and edited by Henry Steel Commager. London, 1959.

Torres Balbas, Leopoldo and Chueca Goitia, Fernando. *Planos de ciudades ibero-americanas y filipinas*. Madrid, 1951.

Torres Saldamando, Enrique. *Libro primero de Cabildos de Lima*. Paris, 1900.

Toynbee, Arnold. *Cities on the Move*. London, 1970.

———. *Survey of International Affairs, 1930*. Oxford, 1931.

Trevelyan, G. M. *English Social History*. London, 1947.

———. *A Shortened History of England*. London, 1962.

Trevor-Roper, H. R. *Historical Essays*. London, 1963.

Turner, Frederick C. *Catholicism and Political Development in Latin America*. Chapel Hill, N.C., 1971.

Ugarte, Carlos. "El cabildo de Santiago y el comercio exterior del reino de Chile durante el siglo XVIII." *Estudios de historia de las instituciones políticas y sociales*, Universidad de Chile, no. 1. Santiago, 1966.

Urquídi Arturo. *El feudalismo en América Latina y la reforma agraria boliviana*. Cochabamba, 1966.

Urzúa, Germán. *Los partidos políticos chilenos*. Santiago, 1968.

Valdivia, Pedro de. *Cartas de relación de la conquista de Chile*. Santiago, 1970.

Vargas, Getulio. *A nova política do Brasil*. Rio de Janeiro, 1938.

Vargas Ugarte, Ruben, S.J. *El episcopado en los tiempos de la emancipación sudamericana*. Lima, 1962.

Vasconcelos, José. *A Mexican Ulysses: The Autobiography of José Vasconcelos*, translated and abridged by W. Rex Crawford. Bloomington, Ind., 1963.

Véliz, Claudio. "Cambio y continuidad: el Pacto Andino en la historia contemporánea." *EI* IV, no. 16 (February-March, 1971), 62-92.

———. "Egaña, Lambert, and the Chilean Mining Associations of 1825." *HAHR* LV, no. 4 (November, 1975), 647-655.

———. *Historia de la marina mercante de Chile*. Santiago, 1961.

———. "La mesa de tres patas." *DE* III, no. 1-2 (April-September, 1963), 231-247.

———, ed. *Latin America and the Caribbean: A Handbook*. London, 1968.

———, ed. *Obstacles to Change in Latin America*. London, 1965.

———, ed. *The Politics of Conformity in Latin America*. London, 1967.

Vernon, Raymond. See Wionczek, Miguel S.

Vicuña MacKenna, Benjamín. *Los girondinos chilenos*. Santiago, 1902.

———. *Páginas de mi diario durante tres años de viaje 1853-1854-1855*. Santiago, 1936.

———. *El Washington del sur: Cuadros de la Vida del Mariscal Antonio José de Sucre*. Madrid, 1893.

Vilar, Pierre. *Crecimiento y desarrollo*. Barcelona, 1964.

Villalobos, Sergio. *El comercio y la crisis colonial*. Santiago, 1968.

Vitale, Luis. *Interpretación marxista de la historia de Chile*. 3 vols. Santiago, 1967-1971.

Wagley, Charles. *An Introduction to Brazil*. New York, 1971.

Walzer, Michael. *The Revolution of the Saints*. London, 1966.

Wanderley Pinho, José. *A abertura dos portos: Cairú, os ingleses, a independencia*. Salvador, 1961.

Weber, Max. *Essays in Sociology*. See Gerth, H. H.

Whitaker, Arthur P., ed. *Latin America and the Enlightenment*. New York, 1942.

———. *Nationalism in Latin America, Past and Present*. Gainesville, Fla., 1962.

Wiarda, Howard, ed. *Politics and Social Change in Latin America; The Distinct Tradition*. Amherst, Mass., 1974.

Wilberforce, William. *A Practical View of the Prevailing Religious System of Professed Christians in the Higher and Middle Classes in this Country contrasted with Real Christianity.* London, 1798.

Wilkie, James W. *The Mexican Revolution.* Berkeley and Los Angeles, Calif., 1970.

Williams, Raymond. *Culture and Society.* London, 1961.

Wilson, Bryan. *Religion in Secular Society.* London, 1966.

Wionczek, Miguel S. "Electric Power: The Uneasy Partnership." In *Public Policy and Private Enterprise in Mexico,* edited by Vernon Raymond. Cambridge, Mass., 1964.

Wright, Thomas C. "Agriculture and Protectionism in Chile, 1880-1930." *JLAS* vii (May, 1975), 46-47.

Wythe, George. *Industry in Latin America.* New York, 1945.

Zavala, Silvio S. *La encomienda indiana.* Madrid, 1935.

———. *Las instituciones jurídicas en la conquista de América.* Madrid, 1935.

———. *New Viewpoints on the Spanish Colonization of America.* New York, 1943.

Zea, Leopoldo. *El positivismo en México.* México, 1943.

Index

Library of Congress Cataloging in Publication Data

Véliz, Claudio.
   The centralist tradition of Latin America.

   Bibliography: p.
   Includes index.
   1.   Decentralization of government—Latin America.
2.   Authoritarianism.   3.   Latin America—Social conditions.
I.   Title.
JL956.S8V44   320.9'8   79-84019
ISBN 0-691-05280-8